BEING SOMEBODY AND BLACK BESIDES

Being Somebody
& Black Besides

AN UNTOLD MEMOIR OF MIDCENTURY BLACK LIFE

George B. Nesbitt

Edited by Prexy Nesbitt and Zeb Larson

With an original foreword by St. Clair Drake
and a contemporary foreword by Imani Perry

The University of Chicago Press   *Chicago and London*

The University of Chicago Press, Chicago 60637
The University of Chicago Press, Ltd., London
© 2021 by The University of Chicago
Published 2021
Printed in the United States of America

30 29 28 27 26 25 24 23 22 21   1 2 3 4 5

ISBN-13: 978-0-226-78312-3 (cloth)
ISBN-13: 978-0-226-71683-1 (e-book)
DOI: https://doi.org/10.7208/chicago/9780226716831.001.0001

Library of Congress Cataloging-in-Publication Data

Names: Nesbitt, George B., 1912–2002, author. | Nesbitt, Prexy, editor. | Larson,
    Robert Zebulun, editor. | Drake, St. Clair, writer of foreword. | Perry, Imani,
    1972– writer of foreword.
Title: Being somebody and black besides : an untold memoir of midcentury
    black life / George B. Nesbitt ; edited by Prexy Nesbitt and Zeb Larson ;
    with an original foreword by St. Clair Drake and a contemporary foreword
    by Imani Perry.
Description: Chicago : The University of Chicago Press, [2021]
Identifiers: LCCN 2021016881 | ISBN 9780226783123 (cloth) | ISBN 9780226716831
    (e-book)
Subjects: LCSH: Nesbitt, George B., 1912–2002. | African Americans—
    Biography. | African Americans—Illinois—Biography. | African American
    lawyers—Biography. | Civil rights workers—United States—Biography. |
    African Americans—History—20th century. | Race discrimination—United
    States—History—20th century. | LCGFT: Autobiographies.
Classification: LCC E185.97.N47 A3 2021 | DDC 323.092 [B]—dc23
LC record available at https://lccn.loc.gov/2021016881

Contents

Illustrations

Foreword

IMANI PERRY

I was invited to write this preface by George Belvey Nesbitt's nephew, Mr. Prexy Nesbitt. I first met Mr. Prexy Nesbitt on one of my trips to Chicago. I have regularly traveled to Chicago for the past forty-three years of my life, and among its distinctions is its tightly networked and multigenerational community of black politicos, organizers, activists, educators, and movers and shakers. Though I never had the benefit of meeting the late Mr. George Nesbitt, I was immediately intrigued when, in a later exchange, Prexy shared details of his uncle's distinguished life, one that was both unique and yet beautifully representative of black Illinois history, and eagerly accepted the invitation to read this memoir.

George Nesbitt's *Being Somebody and Black Besides* is a fascinating portrait of the life of a man who belonged to the category "race man." Race men and women was the designation offered to people who saw their every achievement, and indeed their entire life's commitment, to be framed in terms of what was good for "the race," meaning black people. Race people emerged from the toil and degradation of slavery, the glory of emancipation, through the devastating end to Reconstruction, and in the violent wake of Jim Crow, bearing a profound sense of purpose. They built institutions, and they sought their fortunes beyond the plantations where they once labored as the enslaved. In his story, Nesbitt provides an intimate depiction of the Great Migration and its people, in particular his own family's aspirations, which created in him one of the twentieth century's important men.

Nesbitt's family traveled from rural Mississippi to Illinois; however, they didn't go to the big city. They settled in Champaign, the small-town home of the state's flagship university, the University of Illinois. That detail alone adds an important aspect to our reading of story of the Great Migration. Black people settled in the urban South and the small-town North, as well as the big cities. This is one of a series of important insights gleaned from this remarkable journey. Many others are directly related to the man this migrant became. Nesbitt can be described as someone who transcended Jim Crow, poverty, and adversity to achieve extraordinary professional heights. He can also be described as a vocal opponent of late 1960s black radicalism. Both are true, and yet the power in this story cannot be so neatly packaged.

With painstaking detail, Nesbitt shares the details of his migrant community. He describes their environs, their rituals, and their process of adjustment to new circumstances. His fondness for Southern ways and Southern foods provide a means for Nesbitt to describe the extraordinary resilience of migrants. Their habits, though not always suited to the new circumstances, are the source of Nesbitt's lifelong commitment to unwavering integrity, hard work, and fortitude. He also describes the process of acculturation. The shifting language from South to North that maintains the verve and color of the homeland is matched by shifting relationships between black and white people. Nesbitt notes the relative spatial freedom for black people in the Midwest, but makes abundantly clear that racism and Jim Crow are no less potent forces there. Police harassment, educational inequality, and interpersonal hostility at every stage of his life, including his years in the military and as a professional, provide stark evidence that Jim Crow was indeed a national institution and a widespread public disposition, whether or not Colored and White signs populated public facilities.

When Nesbitt depicts the world that the migrants made, he gives careful attention to his and his peers' socialization and the institutions that held the entire community. Throughout his life, he is rooted in civic associations and a sense of mutuality in community. The domestic norms were supported by community expectations. Educational aspirations lay at the heart of their seeking, and they looked to the university in their midst with pride, even though they had to swallow the bitter gall of its exclusions and, eventually, its cruelly begrudging inclusion of Nesbitt and some others.

Along the way, Nesbitt does have white friends and peers with whom he shares meaningful relationships and some circumstances. And, while he is deliberate about speaking with grace and appreciation regarding white friends and supporters, he is unflinching in his accounts of racism. And in that, his story exposes a too often overlooked part of black political history and life. Though he was philosophically deeply patriotic and an integrationist, the militancy of his integrationism must be recognized. He insisted upon dignity; he saw his role as a racial representative as requiring that he refuse classism, colorism, and petty stratification, moving through life with an unwavering belief in the linked fate of black people that shaped his career as a military man, an attorney, and as the deputy assistant to the secretary of Housing and Urban Development (HUD) in the Kennedy administration.

Though today it might seem less bold than the position of some others, readers would do well to remember that insisting on the full inclusion of black people into the social, political, professional, academic, and legal infrastructure was considered for most of the twentieth century to be so unthinkable that many died for their efforts to do so. It is from that perspective that one ought to read his criticisms of young organizers in the late 1960s who rejected integrationism. There is a tinge of hurt, of the sort often experienced by elders when youth decry their methods. But underneath that is a well of knowledge that to demand inclusion, fully, into the fabric of the United States, was nearly as dangerous as revolutionary politics. There is also the matter of simple generational conflict. Characteristically, Nesbitt worries about change and decline as he approaches his later years. This concern, while sharp, appears to sharpen his memories of what once was. As the social theorist Raymond Williams once described it, there is a "structure of feeling" here, a multisensory evocation of a time and place that could only be fully understood in its aftermath.

Readers will perhaps be surprised also to see that Nesbitt takes positions that are rarely associated with integrationists. For example, he has his own disquisition on the concept that "Black is Beautiful" that reaches back much further than the late sixties, and he has an almost intuitive reckoning with the injustice of colonialism when he is still a child. From his experience as a paperboy for the *Chicago Defender*, once the nation's most important black newspaper, we can glean that that experience was, at least, part of how he became such a race man. As an entrepreneur, a reader, and a distributor of the outlet, in the small town of Champaign he had access to the broad black world, its struggles, its vagaries, and its ambitions.

In the introduction written by the noted sociologist St. Clair Drake, the work is described as follows: "This book is about three generations of a stable but quite undistinguished Negro family. . . . The entire lot lacks a single celebrity; no one of its members has been acclaimed as the first Negro to have done this or that of note. It also lacks the infamous as much as the famed." The point is that there is value in the exploration of un-exceptional black life in contrast to the melodrama and heroism that were often expected in the recounting of the peculiarity of being American yet Negro. However, there is nevertheless a remarkable journey here, one of both the mass migration and upward mobility. These are classic American tropes. And yet, the American success story is never so simple for black Americans, regardless of the achievement, precisely because the life-world and the life chances of the black individual are always profoundly shaped by American racial inequality, both personally and in terms of the world this person witnesses. Hence, though this work is of extreme historical interest, it has ongoing implications for understanding the lives of black Americans even now, generations later. This book will be meaningful for readers interested in African and American history, culture, and politics, as well as anyone compelled by a classic bildungsroman with sociopolitical significance.

Imani Perry
Hughes-Rogers Professor
Department of African American Studies
Princeton University

A Note on
St. Clair Drake's "Foreword"

SANDRA DRAKE

The particular significance of the following introduction by my father, St. Clair Drake, lies in the perspective from which it presents George Nesbitt's account of his life. Its context is the impassioned debate of the era when it was written over how best to conduct the struggle for African American liberation in US society — and even whether that liberation is possible.

What era was that? Although the foreword is undated, intrinsic evidence (as we say in my field of literary study) enables us to locate it closely enough. My father, born January 2, 1911, turned 60 on January 2, 1971. He writes in the first sentence of his foreword that he and George Nesbitt opened their eyes upon the world at "approximately the same time, almost sixty years ago." The latest date, therefore, that the foreword could have been written is January 1, 1971. It was likely written in either 1969 or 1970. In any event, it is a product of the end of the 1960s.

The foreword is not a final, polished version. I have deliberately made only minor changes. The voice is that of St. Clair Drake, and the piece is his. To have changed it further would have altered its relation to the debates of the era in which it was written.

I do not know precisely how a final version would have read. I knew my father well enough, though, to know that the present version expresses his conviction that the African American struggle for liberation in the United States, which began at enslavement and continues today, has always employed a wide range of complex and creative strategies and tactics under profoundly exigent but varying situations; and that these strategies and tactics all contributed to advancement toward liberation. He himself employed a large number of these ways and means throughout his lifetime: he was an activist, a community organizer and supporter of community institutions, a teacher, scholar, and mentor. He knew that all these roles could require great courage, whether in dramatic or quiet ways.

The foreword is of value more than fifty years later—thirty years after St. Clair Drake's death—because it presents the story of a member of the generation that lived and fought for African American liberation during his and George Nesbitt's youth and adulthood in the first half of the twentieth century. This perspective probably accounts for the structure of his foreword, which begins by noting that he and George Nesbitt traversed the century as men of the same age.

In some ways their trajectories differed considerably. In other ways significant similarities derive from what could be described as a characteristic of much of this part of the African American community, raised to esteem and strive to obtain formal education, to hold steady employment within the existing economy, and to struggle for improvement of the status of African Americans in the United States largely "within the system."

This segment of the African American community, its values and efforts, were under attack at the end of the 1960s, after the rise of what has been called "the Black Power movement" (a term that covers a lot of territory). At this time, even the Reverend King was criticized in important quarters as having defended values and strategies that were utterly inadequate to the struggle.

My father's introduction presents George Nesbitt's autobiography as the valuable description of a valuable life, lived in the same period as his, born of similar origins, and lived by a man dedicated to advancing African American standing in the United States in ways that were worthy of respect from a younger generation—with whom my father felt a great affinity—even though these ways and views were at that point, to say the least, out of fashion with many of them.

This foreword, then, like the book it presents, is a "period piece" in the best sense of that term, and a contribution to our understanding of the complexity of the African American community and experience in the United States.

Sandra E. Drake
Professor Emerita, Department of English
Program in African and African American
Literature, Stanford University
August 27, 2020
Menlo Park, California

Foreword to the George Nesbitt Manuscript

ST. CLAIR DRAKE

George Nesbitt and I both opened our eyes upon the world at approximately the same time, almost sixty years ago, both of us in small towns. I was in Virginia, while he was born and grew up in a town where the Negro population was not numerous but was in contact with a highly visible symbol of one way in which Americans "get ahead"—the University of Illinois. Some of the Negro residents worked for the institution or for members of its faculty, and it was inevitable that many of them, and their children, would dream of using the available educational ladder for climbing someday. I attended high school in a Virginia educational center (two exclusive girls' schools and a nationally known military academy) where the black community was under influences similar to those the Nesbitt family and their neighbors experienced in the shadow of the University of Illinois. (There were special Southern wrinkles, of course, such as "No blacks admitted.") Years after I had left the town, one of the college newspapers carried a headline: "MOLLIE'S GRANDSON WINS PH.D." My grandmother had been a maid at one of the girls' schools for over 30 years. Both George Nesbitt and I, however, took it for granted from early childhood that we would go to college someday. We were both atypical American youth in that period in history.

After obtaining a law degree from the University of Illinois, George Nesbitt went on to the nearby big city—Chicago—to seek his fortune. It was there that I first met him, having myself recently come to study at the University of Chicago after several years of working in the South. Those were the Depression years and many of us, despite our college degrees, were living close to the poverty line. It was only natural that we would be drawn close to one of the most significant developments of the late thirties and early forties, the legitimization of the labor movement through the National Labor Relations Board. I was doing some volunteer work for "the redcaps' union," the United Transport Service Employees Association, and George Nesbitt was in the thick of that fight, an experience he describes in vivid detail, for it was a crucial time of decision in his life. Our paths crossed occasionally in other Chicago contexts, too. Then, he went on to Washington where he, a "steady," well-organized, man, rose steadily in the Federal Civil Service. I began a life of academic wandering that eventually took me to Britain and to Africa. One day, about thirty years after our meeting, I bumped into him at a conference on Africa in Washington. He was the same quiet, self-composed George I used to know, grown now a bit more stocky, but still not a person who "stands out in a crowd." He told me he was just finishing his autobiography. I expressed eagerness to read it, for I knew he had been in on the making of some important aspects of contemporary social history. He kindly sent along a copy. I had, of course, read a number of his scholarly and perceptive articles in professional journals, but I never suspected that he had the gift now revealed—of a charming style, low-keyed and sometimes quaint, and the talent to use it for making his own life "live." The style and pace of the work fit his calm, reflective personality, like the pipe does that he smokes or the "somber-hued blue, gray, or brown suit of conservative cut" that he says he likes to wear. But he does not pull his punches; he only gloves them well. Racist episode after episode in his life had rubbed his sensitivities raw, and he is not reticent about relating them, although with rage highly controlled and without rancor. His anger smolders instead of flaming.

In an epoch when abrasiveness is a virtue, I enjoyed, for a change, his handling of what all Negroes call "The Problem." I considered it an honor when I was asked to write a foreword to his book. I had written five, three for reissued works of prominent black social scientists, one for

Claude McKay's autobiography, and another for the life story, *Child of Two Worlds*, of an African friend, Mugo Gatheru. I do it now again, with pleasure, for my Afro-American friend who tells with such effectiveness how, to use his own words, he refused to be "pushed from the realm of humanity and rendered nobody."

Serious concern about the meaning of the "Black Experience" has become an important aspect of the quest for an understanding of recent events that have shaken our complacency—the rapid rise to leadership of a young black preacher whose tragic assassination unleashed nation-wide expressions of mass outrage; the enshrinement among young black Americans of Malcolm X as a martyr; and the recent rejection of "integration" by large numbers of black Americans in favor of Black Power as the only goal worthy of their sacrifice and suffering. A "cult of blackness" has emerged for the first time since the twenties, and it even asserts the *superiority* of values thought to be present in *negritude* and its American variant, "soul." White Americans, most of whom never thought about the matter before making the surprising discovery that Black Protest is nothing new, have had the kind of education that ignored or suppressed the fact of its existence. Slave narratives and historic documents, long out of print, are now being reissued as paperbacks. Anthropologists, sociologists, journalists, and dramatists of both races are continuously laying bare the lifestyles and values of "the ghetto," highlighting the nuances of "soul," and giving currency to its colorful and sometimes embarrassingly explicit argot. Fascinated horror is blended with appreciation of the unsuspected depths of black men's passions. Biographies and autobiographies of Afro-Americans find a growing circle of readers who are being exposed to the fact that a streak of deep resentment and carefully suppressed hatred often lies buried underneath mild manners and ready smiles.

Poverty programs, alarm about "crime in the streets," and teen-aged high visibility and audibility, generate a sense of urgency that focuses attention upon what sociologists call "the lower-class subculture" or "the culture of poverty," and on the social types produced within it. Preoccupation with the violent, dramatic, and exotic aspects of "The Black Experience" has obscured a highly significant fact—the emergence, persistence, and important functions of the black middle class. The newly popular "Black History" finds much more dramatic and "relevant" material in the study of slave revolts than in analysis of the evolution of a black middle class. The one widely known book on the latter subject, E. Franklin Frazier's *The Black Bourgeoisie,* is more often quoted for its satirical caricature of the author's contemporaries among black professional men and women than for its scholarly, informative, historical chapters. Now, this autobiography by George Nesbitt, a Negro professional man in his late fifties, this account of a life that spans two World Wars and a Depression, as well as the present period of rapid social change, presents us with a valuable contribution to the documentation of "The Black Experience," precisely because it provides insight into the middle-class variety of that experience, which is so frequently ignored.

In one sense, "The Black Experience" is the same for all Afro-Americans—continuous subjection to some variety of an ever-present racial prejudice and discrimination that none, however well educated or high in social status, can escape. This straightforward account of one well-educated black man's life makes that fact painfully clear. But, in another sense, there is no single "Black Experience." The accident of place of birth and rearing, as well as individual differences in temperament and personality, make each individual black person's experience unique, as is *every* individual's, while the social position in which he begins life and that to which he eventually moves in this relatively open society, involve types of experience that differ widely from each other. This has always been true throughout the long history of the black man's presence in America.

Every Afro-American grows up within, and lives his adult life within, the framework of "the black community"—an intricate web of families, churches, voluntary associations, and educational and commercial institutions, all of which are repositories of values and norms inherited from the past. There is a distinctive black subculture within the wider American culture, just as there are Jewish American, Italian American, and other ethnic subcultures. But white ethnics may leave their subculture if they wish to do so, by assimilation into the families and institutions of mainstream white Americans. They can "live down" their past. Negroes wear the badge of color. They cannot leave their subculture, except for a tiny minority whose skins and features are indistinguishable from those of white persons. Since leaving the black world is impossible, it becomes "unthinkable." Most Afro-Americans accept as "normal" their participation in what has become a *national* subculture whose values they absorb from relatives and friends, and by immersion in the content of Negro magazines and newspapers (and now "soul stations" on the airwaves), and through membership in local branches of national organizations. The ground of their existence is identification with "The Race." I suspect that the psychoanalysts have overdone and overworked the concept of "self-hatred" as applied to Afro-Americans except for the few of them that end up in their clinics. This story of growing up in a small Midwestern town, and of migration to big cities later, reveals the dynamics of participation in two worlds, that of the Afro-American subculture, which is warm and supporting, and that of "the white world," which is always frustrating and sometimes cruelly punishing.

Embedded in the heart of the many black communities scattered all over America, and with race-consciousness sharpened by residential segregation, is a hard-working, churchgoing core of families with codes of "respectability" who put high priority value upon "making something out of yourself" and "getting ahead." Closely integrated with these families is a more secularized segment that shares the basic middle-class values and forms a front with the "church-goers" against the "shiftless," the "no-accounts," and the "riff-raff." Sometimes, though not always, for size of community is an important variable, a tiny "upper class" is also present, composed of people whose college and professional training or economic affluence gives them high prestige. The author of this autobiography is one of the tens of thousands of Afro-Americans who not only grew up in a family where both parents were present, but where there was also that blend of warmth and firmness that gives children a sense of security. The descriptions of his boyhood are full of cherished memories of a way of life that could only be lived in a small town or the suburbs, but the harmonious interplay between a hard-working, religious father and a supportive mother, intent upon "raising the children right" and eliciting a positive response from youngsters who are ambitious, intelligent, and lively—and sometimes healthily rambunctious—is certainly not unknown among low-income families of "the ghetto." There are more such families than meet the eye or who draw the attention of the most widely read "experts" on the black family. An autobiography like this gives detailed and highly readable documentation to some of the types of families that Andrew Billingsley in a recent work, *Black Families in White America*, has pointed out merit more attention that they have received. George

Nesbitt's own family and those of his four brothers, all of whom live in metropolitan cities, carry on a family tradition, but at a higher level of education and affluence, and George Nesbitt speaks with understandable pride of their achievements.

Students of culture and personality use a professional jargon that includes the key term *socialization process*. It refers to the way in which a child learns the "rules of the game" from his elders and the "name of the game" from his peers, as well as to how an individual internalizes the values of a specific segment of the society in which he grows up. George Nesbitt was socialized as "Negro lower middle-class" during the period of the First World War and its aftermath.

The author sees his family and the black community in which it was embedded as the product of a *group* past that the black middle class knows and cherishes, but of which nearly all white people, and a very large proportion of Northern ghetto youth, are unaware. His people came up from the South and settled in a small town that allowed much of the culture they brought to survive. His family was anchored in an institutional nexus that has a long history. Three hundred and fifty years of historical continuity bind the older black middle-class families to the past. The links are churches and voluntary associations, those enduring structures that outlive both individuals and the family units into which they are born. They conserve the values and norms and lend reinforcement to the families that inculcate them into the following generations. They emerged among "free Negroes" during the period of slavery.

The Englishmen and Hollanders who introduced Africans into the North American colonies had only one purpose in mind—to provide a pool of common labor, field hands, domestic servants, and artisans to supplement the inadequate supply of white indentured servants. By the middle of the seventeenth century, Africans and their descendants had been assigned the status of "servants for life" and a system of chattel slavery that had existed in the West Indies and parts of South America for over a century took deep root on North American soil. But "free Negroes" were not enslaved, and some had been present since the first group of twenty "negars"[1] who came to Jamestown in 1619 served out their term of inden-

---

1. An early spelling of the slur, derived from the French "nègre."

ture. When the Declaration of Independence was signed in 1776, there were at least fifty thousand "free Negroes" living primarily in the cities of the thirteen colonies, with the slaves being concentrated on the plantations in the South. Some were descendants of Africans who had come to North America indentured; a few were "free issue Negroes," descended from children of white mothers by black fathers; a very few were former urban slaves who had been allowed free time to earn wages and were then permitted to purchase their freedom; most were manumitted slaves or their descendants, often related by blood to prominent white families in the South. The Northern free Negro population was always being augmented by "runaways," black sailors who had jumped ship, and a few West Indians who had managed to enter as legal immigrants.

Although subjected to racial prejudice everywhere, without citizenship, and in danger of being captured and sold into slavery, the residents of the small, urban communities of the free managed to produce a stratum of stable, property-conscious, achievement-oriented individuals and families that placed high value upon education and "respectability." The general, middle-class, Anglo-Saxon virtue of "service to the community" assumed a special form—"contributing to racial advancement." They interpreted their own success as proving that the slaves could do likewise if granted their freedom. By 1800, preachers among the free had developed national organizations with local branches—the Free African Society, for "moral uplift" and mutual aid; the African Methodist Episcopal Church, born out of protest against segregation; and the African Lodge No. 459 of the Scottish Rite of Free and Accepted Masons. There were, too, the Free African School and the Free African Theater in New York, and numerous other local organizations in the seaboard cities. All of these groups stressed thrift, temperance, and conventional sexual morality. They held up cherished examples of black achievement for the young to emulate, including the slave girl, Phyllis Wheatley, who became a poetess; mathematician and almanac-maker, Benjamin Banneker; and Crispus Attucks, first to die in the Boston Massacre. These organizations not only embodied middle-class values, but always incorporated a "protest" orientation that found expression in action. Out of the ranks of their leaders came the men and women who cooperated with the white abolitionists in operating the Underground Railroad and in mobilizing public opinion in the North to support a crusade against slavery. Rejecting the pleas and enticements of white colonizationists to emigrate to Africa or the West Indies, they preferred to remain and struggle for their rights and the rights of their enslaved brethren, and to insist upon full citizenship in the country built by their labor and for which they had fought in the Revolutionary War and the War of 1812. The Civil War gave them and their followers a chance to fight for their own freedom.

When the Civil War began, there were nearly five hundred thousand "free Negroes" among the more than four million Afro-Americans in the United States. The top black leadership during the Reconstruction Period came from among their ranks. Lower-echelon leaders included those few blacks who managed to acquire land; other individuals who, though unlettered, showed unusual political talent; as well as a fast-growing group of schoolteachers trained by missionaries from the North and by institutions set up by the black Christian denominations. Schools sprang up all over the South, and ex-slaves and their children flocked to them. This new middle class also drew into its ranks many ex–house slaves and their descendants who started off with a kind of "know how" the field hands lacked, as well as ambitious, upwardly mobile men and women from the "fields." The black middle-class subculture was no carbon copy of the white, though it incorporated its fundamental values. The upper middle class, however, tried to pattern itself upon white models as closely as it could, but the lower middle class developed patterns of worship, play, and family organization to fit its inclinations and its needs, with little worry about what white people did or did not think about their way of life. "Race pride" and "race solidarity" were, from the outset, a part of lower middle-class rhetoric. It was out of the end product of this process that the social stratum to which the author belongs grew up.

Near the end of the nineteenth century, a leader emerged, backed by Northern white philanthropic and church circles and tolerated by the Southern white power elite: Booker T. Washington. He developed and propagated an ideology for "racial progress"—stay out of politics; work hard at whatever kinds of jobs one can find; give the children basic training in literacy, agriculture, and the artisan skills; go into business where possible; and above all, save money. And make it very clear that social equality is *not* the black man's goal. This was a strategy for survival within a Southern milieu that was becoming rabidly racist. It was based upon Booker T. Washington's belief that once the majority of black people had acquired middle-class traits, they would be "accepted." The emerging black middle class in the South adopted the Washington ideology, but the Northern middle class, more solidly based upon a core of old free families—some descended from men and women who had fled slavery via the Underground Railroad—fought hard against the erosion of the rights they already had and pressed continuously for expansion of their opportunities to participate upon a basis of equality in the economic and political order and to buy and rent homes where they pleased. They did not crusade for "social equality," but defended the rights of individuals—black and white—to associate together freely if they wanted to in any and all spheres of their private life. By the turn of the century, as the Southern pattern of race relations was seeping northward, a group of "Young Turks" emerged within the Northern middle class who challenged Booker T. Washington's claim to national leadership. Two young Harvard graduates were in the vanguard of the militant movement. One was Monroe Trotter, lawyer and newspaper editor. The other was W. E. B. Du Bois, who had gone south to teach at Atlanta University. Both were natives of Massachusetts.

In 1903, Du Bois, then thirty-four years of age, published a book of essays, *The Souls of Black Folks*, designed, as he phrased it, to "show the strange meaning of being black here at the dawning of the Twentieth Century." He hurled forth an assertion that "the problem of the twentieth century is the problem of the color-line." Afro-Americans could not have found a more highly trained and eloquent advocate. These passionate and often beautifully written essays affirm young Du Bois's strong sense of solidarity with those black Americans who had never had a chance to come anywhere remotely near to Harvard—"need I add that I who speak here am bone of the bone and flesh of the flesh of them that live within the Veil?" It was to the rending asunder of "the Veil" that Dr. Du Bois devoted the rest of his life, dying in West Africa at the age of ninety-five, still assailing the barriers that divide men on the basis of color and that distort their perceptions of each other, and keep black and brown and yellow men at the bottom of the world's hierarchy of power and prestige. It was *The Souls of Black Folks*, discovered by the author when in his teens, that stirred him deeply and gave him an ideological orientation that remained with him throughout his life. He and his brothers sold the militant Chicago Negro newspaper, the *Chicago Defender*, and read it, too. They were also nurtured upon Paul Lawrence Dunbar's dialect poems in *Lyr-*

ics of Lowly Life (along with the more conventional reading that friendly white librarians helped him to choose), but of his awakening, he writes, "When I was perhaps mid-way in high school, I stumbled across a little black book which held as much needed meaning for me as a Negro as the Bible has for me in humanity. It has influenced me as no other single book save that of the Word. I have returned to *The Souls of Black Folks* time after time since I was a youngster and still marvel at what is there." What Du Bois wrote was a blend of outrage and optimism, indignation and hope, of admiration of efficiency and decorum, but also an understanding of why the masses of black people did not and could not display these middle-class virtues under the load of racial discrimination they bore. Education—of all kinds—plus militancy was Du Bois's prescription for "racial progress." By the time he was eighty, he had despaired of attaining the goal without some kind of socialist revolution, and at the age of 93 he joined the American Communist Party. George Nesbitt has kept the vision and the faith of the earlier Du Bois, and the account of his life is both testimony and testament, asserting his confidence in a type of future and a means for attaining it that both the Marxist Left and the young Black Power militants have rejected. He makes no apology for remaining a "believer."

The kind of roles he was able to play after World War II—the period of Du Bois's increasing disillusionment—strengthened the author's conviction that change *is* possible within the system *if* some important *ifs* are realized. Another black Harvard graduate, a man slightly older than himself, offered him an opportunity to participate, at top policy-making levels, in efforts to fashion institutional structures to relieve somewhat the burden upon the poor, of whom the urban black poor are so large a part. This was Robert C. Weaver, economist, then administrator of the Housing and Home Finance Agency, who would later become the first black man to sit in a U.S. presidential cabinet. George Nesbitt had been fortunate in finding a post in his agency where he could devote his professional career to efforts to increase the volume of decent housing available to his people and at the same time to fight against patterns of residential segregation. In 1959, in recognition of his work, he was awarded leave to accept a Littauer Fellowship at Harvard for a year. Then, in 1961, having been in the federal civil service for more than twenty years, he moved to a very responsible post. During that year, Dr. Weaver, who had been impressed for some time by his quiet efficiency, demonstrated competence in planning, and his published work on housing problems, asked him to take on a crucial assignment—the task of drafting legislation that would legitimize rent supplements for welfare families and facilitating its passage through Congress. The bill went through. He takes great satisfaction in what he was able to accomplish, although he has no illusions about the effect on the total system, which has institutionalized racisms and sustains, for many people, black and white, a poverty-dependency syndrome. With the characteristic sense of humor and critical detachment displayed throughout the book, he refers to his important work in the housing field as "exercises in self-therapy, palmed off as 'analyses,'" and notes that many of his reports were "edited into innocuousness." But on balance, he feels that the vast bureaucracy *did* move. And the record supports him, though the results have been small, as he is the first to admit. These were pilot projects for the future that he believes will come.

This is an American "success story"—the story of a lawyer-civil servant, retired now after twenty-five years of work that brought him satisfaction and was of some social service, born Lucian George Belvey Nesbitt, son of a janitor with only a few years of education and a lifestyle now outmoded. (Dropping portions of an embarrassingly long name was one aspect of upward mobility for the boys in the family.) It is a story of the mobility of George's siblings, too, for older brother Russell became a Social Security official; of three younger brothers, two, Lendor and Robert, became medical doctors, and one, Rozell, an electrical engineer. This kind of getting ahead is not at all unusual in the United States—not even in the black community. The fact that it happens more frequently than is generally known lends added significance to this work, however. But what gives this story its uniqueness is the quality of relationships that has continued between three generations of a close-knit family despite the possible disruptive influence of generation gaps and the economical and ecological pressures that tend to tear black families apart. Of one segment of the family that live in Chicago, he writes, "They have been anchored there for twenty odd years, living caught up in the tentacles of a great growing octopus, the ghettoed slum surrounding the building that is their home. But they have stuck it out." What he describes about that home is as fascinating as it is significant.

This is a black American success story. George Nesbitt's career begins with toting bags in a Chicago railway station *after* acquiring a law degree from the University of Illinois. The account of how he made the climb is, itself, a fascinating story. Yet it is typical of the experiences of many black men and women of "the depression generation." Few have ever put it down on paper, however, and very few would have the literary skill to recreate the mood of the times and the subjective aspects of their experience as he does. The distinctiveness of the work lies in the kind of man the author is as a person rather than in his being a case that illustrates a social type. Any black success story has dimensions to it that no white "success" story can ever have. The first ingredient must be the belief by a black boy that he has any chance at all of being a success. Thousands of young black Americans find it difficult to convince themselves that they really do and have to fight unsympathetic parents in the process. George Nesbitt was fortunate. His family never had any doubt about the matter. His father had the boys in business selling newspapers and doing various odd jobs before they were in their teens, and his mother was "scrimping and saving" to have a little money laid aside if the boys needed it when time came to go to college, even though his father wasn't sure that college was essential to become a success. His mother stood firm on that point. An uncle in Chicago, a follower of Marcus Garvey, always reinforced his racial self-confidence if it seemed to lag. Not all the scurrilous, derogatory terms that white boys hurled at them in that Illinois town (and the author's list of them is long); not all the unintended insults by well-meaning whites (and he details plenty of them); nor the intentional insults and roadblocks from other whites could shake the Nesbitt boys' faith in themselves. They *knew* they could be like those black men Du Bois wrote about in the *Crisis* and that they read about every week in the *Chicago Defender*, if they studied hard and worked hard, and fought and outwitted the white man when that was necessary.

Finishing high school was the first hurdle, and George made it despite some brushes with prejudiced teachers and hostile policemen. Getting a college degree meant gritting his teeth when a psychology professor expatiated on the innate inferiority of Negroes. It also meant studying hard and working almost full time during the academic year and on a variety of jobs during the summers. (Waiting tables was the only kind of job that "got him down.") He won his law degree, too, though his militancy almost lost him that prize. He lived at home while attending the University of Illinois and was an active leader in the Frederick Douglass Civic League, and was always involved in moves to wipe out the demeaning denial of service in downtown restaurants. He drew strength as well as enjoyment from his associates in a black college fraternity to which he belonged and a society that published a magazine with "soul."

Black lawyers already in Chicago provided him with his opportunity to enter the profession, but as a very junior partner. This experience as an attorney gave him a postgraduate education in how exploitation and racism worked, as well as renewed contempt for "all the bluecoated"—the only kind of whites whom he admits have sometimes brought him very close to hating. Black political power as expressed through a segment of the Democratic political machine opened doors that the chicanery of a rigged civil service procedure closed to him. He eventually found opportunities to use his training for what he considered desirable social ends. Beginning as an assistant supervisor during the census taking of 1940, he went on to a post in the Department of Finance of the State of Illinois for a very brief period. Then came the opportunity through the National Youth Administration in East St. Louis to make a dent in the job ceiling in that area. Next, a Department of Labor post allowed him to strike additional blows at job discrimination, and he then became a race relations advisor to the United States Housing Authority. This he liked, but World War II interrupted his career as it did that of thousands of other young men his age. Now he became a failure for the first time. One of the most vivid and poignant sections of the book deals with why the army could not make a soldier of him. He has no regrets on that score. He left *his* mark on what was then a Jim Crow institution par excellence, the United States Army. Once the war was over, he moved steadily into the positions of influence already referred to. Some of his friends who preferred to practice law for other ends are now wealthy men, but George Nesbitt was measuring success in terms of Du Bois's goals, not Booker T. Washington's.

This life story is a vivid reminder that there is no such thing as a "self-made man"; that we are all fashioned in a process of interaction, and that in response to our actions for which we *can* be responsible, come reactions which, in turn, help to shape our future actions. The author gives generous credit to individuals—black and white—who opened doors for him, as well as to the family that was the matrix of his existence. Yet in the final analysis, it was his own intelligence, competence, and resilience that brought him through. He is too modest to emphasize that fact. It is his awareness that he owes something to others that has made him determined to shape his life so that he would pay something back. A white success story would laud "the land of the free and the home of the brave, this land of opportunity." There is very little of that flag-waving which immigrant success stories particularly are full of. Even very patriotic black Americans seldom wax *that* enthusiastic, and with good reason.

There are two models with which the American system of race relations might be compared. At one extreme is South Africa—frankly, aggressively and viciously racist, determined that wherever white and black men interact within a single society, blacks must be subordinated, and that the long-term goal should be complete separation, *apartheid.* At the other extreme is Brazil, where official policy is verbalized as favoring cultural assimilation and physical amalgamation, the stated end product being one Brazilian "race" sharing in one homogeneous national culture. Neither alternative is acceptable to white Americans. Their conscience cannot accept the former, and their prejudice will not tolerate the latter. The most advanced "liberal" position, since 1954, has official government sanction, however, and is usually referred to as "integrationist." This seems to mean acceptance by the dominant white group of Negroes into the economic and political order on the basis of free competition, unrestricted by considerations of race, color, or ethnic ancestry; free access to all public facilities, including schools, on the same basis as whites; and a free open market in housing. On the other hand, participation in churches and volunteer associations, and marriage choices, will remain in the private domain, with no legal barriers against freedom of choice by individuals. Strong informal social controls, however, will keep these areas of life highly "segregated." The shift to the legitimization of a doctrine of "integration" is very recent, having proceeded slowly since World War II, and it is an official policy, *not* an operative reality.

George Nesbitt's life has been devoted to the struggle for "integration." His role in the fight comes through clearly in this, his life story. In this respect he is typical of the college-educated black men and women of the thirties and forties who gave that struggle moral and financial support. Despite the efforts of the federal agencies with which he was associated to foster "fair play in housing," the extent of residential segregation increased during the 1950s and 1960s as whites fled from the path of the expanding ghetto; others stayed, but only temporarily. Customary controls have kept the rate of associational integration and intermarriage very low, and some of the author's descriptions of his experiences indicate vividly how these controls operate.

The pattern of race relations in the United States seems to be moving in the direction of a greatly increased degree of "integration" *on the job* in professional and semi-professional occupations and at upper managerial levels, with some quasi-social extensions—but not below those social levels. George Nesbitt was one of the pioneers who made the first breakthrough into some of these areas, and the account of his experience emphasizes the psychological costs that had to be paid.

Today, a new social type is becoming institutionalized—"the half-integrated Negro." Individuals living this style of life will be far more prevalent than they have been in the past. The masses of black people, however, are likely to remain "ghettoized" in body and mentality, and "un-integrated" except in work situations. That mentality, aggressively black nationalist today, and not quietly accommodative as in the past, is a phenomenon Americans will have to learn to live with, since they prefer this to the complete abolition of all forms of segregation. Malcolm X, LeRoi Jones, Eldridge Cleaver, and other gifted, angry young blacks have made the nation aware of what is going on in the minds of these black men who pour scorn upon what America has to offer as "integration," and counterpose to it a defiant and proud affirmation of their preference for segregation with dignity. This autobiography is a valuable document in that it portrays the lifestyles and the thought styles of those who will choose to live "half-integrated" and who insist that such a style of life can be lived with dignity, too.

Young black militants will not share George Nesbitt's integrationist choice, nor see any percentage in the goal he sets for himself in the writing of this book—trying to make Whitey empathize and understand—for it is a book directed at white liberal readers. (I am sure the author did not have lower middle-class, white proto-fascists in mind when he wrote it, nor black militants for that matter.) There is a strong middle-class bias to the book and an implicit plea: "Stop treating us all alike. Treat us as individual men and women, giving us equality of opportunity, so that each can express his fullest potential, and then let each man be rewarded and punished on his merit." He is saying this indirectly, gently, circuitously, and subtly, but insistently. And he is also saying that until such conditions do exist in America, black people will have to organize themselves and cooperate with white allies to fight for it.

Understanding a person like George Nesbitt also helps in understanding black men as unlike him as the Black Panthers. Most never had a chance to internalize the kind of restraints that made the author what he is, and they react all the time as he reacted *some of the* time, for he mentions occasions upon which even *he* "blew his cool." One is led to say, "If *he* reacted that way, my God, what a load of dynamite must lie within the bodies of other black men!" It is this common core of resentment shared by all Afro-Americans that makes it possible for them to understand, even when they do not approve of, the way some of their brothers express it. Thus, the author has deep sympathy for and profound understanding of that younger generation which he is sure regards him as "an old fuddy-duddy, short on identity, and Uncle Tom-ish, all rolled together for a quick write-off." He certainly doesn't consider himself any of these things, and he isn't. He explains with care and insight how diffuse prejudice and institutionalized racism have created a situation that has driven this generation of black youth to the point where the faith of their elders in "the system" seems like "treason to the race." Yet, he still clings to that faith, believing that white Americans who wield economic and political power will eventually make the kind of necessary, basic structural transformations that he discusses in a postscript. He has witnessed enough changes in his own lifetime, in some of which he played a key role, to sustain such a belief in the country's future. Yet, there is no repudiation of the stepped-up search for identity among black youth, though he does "kid" them a bit—using his beloved nephews and nieces as the objects of his observations, reminding them that "soul is something a little deeper than eating, dressing, and talking." Nor does he have any apology to make for his own life: "I celebrate my Negro self just as it is!"

George Nesbitt has enjoyed some aspects of being a black man in America—the families and friends within the warm subculture of the black world, and the challenges of fighting the white world. He has not had the ghetto experience that produces so-called "extremists." But he feels that apartheid must not be allowed to last forever. He is explicitly for "integration" as a long-term goal. Like virtually all middle-class Negroes over the past two hundred years, he stands firmly for "organizing unorganized resources where they are in the ghettoes—but toward the end of ghettoism." And he is also emphatic in his expression of abhorrence for "black racism," or "black violence," or "black separation." He sees Afro-Americans as being in the midst of what one writer has called "the summer of their discontent." His formula for survival and intelligent action is as relevant to white liberals as to all blacks, including black militants:

> "The certainty of uncertainty is what he must know and expect,
> learn to roll with, and manage to bounce back from, if he is to
> live strongly through the long summer."
> That is, as a Negro, *he* becomes somebody, too.

A Note on the Manuscript

PREXY NESBITT

George Belvey Nesbitt was born in Champaign, Illinois, on February 24, 1912, and died from pneumonia March 15, 2002, at ninety years of age, in Evanston, Illinois. Throughout his fifty-year legal career, he battled for the civil rights of poor and working people. This included taking the cases of US soldiers victimized by racial violence in Texas and elsewhere, until the US Army in retaliation stationed him in Australia in a tent by himself. Later, he worked on housing and employment discrimination.

Uncle George Nesbitt was unlike the other dozen-odd uncles and "yard kin" uncles that were around the Nesbitts and their circles growing up in the 1940s and 50s on the West Side of Chicago. But then those Nesbitts and their friends were not the usual type of American family, anyway. George and his wife, Josephine Ball Nesbitt, despite their hopes, never had children. But they had some sixteen nieces and nephews and an additional ten or fifteen "yard" nieces and nephews. I was lucky enough to be one of the "authentic" nephews, though those distinctions never mattered very much to my uncle. They took very seriously their interactions with their siblings' children and the children of their siblings' associates.

Thus, when Uncle George said to some of us nieces and nephews as early as 1966 that he was writing a book about the whole family history, most of us were attentive. Then when he self-published his book of poetry, *Praise of Worthy Women and Other Poems*, in 1985, we began to better understand how serious he was. He wanted to tell our family's story, perhaps because it wasn't typical (whatever that means), but also to make sense out of African American life in this country. The setbacks encountered by Martin Luther King Jr. in Chicago deeply affected him and made him want to offer his own perspective on racism in his home state.

We knew he had written many articles and essays and was never fearful of letting people know his viewpoint. We knew that the NAACP archives had a collection of letters, court documents, petitions, and other writings stemming from his legally representing large numbers of Negro soldiers attacked by whites during the 1940s, when Truman and Eisenhower initiated the desegregation of the US Army. But an entire book on the family was another matter altogether. We began to understand how big a project he was undertaking when he showed us the introduction to his book that his friend St. Clair Drake had written. He also related to us that he was writing the book as a response to the "black power" direction that the civil rights movement had taken. Further, he was challenging his nieces and nephews attracted by this perspective to ready their rebuttals to what he would presciently assert should be the principles and the goals of the struggle for racial justice.

Uncle George had finished writing the manuscript by the early 1970s, though he returned a few years later and added a brief postscript about various family members as well as some deaths in the family. He captured our family at a moment of incredible change and turmoil in the United States. From the time that he finished writing until the early 1990s, he took the manuscript to multiple publishers but was repeatedly rejected.

Family members all had copies of the book, but outside of the inner circle of Nesbitts, it was unknown. In 2018, I began working to try and publish the book. Uncle George had left us a manuscript of more than 175,000 words, with some handwritten corrections in places. Together with Zeb Larson, a historian and friend, I worked to prepare the manuscript for publication. Some sections have been condensed for length, some anecdotes were pruned from the final draft, and chapter titles have been added. Descriptions of Uncle George's childhood were shortened, as were later descriptions of the Nesbitt family in the 1960s and 1970s. However, every effort was made to preserve the feeling and ideas that he wanted to convey with this manuscript. The language and writing style were not changed except to correct a few minor typos: George's authorial voice has otherwise been preserved.

Readers may note that George Nesbitt quotes from a number of Jewish theologians throughout the text. He and his brothers were influenced by their father's membership in the Church of God and Saints of Christ, a black Hebrew Israelite denomination. They were also deeply influenced by both the African Methodist Episcopal and Christian Methodist Episcopal Church in Champaign. The teachings of black churches stayed with George Nesbitt throughout his life.

The chief difference between this book and the original manuscript is that the chapters on the family in the 1960s have been rearranged and consolidated. Capturing the family at this moment of change was as important to me as it was to Uncle George. It speaks to generational change, but also to generational continuity.

Uncle George was complex. Like other African American leaders in his generation, the United States in which he so deeply believed was rooted in beliefs envisioning a far different place from the polity that provided such tough lessons as he grew up. He tried to reconcile his admiration for figures such as Abraham Lincoln with the complicated reality of their own racism. He found pride in his race while living in a country that often tried to relegate him to an inferior status.

A quotation from the manuscript says it all. In his various jobs in the government, Uncle George was often required to respond to "interrogatories" from loyalty boards and security officers. Had he ever belonged to the National Negro Congress? The NAACP? The National Lawyers' Guild? The American Student Union? As he says,

> The need for these queries I rather accepted but they were nonetheless irritable. One set of interrogatories invited my adding to my answers anything which I felt pertinent to my loyalty to the Government of the United States. In that space I wrote, "I have nothing to hide and little to add. My loyalty to my Government is inevitably of the highest order. All that I am, as the college-bred descendant of slaves, I owe to its ideals and workings.

Much of what I am not yet, as a second-class citizen, can be obtained the same way. What I am obliged to count on so heavily, I am committed to preserve."

Prexy Nesbitt
May 30, 2020
Oak Park, Illinois

Preface

This book is about three generations of a stable but quite undistinguished Negro family and one of its members of no greater distinction. The entire lot lacks a single celebrity; no one of its members has been acclaimed as the first Negro to have done this or that of note. It also lacks the infamous as much as the famed. To dare the writing of a book about a Negro family that is neither celebrated nor sick surely requires explanation.

The effort was hardly escapable in the first instance. Not being burdened with children of my own but instead blessed with nieces and nephews who repeatedly urged me to set down for them the stories which I have from time to time told them, I have simply succumbed to their blandishments.

But in more truth, it has been conversations with several adult friends of mine which persuaded me to go to work. These pressures have had their way, despite my fear that well over two decades of expressing myself within the Federal bureaucracy have left me unfitted for writing readably, if ever the facility was at all mine.

Those discussions have taken this line, as I am able to reconstruct it.

The stories of my telling belong to a wider audience than to the children of my brothers. For as the urgings of my young kinsmen suggest, they are of a generation whose members grope and yearn for comfort and clarity respecting the duality of their beings as American Negroes. They reach for a sense of continuity for themselves, to better accept themselves, and to know more of their particular past for strengthening their position in the future, as is most plain in so many of younger Negroes who rather frantically seek roots in the long, long ago, and as far away as Africa.

What it was like for poor Negro parents, a generation removed from slavery, to move from the rural South to the urban North, there to engage themselves and their children in incessant striving for self-esteem, respect from whites, and material well-being, is a part of that continuity. For this movement from the South has been a course steadily run by hundreds of thousands who represent both more of the plainer people of America still behaving in essentially a pioneering fashion and her darker people ever protestant against the withholding of the American promise and continuing, stubbornly, to pursue it.

Northbound Negro migrants have not conquered forests nor crossed a barren expanse. They have traveled a route far worse, across rough mountain and frightful morass, to sight bright rainbows beyond stretches of quicksand, and meet with posted signs which both urge them on and forbid their passing. Along their way and at the journey's end, they have encountered again and again an enemy worse than nature, an alliance of callous indifference and the nurtured evil of man against man. This has been pioneering. South to North, country to city, within the color line.

Many of these travelers have made it, survived and persisted, striven and succeeded, even according to the measures for those who are allowed the easier, white ways, free of restraints. Some of those who did not faint were once pointed to in community after community, with hidden guilt and show of pride, as "the hard-working, respectable ones."

But today those Negroes on the move and who prove the will and strengths of a people, those called "upwardly mobile" and "the Negro middle class," are nearly forgotten. The white community, distant and aloof, and with fear and trembling, looks upon what it has wrought in the great black ghettos of our cities and eases its guilt by seeing all caught within them as great, simple masses of helpless and hapless humanity. This is done even while elaborate means for the restoration and release of the hemmed in are proposed and somewhat implemented; while the protest and push continue, with increasingly frequent violent outbursts; while others still arrive, moving from subjugation to alien and hostile environs in search of greener pastures.

Worse than being lost in the eyes of those outside the ghetto, its respectable residents are spurned and all but spat upon by the youthful activists who shout "black power" on campus and in the streets, and by would-be Negro Messiahs. These young assertive ones say that their elders woo false gods and hate themselves. They see the struggle for racial equality as something commenced only a few months ago and tag their elders as "Toms." Those institutions built by their fathers and grandfathers to carry forward the struggle are denied and disdained, despite the long proof of their capabilities.

Now black power ought to be celebratory too, as white power has so long been and so patently is. Moreover, the exercise of rights and responsibilities requires a sense of identity and self-esteem. And it is good to see the rebellious young ones engage themselves in aptness of self-celebration, the resurrection of which has been long due.

But the rub is that too many of the celebrants are drinking wantonly of the good medicine and having themselves a binge. They confuse ends with means and go on to make their color distinctiveness the end-all of their efforts. They would overcome white racism with black and seek race separation. By this token, they are entangled in their narcissism, seek insularity in a fluid and mobile society, and lose hold on the leverage which the American creed gives the Negro cause, while young whites and even a part of themselves reach for the goodness of life beyond abundant bread, and at the very hour when a brotherhood of plurality and equality presses for acceptance around a shrunken world.

To tell the story, across three generations, of one Negro family which came and persists in the pioneering path—of thousands upon thousands—whose weary ones were never celebrated, are too little understood and now questioned, when not altogether forgotten—may be helpful in the midst of the current turbulence of Negro-white relations.

In addition, though many, many are the Negroes who can truly tell stories which match and indeed excel those told here, my friends remind me that too few of such Negroes can bring themselves to tell them. They fear so to pinch themselves lest they waken from dreams more to their liking.

Lastly, the time and place for these stories perhaps strengthen their character. The nineteen hundred and twenties, thirties, and forties embraced the Great Depression, which was yet longer and deeper for Negroes. In those decades "the times were hard" indeed, to test the fiber of the poor and aspirant, especially the color-burdened among them. Negro-white relations in the Midwest, the setting for most of the narratives, were awkward and tricky, in some part harsh and rigidly separate but unmarked so, thus combining the worst of the essence of the color system in the South and the nature of that more prevalent in the East and the Far West.

For these reasons, then, I was persuaded to write this book.

The first chapter describes a bit the community and neighborhood in which my parents settled and reared their children, and the forces which earliest began their shaping.

The second and third chapters tell of my parents, of that strong and heroic but warm figure who was our mother and how she skillfully managed our family, while relegating to my father the central responsibility for rearing, disciplining, and making men of his boys, by teaching them Biblical wisdom and injunction, the frailty in the notion of color supremacy, to despise hypocrisy and be wary of superstition, and to accept the dignity and worth of labor, if one was not, in his heart, another man's servant.

Chapter four relates how I chanced never to find my blackness either a pitiable or a despicable thing, for myself or others, but something instead to be bravely borne and acclaimed as long as whites made it a burden.

The fifth and sixth chapters are of the same span of time. The fifth recounts the unwelcome presence of a handful of Negroes in a prairie state university, where some scientists discovered and some teachers taught their students how to raise greater yields of grain and bigger hogs faster, while others insisted that not much could be done for a Negro and not much was, though we Negro students fought against the tide. The sixth is the story of how I sought to cling to, serve, and identify with the Negro community, as my university training pulled me from it, and how, in the end, my independence of thought and action brought upon me its censorship.

The seventh is the story of a Negro child's head start in the world of hard work; who's fooling whom when a Negro is the hired personal servant of a white; the discomfiture of being all dressed up with degrees and no place to go in the midst of the Great Depression; how it took a "drag" to become a lackey in a railway depot, and loss of the soul was risked in the process; and how a certain vicious circle of no jobs for untrained Negroes and no training for them because there would be no such jobs was broken, and without bringing to a community its second race riot.

The eighth chapter pictures me as a made-to-order misfit in an apartheid army, unable to cease fighting Jim Crow, and the exorbitant price exacted for the privilege.

With the ninth and tenth chapters some departure is ventured from the restraint exercised in those preceding them. In the ninth something is told of the mistreatment I have suffered in places of public accommodation in Northern communities, where law forbade it; in the tenth, I tell of how firmly fixed the racial slur remains and how countless are its ways, as whites and blacks intermingle wherever in newer-day America. But with each I was tempted variously to note also that a hard residuum of more subtle persecution is part of the foreseeable future for Negroes in America, perhaps to last as long as Negroes visibly differ from their fellows. This seems to me the irreducible element of "the strange meaning of being black" in this country of ours. Still it is never to be accepted by *us* nor by any who would make America what she is acclaimed. And it is a measure of how far all America has yet to go in the pursuit of human decency and a sign that the goal is one perhaps never fully to be grasped but always and unceasingly to be sought.

The eleventh chapter tells of my brothers and how each has remained the husband of his first and only wife for nearly a quarter of a century; how these professionally trained men and women have lived for more than twenty years in the midst of Chicago's sorriest racial ghetto, rearing their children there and serving as supporting members of the community.

The last chapter is devoted to the children and how they were reared through a blending of old and new ways; how each, without a miss so far, heads for college and service to people; how they have met and mingled at home with people from thirty-five countries, seventeen of them on the African continent; the ease with which they traverse the color line; their youthful activism and flirtations with black power; and finally how the latter little dismays me and why.

* * *

I must now acknowledge the help of those who enabled me at long last to "make" the book my nieces and nephews demanded as little ones. Several of the older ones read several of its chapters, giving them their blessing. Though this accolade held no promise that my manuscript would ever be printed, it assured me that there were those who would read and even treasure it.

My wife, Josephine, patiently allowed me to reduce to writing the stories too often heard by her and learned not to interrupt the writing as she so often had the telling of them. My friends of long standing, Frank S. Horne and Mrs. Marian Perry Yankauer, encouraged the undertaking, though neither is in anyway responsible for the results. Mrs. Levergne Walker read several early chapters in roughest state and urged me on. Henry Minton Francis also critically reviewed a chapter for me.

My thanks are also due a bevy of lady associates of mine who were kind enough to type for me during their evenings and after long hours of the same for Uncle Sam. Mrs. Catherine W. Jones typed almost the entire manuscript as it was first scrawled, distinguishing my quite alike r's from n's, a's from o's, and e's from undotted i's. Miss Pamela Johnson did the bulk of what she more desperately hoped than I would prove "the final" it was called. There were other girls who pitched in to do for me a few pages, a chapter, or two. These generous young ladies are the Misses Lea Abrams, Cheryl Arrington, Sarah Goins, Frances Maltese, and Mrs. Catherine Daniel Brooks.

Our Family's Great Migration

GROWING UP BLACK IN THE
SHADOW OF THE UNIVERSITY

A man should remember the place from which, he has derived a benefit.
—Bereshit Rabbah 79:6

Lucian and Christine came north as teenagers, up from the South, early in the century. They came along a path long and still used by the black peasantry of the Delta and the states between it and the Mason-Dixon Line, the Illinois Central railway. They were born in the in-between area, he in little Huntingdon, Tennessee, and she somewhere in the country-side of Flint, Alabama. They first stopped among relatives in Pulaski, near the southern tip of Illinois in its Little Egypt section. Finding the poverty and the color ways of Pulaski too much like back home, they soon moved farther north and again by way of the I. C. This move left them still short of Chicago, terminal for the I. C. and Mecca for Northbound Negroes by the thousands.

They were never able to explain this failure to go all the way to the I. C.'s Twelfth Street Terminal Station in Chicago. But the shortcoming was likely of great fortune for them and for their children to come. For Chicago, oasis of freedom and opportunity along the shore of Lake Michigan, even then was quicksand for many wending their way there from the rural South. Besides, the place at which they stopped was Champaign, small and still country enough for liking, the home of the University of Illinois. Here they put themselves down in 1906, with their hopes and fears, two mules, a cow, and a flock of chickens.

Three decades and five sons later, the sons themselves could explain the anchorage in Champaign. Half in fun and half seriously, we could agree that Mom and Pop wound up there, each for a good reason. Pop preferred a livelihood of cleaning and dusting in the little business establishments and the homes of the professors and others about the university campus to back-breaking labor in the industrial mills of the Chicago area. Mom was bent upon having one boy-child after another and a university handy for their education.

Today the proof of a wise choice in each case is in. My father is still alive and kicking in Chicago, after twenty years of janitoring and as many years more of contracting to wax floors and wash windows here and there in Champaign. My mother, who herself knew only six years of on-and-off Negro schooling in the cotton country of Alabama, died in 1947, shortly after seeing her last son through the university, having had for herself altogether two sons trained in medicine and one each in physics, electrical engineering, and law. She largely managed it herself, partly by pointing and prodding her children, and partly by cooking day in and day out for the members of a white fraternity in order that she could put together and push along a small but real brotherhood of her own.

THE NORTH END

We lived in the northeastern-most portion of the city, bordering Urbana on the east and open country to the north. It was fittingly and inescapably a neighborhood for the poor and the Negroes among them, leaving them twice located on the wrong side of the tracks, the Big Four railroad for its southern boundary and the Illinois Central for its western.

The small frame houses in the North End were without central heat and inside plumbing, and most also lacked electricity at the time. Only the central street, Fifth, was paved, and even it was without a sewer. There was city water throughout the area, but the taps, like the toilet facilities, were mainly outside. Only a select few of the homes enjoyed telephones. There was not a single park in the area, the nearest being completely across town.

Lawhead, the neighborhood school, stood impressively tall and of sturdy red brick construction, with inside toilets served by a cesspool. It was in a central location, though it had only four classrooms. Once a child advanced beyond fourth grade, he had to go beyond the neighborhood for his schooling. Lawhead also had ample grounds for play space and even a set of swings. But use of the school grounds outside of school hours was prohibited, a rule that applied throughout the city, but was most strictly enforced by uniformed city police at Lawhead. Except between the hours of 8:30 a.m. and 4:00 p.m., the city's then lone squad car or one of its two motorcycle "cops" would regularly turn in the school's driveway and shoo away the children. During the long, hot midwestern summers, even the few privileged hours of play during school term (before the a.m. session, before the p.m. session and a half-hour recess period to breach each) were shelved. Most of the summer, most of the smaller children were forced to play in their tiny yards, out in the dirt roads, or on the vacant lots too often liberally anointed with tin cans, broken glass, and other debris.

Most North Enders bore nicknames. They were not the easy, familiar ones which start in the family. Though there were "Bobs," "Buds," "Billys," "Jacks" and "Johnnys," "Jims" and "Joes," and a "Jerry," such polite and parental handles were often themselves replaced. For a fellow who was accepted had to have a name that was not only short and bendy but which fitted him, fitted nobody but him, whether he liked it or not. The label was better the more the subject disliked it, if he could take it. He then belonged with us, not just to his mama and papa. Many a guy wore the jibe proudly. In our neighborhood we helped a fellow's folks to make a man out of him.

Johnny Baxter was a four-letter man at high school, agile, fast, and rough, but he was also a braggart. He had proven himself the best fifty-yard dash man in the state but let a nobody from the high school in little Tougaloo beat him. So Johnny was promptly dubbed "Tougaloo Kid." "Dutch" Waumbierry rode a motorcycle like it was a bucking bronco, chewed tobacco, cursed like a sailor, and all in all was as tough as they came. He made "Dutch" a respected name. One of the Barnharts did the same with "Mutt."

3

There were, of course, lots of fellows called "Shorty," including my brother, Lendor. One of the Lewis boys was called "Fat." But fat was not greasy enough for one of us bearing the honored name, Homer. We called him "Lard." Another had a head of ample size and so was tagged "Jug Head." The fellow called "Hots" for the small, peppery, heart-shaped candies we ate, known as red-hots, simply had extra-thick, extra-red lips prominently seen against his glistening black skin. The "Hooks" which R. B. Scoby bore was a remarkably accurate description of the thin and crooked legs he could move so fast. "Jabber" Hegmon stuttered badly to achieve the name. "Piggy" was stuck on a white youngster who helped his father at truck farming enough sometimes to have plenty of black Illinois dirt all over himself. "Gates" Wade's feet were as big and leathery as suitcases of alligator.

Occasionally there was compliment in the nickname. "Flap" Burgess did swim like a fish and "Whiz" Clark was really fast on his feet. "Zip" Lewis had plenty of zip. "Hoppy" and "Hop" abbreviated James Hopkins' last name but they also characterized his alacrity at baseball.

George Evans was called "Spinach" because he did not like it. I was "Artichoke" but not because of any association with that fancy vegetable. I was merely so small as to be deemed hardly a "hearty choke." I was also dubbed "Yatsy" for some forgotten reason. I also forget what gave rise to "Chicken," "Salty," "Soapy," "Sally," "Snapper," "Preacher," and "Coot," and many another such soubriquets. I do recall that my oldest brother, carefully christened Russell Aaron, became "Rusty," sometimes stretched to "Rusty Butt."

The bigger children took more to Fifth Street, competing with wagons, autos, and delivery trucks for the use of its solid footing. Much of their play took place out in the center of the busy street and along its curbs. In the spring and summer, it was marbles, shinney and rounders, top spinning, auto hopping, and bike racing up and down its brick-paved expanse. Occasionally an auto and a cyclist would get all mixed up out there in the middle of the street. One day Johnny Willis and R. B. Scoby were racing each other on their bikes, pulling hard and with heads down. Neither saw a car pulling out of an alley as they neared it. The driver blew his horn and came to a stop almost squarely in their path. Johnny looked up and was able barely to miss the car but Scoby plowed right into its hood, to turn a neat somersault and find himself and his bike suddenly sprawled in the street. The frightened driver jumped from his car and rushed toward Scoby just as he pulled himself up from the street.

"Are you hurt, son? Are you hurt," the auto driver anxiously asked.

"Naw," said Scoby, "I'm okay," and he was.

It was then that an old man, who had looked on, said to the auto owner, "He's all right. But you'd better see about your car. It may be banged up good."

The parking strips and sidewalks of Fifth Street were the places along which the bigger boys would prove their strength and agility, seeing who could jump the farthest, stand on his hands the longest, and do the best cartwheels, especially after the police had chased them from the schoolyard. Many a fleet-footed, springy-legged youngster first showed his wares out in the center of Fifth Street and then went on to win blue ribbons at the annual Champaign-Urbana-wide track meet, competing for Marquette, Willard, and Central schools. Lots of them as grade schoolers ran the hundred-yard dash in closer to ten than eleven seconds, yet never reached high school or became varsity trackmen for one reason or another. I saw one of them, the youngest boy in the athletic Pickens family, broad-jump more than twenty-three feet when he was a mere eighth grader. Besides his method was that then in vogue and known as the "double-hitch-kick." But nobody had taught Clyde such a fancy style. He was just doing what came naturally.

Sometimes in the evening the big boys would sit telling stories along the curbing and under a corner light. As the hour grew late, the younger ones hanging about, with eyes and ears wide open, would be called home or sent on their way there by the older fellows. Then the bigger fellows would "play the dozens" among themselves and tell stories about traveling salesmen or jokes that they had read in *Whiz Bang*. When a smaller fellow was permitted to stay and hear the likes, he could know that he had arrived. He was "in," as it is now said.

A UNIVERSITY FOR A PLAYGROUND

The University of Illinois was no small part of the earliest influences of Champaign upon us. This was not because the university made of the North End a laboratory for study of the poor. Nor was it concerned about the lot of Negroes in Champaign-Urbana. The truth is that once Negro residents of the community, like other Negroes from wherever, sought to make of the university their "alma mater," they found themselves little more than stepchildren. Moreover, at the time any Negro big enough to be on his own near the campus during the twenties had to suffer student groups—most always groups—calling out "Nigger!" or any of a dozen such other names then in white vogue.

Nevertheless, my brothers and I and many of our buddies adored the university. We claimed her in fun and frivolity and in our reachings too.

The campus and its environs were a wide and wonderful playground for any curious youngster free enough to be on his own a bit. Its big, open buildings, the tall bushes near them, its many trees and spacious lawns, here and there with a bench and bordered by low, piped railing, gave North End youngsters a new and bigger world to tramp, romp, and explore. We took on the campus at every chance a group of us could get. The opportunities came often enough, because "out on the campus," as it was put, were many a Negro mother and father, cooking and cleaning in the fraternities and sororities, the rooming and boarding houses, and the restaurants serving the students.

We sometimes made our way out to the huge Illinois Armory, a place made-to-order for a kid's yell and its echo. Besides we saw there the R.O.T.C. units at drill and the indoor track team at practice. Nearby was a building where the Illinois band practiced. We could always stop and listen to it and some days see it practicing its fancy formations.

There were university games we were certain we had to see and ways to do it without so much as a dime. It was as much fun making the ruse work as seeing all there was to see afterward. At Illinois Field, surrounded by its tall, iron picket fence, we saw many a baseball game despite the fence and the canvas stretched behind it. Some of us would provide business for "Pete," a campus policeman, at one point along the fence, while others slipped over it at another. Or we would make fun and friends with the student gate attendants who would cooperatively turn their backs long enough to let several of us make it inside the Field. Or friendly students on the inside would pull apart the canvas at one of its joints. The peeking through the opening would be good for the rest of the game, if there was no noisy fussing and fighting for the front-most position.

One time several of us literally dug our way into a football game, a big game such as Illinois against the University of Michigan. At the football end of the field, the bleachers made it impossible to see from the outside, and the game was too much a "must" to trust to the luck of a slip-in. So several of us planned and engineered our way in. We located a spot along the fence and at the end of the field farthest from the bleachers and where the earth was fairly loose. We loosened it more with sharp sticks the evening before the game. The next day several of us pulled aside the earth and made it safely inside before the leak-in was discovered.

But the peeking and the slipping in were all over for my bunch once the Memorial Stadium was built. Its walls were brick. We would no longer peek through, nor could we go over or under.

I remember the big football game for the dedication of the stadium, and how we tried every trick in our bag but still were outside when time for the kick-off came. We stood in a little knot, looking way up to the top tier of the stadium. Here a sympathetic fan stood and began periodically to shout down upon us announcement of events inside. He yelled down, "That was the kick-off!," as we heard the crowd cheer. Soon his shouting account was of one Illinois touchdown after another, and only minutes apart. We were being joshed for sure, we thought, and soon we broke up. But I later learned that it was all true. It was the afternoon the famous "Red" Grange ran rampant-over the Michigan team in 1928.

The university influenced as well as entertained us. My brothers and I perhaps felt the university even more closely, more often, and in more ways than many other Negro youngsters. We were in and about the campus with frequency. Wright and Green, the hub of the campus, was as familiar to us as Lawhead School, the center of our neighborhood. We would play-march to the famous "Illinois Loyalty" song and could sing it too. We wore on our heads the green "spots," marking the wearers as freshmen at the university, before we left fourth grade at Lawhead. These "spots" of ours were often tightened up with a safety pin and invariably were pieces of rummage, with tears or holes in the felt, bills crushed, or felt cover missing from the center button. But they were as proudly worn by us in the streets, as we were also to have at home a navy blue blanket with a huge, block "I" of orange color at its center, though it must have been moth-eaten or a cast-off of some other kind.

For Papa was janitor at "The Coop," the University of Illinois Book and Supply Store, situated at the Wright and Green Streets corner. He regularly brought home salvaged items that became treasures to his boys. We went to the Coop as often and stayed as long as we could in the midst of the books and the students. Papa would come home each evening telling of this or that about the Coop, the university, or Professor So and So.

Near mid-high school for me, I took to the university in another fashion. My older brother had been hospitalized for several years, during which he had become acquainted with several of its younger faculty members who would visit the sanitarium and had commenced supplying him reading materials. He would pass this literature on to me, including *Atlantic Monthly*, but also *The Nation* and *The New Republic* and now and then a copy of the socialistic *Milwaukee Leader*. Somehow, the *Leader* led me to a book whose title now escapes me. But it was written by Glenn Frank, then president of the University of Wisconsin. The book talked of the "social fluidity" inherent in the American social system in a way which deeply impressed me. I don't remember its talking specifically about Negroes. But when it spoke of poor people, their struggles to improve their working and living conditions, and how this was to be expected and was really good for the whole country, it all seemed to mean Negroes too.

By this time, too, I had come completely under the spell of the legend and lore of Lincoln pervading Champaign-Urbana. Lincoln's likeness, in pictures and statuary, was present in many places, and here and there in the community there were quotations from his speeches. Lincoln places abounded. The Urbana-Lincoln was and still is a local hotel. Lincoln Hall is one of the university buildings, and there is a Lincoln School in each of the twin cities. Lincoln Street is in Champaign and Lincoln Avenue in Urbana. Lincoln had ridden the circuit as a country lawyer and pleaded cases in Champaign County, our teachers told us. Certain families proudly claimed that their antecedents were his hosts on such occasions.

In February of each year, the local newspapers would editorialize on Lincoln's virtues and copiously recount the legends about him, usually taking care to identify him with Champaign and its surroundings. One of the history professors at the university was a Lincoln scholar, and his talks on the subject would be fulsomely reported in the local papers. I was moved also to read several books about the Great Emancipator. As a Boy Scout on a weekend camping trip near Monticello, Illinois, I think it was, I stumbled into a plaque marking the site of one of Lincoln's debates with Stephen Douglas, and wherever I was along the Sangamon River that weekend, I felt that Lincoln had been there in the very spot before me, for sure.

So I picked him up through a sort of osmosis. I was in Lincoln water and got thoroughly wet. I believed all the stories I read, imparting his virtues, the one about the return of the pennies and that of the pulling of the hog from the mud. I still believed it all, even after reading one biography rather in the muckraking tradition. What was much more for me, I felt a superior claim on him, for he had vowed to strike a blow against slavery when he saw black people herded together and sold off like cattle at New Orleans. I soon began to sense the hypocrisy and weaknesses in those who made such fuss over him, while having little use for me.

A bit later, of course, I learned more of Lincoln than all the lore and legend. He had declared himself a believer in a basic white superiority; blacks were unfit for political equality. He had preferred the colonization of Negroes rather than to free them. He had lagged way behind the northern preachers, press, and politicians during the war which so vastly expanded his power, at first even stopping the Union generals from turning slaves into badly needed soldiers, so hesitant was he to bring slavery to an end. His big feet were of clay; he either was short on moral courage or played politics with the problem of color, as did many another man before him and since.

Yet, though my reading brought the Great Emancipator down to earth, if Champaign-Urbana whites wanted to keep him on a pedestal, I'd know no better and hold them to Lincoln as they saw him and wanted him seen.

It is fair to say also that life for us in Champaign drew some of its meaning from the fact that though Negroes were set off, they were by no means completely isolated. Even as children we freely circulated wherever in the community.

KIDS AND COLOR

In the twenties, the North End, which is now a little racial ghetto, was perhaps as much white as Negro. There were lots of families of German origin. We lived in the Vredenburgh addition and went to school with Schaedes, Gaults, Glandts, and a younger Schalk, as well as the Vredenburghs. Most of us were delivered by the good Dr. Schowengerdt, who lived just below the neighborhood. There were also Irish and Italian youngsters. We played with them, too, though mostly they went to school at St. Mary's, just across the tracks at the lower end of the neighborhood. There were also many more common whites, mainly of English origin, or its claimants.

With all of them, the play was rough and tumble. Shinney played in the middle of Fifth Street with tin cans for pellets was a favorite game. When we engaged in what is now known as "touch football," it always finished up as pure and decided scrimmage. "Rassling" was frequent and it went on until the fellow underneath would "give," saying as much if he had breath enough left. There were fights, too, especially when someone "niggered" or "dagoed" another or "dirtied" a kid preferring to be left simply Irish, though these scraps were as cleanly as hard fought. When someone came to the top or bloodied a nose in such a scrap, part wrestling and part pugilism as it was, it was all over.

But I remember one of them which was different. It was not enough for the Negro boy called "nigger" to get the better of the white one making the slur.

Paul was a younger one of several sons in the big family of our new minister who had recently arrived all the way from South Carolina, where Paul was born and reared. He was my age and in my Sunday School class—as well as a fourth-grade pupil with me at Lawhead school. I was beginning to know Paul, I thought, as a bright and friendly fellow though he did seem sort of hot-tempered. I had learned that he would fight at the drop of a hat, but so would others.

That day when the white youngster "niggered" Paul, he got himself the fight for which he asked, but of kind I am certain neither he nor any of us gathered about had ever seen. Paul was lean and wiry and fast with feet and hands. He tore into the white boy with the fury of a black storm suddenly loosed, striking him again and again without let-up until shortly the lad was knocked to the ground, where he lay crying and cowering, obviously whipped. But Paul was not finished and still in the midst of his fury. Grabbing the beaten boy by the shirt collar, he pulled and jerked him to the sidewalk, where he first kicked him several times, then jumped astride him and began bumping the back of his head against the sidewalk, while choking him with both hands clutched about his neck. The brutality of it was terrifying until several of us together managed to pull Paul off and away. We talked about it for days, not being able to understand it. Finally I asked about it at home. My father said, "He did that white boy the way he's seen Negroes whipped in South Carolina. Maybe by more than one white at a time too."

My brothers and I enjoyed close relationships with several of these white youngsters with whom we played.

The youngest boy in a German-descended family sometimes slept at our house, as one of my younger brothers would at his. This friend was immensely fond of my mother's biscuits. In a sense he liked them more than we did, for he liked them cold, and we wanted them only as a hot bread. As this lad became a teenager, his older brother, who also had been close to Negroes among his contemporaries, began to avoid them. It was rumored that he had become a Klansman. During the same period an all-Negro troop of Boy Scouts was formed, which the white lad wanted to join but was forbidden to do by his older, color-conscious brother. Several years later, the lad drifted into bad company, despite its all-whiteness, and was placed in a penal institution. Later his brother, remorseful over what had happened, told me that he had indeed kept our buddy out of the Scout troop and by then knew it to have been a mistake. No repentance respecting the Klan membership was offered, if he had in fact belonged to it.

Across the street, my brother had a white chum, and the two were rather inseparable for a long period. Down the street and on our side at the end of the block were Swedes with whom we were friendly. I remember being sent to read and explain a public notice of some kind or other to Mrs. Pedersen. We were especially on good terms with the Burgesses. Mr. Burgess was a contemporary of my father's with two sons of our ages, who lived nearby and distributed newspapers throughout the neighborhood.

One of the Burgess boys had made himself my friend almost as soon as the family arrived in our neighborhood from southern Illinois. I shall never forget him. It isn't simply because "Flap," as we called him, was my age, my classmate, seemed pretty smart, and was a regular fellow. It was more because he was an excellent swimmer and brave along with it.

Flap had jumped into our favorite swimming hole while a bunch of bigger boys sat on its banks, afraid to go in. I did not see his daring, I felt it, for he was after the drowning me. He pulled me out and safely to shore after I had gone down twice and was full of water.

A Saturday in late spring had turned warm, warm enough to make boys itch for the first swim of the season. We had abandoned Fifth Street and hiked the country road that wound around the corner of a cemetery until we reached a point just south of the Urbana Country Club. The hole was there all right, but the water was high and swift, swollen by recent rains. Most of us undressed ourselves anyway, down to the very skin. (A fellow in swimming trunks would have drawn a laugh.) We sat tempted but wary. First light pieces of fallen tree limb and then heavier ones were thrown in the water, all to be tossed about and soon swiftly sucked downstream, so deep and fast was the water. Several of us gave up and began dressing. But all at once someone held a ball in the air, yelled that he was about to throw it in, while daring anyone to go after it. When he let it go, I was the sucker who dove in and started for the bobbing ball.

I was never much of a swimmer and panicked as soon as the churning water began to toss me about. It was then that "Flap," a little white fellow, almost alone, if not that, among fifteen or twenty Negroes, most of whom were twice his size, and to whom he was still pretty much a stranger, showed his mettle.

ERRANDS AND FOLKS

But much of our getting around was on errands.

My older brother and I at a very early age commenced regular trips back and forth through the business district carrying laundry which my mother did for a West Side family or two before she commenced cooking "out." The head of one of the families was a lawyer, whose many white shirts I envied. Delivering those shirts was not the proximate cause of my studying law but perhaps contributed to my deciding to wear a white collar someday.

We soon discovered the Main Library on West Church Street. It overlooked the West Side Park and had so many more books, tables, and ladies-to-help than our Branch Library room at Marquette School that we transferred our cards to the Main Library. We also had to go downtown regularly for Mama, especially to "the A & P" for groceries, where she said the prices were better than in the neighborhood stores.

Papa would have us meet him after school at one of the West Side homes where he tended the lawn or at the big apartment house where Papa was janitor, and Zuppke, the renowned Illinois football coach, lived. Papa would want us to help pick fruit or to bundle up books and magazines to take home in our wagon. Later, after I was in high school, I went regularly on Saturdays to clean the foyer, halls, stairway, and back porches of a small apartment building on the West Side.

But what really made us circulate throughout the whole community, at least once a week, was a Negro news weekly, the *Chicago Defender*. The family was its agent and at one time sold and delivered more than two hundred copies weekly. Our customers were located most everywhere, it seemed to us. Negroes lived not only in the big North End section but in three small clusters elsewhere in Champaign and in several locations in Urbana. We also delivered in some instances where our customers worked, in West Side homes, in barber and valet shops downtown, at fraternity and sorority houses, and, in several cases, professional offices.

So we began to learn something of the way the West Side people, the white and well-to-do, lived. We saw their big, spacious, and well-kept homes with neatly landscaped yards and, inside their homes, would glimpse rooms with carpeted floors and some with book-lined walls and magazines lying all about. These people all seemed clean and neat, too, like their houses and yards. They, and even their children, spoke English like our schoolteachers and people around the university.

Some of these West Side people gave us books and copies of magazines like *National Geographic,* old copies but still clean and fresh like. They would sometimes ask if we liked to go to school and even what we would be when we became grownups.

Most of our paper customers became our friends. Many would take up time with us, or make us come in and stay awhile and warm up during cold weather; and some would give each of us an apple or a banana, now and then. I remember that when I graduated from high school, my customers gave me two five-dollar gold pieces and several shirts, including one that I learned was a $3.98 shirt, the first "fine" shirt I ever had. Occasionally one would want to know what was in the paper he was buying, and I could tell him or her.

One old man once said, "Well, son, was there one of us lynched somewheres this week like last?" I went home and mentioned this to Mama. She talked some about lynchings. What she said has long been completely forgotten. But I deeply remember the several big tears I saw start down her cheeks before she rose and left the room.

At the places of several of the customers, I would linger as long as I could. There was Dr. H. E. Rowan, who sat several times and talked to me about a place called Meharry Medical College and showed me some pictures of it and his graduation class. Mr. Herman Harris, who ran a little cab company, was a favorite customer and once employed me to answer telephones for him at night. I looked up to a Mr. Albert Lee who clerked in the president's office at the university and was a committeeman for our Boy Scout troop. Two of my customers owned and operated cleaning and pressing "establishments," as they were called: one was Woodie's on the campus, and the other Allen Green's, downstairs on the main corner downtown. These two places were intriguing to me. They seemed more like "real" businesses than the neighborhood stores run and patronized only by Negroes. They were located on busy streets, the people working in them moved in business-like fashion, though they also were Negroes and simply pressing clothes and shining shoes. The customers were mostly white.

Several of my women customers were especially nice, I felt. One ran a little store where I bought cookies, and she talked to me about school every time I saw her; like my mother, she made school seem important. Another was "Mother" Hopkins, whose home was always so clean and neat, with flowers inside and outside too, and who spoke such good English for an older person, I felt. Still another woman had two boys of my age with whom I would stop to play because her home was the end of my route. But I became close to her also; she seemed busy always but stopped to talk to me about things like the mayor, taxes, and politics. Then there was the customer who lived in a big house with white men going in and out almost every Saturday afternoon I delivered the paper. For a long time the place had puzzled me. When I first started carrying papers, going along with Papa, he would not allow me to deliver to that house and would do it himself.

Yet the big woman who, I later learned, "ran" the house was certainly always nice to me. More than once when it was very cold she made me come in to get warm—she had almost to pull me inside. As I would enter the door, the ladies Papa later called "painted women" would all leave the big parlor with its big stuffed chairs and ashtrays all about.

Champaign-Urbana was a good place in which to grow up, a good place for any boy to start out. It was a place of tallness, oak, elm, and field corn, and men too, the learned ones about the university and Lincoln, the legendary one, to whom the community made avid claim. It was a good place also because it was some country and some city, not too much of either.

It was not the worst place for Negro youngsters to start out. It set us off but did not hem us in. It denied us, but it whetted our aspirations too, pushed us back but pulled us along. It was the Midwest, unwilling to handle Negroes as in the South but unable to treat them in the ways of New England. I like to think that it prepared me to live in my country, all over and anywhere, not to expect too much nor to settle for too little.

So I came early to know people on both sides of the tracks and each side of the color line, different kinds of people, living in different ways, in different kinds of houses. I found some to have fun and be friends with, and some to look and listen to. I began early to know that the right people were not wholly so, nor the bad ones altogether without goodness.

A Family Which Stayed Together

Whatever blessing dwells in the house comes from her.
—Baba Mezia 59a

Ours was a family which stayed together, though it rather prayed apart and was poor and Negro besides. As my father said not long ago, "If your mother had not died in 'forty-seven, we would be married nearly sixty years by now."

The family continues together in another way, not altogether common. My father is eighty-five years old and moving into senility. But he is not stuck away. He had five years, off and on, of what at most was merely "colored schooling" in the rural South in the 1880s, speaks simply and ungrammatically, though dogmatically, and is a bigoted follower of a bizarre religious faith. Yet for twenty years now, he has lived in an apartment building with his college-bred sons and their schoolteacher wives. He mingles freely and frequently with them, his grandchildren, and their guests. When there are dinner guests, Papa is often invited, and his presence awaited so that he can bless the food in the strange manner of his faith. He has sometimes been difficult and had to be explained. But he is never slighted or hidden away, even to smooth the way for a special occasion.

MAMA'S BEING IN CHARGE

The family's strength was founded in Mama's being in charge, rather than its being strong in spite of the fact. It was not so much her domination as her leadership, including a capacity for keeping Papa happily under the illusion that he was in control, as he followed her planning and direction. This was the way of it, despite Papa's firm and oft-repeated view that "the man is head of the house" as God intended, he was certain, the latter being so clearly evidenced by the prior creation of Adam. But Papa would have his ample say and then almost always go along with Mama's program. This was perhaps the result of his recognition of her superb capacity for household management. Sometimes I strongly suspect that altogether each took proper advantage of the other.

Papa once plainly revealed his willingness to cooperate once Mama had made a decision. His first place of steady employment in Champaign was a bookstore, which soon purchased an adjoining lot for construction of a larger building. A big frame house had to be removed from the lot, though it was in good condition, and it was offered to my father for next to nothing, provided that he would arrange its removal to his own vacant lot. However, he said nothing to Mom, and himself unduly delayed a solitary decision until the store turned the house over to another fellow.

A bit later Papa made the mistake of revealing to Mom the opportunity he had missed. For years afterward she recurrently chided him about the house he could have had for a song. But apparently he couldn't sing a solo. After one of the beratings, before us children and to his considerable embarrassment, he waited until my mother left the room. He then quietly defended himself in this fashion: "Your mother shouldn't keep bringing up the subject. If I'd remembered to tell her soon enough about the chance I had to get that place, we would have managed to get it for sure. She knows that."

There were five of us, all boys and born pretty much every two years beginning in 1909, except for two still-births to disrupt the pattern. We called a girl cousin who was reared with us "Sister," and knew her only as such for the first of our years as children. She was the daughter of Mama's youngest sister, who died in Missouri when her baby was only nine days old. When Sister's brother was fifteen or sixteen, he ran away from his father, and he too came to live with us for several years, as long as he wished and until he was a young man.

Sister's brother came to join us suddenly, arriving in the black of the night. We children got up to find the newcomer whom we had never before seen, telling my mother and father of the mistreatment from his father which led him to flee and the tribulations of his trip to Champaign by freight train. My mother was weeping great tears of pity upon him and joy that he had come to her. The next day she wrote his father a letter which I am certain was a scorcher. Subsequently she several times mentioned his father's writing in reply and asking the return of his son, and once I heard her say, "Never! Not as long as I live."

After we learned that Sister was really only a cousin, one of us made a strong point of the remoteness of our kinship with her, during a quarrel and in the cruel manner at which children are so adept. "Anyway you're not our real sister, you're just a cousin," it ran. Sister promptly burst into tears and bellowing. My mother flew into the offender and quickly and literally left an impression serving never again to let such an argument be used by any one of us.

And never to my knowledge did Papa do other than willingly share with his wife the responsibility for her motherless niece and nephew.

The only notably continuous strain between my parents stemmed from their religious differences. Mama was a Methodist when she married Papa and only more so when she died. But Papa was successively a member of the Baptist Church, the Disciples of Christ, and a tiny and little-known sect called the Church of God and the Saints of Christ. Whatever path to salvation my father found himself on at any time, he was always certain it was the true and only one, and would extend my mother repeated invitations to accompany him. But Mama was so comfortable, devoted, and busy in her Methodism, as a founding member of her particular church and a member of its stewardess board, that Papa never once came near persuading her to join him.

Occasionally we children would be permitted to speak out and to attempt assailing the logic of my father's religious position, especially after he gave up being Baptist and became a Disciple. We would suggest that so few people belonged to Papa's new affiliation, as compared to the many Methodists and Baptists, among Negroes, that he was giving himself, not to speak of God, a decidedly tiny minority of the heavenly potential. He would rejoin about the narrowness of the Way and that "few there be within it," followed by a citing a Biblical book, chapter, and verse. We would indicate that those switching from one denomination to another were obviously uncertain of their way; how did he know but what he was not still lost? He would then turn upon those who were mere "joiners," or simply "born" Baptists, or "poured on" Methodists, instead of being "really born again."

This tilting with Papa was always an exciting pastime for us, if Mama did not get upset, and until Papa would pull the very ground out from under us. Finding himself hard pushed and outnumbered, he would turn the discussion so as to make *argumentum ad hominem* out of one of the Ten Commandments. "Honor thy father and thy mother; that thy days may be long upon the land which thy God giveth thee," he would sternly remind us, quite overlooking the esteem we were showing Mama.

The divergence in religious affiliation was occasionally burdensome on one of us in a very pragmatic way. The people in Papa's Church of God and Saints of Christ, "keep the true Sabbath," as he still rather belligerently puts it, while Methodists are, of course, Sunday worshipers. This difference, coupled with the wish of both parents to attend church with their children, meant worship two days in a row for those of us without Saturday jobs or other escape.

For of the religiosity that was my father's, one early summer day in 1918 or so left it clear that his then little children thought more of their mother's ties than his with the God they both so devotedly, though differently, worshiped. That day a tornado twisted its terrible way through Champaign. The rough winds pushed through the neighborhood with great whooshing sounds, accompanied by repeated flashes of lightning, seemingly headed straight for our house, as the whole place shook violently. All of the family lay on the floor of the living room huddled closely together in fear and trembling. Suddenly one of the children begged: "Somebody pray! Somebody pray!" Certain, I am sure, that this could only mean him, Papa commenced a prayer, only to be quickly interrupted by another fervent cry: "No! No! Not you Papa. But Mama! Mama!"

Long ago a poet wrote in praise of a worthy woman:

> The heart of her husband trusts in her,
> and he will have no lack of gain.
> She does him good, and not harm,
>   all the days of her life.
> She rises while it is yet night
> and provides food for her household
> and tasks for her maidens.
> She considers a field and buys it;
>   with the fruit of her hands she plants a vineyard.
> She opens her hand to the poor
>   and reaches out her hands to the needy.
> She opens her mouth with wisdom,
>   and the teaching of kindness is on her tongue.
> She looks well to the ways of her household,
> and does not eat the bread of idleness.
>   Mama was like that.

HER WAYS

She did indeed rise before dawn to provide food for her household. She was, if you will, busily seeking what it took, not only to feed but to clothe, shelter, and educate her household. For she would be off to her cooking at the fraternity house before daybreak so that forty or so other young men could have hot breakfasts before classes.

At the fraternity, she was enough of a home economist and kitchen manager to make the job pay beyond the salary check. Unlike the arrangement followed in most of more than a hundred fraternities and sororities about the university campus, that frat brother in charge of the dining service passed on to Mama part of his monthly pay because she could and did plan the menus, buy the food, and handle the rest of dining management. All he needed do was to bear the title of "dining manager" and keep winning election to the post, a feat simple enough once he learned that Mama was more than a mere "colored cook" and gave her more rein. She was somehow able also to get "time away from the kitchen" in the afternoons and come all the way back to the home area. There she sold cosmetics and dresses to her neighbors during a spare couple of hours before dinner back at the fraternity house.

"'Tasks for her maidens" were left too, despite the fact that, except for Sister, they were all boys. One of us would be left to finish the wash or the ironing she had little more than started. Another would have to straighten up the living room and kitchen, beds having been made shortly after the arisings, with the airing and changing of them a part of the Saturday cleaning schedule. An older one of us would begin his day by driving Mama to work, whenever the old Dodge sedan someone had foisted on us was in running order and could be started on cold winter mornings.

She stretched the clothing dollar in various and sundry ways. If work kept her from going herself, she would send one of us downtown for "dollar day" or other sales, or to a neighborhood church basement or vacant store building in which West Side ladies would occasionally stage a rummage sale. Flour sacks, both our own and bigger ones from somewhere on the campus, made summer underwear for us, during our younger years, and pajamas for a while longer.

The biggest savings were made in feeding the family—a family that was fed well. Most of our groceries were purchased at an A&P store and, in the bulk, such as large bags of flour, sugar, and salt, potatoes by the bushel, and cartons of canned peas and pink salmon. Milk was bought at gallon rates from a nearby dairy. Occasionally it was only "blue john," skimmest of skim milk. Meats came mainly from still another place, Roberts and Grant, a wholesale-retail meat market. It was the same market supplying meats to the fraternity for which Mama worked, and she had arranged to have her own little brotherhood enjoy the same wholesale rates. We would simply ask for Mr. Roberts, Mr. Grant, or the head butcher and reveal whose sons we were. When we ordered a slab of bacon and had it sliced by machine, extra bacon ends and skins, paid for but declined by West Side folks, would be wrapped along with our purchase. The "seasoning" meat in many a boiled dinner eaten on East Tremont Street was bought and paid for by a West Side family, completely unwitting of its benefaction.

We bought the cheaper meats, hamburger, short ribs, chuck roast, beef brisket, picnic shoulders, and sometimes beef liver, though more often it was pork. The latter was not for our cat, either. Leftover breads were never overlooked. Whether they had started separately as hot cornbread, biscuits, pancakes, or "store" bread (that homemade never achieving a leftover status), when they hung around they wound up together, though not always as a meat-stretcher. Sometimes, they became bread puddings, with or without raisins or lemon sauce, or as a breakfast dish called "cush." "Cush" was sort of make-shift, quickly-come-by scrapple.

Mama practiced canning with the care of a squirrel putting away nuts for winter. When, she died, she and my father had been living at home without any of us for three or four years, but the hang-over from her canning left several hundred jars of jams, jellies, pickles, fruits, and vegetables in the basement.

The truth is that Mama's economy was pretty much a frugal one, with jelly coming from apple peelings, soap from bacon drippings, and dish cloths from salt sacks. The worn rugs given to Papa were turned about on our floors until they reached a uniform state of threadbareness. It was not until I lived in New England for nine months that I was to see such frugality practiced more as virtue than out of penury. There I saw sturdy old cast iron stoves converted from coal to oil burning and, in Boston, detected comfortable looking men, real Yankees, wearing shirts with collars and cuffs neatly turned, just as Mama had done ours.

Papa's pay as a janitor was little enough. Mama's cooking paid little and was only seasonal, nine months of the year. But the two spent sparingly. Even that bit of income from the weekly newspaper, two cents out of each nickel, was not for dissipation.

This kind of economy for a family meant that it pretty much paid its way as it went. Only the most costly convenience and comfort, like the furnace, were bought "in time." Indeed, Mama was always able to have a savings account, and so were several of the boys, at times. There were also a few dollars in that jar in the china cabinet, and always a larger amount in a little sack tucked underneath the mattress of Mama and Papa's big, wrought-iron bed. It was added to, spent closely, and some of it hung on to, because schooling for her children was the purpose behind it all.

Mama also kept as close a watch on what school and the children did to each other as her long work hours permitted. The report cards were read before she signed them, with a low mark in deportment drawing close questions just as one in arithmetic. She occasionally used her precious time off in the afternoons to make a PTA meeting and several times for badly needed conferences with teachers. When one of us had a heavy bit of homework on his hands, she would transfer the responsibility for the evening dishes to another one of the boys, if the two could not work out the problem themselves.

All of the boys except the oldest were started to school before they had reached the minimum six years required. This practice was doubtless of convenience to the family, but it also reflected Mama's anxiety to push her educational program along. When she sent the fourth son to start the first grade before he was five years old, she was in trouble. The little fellow, of squatty build and later to be dubbed "Shorty," was promptly sent back home in spite of his tears and protestations. The next day he was sent back to school and allowed to remain. One evening a few days later the teacher called to tell Mama that he seemed to her to be the smartest in his class. He graduated from high school as one of four or five Negroes and was second in scholarship in a class of perhaps two hundred. He never quit trying to prove himself big and ready enough for school.

She would sometimes ask us to read the evening newspaper aloud to her; to write letters to one of my uncles, upon occasion saying not to seal the envelope, as she would add something before mailing it; to pull off her shoes and put her slippers on; to tie her shoelaces for her and brush her clothing before she left for church. We learned to shine her shoes too, as we shined our own.

We helped her to pit cherries, peel peaches by the bushel, string apple slices to dry in the sun, and wrap pears in tissue for hiding away in the dark until they mellowed. Many were the times I mixed the yellowing into the white margarine, two pounds of it each mixing, and often also exercised my right as assistant with the handbeating of cake batter to claim first chance at the frosting bowl.

Mama not only let us help in ways that sometimes were fun, she also would listen to what her children would tell her. She was always growing. When the hygiene teacher taught our class how really to brush the teeth "not just around and up front, but up and down, inside, and way in the back," I took it all straight to Mama. Mama and I got out our toothbrushes and practiced together. When my brother saw and read aloud to the family a recipe for strawberry jam cooked by putting the berries and sugar mix under glass for long hours in the hot sun, we thought the process fascinating and were all for Mama's trying it. Papa said, "Yes. Eggs can be fried on the sidewalk, too, when the sun's hot enough. Not mine though." But Mama told my brother to clip the recipe and save it. That year our strawberry jam was cooked in the sun. Indeed, Mama's cooking altogether was a Southern style that was Northern-modified, the same food but not cooked so long, nor with so much fat. After she learned that steel cans could be used at home for canning, they replaced the glass Mason jars. But only for two or three seasons. I think that she found that being able to see the vegetables as well as the fruits of her labor through glass was more satisfying.

Besides teaching us by example to work hard, spend carefully and always save a little, and to love and serve those about us, Mama taught us by both precept and example to live cleanly, in speech, person, and surroundings, and to accept responsibility. "Cleanliness is next to godliness" she would remind one of us almost daily. Though the language came from Franklin, she likely thought it was from the Apostle Paul. She had considerable help from Papa in keeping our speech clean, and the proscription against bad words was broad indeed. It ran from "taking the Lord's name in vain," at very worst, down through the familiar four-lettered obscenities commonly used on the street—and heavily so in our neighborhood. Even "fool" was forbidden, while today's familiar "stupid ass" would never have been dared within hearing of our parents. "Nincompoot" was about as sharp as we could get and as far as we could go with trouble-free name calling. Its several syllables left it fancier and less blunt than "fool" and hence permissible. We also got away with "simple" which, in effect, stood for "simpleton," though we did not use it so much as an abbreviation as out of disrespect for grammar. With all such impugning, we were also able quickly to shift to a tone beguiling to our parents whenever we suddenly noticed that one was about. "Nincompoot," even "simple," could be elongated and sweetened, as it was spoken, to convey a mix of disappointment and brotherly affection for the dullard who was its subject.

Even after I was in college, I felt her watchfulness. Mama, like many of the Bible-readers of her generation and background, placed considerable stock in her dreams. She needed no Freud to live by them soundly and sensibly. In the main she received guidance from the water or the weather in the dream. If either was clear, something good was ahead for her. However, if she saw dark or murky water, or dreamed of a stormy or cloudy day, it meant that she must move with care in the days ahead. Living with hopefulness and carefulness was fairly practical, I've always thought. But sometimes Mama's dreams could get pretty pointed, as one did for me. She told me one evening that she had dreamed of a certain young divorcee's screaming at and attacking me, clawing and scratching me until my face bled. I had seemed helpless, she said, and wanted to know if I knew the woman. Well I did know her indeed and also knew that Mama had had no dream. The revelation was earthly and most un-divine. Some gossip had gabbed, for the truth was that I was in the midst of a surreptitious ado with the lady. Nevertheless, Mama's "dream"—the unspoken disapproval of the affair—brought the trysting to its end.

Mama was helpful to the needy beyond her own family. She was a warm though crude social worker, I suppose, though she wouldn't have understood the compliment. She was simply helping friends and neighbors when they needed it and she could provide it. She would see to families, other families besides her own, getting on the list for Salvation Army Christmas baskets and knew how to get a girl who had achieved the pregnancy but not the marriage placed in a home for such girls in Chicago. Good Methodist that she was, she could go the Sisters at St. Mary's to try to get a troubled youngster in the Catholic school and at as little cost to his parents as possible. She felt the Sisters and the stricter discipline might help the boy. Now and then a youngster would stop just to talk with her. Once when she was at home sick, a youngster of my age, pursued by a brutish, bigger fellow, ran into our home for protection and sought to hide himself under her bed. She made him come out from his hiding place, got herself out of bed, and sent his pursuer home.

She was also close to many of the neighborhood's younger married women from time to time. A young woman married to a wife-beater fled from her home across the street in her nightgown to Mama late one night to escape her husband's wrath. We boys were at once awakened and let in on the drama by my father. He had been forced to come upstairs to share sleeping space with us so that the woman could sleep the remainder of the night in the big bed downstairs with Mama. One of us then slipped downstairs seeking fuller intelligence and hoping in all likelihood to see the lady. But the nosy emissary was met with stunning news. Mama was not there, the woman explained from behind the bedroom door. Mama had gone across the street to lecture the lady's miscreant husband, before returning to comfort his wife and resume her sleep.

During the early part of the depression of the thirties, Mama frequently intervened with the township supervisor on behalf of people seeking relief, especially those less well established in the community. Here I cannot feel comfortable that her successes were due entirely to her native capacity for social work. For both she and the township supervisor were active Republican party workers and she was in part tapping her political due.

It was also in this period that our family, like so many other North End families, subsisted in part on surplus commodities, cans of beef and pork; boxes of peanuts, prunes, and raisins; and sacks of whole wheat flour, distributed by the government. Mama made a variety of dishes from these commodities, especially by combining garden items with them. But many needy recipients were nevertheless unable to use them and either allowed them to spoil or gave them to other families. Here and there Mama would suggest use of the commodities in ways more closely akin to Southern cooking. She occasionally set down on paper such a recipe for someone. Finally word about this kind of guidance of hers reached those distributing the surplus items. As a result, Mama one day found herself demonstrating several of her surplus commodity recipes before a group of neighbors.

My mother kept herself close with all of her kinspeople. The degree of kinship meant nothing. "Cousins" of whatever degree and whether or not she could trace the relationships, they were hers with affection.

She was thoroughly devoted to her three brothers who lived in Chicago, just as they were to us as their nephews. That one who, as she would quietly whisper, "had always been peculiar," she induced to come and live with us. He was keen-minded and had a wonderful sense of wit, yet forever suspicious that many of the people he knew, including his sister, were bent upon harming, even poisoning, him. She suffered and cried over his suspicions of her, while humoring and hovering over him, and insisting that we understand him. After he left us and was near the breaking point, I was sent as a seventeen-year-old to spend what became a most trying summer with him. Before its end he was found of some paranoiac type and placed in the institution where he has now been for nearly forty years, outliving by far all of his sisters and brothers. The other two brothers, one a stationary engineer with some training at Tuskegee Institute, and the other a stationary fireman, were sober and hard-working. One of them was a "moonlighter" for perhaps thirty years, and the other also worked two jobs from time to time. Both were always generously helpful to Mama, a source of cash or clothing for her children in time of need.

Mama's church, St. Luke's Colored Methodist Episcopal, had a place deep in her heart also. Her love of St. Luke's was as constant as her Methodism was firm. When dissension sometimes arose within the congregation, over such a question as whether the bishop should be asked to remove or return the incumbent pastor or presiding elder, she talked long and earnestly to those sisters and brothers she best knew in terms of "doing what is best for the church." Her feeling that the "good of St. Luke's comes first" was as unshakeable as her belief in Methodism against the onslaughts of my father, who tried off and on as long as she lived to pull her into his varying ways of worship. When she sang "blessed assurance, Jesus is mine," it meant also the Wesleyan way and St. Luke's.

As our elders would say, we children "grew up in the church." We attended Sunday School in the morning, Epworth League in the evening, and church service proper when ordered. As youngsters, each of us sometimes went and stayed with Mama through prayer meeting, during a revival service, or when her board staged a fish fry or chicken dinner on Saturday evening. Once a brother was left alone as a little fellow in the church, Mama thinking he had slipped off and gone home. He was picked up in the wee hours of the morning as he awakened from his nap and sounded off as only a frightened child can. When I was first privileged to attend "watch" service on New Year's Eve, I was disappointed. It was good to be allowed to stay up so late, but I never really saw what I had "watched" for, and it seemed simply a longer than usual prayer meeting. Being permitted to be up all night before the Fourth of July with the church stewards, who barbecued several pigs, was appealing and satisfying as long as it, or rather I, lasted. Long before daybreak, I fell asleep and was carried into the church basement and "benched" there.

As it happened, I was the son last to see Mama alive. Two days before her death, as she lay the victim of a second stroke, she recognized me as I walked into her sick room, just off a train from Chicago. Her first words were not addressed to me. She looked at me, but she spoke thusly: "Thank you, God, for letting me see my *children* once more."

I do not forget the funeral. It was simple and quieter and briefer than those to which I was accustomed. My brothers and I bore the body the few feet from home to church, followed by our wives, most of the women with whom as our cousins she had been so close, and some of those long her neighbors, her sisters in her church. Within a few minutes the service was over. A psalm was read, several of her beloved hymns sung, and the minister spoke sparingly. He reminded his listeners that Mama had seen and helped shoulder the movement of St. Luke's from a mere mission in a frame house to the edifice in which they were seated. No summation of her life and its character was needed from him. It was woven with the lives of those assembled. I left the church filled with pride and comfort.

Even Mama's burial was beautiful. She was put back into the earth in Mt. Hope Cemetery, once bordering and now virtually surrounded by the campus of the University of Illinois, to which, through her children, she had staked herself a claim.

CHAPTER 3

Learning to Be Somebody

And thou shall make them know the path they
are to walk in and the work they are to do.
—Exodus 18:30

The abiding difference between Papa and Mama as to whether Saturday or Sunday was to be observed as the sabbath day disturbed not in the slightest their common hold on the other nine of the Ten Commandments. Indeed the meaning of no other Biblical injunction was ever questioned by either so far as we children knew.

The whole of the Bible, its Old as well as the New Testament, was a singular source of morality and wisdom for our family. We had no great, heavy, leather-bound copy of the book containing genealogy, our names and birthdates, with which to run the risk of an easy and assumptious connection with God, as well as self-worship. We were more richly endowed, always having several worn and tattered copies of the Bible available in handy places. Mama read them off and on and thus provided example. Papa studied and read from them aloud and to us children with frequency.

Papa's readings to the children were neither ceremonial nor lengthy. They were instead short and to the point, brought to bear on the errant all at once, whenever and as he felt needed. The gospels, Paul, the Ten Commandments and Proverbs were most often read and cited, book, chapter and verse. He made the Bible a rule book for the training and guidance of his children.

Nevertheless, Mama did a better job of using it to draw lines for us as little children than Papa did. She was more effective because she was less pointed and better met us on our own—a Sunday School—level of Bible understanding. Once we had learned that God is love and loves little children especially, she could make productive use of a saying premised on those teachings. The saying was utterly simple. "God doesn't love ugly," it ran. We never learned who said so, but believed it deeply. We wanted God's love and feared appearing "ugly" inside ourselves where God could see, as we had also been taught. We were convinced that God did not love ugliness, and from there on Mama had her way.

Mama made the "ugly" that God cannot accept cover far more than the lying and stealing, in stern condemnation of which Papa so often cited the Decalogue. She used its flexibility to embrace all the naughty little deeds at which children are adept. She applied "God doesn't love ugly" to that one of us who used a nasty word, landed the first blow in a fight, struck a smaller playmate, vowed to "get even," refused to share, declined apologizing, and cheated as well as fibbed, stole, or sassed his parent or some other grownup.

THE TRUTH, THE WAY, AND THE LIGHT

But the Bible was also the fount of all wisdom in most the Negro homes on the North End. Our neighbors prided themselves as people living in Christian homes. Color prints of Christ or the Last Supper, in dime-store frames, adorned their walls. Printings of the Ten Commandments or quotations from a Psalm or a disciple hung where they could be seen. In some houses folks fairly certified themselves followers of the Way. A framed proclamation was posted reading "Christ Is the Head of This House," "This is a Christian Home," or the like.

They were fundamentalists, unashamedly, even proud, followers of the old-time religion. It was good for Paul and Silas, and good enough for them. For they were of the rural South and had brought with them to Champaign-Urbana their simple religious beliefs and practices. Three of the churches were Baptist: Salem, Mt. Olive, and a "Free Will" unit, and two were Methodist: Bethel A. M. E. and St. Luke's C. M. E. There were mild variations among them in the fervor of preaching felt acceptable, and, in one, "shouting" was frowned upon by the members, who were less Southern, more of them having been born and bred in Illinois or of longer residence there. Moreover, these churches did have strong differences respecting the precise form for the baptism ritual. I still retain in my mind's eye the Biblical quotation inside one of the Baptist churches, painted in bold, black letters where every worshiper could see it every Sunday: "One Lord, One Faith, One Baptism." As this dictum was interpreted, the threshold to salvation is crossed only by way of immersion in the water: sprinkling and pouring are insufficiently symbolic.

But in substance, Baptists and Methodists were more alike than they knew. The common religion was close to "old time" and the law for all was the Ten Commandments, sometimes enforced, subtly, by a sermon "reading" the especially wayward out of the church and occasionally through simple but formal church proceedings.

More important for me, as a child, was the complete agreement among these people, as adults, on how children should and should not act. The Bible was not only the rule book for grown-ups; it left no need for the likes of a Dr. Spock. Children, it was plain, were to live as Jesus taught, learning the Way by attending Sunday School in the morning and the young people's meeting in the evening, with those who also attended the regular service being blessed indeed. Christ had ordered suffering little children "to come unto" him, and those of his followers that I knew as a child hurried us along.

We children were expected to keep the Commandments quite as much as the grown-ups. Thus we were taught more "shall not" than "shall"— and under threat of eternal damnation for the disobedient. Still the fifth commandment, that positive direction centered upon the young and accompanied by its own earthly sanction, received a most decided emphasis. We were to honor our fathers and mothers, if we were to live long. Moreover, this absolute requirement extended to the parents of one's playmates. Indeed all adults were always to be respected, especially those who were church people, the more elderly among them, and particularly those of common church membership with one's parents. Any grown-up was privileged, and many felt obliged, to watch over us children, to keep us in line if possible, and to report its breach to the parents, if not. If he willed to do so, he could punish—and physically—the child on the spot.

The result, it now seems plain to me, was a wide web of influence upon us children. We had lots of people to respect and some almost to fear. But we had many people to live with, to learn from, and to "go by" as well. Most of them were strict and restraining, but some were also warm and friendly. It WAS a system of child-rearing, I suppose, and, I think, a good one.

WEB OF WATCHFULNESS AND WARMTH

Whether the system was good or not, it heavily influenced the little Nesbitts. This was not because our natures were any more angelic and yielding than those of the other children; the system often sorely chafed us. It worked well on us merely because we were under its surveillance at so many points. With Mama a stewardess at St. Luke's Methodist and Papa, at first, a deacon at Salem Baptist, our parents were calling people "Sister" and "Brother" in twice as many churches as those of most of our contemporaries. But what really extended the chain of watchfulness over us— and for us—beyond its encirclement of other children was our *Chicago Defender* agency. The two hundred customers we saw each week were men and women who knew my father, and if they were not members of his or my mother's church, they worshiped at one of the other three. Away from home then, whenever we were in the home neighborhood or far beyond, our paths were apt to coincide with the presence of an adult we knew to know us and our parents.

Petty theft, vandalism, property trespasses, profanity, fighting, loud and boisterous behavior, and gambling, even penny-pitching, activities of such likely exercise by regular fellows whenever they gathered and had little else to do, were strictly forbidden. My brothers and I occasionally indulged in such activities, but only occasionally, and no one of us ever succumbed to any one of them. This was partly because we were kept so busy, in school and at schoolwork, carrying papers, and working at odd jobs. But mainly we were saved because Mama had her church, Papa his, and both knew so many of all of those paper customers.

The many people other than our parents who helped see to our proper behavior did more than to watch for infractions and help enforce the rules. The web, especially those in it who lived close by in the neighborhood, included some who cared for us children, who nurtured and supported as well as kept us under watch.

The childless wife of one of our better-off neighbors was much concerned with the doings of neighborhood youngsters, inevitably so. She kept an immaculate house, outside as well as inside, but it was located on a principal corner, one frequented by the children. Here was a daily struggle to keep us out of her young fruit trees, from trampling her reseeded grass, and from being too noisy for her comfort. She reprimanded us with regularity and always in no uncertain terms. The smaller ones were quite fearful of her.

But this lady was as nice to me as she was strict with all of us. One morning I started around her corner on the fly, headed for school. Though I was moving fast, her scrutiny did not miss what to her was a serious deficiency in my appearance. A hole in one of my black stockings glared forth against the whiteness of the leg of my long underwear. She summarily called me to a halt and ordered me to return home and sew up the hole. I politely countered that this would make me late for school. However, she insisted that with that hole in my stockings I was not really ready for school anyway. She also reminded me that my mother, by then at work for several hours, would want done both what she was doing and the sewing she was ordering. In fact, I should have done the sewing before leaving home.

Papa was strict with many matters, day by day, beginning with dawn. He arose before Mama to start the fire in the coal-fired kitchen stove and to put on the coffee. As soon as a hot cup of coffee was in his hand, if not before, he would call us boys from our slumbers. Early to bed and early to rise was our household practice, at first simply because it was the way he himself had learned to live in the country in Tennessee. But he made of it a virtue. Occasionally on the weekends, especially as we grew older and stayed up later, we would resist rising with the day. "For what, Papa?" would draw a variety of reasons valid enough with him. "Because the sun is up," he would say. Or "Because God has given you another day, get up and be thankful in it." And, if need be, the ultimate reason was, "Because I said get up, and I am not going to say it again!"

Papa's strong belief that "the man is the head of the house" told him that he should do little inside it. He leaned over backward never to put his hands in dish or laundry water, to make a bed, or cook a meal for himself, so long as Mama or one of the boys was within beck and call. But by the same token, he was forced to perform outside of the house and be a man before his boys. He was thus the victim of his own propaganda, with much the burden of chores falling also on us, though we were bound also to help Mama inside the house.

I remember once begging him to take me to hear Colonel Roscoe Conkling Simmons, a then well-known Negro orator, who was scheduled to deliver one of his speeches in our community. He had no interest himself in hearing Simmons but gave me the admission fee and arranged for a neighbor to take me along to hear the colonel. The speech was stirring, an exciting blend of allusions to Negro heroes of the past and shrewd counseling of his cheering Negro audience to trust to the future and the Republican party. The next morning at breakfast, just as he often would ask following one of his children's hearing a sermon of a preacher other than in his own church, Papa demanded of me, "What did Roscoe Simmons have to say?"

I began my answer recalling the titans of Negro history Simmons had mentioned. But Papa interrupted with, "Yes, but what did he say of today?"

"'It is patience we must have! Patience! Patience! Patience!' That's what he kept saying all through his speech," I replied.

"I was afraid of that," Papa said quietly, and nothing more.

In a little while I got the point.

There were other slow-burning candles with which Papa lighted the long way ahead of us, and more often than not I am unable to divine where he got his light to start with.

Despite his simplistic, word-by-word belief in his Bible as holy and historical fact, the creation, the miracles, and even the parables, he was impatient with much of the fictional folk belief that was a larger part of his Southern rural background. He had little use for many superstitions, and especially ghosts.

Late one dark night, when nine years old or so, I came home alone and full of fear and trembling. I had just seen a ghost and insisted on the certainty of it. Papa patiently allowed and helped me to relate "the facts"—

the neighbor's backyard in which the ghost was seen, how near it was to the back porch, how tall it appeared to stand, and without motion or sound—though all these "facts" were doubtlessly rather rapidly gathered. Then he said, "Tomorrow night we'll watch for it, if we don't see it before then." This was a bit puzzling to me; he should have known that ghosts were out only at night. But I was pleased and comforted that my story was accepted and that something would be done about a danger so nearby, though I was not eager to look for the ghost the next night, even in Papa's company.

But the ghost-watching never took place, for the next morning ended the matter. On the way to school, I passed the neighbor's backyard and saw better and fearlessly what was so frightening the night before. There, standing exactly where the ghost had stood (though, of course, hardly so tall), was a freshly placed, whitewashed post, about the size of a railroad tie, with hooks in it for laundry lines. Papa never admitted that he saw the big, white post being placed in the ground. He let on merely knowing all along, as he had shown me, that there is no such being as a ghost.

Another then rather advanced scientific notion with which our utterly unscientific father early endowed us was that white folks are no better than other people because they are white. He did, of course, occasionally allude to the Bible as the source for his belief in the universal weakness of man as well as his brotherhood. But mostly he did his own reasoning and provided his own expressions of belief in the commonness of man. He explained to us that the white man had power, wrote all of the books, and drew the pictures in them, Bibles included. Thus the white man made everything good white and everything white good. Once Papa vehemently declared "The white man is no god for me, as much as he worships himself." But it was that constant admonition of his which I have mentioned earlier that lastingly impressed us. Over and over again, he stopped us, as we related an event or passed on a story in terms of what a "colored" or a "white" man had done, with the question, "What difference did his color make?" Usually it made none, though sometimes it did. These then became early lessons in objectivity but also in color prejudice and discrimination.

Indeed, Papa's Bible-reading told him that most men were the same, weak and sinful, destined for a hereafter of fire and brimstone. He felt that class as well as color lines were unworthy of a true Christian. "It takes a big man to be a Christian, big enough to behave like the Samaritan and to wash another's feet," he would say.

Papa required two things of the West Side matrons who employed him which must have disturbed them. If the first insistence did not make his first employment by many a lady the last, then his second one surely did. For the ladies were neither to call Papa by his first name nor to seat themselves apart from him as lunch was eaten.

He invariably told his ladies, when they asked his name, "Nesbitt, just L. B. Nesbitt. Call me either one."

The seeming generosity often worked easily. When it did not, the resistant ones, who could not bring themselves to call him "Mister," were forced to settle on "Nesbitt." Occasionally one would try out-maneuvering him as she wrote his check. "Now," the tactic ran, "what is your full name? It should go on this check." He would reply, "L. B. Nesbitt will do. It does with the banks and it's that way in the phone book too."

Papa took no lunch with him as he headed for the West Side to do housecleaning, since he liked to eat "on the house" wherever he was. This was likely the custom among day workers and housecleaners. But that fringe benefit was doubtless a tall and shocking order when a Negro extended it to expecting a country club matron not only to fix his lunch but to eat hers at the same time and across the table from him. Enough of them learned to put up with it, though I am certain that in their own circle they must have explained that "He's a bit peculiar but a good cleaner."

I also used to think Papa's demands a little too much, but now they fall into place. They underscored for Papa that he was up North, no longer in Tennessee; working under a contract of his own making, not bopping for the "Man"; and being accorded a bit of *equal status*, a phrase Papa couldn't have used, but a notion he understood.

Papa was determined to be no man's servant. He wanted to earn a living as independently as possible, and I remember that he admired unions, while despising their color barriers. He had once become the head janitor at the post office in Champaign but gave up the job, complaining that he was neither paid the wage rate to which he was entitled nor as completely in charge of the custodial responsibilities as he should have been. He twice attempted small businesses, as a partner in a little grocery and notions store on North Poplar Street and as a restaurant keeper on North Fifth Street. He became, in fact, a cleaning services contractor. Besides knowing how to exploit his children for his labor, he was a shrewd bidder on a floor-waxing, wall-cleaning, or window-washing job.

Indeed it was Papa who started us to peddling the *Chicago Defender*, which, for all of its modesty, was a real business enterprise and kept us from having to shine shoes, as so many of our schoolmates did. Ours was much more than hawking papers at a stand or handling a route, the delivery of papers from door to door, under someone's supervision. Each week we wrote copy for the *Defender* about Negro happenings in Champaign-Urbana; ordered our papers, estimating the number we could sell and taking a loss on any unsold; purchased a money order for the purpose at the Post Office; kept our bicycles in order; kept the collection records, and made follow-up visits with slow payers; and delivered the papers with dispatch to as many as two hundred customers, came rain, snow, or shine, and as widely scattered in the community as Negroes were permitted to live. The little business bought many a blue serge suit and second-hand schoolbook, besides helping to make men of us. But for Papa, I suspect, it meant independence for us.

Papa was no joiner, except of churches, and left to Mama and me, as I grew older, active membership in the Frederick Douglass Civic League, the local NAACP, and other organized efforts against color discrimination. But this failure to associate with others in anti-discrimination action by no means meant that he did not protest for himself when he was directly involved in color mistreatment. Several incidents of the kind impressed me.

Late one Sunday evening Papa had finished some chores for a West Side family and was walking away from work when he encountered a white policeman. The officer presumably was merely walking his beat, no misbehavior of urgency had occurred to bring him there. But with Papa being Negro and the neighborhood white, besides well-off, the policeman wanted to know of Papa, "What are you doing in *this neighborhood*?"

"The same as you are," retorted Papa, "walking down the street."

"I am doing my job," said the policeman.

"Well I just finished mine," said Papa. Naturally, there were other words, for as I now well know, no run-of-the-mill white policeman finds such conversation acceptable from any Negro. The white policeman, more often than not, is a white man left behind. When such a fellow is endowed with a cloak of authority and armed with club and gun, he not only suspects each Negro he encounters but feels privileged to browbeat him and to push him about at the slightest provocation. But somehow it did not happen. Papa stopped off at the police station and left a complaint with the desk man.

On another occasion, two policemen in a squad car similarly accosted Papa, out of their idle, unbridled curiosity, as he was on his way home. The details escape me, though I remember that Papa suggested to them that since they had delayed him so unnecessarily, they should drive him home. They did so, and I have always wondered who got the better of the deal. The two policemen likely felt that all who saw Papa in the car would feel that he was guilty either of a wrong done or need for restraint from the deed. Papa may well have known what was in their minds and looked to his stature in his neighborhood to leave their judgment in error. Besides he was tired and needed the ride, and doubtless enjoyed being chauffeured home by those who ordinarily transported cargo quite beholden to them, their powers, prejudices, and fears.

A third occurrence was most reassuring because my own protest occasioned Papa's action. He had sent me to give a yard its first cutting in the early spring. I worked until noon, when the lady of the house called me to eat a lunch she had prepared. As I walked into her kitchen, she invited me to sit at the table already with the food upon it. She herself took the opposite seat, as would have pleased Papa. But her first words were no grace. They were, "My, I'm tired and hungry as I can be. I've been working like a nigger!" Thereupon I said not a word but arose, retrieved my cap and jacket from the back porch, and walked away, leaving the lawn mower in the middle of a yard only half cut.

After I reached home, I learned that she had called to express her concern. I had appeared to the lady to have become sick. Later, Papa called the lady to tell her that I had indeed become sick but made plain to her that she herself had caused the malady. He allowed her yard to remain in its uncertain state until the following week, when he finished the work, collecting his pay and my bit from the apologetic woman. Her home never became one of Papa's "places."

When Papa and Mama left "down south," neither was much of anybody, like thousands upon thousands of other young Negro men and women who made the same journey. Each was nobody much but wanting to be somebody, and this is why they picked up and pulled out. They left the poverty and the hard and ugly white ways of the south; they were pushed out by them. But they also gave up the warmth and goodness of the place and its people, their own people, and some whites too. They put behind them the huts and the big houses, the fields and roads they knew inside and out, and only, among all the places in God's great world, and the people about them who knew them inside and out, their kin folk, those "like a brother or sister," and the whites, those watching out for them and those they had learned to watch out for. It is not easy for people who have nothing and know little to turn their backs on the people who are theirs and the only places they know. Something has to draw them away.

So there was something which was pulling them on. It was not the "bright lights" of the city, for Pulaski, Illinois, where Papa and Mama first stopped, was a country town, cotton country besides, and they soon moved on. They were not simply following after their relatives either. Each left behind close kinfolk in and about Pulaski, and neither had them in Champaign ahead of them. No, it was being done with being nobody much and wanting to become somebody that picked them up and put them down in Champaign.

My memories make this plain for me. For as Mama and Papa talked, with each other, other folks, and to us, the talk was full of "nobody" and "somebody." This fellow was a "nobody" but that one would be "somebody" someday. A grown-up somebody had a job, worked hard, cared for his family—or, as a woman, helped the husband. A somebody coming along went to school and made a serious business of it.

Learning was the route to being somebody. For Mama, how to cook in a Northern style but with the seasonings of the south; manage not just the cooking but the whole dining operation on the campus, for better pay; handle her own household with enough prudence always to keep a sack under her mattress out of which school books could be bought; and now and then to learn something new along with the children. For Papa there was no "Man" in Champaign to crop for but housecleaning skills to learn and how to bargain and contract with many people and belong to none of them. For us children, there were the wisdom and ways of the Bible to learn at home, at Mama's church and Papa's too, from the neighbors, and at the feet of this *Defender* customer and that one. And there was school. "Go on to school so you can be somebody," everybody who was anybody kept saying to us. "What grade will you be in next fall?" paper customers would ask during the summer. "Get an education and nobody can take it from you, folks would say over and over again. This was the way to prepare for a hard world.

So it was good to get away from Poplar Street as it started downhill and up on Tremont Street, near the countryside, church, and school.

The Comfort of My Negroness

He simply wishes to make it possible for a man to be both a Negro and an
American, without being cursed and spit upon by his fellows, without having
the doors of Opportunity closed roughly in his face.
—W. E. B. Du Bois

It seems to me that I have been aware of my Negroness as long as I have
been a Negro. I recall no sudden awakening, rude or otherwise, to a realization of being different from other kinds of people. Moreover, the
abundance of melanin in my skin, indeed my Negroness altogether, is
quite comfortable and always has been. It is as accepted and easy with
me as the color persecution I suffer has always been difficult to bear. The
two, the color that is mine and the mistreatment it occasions me, are not
to be confused.

COLOR AND COUNTRY FOLK

That skin color, my own and those of all the rest of man, has bothered me
little is no small matter with one in a group where it inevitably is counted

too much. In our society of white and black, the one blessed and worshiped and the other disparaged, even the victims of the color line have long tended to measure themselves in large part by the colorings of their skins. Mine is black enough (being somewhere between the colors of, say, Sammy Davis and Jackie Robinson) to leave me accounted a lesser man by the white world as well as by some people within my own.

But I have never discounted myself because of my pigmentation, nor have I drawn lines against other Negroes because of theirs, not even among those with whom association is selective, close, and a matter of pride.

Take this, as example. As long as I have been able to enjoy and suffer female attractions, the colors of their skins have never mattered. Many other things have intervened but not the hue of one's covering. Liking girls is something early engendered and allowed in the kind of setting in which I grew up. Still, for all my shyness, I always made the most of my options, the pink-as-pink comes ones, the "high yellow" and the olive, those like creamed coffee, the nut, mahogany and chocolate browns, those a satin smooth, berry-black, and several of the in-betweens. Twice the girl's complexion was what Negroes call "mariny," with a sandy-red color for hair and skin, and freckles more often also part of the picture. Once she was quite fair-skinned and with blue-green eyes; the defiling drop that made her a Negro was indiscernible. In Chicago late one night, we sat in an elevated car, holding hands and whispering, until I became aware of a charge filling the air. As I looked up and about, I could not only feel the hatred of the white men surrounding us, I saw it turgidly hanging there, all over their faces.

As I grew older, I did take to declaring a certain color preference. "There is no pretty, there is no pink, prettier than pink brown," I would assert at parties. And she was a pink brown for whom I settled until death parts. But I did not really believe in the line I laid down. It was merely so palatable, encompassing, and convenient, loose enough to take in so many of the brown ones, there being so many more of them. Still I did not permit it to leave out others who struck my fancy and allowed it a chance.

The truth is that when I was young, Negro skin coloring, that continuum of color, shade, hue, and tinge which is made the essential mark of a Negro, nearly went to my head. As I made more trips to Chicago and saw thousands upon thousands of *us* there, *we* seemed more and more fascinating. Our rounder, fuller features seemed handsomer, more life-filled than those of the others, especially their thin, tight lips. Most white lips appeared mere slits under their noses, a mouth unfinished. Our pigmentations appeared to me of richer and warmer beauty than that of others. Whites began to appear a dull and colorless sameness, looking doughy, undone, lacking the lively brownishness of people done to a turn. I was selling myself in all seriousness that line later to sell a cosmetic. "Don't be a pale face. Don't be a pale face. Use Coppertone!" I was about to turn the social order around and do unto others as they did to me. Had I stayed in Chicago long enough for heavy enough doses of the exaggerated and simplistic history and wonders of the darker people, provided by certain small coteries of medicine men then active there, I would have become a little black racist—pitted against a multitude of white ones. I would have turned on a black wheel as so many Americans do on the big white one.

But it didn't happen. There were other stimuli, including Papa. He preached Negro pride, as best he could, and poked hard at white superiority. But, for some inscrutable reason, he tempered it all with what I have heard him say a thousand times, often with wonderful timing, "What difference does color make?"

Certainly it took more to save me than that oft-repeated mouthing from Papa, more than preachment, for the world about me as it went on was pointing the other way.

The earliest, protective influence was mere fortuity. Both Mama and Papa and all the members of their families we saw as children appeared uniformly and assuredly Negro. Their colors stretched from an English walnut to a deep chocolate. None among them was mulatto, and I remember only two as having freckles. We have neither boasted nor suffered the problems of those light enough to pass as whites. Moreover, I never heard an adult on either side lay claim to Indian ancestry, as those in many darker Negro families were so wont to do. I came up among kinsmen content with their colorings and at ease with their darkness.

None of my elders, parents, the one grandparent I ever saw, the uncles, aunts, and older cousins, ever sought in my presence to trace that bit of the white lineage that is surely in us as in most Negroes, with a single, and only somewhat of an exception. When Papa several times told a story about a trace of whiteness in his family, it was a matter of amusement, a laughing at its unhappy exposure rather than reaching out for any back-door but superior antecedents of the kind. As a child in the little back-woods community of his birth, he had had a white playmate with whom he was very close. Gene, as Papa called him, was rather a precocious youngster and certainly a little rebel among Tennesseans, since he was looked upon as an infidel. One day the bright little upstart told Papa that Papa was really his cousin. Afterward little Gene was not allowed to play with Papa nor Papa with him. Gene became known as worse than an in-fidel, he was crazy. Naturally Papa is convinced that the much ado meant that the truth had been revealed. Perhaps the several freckles about the noses of Aunt Lula and Aunt Peola, Papa's sisters, are thus to be explained.

In our home, being colored was accepted, not without some pride and a modicum of easy cultivation. My Bible-reading father spoke of Solo-mon's being wise, black, and comely, all of that together, and knew to reveal that Simon the Cyrenian was dark hued. He also suspected the Christ of being colored. We learned and believed from him too, as little ones, that Egypt was the cradle of civilization and Ethiopia would some day stretch forth her hands. What most impressed me was when he would snort at the pictures in color on cards and in lesson books brought home from Sunday school. He would explain that the white man published them and made everyone in the Bible look like himself.

Mama would see to the pink-jowled Santa's leaving my cousin, Sarah, who lived with us, a brown-skinned doll for Christmas instead of a blond one. This required a special effort, for in those days make-believe people in the toy departments were no more racially integrated than real ones in the suburbs. The stores carried pickaninny ragamuffins for little white girls, but no beautiful brownskin dolls. Mama had to order Sarah's doll in the fall from a distributor advertising in *Crisis*, the NAACP magazine, to assure Santa's leaving it for Sarah.

Then there were the give-away calendars of which even the poor and Negro families would get enough to throw most of them away. In our home those calendars kept and hung on the walls usually bore pictures of Negro subjects, most often in color, an advertising approach the Negro undertakers and insurance companies early learned to use. The pictures most often remained there long after the year had run. In addition, among what otherwise were pictures of relatives hanging on the living room walls, there was a big, framed picture of the officers and men of the Eighth Illinois Regiment. This picture of the all-Negro unit, which had distinguished itself in France helping "to make the world safe for democracy," was in color too and included an American shield in red, white and blue.

Darker-skinned Negroes were plentiful, if not predominant, among those in Champaign-Urbana. Many of them were strong and respected people in our church and the community, as if to prove the blacker the berry the sweeter the juice.

John Rivers was as black as the fez he always kept on his head in his grocery store a half block from our first home. Big Bob Smith was a neighbor of ours too when my brothers and I were little ones. He hauled coal with horses and wagon, and the coal dust hardly showed on his skin. But he was big and manly, friendly, generous, and jolly, and would give us rides, letting us hold the reins to his team once in a while.

In our church the shiny black Brothers Robert Ewing, Sam Johnson, and Jimmy Jones were sturdy members of the board of stewards. Just as ebony-hued were Brother Pete Carey and Brother Jeptha Tisdale, who required and drew respect from us as strict and stern churchmen but also as skilled carpenters and owners of rental properties in the neighborhood.

There were many other darker-skinned men of community distinction. The Reverend M. A. Crowder was a man I had seen move from barbering to an assistant pastorship, to ordainment and a presiding ministry. B. P. Bayne was a barber and a Masonic leader. Ray Scott carried mail on the university campus and played saxophone in his own band. The college-trained Art Woodruff was the lone Negro postman in town for many years. Charlie Martin ran a restaurant; the Hite brothers, a valet shop; Cliff Jordan, a downtown barber shop; and Allen Green, a cleaning and pressing service. All of these bought the *Defender* from me week after week and early showed me that blackness was something neither shameful nor any more of a penalty than other pigmentations.

The easy and certain acceptance of the dark skins that are ours was not only a matter of what we saw but also of what we read. The family possessed few books, besides Bibles. But one of those few served as an antidote for Little Black Sambo; it made for comfort of color and culture as well, the Negro folk culture that was the background of our parents and most of our Negro neighbors from Alabama, Tennessee, Mississippi, and Louisiana.

That book was *Lyrics of Lowly Life*, the poetry of Paul Lawrence Dunbar. Papa now tells me that the book was bought new from a door-to-door salesman, some fellow smart enough to know what would sell in the North End. But I can visualize it only in a thoroughly worn condition, a faded red backing into which the pages were no longer bound but would simply fit and were kept. When we wanted to read aloud some of the poems we liked so much, we had first to locate and put the pages in order. But it was well worth it, then to lie in the floor and read "When de Co'n Pone's Hot," "When Malindy Sings," "Little Brown Baby," and many other of Dunbar's verses in simple, lyrical dialect. There is little wonder that we read Dunbar with such delight over and over again. The folk Negro pictured in the book, the life problems and patterns of living treated in verse, and the dialect itself, all of these only slightly removed, were much like our early surroundings.

I have strong memories of some of the country ways brought to our neighborhood. One of them was of inescapably deep meaning. Some of them were disturbing to the school breeding in us, and we children resisted and avoided them as best we could. Others were fascinating, easily when not eagerly accepted, and they remain with us today.

One of my brothers was delivered by a white physician, then the family doctor, but the nearing of his arrival, and, in truth, the success of it, was a matter for a midwife. Mrs. Lewis was a vigorous, little old lady of coal black color who wore long skirts and a bandana, to look for all the world like a mammy, dear to the heart of a status-seeking Southerner. She came to our house, as a neighbor, to help out until the doctor came. But she stayed through the delivery, and "It was a good thing that she did," Papa said many times. For the doctor had pronounced the new baby a stillbirth, but Mrs. Lewis pinched and spanked his tiny bottom until he gave a little cry, halting the doctor who was preparing to leave.

We used to look upon Mrs. Lewis with awe and deep affection and worshipfulness. The older I grew and the longer I lived in a world of color differences, the more often I wondered whether that doctor had not too lightly borne his responsibility because of it.

A piece of Irish potato to allay a boy's muscular disability with a leg was acceptable; it was simply hidden in the pocket of the trouser leg. But it took exertion of the strong parental hand, almost literally, for a child to get down the bitter brews from weeds or to accept administration of the smelly poultices, salves, and liniments made from seeds and weeds, roots and barks. The fetid asafetida, to ward off various diseases (a most plausible assumption!) was especially abhorred by the kids. It was carried about the neck in a little sack, generally a tobacco sack obtained from a cigarette smoker who rolled his own from tobacco makings. The boys could hide the sack under the shirt buttoned up all the way, but there was no way to smother that cutting odor. Still there came a time when almost every child at my school carried asafetida about his neck. It was when influenza raged throughout the winter following the first World War. Copper wire about the neck or wrist was another folk treatment, protector against or palliative for what, I don't remember. The older children resented the fact that the copper adornment too much resembled bracelets and necklaces worn by their "savage" cousins, as they appeared in our geography books and an occasional issue of *National Geographic*. But those who needed it were thusly wired up.

Chewing and snuff dipping were distinctly rural Southern forms of the tobacco habit. So in the North End the boys preferred licorice candy cut into plugs, like chewing tobacco. But whether we bought it as licorice drops, twists, whips, or plugs, we chewed and spat out the dark brown goodness along the sidewalk, mimicking our tobacco-chewing elders. The snuff was something else to me. Women often dipped it, sometimes rather slyly. One of them was a friend of Mama's and mine who frequently grabbed and snuff-kissed me, and always the taste of her powdered tobacco was disturbing, as much as I like her.

Folk singing and the folk foods—"soul food," now sometimes called— I learned early to enjoy as *our* eating and *our* singing.

It was a real gift, like a box of fancy chocolates, to get a piece of sugar cane sent up from the country in Tennessee. Once a whole barrel of sorghum was sent, and two gallons of it came to our family. Papa pronounced it "sopping good" and it was. Cornbread—hot water or egg, as pone, cakes, or in the pan; biscuits; sweet potatoes; greens that were mustard, turnip, or a mix of wild ones; collards, after frost; and bacon and pork were familiar items in our kitchen, as many another. But it was that winter following the raising and fattening of thirty or so young hogs belonging to a half-dozen families in the neighborhood which brought so much "down home" eating to the older folk and taught us young ones that there is so much more to a hog than his greed and grunts. This was the outcome of "keeping" sows "on halvers." A farmer had assigned a sow readied for a litter of pigs to each of the families, for tending and feeding until the litter came, after which he took back his sow and half of the litter, leaving the remainder to the family. These pigs were killed by the men in all of the families and home-butchered by them and their wives after the first cold snap. In their hands those hogs turned into head, snout, and feet; souse and head cheese; kidneys, liver, and lights; salted shoulder and sugar-cured ham; salt pork and fat back; brains, to fry in an egg mix; and, of course, the chitterling set, the Kentucky oysters, and the maw. There was one item which came only from the boars and that only "Pa" Pickens was old enough to know how to dress and cook. "Mountain apples," he called them, and he had plenty of his delicacy that winter.

The singing I heard so early and is forever to move me was mostly gospel and spiritual, but sometimes included work songs and the blues. The spirituals came more often at the revivals when the preacher himself would raise one, though when the spirit was strong at regular church service, some older person in the congregation would raise it on his own. Afterward two or three more might simply start up and on their way home the members would say, "The church rocked this morning!" For several years there was a male quartet which sang from church to church in the neighborhood. We children followed them about, fascinated by their work songs. There were several fellows in the neighborhood who played the banjo and sang the blues, those sung by all of those Smiths on the records (Clara, Bessie, and Mamie and no trio) but others that had no titles. I liked the blues especially, the plaintive melodies and the lyrics as well. Whenever a "colored show" was part of the carnival at the county fairgrounds, I would most enjoy the woman, usually rather fat and dark brown, who sang the blues. I would stay late to see the show and hear that singer, though I would not tell about it at home. The blues were too bawdy for a Christian home. We had a phonograph, a Victrola it was, but no blues or jazz records. We did have several Bert Williams records, because Papa enjoyed them too.

DU BOIS, AN UNCLE, AND A NEWSPAPER

Later, when I was perhaps mid-way in high school, I stumbled across a little black book which held as much needed meaning for me as a Negro as the Bible has for me in humanity. It has influenced me as no other single book save that of the Word. I have returned to *Souls of Black Folk* time after time since I was a youngster and still marvel at what is there.

This book, which William Edward Burghardt Du Bois wrote just as the twentieth century began is echoed today in hundreds of books and articles. In 1903, he had written in *Souls of Black Folk* that "The problem of the twentieth century is the problem of the color-line, the relation of the darker to the lighter races of men in Asia and Africa, in America and the islands of the sea." No more need be said. Moreover, the Negro problem is now accepted as not only partially economic but as that of the whole nation; Du Bois had that long ago seen it as "the dead weight of social degradation partially masked behind a half-named Negro problem." In these sixties hindsight tells us that black poverty in the midst of white affluence causes disorder; Du Bois had observed that "to be a poor man is hard, but to be a poor race in a land of dollars is the very bottom of hardships." The loss of Negro self-esteem that so concerns those most honest about correctives for the color problem Du Bois had seen coming. He was even then fearful for the Negro "in this American world—a world which yields him no true self-consciousness." He saw even then that the color problem "has wrought sad havoc with the courage and faith and deeds of ten thousand people—has sent them often wooing false gods and invoking false means of salvation and at times has even seemed to make them ashamed of themselves." He foresaw the pathological plight that the ghettos were to bring and, what is more, he did so with some sense of balance. "So dawned the time of *Sturm* and *Drang*: storm and stress today rocks our little boat on the mad-waters of the world sea; there is within and without the sound of conflict, the burning of body and the rendering of soul; inspiration strives with doubt, and faith with vain questionings," he wrote decades ago.

At fifteen or sixteen years, I could not grasp Du Bois easily or wholly. His classical references were too much for me, and his Latin and German phrases were simply skipped. But already I was being buffeted about as a Negro. Already I had felt what he called "a peculiar sensation, this double-consciousness, this sense of always looking at one's self through the eyes of others . . . ," my "two-ness—an American, a Negro . . ." I was reading Negro history and liked hearing that we darker ones are "not altogether empty-handed." I had started among Negro folk and could appreciate his labeling as "the soul-beauty of a race" that which "set the ruder souls of his people a-dancing and a-singing." When Du Bois spoke of the "ideal of book-learning" and the power in "the longing to know," it made all that emphasis on school from Mama fall into place. I certainly sensed what he meant when he spoke of racial prejudice as "that personal disrespect and mockery, the ridicule and systematic humiliation, the distortion of fact and wanton license of fancy, the cynical ignoring of the better and the boisterous welcoming of the worst, the all-pervading desire to inculcate disdain for everything black." And I could eagerly accept, as I would badly need for the long haul, that

> merely a concrete test of the underlying principles of the great republic is the Negro Problem, and the spiritual striving of the freedmen's sons is the travail of souls whose burden is almost beyond the measure of their strength, but who bear it in the name of an historic race, in the name of this the land of their fathers' fathers, and in the name of human opportunity.

Perhaps it was as much my adolescent intensity as the chapter I was reading in *Souls of Black Folk* which one evening brought me to tears that I did not succeed in hiding from my mother. She made me put it away for a while. I have ever since gone back to it again and again, always to find it moving, sometimes stimulating and stirring, and at others succoring and saving. More of "the strange meaning of being black" seems to be there than in any other single place of my knowing.

After *Souls of Black Folk*, I began to follow Du Bois in the *Crisis*, turning its pages as soon as I got my hands on it to his column, "As the Crow Flies," to read his tightly reasoned, trenchantly expressed observations on what was happening to Negroes.

During the same period, my brothers and I commenced visiting Chicago to spend summer vacations with Uncle Robert, Willie, and Rufus, my mother's brothers. Uncle Robert was of most influence on our self-images. He was a graduate of Tuskegee Institute and remained much impressed by Booker T. Washington and the wisdom and respectability of the Negro business entrepreneur. Tuskegee had made a stationary engineer of him, and he worked at it sixteen hours out of twenty-four, five days a week, for perhaps thirty years at a yeast company and for the city of Chicago. But the fruits of this labor were meant to get him into business, something he finally but failingly tried. Meanwhile, he was taking his nephews during the summers to meet Negro keepers of small retail and service establishments which he patronized, but not omitting also to take them to see the larger and more significant enterprises such as the Binga State Bank and Building, the Overton Hygienic Company, and the Robert S. Abbott Publishing Company. He would also point out and identify the operators of these places as well as lawyers, doctors, and dentists he could recognize. I recall a neighboring playmate who switched his career aspiration from that of Pullman porter, an impressive functionary he would see on the trains back and forth to visit in Tennessee with his mother, to dentist, after his tooth was pulled by the Negro dentist in nearby Danville, Illinois. When he informed us little Nesbitts of his lifted sights, we could tell him of the wonders of Chicago we had seen with our own eyes, not only Negro dentists but lots of doctors and lawyers, even business owners besides.

Uncle Rob also took us to a building on State Street which had once been a store of some kind but where what was called the Universal Negro Improvement Association met, and I once went with him to Washington Park to hear the boldest, most blunt-talking black man I had then ever seen, Marcus Garvey. Uncle Rob admired Garvey because he was bent on getting Africa back from the white people who had stolen it, especially the English. Most of what Garvey said was frightening thunder to me, though Uncle Rob could almost convince me that Garvey's ambitions were right and just. In fourth-grade geography I had first seen a map of the world, most of which was in red (except for all the blue water) and belonged to Great Britain. Yet England herself was a tiny little place and, in my child's mind, I had never found acceptable her having so much dominion. It did not seem right and needed correction.

The *Chicago Defender*, a Negro newsweekly, was inescapably part of our shaping. We distributed it weekly and read it as regularly and fully as did our customers. At first, it simply made us feel good and helped us to know and accept ourselves as Negroes. Week after week, as little children, we read the *Defender*, early to learn of Negro educational institutions, doctors, and lawyers, and other professionals, even banks, and other businesses in various of the larger cities. Its pages also began to give us some sense of a past for ourselves as Negroes other than that of the humility and subjection of slavery, some consciousness of history neither taught nor even to be suspected from what we were learning at Lawhead and Marquette schools. Through its feature stories and pictures, and even its editorials, in celebration of the birth anniversaries and observing the deaths of notables among "race" men, as the newspaper would put it, we began to learn of Nat Turner and Denmark Vesey, the insurrectionists, Crispus Attucks, Frederick Douglass, the abolitionist, Benjamin Banneker, the early inventor and surveyor, and even women like Phyllis Wheatley, Harriet Tubman, and Sojourner Truth, the underground railway workers. My older brother and I were permitted, I remember, to name a neighbor's newborn baby Harriet Sojourner, and the latter became the beautiful name of "Sidgee," the most her little brothers and sisters could make of Sojourner. Had the baby been a boy we would have named it Nat Turner or Denmark Vesey, I am certain.

But soon the same *Defender*, abhorred as too radical by many people, including Negroes, was to do more than make for color consciousness and security: it was to excite us about the mistreatment of Negroes in a way I am certain yet marks me. It is what I read so much of in that newspaper, beginning when I was only seven or eight and continued week after week until I was twenty, as much as what whites have directly done to me, that first put me on guard against them, perhaps to leave me still that way. I have sought to have something less than a chip on the shoulder for them and, I think, succeeded. But the withholding of judgment, the burden and armor of watching and waiting to see how long it will take this white one and that, no matter how warmly and wonderfully human he may seem and really be, before his white feelings slip through, is something with which the *Defender* early endowed me.

For over and over again as little children, we lay on the floor and read in the *Defender* of white brutalization, the beatings, the floggings, the shootings, and the lynchings of Southern Negroes. We read long, sickening accounts of the Southern peonage system and had an uncle to explain, "Yes, it's like slavery, but it's worse. A slave was a human machine that had to be cared for to keep it going and protect its value. But on the peonage farm, the people aren't owned. There's nothing to lose. So they just drive them and drive them until they die." We read the stories of men, women, and little children who had managed to escape from plantations and made it to Chicago.

We learned the word *extradition*, as we frequently studied a story about an escaped Negro that a Southern state was trying to get back in its white clutches. We saw frightening-looking pictures of black chain gangs, watched by rifle-armed white overseers, and of black men hung, beaten, burned, and mutilated by white mobs, in sheets and without them. Upon occasion, the pictures would be difficult to believe, but the whole pattern of response by Papa and Mama, more than the specific answer to "Is this real?" was more than convincing—their own stories of other such events, involving their own relatives and friends back in Tennessee and Alabama and especially the tear or two Mama would sometimes shed in the telling.

The *Defender* at any time would have deeply affected an eight-year-old reader. But I was eight in 1919. This was the time of return for the Negro soldiers of World War I, looking at home for the democracy for which they had helped Mr. Wilson make the world safe, but all too often only to be greeted by lynch mobs for all their pains. Some of them were lynched in uniform.

That summer, a series of race riots swept across the country, not only in the South but also East, West, and North, and especially in Chicago. In Chicago, the riot was the worst of all, running thirteen days and bringing death to twenty-odd Negroes and injury to several hundred more. The gruesome details of this blood bath we not only read in the *Defender*, the family, with Mama foremost, was intimately involved. For her three brothers were all in Chicago, and there were several long, anxious conversations between them and Mama during the long days and nights of rioting. After each, Mama would tell us what she had been told. While on his way from work, Uncle Rob had once been chased by a small mob. In this way the meaning of what the *Defender* had been saying reached us with new force. What whites did in the South to Negroes they could do in the North, in Chicago, and to members of our family.

SLURS, SMILES, AND SUPPORTS

In Champaign itself, of course, there was little or nothing of the same cloth of the physical mistreatment of Negroes reported by the *Defender*.

Still, whites were whites in Champaign-Urbana and run-of-the-mill at the university, as elsewhere, it must be added. Color-based prejudice and practice were there. Their most common expression was the racial taunt and slur, verbally and in symbols. This kind of mistreatment was so pervasive that no Negro youngster circulating as I did could escape it. Anti-Negro brutality had little or nothing to do with the Champaign I knew as a youngster. But, as I look back on it, it was slow strangulation of the spirit that was the risk.

Among the youngsters in the North End, who roughed it and roughed up each other there, name-calling was to be expected as much as the thick black mud in its roads after rain. It was a dish-it and take-it process, "you black nigger" for "you dirty piece of white trash" and vice versa, when angry feelings found the happenstance of color difference for adding fuel to the fire. Slurring was sometimes followed by slugging, usually remaining "man-to-man." The antagonists, one poor and black and the other white but with little to show for it, were not really so different, especially so long as they remained in the North End.

But beyond the North End, the insults we recurringly received were of another order and usually had to be taken. They were always cruel, because they were unprovoked. They would come unexpectedly, out of a clear blue sky, in many different places and from all kinds of whites, nobody-whites but those who were somebody too.

They came upon us from time to time in the funny papers, the cartoons, the advertisements, and, of course, the jokes that we saw in the local as well as other newspapers. They came occasionally in pictures, drawings, and scratchings upon school walls and sidewalks. They popped out and upon us—into us—as a pickaninny doll in a department store window, a huge figure in black licorice with lips of red-hearts and big white eyes lying in a confectioner's window, or a picture of Little Black Sambo on the cover of the book and scattered through its pages—a book distributed by the public through its schools and libraries.

The cheap whites who loafed about the I.C. Depot, the Varsity Theater, the nearby poolroom and the Coney Island restaurant—cabbies, delivery truck drivers, and the like—found sport in calling out "shine" and "blackie," extending their flat, western speech to southern dialect, in loud tones, or softly singing or humming "Bye, Bye Blackbirds," as we passed within hearing.

This kind of white could go farther. I remember once when a couple of garage fellows, along Hickory Street, offered several of us, all Negroes, a ride to school. We leaped into the back seat of a top-down, T-model Ford, with an extra-loud muffler and what passed as clever phrases painted on it, such as then was popular. No sooner were we driven several blocks into the heart of downtown, when suddenly we were receiving electric shocks from all directions. As we screamed, jumped, and scrambled about unable to escape the moving vehicle, we surely were the laughable spectacle, of choice order, that was intended.

Occasionally mature, well-dressed people of apparent quality could be heard in all sobriety to refer to "the little darkies" in distinctly Northern accents. And little children would call us, as best they could, "nidder, nidder."

Then there were the gangs of students on and about the university campus who would make sport of us. Nothing more was required of us than to come within sight and yelling distance of them. They would then display learning and literacy superior to that of the poor whites along Main Street by making us little Negro youngsters the butt of contemptuous epithets more colorful and varied than "shine" and "blackie." Theirs was a range from "Asphalt" to "Zulu Boy." They called us everything imaginably black, dirty, or otherwise disdainful. Anthracite, Bituminous, Blackbird, and Black Boy, Chocolate Drop, Coal Baby and Coal Dust, Cloud, Coon, Dusty, Ebony, Eight Ball, Hershey Bar, Jig, Jigaboo, Licorice, Midnight, Mose, Rastus and Rufus, Sambo, Spade, Smoke, Spook, Sundown, Shine and Sunshine, and Tar Baby—a little darkey by any such name was something funny.

We threw "dirty white trash," "white son-of-a-bitch," and rocks back at them, this from a distance enabling escape should chase be given. But, of course, we were no match for them. We were outdone even on those rare occasions when a rock found its target. We were licked from the start, for we were up against too much: not a handful of students, but the white supremacy system. We heard the raucous laughter, saw the smirking countenances, and felt the scorn. It was beginning to cut deeply.

During this same period, I first resisted what seemed to me clearly to be racial mistreatment at the hands of the public, its police. Never since have I had much use for them, a position they see to my keeping.

As I made one of my trips for Mama with laundry for a lawyer living on the West Side, I had seen a motorcycle policeman amiably chatting with the white children gathered about him, as they admired his machine and fingered its gadgets on the spacious grounds of Avenue School, where the attendance was nothing but white. I recognized him as the same officer who frequently during the school term and almost daily in summer would send the children, mostly Negro, scurrying away from Lawhead School as if they were rats. It was a stupid policy he was callously enforcing, for there was no other recreational area accessible to us. The fact was that children were not allowed to play on the grounds of any school in Champaign outside of school hours and I well knew it. I had seen a post bearing a large wooden sign containing such information on every school ground on which I had been. But it seemed to me even then that if a rule which was unfair and of no sense to begin with was to be overlooked at any place, it should be at Lawhead, in a neighborhood so lacking in play areas as it was. Besides, if a policeman, the same policeman, could tolerate play on the grounds at Avenue during off-hours, he should allow it at Lawhead. He did not, and to me this was racial discrimination.

Then and there, as I looked upon that event at Avenue School, I decided that I would never again run from the grounds at Lawhead, certainly not from that policeman.

A few days later, my determination was put to test as the same policeman wheeled his motorcycle onto the grounds where a huge group of boys, most of them much larger than myself, were playing. Immediately, and without a word from the cop, everyone fled but me. He then called me to him, demanding, "Why didn't you run?"

"Because I haven't done anything wrong," I replied.

This drew his reference to my certain knowledge of my wrong-doing, backed by his pointing a few feet beyond to the familiar posting against play on the grounds outside of school hours. At this point those who had fled had begun returning out of curiosity and in time to hear me charge the policeman with treating us differently from youngsters at Avenue. When the angry, red-faced, red-necked policeman rejoined, "What I do out there is my business!" a chorus of protest from the increasingly emboldened group arose. They had joined the revolution. Outnumbered and having indirectly admitted guilt of discrimination, the angry policeman suddenly halted the proceedings. Ignoring everyone else and centering his attention on me, he said, "The next time I come out here, I want to see you run like the rest."

He then drove off with a great spurt, as those who once so feared him laughed at his obvious discomfiture.

I do not remember his or any other policeman's coming back to Lawhead to treat children like rats. That was the last of the mad rush of children from the Lawhead grounds as the cops approached.

Thus, though I had come to be satisfied with my Negroness, to accept and live with it easily for myself, I also had begun early and swiftly to learn from a newspaper and books and from those whites with whom I brushed that the blackness which pleased me was something that they felt compelled to laugh at and look down upon. Nor was that all. They would withhold from me what they found good, convenient, and necessary for themselves, their children, and most others at all of the same mold. This I could not stomach and began early to resist.

Such early resistance against what was so all-pervasive, what even then clearly was to be encountered in so many ways and so many places, might well have torn me asunder, as at later times it came dangerously close to doing.

Much of what has saved me and served me well the remainder of my life was the gift of other kinds of whites, those seeing me other than as a funny piece and a thing to abuse. This gift came early, too. This does not say that whites have not accepted, understood, supported, even joined me all along my way as I have protested racial mistreatment and demanded respect for beings of my kind. They have. But the decent ones whom I knew early were those I so much needed and who by their example taught me that strong and secure people standing up for decency would usually be there to count upon. They were among those who shaped me.

So I must now tell of some of them, white people who protected, smiled on, and sustained me when I was young, rebellious, thin-skinned, on edge to act, and able to react quickly. They made a kind of place for me. Some of them simply let me be; others took care to include me in, at least to avoid shutting me out; still others reached out for me. And one stopped to give me a hard push in the way of the Negro protest, the way I am proud to have come.

There was W. W. Earnest, the superintendent of schools, distinguished for his ability to relate himself to all of the students in the system and, I learned, especially to the bad actors among them. He regularly carried his fatherly appearance before the children throughout the system and involved them in his inspections, if such they were. For myself, I saw him at least once or twice every year, from first grade through the senior high school year. On each of these occasions with students beyond the first grade, he would invariably ask them, "What is the business of the schools?" Thereupon, no matter the academic level of the assemblage, he would at once and unfailingly get from them en masse the one and only answer. It would be repeated in the same sing-song fashion of its rote learning directly from Mr. Earnest himself when they were first graders: "The business of the schools—is to help boys and girls—to grow up to be—the best men—and the finest women—they ever can be."

As a fourth-grader at Lawhead, I came to know the superintendent from closer up, because I could not restrain myself from striking a teacher during a recess period. For some reason, she had jerked a brother of mine in the second grade by the collar of his shirt, sending the buttons flying off his shirt down to the waist and leaving him screaming. The next day I was ordered to the office of the superintendent of schools to see Mr. Earnest, amid schoolground rumor that I was certain to be sent to a reformatory.

I went alone, a little eight-year-old Negro villain, charged with striking a white and female schoolteacher, and not to a hearing but to hear what the white man in charge of the entire school system would say was to be done to me. And I received in thirty or forty minutes an educational experience which was at once warm and apt and of long reach. It was more skillfully conducted and of more lasting impact certainly than any single lesson I had received previously, and perhaps since.

This superintendent began by taking care to relieve my fears and tension and to leave me able to learn, though how it could be done so advisedly I have never known. Said he, "First, let me say that you are not the worst boy who has had to come here to see me and you are not to be sent to any reformatory." Those words I shall never forget.

Then he kindly, clearly, and challengingly made one point after another. A reformatory meant a place to reform bad boys. But until the boys were worse than I was they could improve themselves. The teachers at Lawhead had said that I was hard to control. Well, a strong and good person ought not be easy to control. But he ought not need much control from others, his mother and his teachers. He ought often to know when he's about to misbehave and control himself. "That's called self-discipline," he said.

"Your own teacher also says that you're stubborn. Now let me show you something," he went on to say. Then, handing me a sheet of paper bearing all of my grades in the basic subjects since I had started school and then taking it back, he added, "This shows that you are a good student but you are weak in arithmetic. You need to work harder and longer on your arithmetic. This is where you need to be stubborn. If you are stubborn, where it's needed and for a good purpose, people call that persistence."

After cautioning me to go on back to school and to get along with my teachers, he dismissed me with "Remember now, self-discipline. And be stubborn about that arithmetic, be persistent."

A year or so later, the transfer of my public library card from the

Marquette Branch to the Main Library was to bring me within reach of Nellie Amsbary. This woman need not have reached out for me, for she was an Amsbary, a local family of importance said to own the water works. She was in charge of the library, with enough to do I suppose doing whatever head librarians do. If she were voluntarily to extend her devotion, the social position that was likely hers, or at least her family status, would have reserved her special favors mainly for the first ladies on the West Side who wanted sooner to see the latest must-be-read novel than their positions on the waiting list merited. As far as children went, extra effort at pleasing, if not serving the best literary interest of those with the right names was likely expected.

As for me, as one of Miss Amsbary's patrons, I was surely a bit untidy, black, and barren of distinctiveness except for being out of place at the Main. I might well have been closely watched, kept silent, and served promptly, so that as quickly as possible I could be dispatched back toward the wrong side of tracks from which I had come. But it was not so.

Miss Amsbary did keep an eye on me, a friendly one. She doubtless had done so for weeks, if not months, before that day when she intervened with the little interloper that I was. I had approached the desk where she sat, surrounded by books and readying herself to charge out the stack which I placed before her. She quietly and quickly surveyed the titles and authors, more often than not Zane Grey; it was his turn with me. I had finished "the Rover Boys" and had quit the endless flow of Horatio Algers.

"Well, you may take them all. You do come a long way for books, and you do get them back on time," she said.

But then suddenly she bent down beside her desk and raised up with two books in hand. Thrusting them toward me, she added, "But I wish you would take these to read and put back two of those you have. I've been saving these two books just for you."

I hesitantly accepted the two books Nellie Amsbury had set aside for me, examined them cautiously and to no avail. They were utterly foreign to me, an East Sider; they were likely two of the classics for West Side children. I have long ago forgotten their titles. But I read them and the first was by no means the last time Miss Amsbary saved a book, of her own selection, for her little colored customer. Later she occasionally reserved a title for me but of my own choice or complimented me on a tentative selection of mine—all I am certain under an influence that was hers to start with.

But for Nellie Amsbary I might have gone on and on with the man who wrote *Riders of the Purple Sage* and that seemingly endless series of stories of cowboys and Indians, rustlers, and gunfighters. What she had done for me I suddenly realized one summer when for three weeks I substituted as houseman in a West Side home. I was then a high school senior, seven years older than that day when Miss Amsbary so gently steered me toward books more worth my reading. As the mistress of the house took me on an initial tour of it, to show what was expected of me in this room and that, I lingered a moment for a critical scrutiny of one side of the thirteen year-old daughter's room. The whole wall from floor to ceiling was in bookshelves filled with books, good books. And there they were, the same ones that Miss Amsbary had begun pushing my way, *Tom Sawyer* and *Huckleberry Finn, Hans Brinker, Black Beauty, The Call of the Wild*, and a lot more of them.

I am not to omit here several of my eighth-grade classmates who were to become the core of scholastic and activity leadership in my high school class. I met them first at Central, the single eighth-grade school in the city, as the lone Negro assigned to its first division, each division being numbered in rank order based on the seventh-grade scholastic achievement of the pupils assigned to it.

The children in the first division were not only quite bright, they were for the most part the offspring of the better-off. Many had the same last names as those I had seen on doors to downtown offices and business places. Most had never attended school with Negroes nor been taught to fear and despise them.

They easily made room for me among themselves in a natural and spontaneous fashion. In the early twenties this acceptance, mind you, would not have been the conscious, guilt-easing acclaim of token Negro presence which occurs today in those occasionally integrated oases within a school system, where it is ever so tenuous and often guided by the teachers, if not also the parents. It was a real acceptance, as complete and easy as our color system allowed.

It began with our homeroom teacher, who simply seated his class alphabetically, a fact which happened to leave me in the center of a bevy of girls. On February 14 of that school year, a special day which had never meant anything to me as a boy in a family lacking girls as well as money for buying valentines, I found myself the recipient of eight or nine missives of affection, each from a girl. This surely had not been "managed" from any of the homes of my classmates nor by the gentleman who was our teacher as well as principal and coach and who was at once crusty, likeable, and jocular.

As I started high school these bright girls and their closer friends continued to display an easy willingness to allow me a degree of belonging in other ways. The morning after the freshman class election, one of the girls revealed that I had been a nominee for the vice presidency, an occurrence with which she likely had to do. I had not bothered to attend the meeting. As teams were picked for a spelling bee staged in my sophomore English class, another of the group laughingly told the teacher that she had skipped me twice, in deference to the captain of the other team, and still another of the group, who she was sure liked me and wanted me on her team. The girl presumed to like me blushed and chose me promptly. Once or twice it was suggested that I join a school club. When a popular fellow in our class died, and word got out that I had written a poem in his memory, I was asked to read it at the high school assembly but declined. Thereafter, one of the girls demanded the poem and herself read it, after crediting it to me and noting my refusal to do so.

It was the tumultuousness in me which brought me face to face with the high school principal, not once but several times, before he was to hand me a diploma. I had not struck another teacher. Instead it was my striking out against discrimination.

Charles S. Dale commenced his principalship as I began my freshman year, succeeding an affectionately regarded woman principal who in her later years was hardly able to control the more rambunctious high schoolers. He had been drawn from principalship of a technical school in Portsmouth, Ohio, I suppose, to strengthen discipline, if not also athletics, the latter being an acceptable means to the former, not to speak of its being pleasing to the alumni about town.

Mr. Dale looked the commanding part of a disciplinarian, tall, straight, and lean-figured, with his rather handsome features overall, including angular lines with firmly set jaws and tightly fixed lips. But his coming had been well publicized, including the fact that he was in fact a Kentuckian. I then concluded that he looked lean, hungry—and would be mean to Negroes—like the Southerner he was should be expected to be. I was certain that he would have no use for Negroes.

But I could hardly have been more mistaken about him. This I quickly learned as I began to react against what seemed to me color mistreatment.

Twice I went to him alone, without representative capacity whatsoever, to make issue of and protest against practices about which there was wide complaint among Negro students, voiced among themselves. He easily and squarely faced both matters and readily resolved them. The first complaint was against the segregated seating of Negro students on the part of some teachers. This practice was clearly revealed at the weekly assemblies, "Jim Crow" pockets, little thickets of Negroes, would show up scattered throughout the student body. An instruction for seating of homeroom groups alphabetically took care of the matter. There had been no beating about the bush, no passing the buck to faculty meeting. No semester change was awaited to effect it. It came soon after we talked.

To the credit of the principal also, he did not regard me as so much a little monster in advancing what became my anti-discrimination program that he would not stoop to have me help him carry out one of his own projects. At his request and just before school started one fall, another Negro student and I went on a mission comfortably strong in the tradition of varsity athletics at the college and often the high school level. In short, we went to the North End and located the star Negro athlete for Central the previous year, who had decided he had enough of school. We convinced this dropout that he should go talk with Mr. Dale; in turn, Mr. Dale convinced the young man that he should continue school, and a few days later a successful football season for Champaign High School was clearly in the offing. This recruit proved highly versatile, a stellar football, baseball, and basketball player and in track, a sprinter, hurdler, broad jumper, and javelin thrower of first rank.

As my junior year of high school neared its end, I began to face the reality that I was more than a half-year behind in credits. As they stood, I would not be able to graduate with my class. The rather decent scholastic record which the superintendent had used in his noble effort to get me on a better emotional course had persisted through the eighth year, though including the weakness in mathematics. But thereafter, I had demonstrated not only a weakness with algebra and geometry but had failed other subjects. It is not an excuse but accurate, I think, to say that the discrimination-centered turbulence that was mine was no small part of my trouble. There were times, I know, when I was indifferent to the extent of not making the presentation I was prepared to make, when the teacher was not to my liking. Indeed this confusion was known and met with sympathy if not understanding by some of my teachers, as I later came to appreciate.

In any case, the willingness to give a Negro youngster, a confused and a rebellious one at that, a second chance and very large benefit of the doubt was there. When I went to Eleanor Chaffee, the vice principal, who was in charge of the problem people as well as the academic records, and told her I wanted to graduate with my class despite the heavy arrearage in credits, I shall never forget what she said.

"If you are really certain that is what you want and are determined to do it, you can. I believe you have what it takes. You may have the opportunity, if we can work all you need into a schedule. The problem will be that of scheduling," was her decision.

She then managed to work out the schedule by getting a male teacher of one needed subject to make me a class of one during his lunch hour. This man not only taught extra and yielded his lunch hour for my sole benefit, but in so doing he had that much less time to share unimpededly at noon with the lovely young faculty member he was courting and shortly was to marry. And he was a Southerner!

The outcome of the favor done me was this. During my senior year and under the pressure of measuring up to the special privilege I was given, I earned six and a half instead of four credits and made grades that averaged close to honor level. I had turned out at long last a pretty decent student.

* * *

Comfort with my color and a liking for some of the simple ways of black folk remain strong and settled parts of my being.

Black people seemed beautiful to me long before the urgings of those preaching black power. Years ago, the continuum of color, shade, and hue among Negroes, the hair that is kinky, curly, limp, straight, or hard to know just which, and the facial features and contours which shift so within a single family as to leave its members quite unalike, all seemed to me to produce striking compositions to look upon. So I learned to protest skin bleaching and hair conking long before Malcolm X came along. As I saw *us*, *we* seemed good, and I felt that we should let ourselves be.

My preferences in food lean to the South and the fare of its field hands, especially the pot of this or that vegetable with smoked meat for seasoning. Every spring I take off for the Maryland or Virginia countryside to gather a mess of wilder greens to put with the dandelions from my own yard. I have never been tempted to have my chitterlings or pig feet behind closed doors. As my wife knows, corn bread is a delight with me, even as an allowance.

I can sit and listen to music from the masters, as it is called. But nothing musical moves me as much as do the slave songs, the spirituals, and the gospel hymns. I like them left simple and sung without stilt, restraint, or stepping-up. Many a Negro female vocalist, it seems to me, begins with a voice that is rich, strong, and rangy but allows it spoiling with a "style." I would prefer hearing them back in the Baptist choir where they began, singing our songs like they are—or were—singing like "Malindy sings."

Dunbar's verse and that of younger poets in dialect, when it sounds real, are an enjoyment of mine. I like to read it aloud to whomever will listen. Though the first lines are difficult, the adjustment is fast, since I have but a recovery to make.

Langston Hughes's Jess Simple was a favorite of mine. His authenticity never ceased to impress me, and Simple's folk expression and flavor, kept abreast of times in the ghetto, were always intriguingly delightful. Now that Simple's creator is dead, I must do more of what any bonafide-appearing Negro is free to do, get to a certain kind of barber shop in the ghetto to hear the folk woes, wisdom, and wit straight from the folks. The right barber shop is that in which the speech is mostly wrong, but free and honest, relaxed and lively, with the fellows saying what they mean and meaning what they say. Since the mask is off and the storytellers up North, what "th' colored" says about "th' whites" is sometimes bitter. But most of the chatter is rolling fun and affords me more relaxation than the gabbing in any other place open to me. The public accommodation law and the habitués of a white barber shop can never take the place of the bunch in the barber shop in the ghetto.

Lastly, I must admit that I have my soul served in the ghetto less often than I get my hair trimmed there. Most often I choose to worship by way of a carefully selected radio program, in a university chapel, or as a transient member of a Unitarian congregation. The sermon I hear is neat and well ordered, addressed to a current great issue, and unaccompanied by scattered, vocalized affirmations. But whenever I do attend church "in the inner city," I am well served. The fervor with which the message is delivered leaves it convincing, and the issue may be old but is ageless and impacts me. The bursts of participation from the older worshipers about me are unscheduled but not unexpected. And the simple songs of simple faith are familiar, sung as handed down. I always feel at home in such a church; it has a strong claim on me that is always deeply felt.

Going to University

LABOR AND LEARNING

If you have acquired knowledge, what do you lack?
If you lack knowledge, what have you acquired?
—Leviticus Rabbah 1.6

In September of 1928, I became a freshman in liberal arts at the university, an event not as much the result of decision as nature taking its course. No chosen career requiring college training was envisioned, nor had I received any counseling in that direction. Neither was to be expected in the face of the bleak outlook for a Negro in a professional or other white-collar position in Champaign-Urbana.

For though the university was the focus of the community, a public institution, and the major employer in the area, it had not a single Negro faculty member, not even a lowly instructor. It did have a Negro employed in the Office of the President in a position bearing the title "Chief Clerk." But he was the lone such white-collar employee on the entire administrative staff, and we felt certain was thus to remain. Moreover, while many a Negro youngster came to respect this man who devotedly served the Negro community as a Sunday School teacher, Masonic leader, and troop committeeman for the Boy Scouts, his chief clerkship was suspect-edly phony and a sop to Negroes throughout the state. The man was in-spiring, not so much his position.

Beyond the university and in the larger community, there were few black figures for career inspiration. For a while we were without a Ne-gro doctor, and we never had had a dentist or a lawyer. Even the ubiqui-tous Negro public school teacher of Negroes was lacking in Champaign. Looking to do as adults what Negroes did in our hometown meant ser-vice occupations. Our fathers were barbers, table waiters, porters, jani-tors, pants pressers, and boot blacks. Most of our working mothers, and many worked, were maids, day cleaners, and cooks, as were some of the men, especially in the fraternity and sorority houses.

Little wonder then that few of us completed high school, and only now and then was one of those moved to enter the university within whose shadows we were growing up. Those of us who were part of the high school class of 1928 were but typical. Two of the six of us went to col-lege, and the six were the residue of perhaps as many as twenty who had started high school.

It need hardly be added that my entering college was also not merely to please my parents; poor parents cannot afford the pleasure. Nor had there been any alternatives to weigh as between the university and this or that college offering this or that advantage. I was too poor to have such choices.

I went to the University of Illinois out of compulsion. Mama had pushed schooling, and most everyone who counted saw it as the way to being somebody. Nobody had said where to get off the learning road. Be-sides I had seen and felt enough of the university throughout my child-hood that high school graduation left entering the university the next, natural step to take. Those cast-off, freshman "spots" I had so long worn atop my head I was bound one day to wear of right. The university and I had been so much on the doorsteps of each other that one day the twain had been certain to meet. To be sure, it is also to be said that its modest tuition fees ($35 a semester I now find hard to believe myself) and the fact that I could live at home were circumstances which made things easy for the compulsion.

Since North End youngsters so rarely went to the university, my in-tention to go had required explanation among my friends. When someone would ask the why of it, I would quickly say, "Because I have always wanted to do it." But early that summer before I started college, Papa had raised the question of why. With him my stock answer of having always wanted to go to the university was quite insufficient, especially since my intention did not square with his.

"You are big enough to help me now. You can help take care of the smaller ones," he said. He knew whereof he spoke, for already I was helping him with his custodial chores at the local business college and a haberdashery. Besides, I could wash walls and wax floors as well as he could, for which he charged as much, though more often than not he paid me less. Besides this direct profiteering from my labor, he also had begun to enjoy my willingness to contribute to major household expenses such as the real estate taxes, a practice which all of my brothers later followed.

For several days running, Papa and I discussed the issue, in the presence of Mama, but with her saying little. Finally, one evening after dinner, Papa introduced a consultant opinion in support of his position. He revealed that his friend, a self-appointed minister known as Reverend B. J. Williams ("Bee," we children called him, when outside of Papa's hearing) had also concluded that I should go to work. This intervention was indeed a mistake, for Mama had little use for the officious, arrogant little man, who was a Seventh Day Adventist and had more than once told my faithfully Methodist mother that she should "keep the true Sabbath" as he and my father did. She did not flare up, but quietly said, "Perhaps you should stop arguing with your father about the university."

Later that night she talked to me outside of the presence of Papa. After a quick word or two, airing her anger over the clerical intervention, she said, "If you want to go to the university this fall, get all the work you can find this summer and save every penny from it you can. I'll help you as much as I am able to. You know that."

That settled it. "Bee" Williams's meddling had accelerated Mama's announcement of her position and pledging of support by way of that sack, her "school fund," kept underneath the mattress of her bed. How she made known to Papa that she stood with me I have never known. But he certainly yielded to her, and with me, for never again did he make an issue of going to college, not for me nor for any one of the four brothers to follow me. Indeed, as one after another of us finished the university, he began to convey to those unwitting of the truth that he had so planned it all.

One day, years later and with all of his sons well on their respective ways in Chicago, where he lived with them and almost totally at their expense, he and I made a quick visit home to Champaign. After a few hours stay, during which I had visited friends in the North End and had thought he was similarly engaged, I was alarmed not to be able to locate him as time for the return trip to Chicago neared. Later I learned that he had been downtown in Champaign, standing on the principal corner, where several of the well-to-do people for whom he had worked had greeted him. They had inquired about his boys and he had proudly related their successes. Still later, after talking with my brothers, I found out that this was his favorite pastime on visits home, telling *his* success story to all those he knew and could buttonhole as they passed that corner.

Mama stood ready but did not have to make direct contributions to the cost of college for me nor for those that followed. She only had to help board and room us, a large enough order for her with the small fraternity house of her own that five boys in college and professional schools became. What happened was that each of us worked his way through school. We made literal application of the university's motto, "labor and learning."

A JANITOR AND THEN SOME

Each of us, with one exception, successively served as a student helper to Horace Long, the janitor at the University of Illinois Book and Supply Store, or "the Co-op," as it was called.

The Co-op was a good place to work. Its location at Wright and Green Streets, across from the campus, left one able to work until close to the hour for his next class before shedding coveralls, a quick wash-up, and heading for the nearby classroom. Beyond a routine two hours in the mornings at sweeping walks, dusting counters, and the like, the hours were flexible.

I could work pretty much when I had time to spare: at noon, between classes, in the evenings, and on Sundays. On Saturdays, I would often go to wash walls or wax floors at the home of the boss. I made the most of all of the opportunity, and less of my schooling in the process, working an average of at least thirty hours a week.

The work paid forty cents an hour, an average of twelve dollars weekly.

In the thirties, this was not bad pay for a student; it would perhaps be better understood as equal to at least a dollar-fifty an hour or forty-five dollars weekly today. Moreover, the pay rate was the same as that for the student clerks, who were all white. Thus, while fair employment was lacking, the separate work drew equal pay. I could settle for that half-loaf, did, and liked it. Many of my fellow Negro students often expressed envy of me in the handy employment.

The working conditions were pleasant. The white student co-workers were cordial and easy to get along with. They respected me as a fellow student, and none ever tried to make a lackey of me. We did favors for each other and occasionally complained together about a tough course or a hard professor. We worked, chatted, joked, and laughed together with considerable ease and freedom.

Sometimes we would seriously discuss current events, and the discussion would take a turn bringing to the surface color problems. Or, one would mention what a professor said or an observation in a book or newspaper about disenfranchisement, a lynching, or other mistreatment of Southern Negroes. In these discussions, I learned to employ the same tactic over and over. I would not let them condemn the harsher color persecutions that were Southern and pass over the discrimination patterns in their hometowns and in Champaign-Urbana. Yet they never stopped opening up the color question, and I would always try to shift it right into their own backyards. I well knew that except in a few places in downtown Chicago, Negroes were not treated in the same manner as whites, if admitted at all in restaurants, theaters, and hotels throughout Illinois. So as they would deplore a lynching in Mississippi, I would have them face up to the uncertain prospects of equal treatment before me should I visit Streator, Oak Park, and other communities from which they came. Thin-skinned about color mistreatment as they knew me to be, they doubtless as often baited me, as I sought to confront and embarrass them with the hypocrisy prevalent in their hometowns.

Both the supervision that I received and my relations with the other employees as the bottommost among them were satisfying. The proprietor himself was present day by day, walking about the store, missing nothing out-of-place, but saying little unless he was spoken to. He never sought personal services from me and rarely directed that I perform a cleaning chore. Only once in seven years did he censor me, and then it was done ever so gently though most effectively. He did not open his mouth. Upon that single occasion, he merely pulled his forefinger across the dust-laden surface of a long light shade fixed over a cash register. This he did within my presence and walked away. He may have subsequently checked that shade in the same fashion but, if so, I am certain he never again found as much dust on it or any of its counterparts in the store while I worked there.

There were six departments in the store: textbooks; paper, tobacco, and notions; art supplies; athletic goods; a gift shop; and a book shop. The latter two were run by women, and each occasioned me some mild discomfiture. The lady who ran the gift shop, though with intermittent intervention from the wife of the boss, had status needs, and was a little pretentious; she seemed to think she was herself a gift. She obviously enjoyed summoning me before lady customers to wrap a package, and her instructions were sometimes unnecessarily detailed. Once as a group of lady customers hovered about, she called me from my dusting downstairs and rather whispered, though audibly, "We are out of T.P." The "T.P." threw me momentarily, but when its meaning suddenly dawned on me, I just as quickly sensed a long-awaited opportunity to poke fun at a phony. "Oh," I loudly said, "You must mean toilet paper. Everybody uses it, you know." The lady customers simply snickered a bit. But once the story reached the men employees, they laughed about it for days.

The other lady of some irritation to me ran the bookstore. She was the quiet, genteel niece of the proprietor and not too much older than myself. I respected her for herself, except for one little rub. Though married, she was called by her first name by everyone in the store, including Horace, the janitor, who like the others had known her when she was a child. But she insisted that I call her "Mrs." This was at first difficult only because I naturally tended myself to use the same labels for the people, as well as the goods, in the store that the other employees did. Later I realized that she allowed the white student employees to call her by her first name. I resented being singled out as the sole source from which she was to get the "Mrs." because it was my blackness she pushed back. The result was that whenever I addressed her as she preferred, I was indeed singling her out, and with coldness of tone conveying every bit of the distance she required and as much more as I could muster. Most often, at the bottom of the heap though I was, I skipped salutations and said nothing whatsoever to her unless she did to me. Even then I managed rarely to have to speak to her by name.

My relations with the male department heads were uniformly friendly and relaxed. They made me feel respected as a student, even while I dusted or washed the showcases in their departments. They, like the boss, rarely gave me directions.

Now the weightiest burden of the porter in a business establishment is often more social than physical. The load is not so much what he has to lift and carry as that everybody in the place including the cheapest of the customers—and with the porter the customer is indeed always right—tries to boss him. Somehow this did not happen to me, even though I was lower than porter, the porter's helper. I am certain that it was because the porter himself commanded so much respect from those above and about him as to leave cakish crumbs enough for his helper. Everybody was decent toward Horace, and there was some left for me. Besides, I have never worked for any man whose supervision I more respected and found easier to accept than that I received from Horace Long, the bushy-headed black caretaker at the Co-op. Nobody needed to push or prod Horace, nor did he anyone who worked for him.

Horace was much more than an able janitor; he was a gifted and competent maintenance mechanic. More than that, he was "butcher, baker, and candlestick maker" at the Co-op, and occasionally an advisor on some aspect of the business operation itself.

He kept the Co-op clean, of course, its floors swept, windows washed, and its furniture and fixtures dusted. But also, without orders and following schedules of his own making, he kept the store's mechanical systems in good order. He cleaned, repaired, and renewed the plumbing; wired, rewired, and replaced electrical fixtures; and kept working the store's radiators, boiler, furnace, and stoker. Periodically, too, he painted its walls and would refinish its floors, woodwork, and show cases.

Besides being a maintenance man, Horace handled a wide range of wrapping, packaging, and shipping activity, ranging from neatly beribboned gift items to huge crates of books for shipment to other stores or back to the publisher. He prided himself on accuracy with his labels, spelling included, and his parcels and boxes never reached destination in a damaged state. He strung and repaired tennis rackets, fixed bicycles, and did the picture framing. The sign "Fountain Pen Repair" hung over the jewelry section because he could do that also. He could make a balky cash register work again, if the problem was one at all within reach of anyone short of a National Cash Register man. He not only cleaned show windows—now and then he dressed one.

This Negro janitor not only routinized his own work, he also ordered his own supplies, chose the cleaning equipment he wanted, and hired his student assistants, like myself. He opened the store each morning and closed it at night. But besides door keys, he possessed the combinations to the safes, the big one as well as smaller ones for jewelry and other valuables. In his head, too, was the Co-op's price code and I often saw him start off white students at price marking a new shipment of books. He knew how to, and in squeezes would help, not only to mark stock but also with shipping records, inventory, and even waiting on customers.

He was highly intelligent, knowledgeable, experienced, and judgmental enough to provide advice, and wise enough to do so only when he was asked. He could, for example, give opinions as to what was "off" about a window being trimmed or why a gift item sold slowly.

This complex of resourcefulness, skills, and capabilities was available to the Co-op day in and day out. Horace was rarely late or absent. When he stayed away because of sickness, he was in bad shape for sure.

So here was a boss to respect just as everyone about the place obviously respected him. He had broken out of "his place," in terms of what he was permitted and expected to do, not only because of his loyalty and devotion but because of his demonstrated mechanical skills and his braininess. It was then easy to listen to and follow him. He was a good supervisor, too, gave his instructions clearly, accompanied by quick, easy observations as to why this or that and not the other was the way to load a paper baler or the stoker. He would give me an assignment and go off to what he had assigned himself, leaving me on my own and determined to measure up. He was also kind and considerate, occasionally breaking any heavy labor with something light for a while, such as picture framing or marking books. We swept and mopped all day on Sundays, but when Sundays fell before examinations, I could take the day off or study a bit off and on during work.

On Sundays, with the long hours to ourselves in the store, we talked about many matters. He read lightly, *Argosy* and another pulp magazine or two, but he could intelligently discuss almost any subject I could venture. Moreover, he enjoyed being an unannounced devil's advocate and was smooth enough with it that I would often not discern his role until his eyes twinkled or he broke into a grin.

The wonder I saw in Horace struck me all at once early one morning as I watched him at the notions counter, selling a newspaper to a customer. The depth of my appreciation was not triggered by the simple transaction, I had seen Horace sell hundreds of papers. No, it was the customer upon whom Horace waited that set me thinking. The customer was a certain psychology professor who taught his students that all Negroes were highly emotional, simple-minded animals, of limited, naive learning capacity. I knew this; I had taken his course and suffered the indignity it provided me.

I looked at the white professor, seeing him as the purveyor of prejudice in the name of science that he was, as he stood across the counter from the Negro janitor, intelligent and responsible as I knew him to be. The professor is a phony, and worse, he's all tangled up in his prejudice, I realized. Horace, standing there before him, makes him out a liar.

I laughed aloud, a bitter laugh that covers a curse. The professor turned and looked at me, his face puzzled. Then I quickly walked away. I didn't want a question from Horace. Still, there was a question I often wanted to ask Horace on those Sundays of ours together, though I never did. I wanted to ask him what salary he received, but I was afraid the answer would hurt me. For here was a Negro porter who could have been manager of a department, almost of any one of them. Indeed, he could have gone to the very top of the Co-op heap had his color allowed him the opportunity. If the answer showed that he was not adequately paid for all he really did, as I feared would be the case, it would upset the warmth and appreciation I held for the whole Co-op, virtually part and parcel of my schooling.

I have long since realized how legion are the Horace Longs, intelligent, hard-working, all-giving Negroes, as reliable as the passing of time. This kind of Negro menial performs beyond expectations from the simple, doing far more than is deserved by the employer who leaves him pinned down where he begins. Such menials find it easier to perform to capacity than to yield to bitterness and hold back.

I have met and noticed them at many a turn. They included the household servants who clean and cook with perfection but also give character to the children, while serving as anchor to their parents in times of stress. There also are those maids and stock girls grown gray in the Avenue dress shops, who began attractive and bright enough not only to find, brush, and press Madam's dress but to have bought it abroad, sold it on the floor, fitted or modeled it, had the chance to do so been allowed. Even in the federal government, messengers still depart its civil service as messengers, though carrying away with them a gift of luggage and a citation for "loyalty, devotion, and efficiency" for thirty years of service, during which they started many another up the ladder to the bottom rung of which they were stuck fast.

A TRICKLE, TROUBLED AND TROUBLESOME

In the thirties, Negro students at the university were but a trickle, yet they remained almost completely outside of the mainstream of campus life.

There were only one hundred blacks in a student body of ten thousand or so. Today, at a good private university, that one percent would amount to easy-does-it token representation, useful to assure for the school a "fair image" as a repository of all the Great Society portends and to complete a laboratory in which children of the white middle class can put in a little practice at equality, not to speak of relieving their parents of a bit of their guilt feelings about color prejudice.

But this was a state university—a highly conservative one at that. It was financed and its tune called by a rural-dominated state legislature. It was largely concerned with increasing corn yield and pork production, and little with human relations. The administration and the faculty were doubtless expected to keep student life as much like life in the towns scattered over the state wherever Negroes were, safely and securely in racial separation. For this was not the sixties, when white and Negro students alike and often in coalescence would stage sit-ins and hit the streets for freedom. Instead it was the thirties, when, as the psychologists were finding, substantial percentages of white college students viewed all Negroes as musical, superstitious, lazy, happy-go-lucky, ignorant, and stupid.

We black students were at best pretty much overlooked or left out, and at worst a troublesome presence upon occasion.

The sixty or so males among the Negro students found lodging in three Negro fraternities supplemented by several rooming houses. In this instance, there was little difference in the quality of the abode for Greek and barbarian, both being Negro. A Negro of potential worthiness as a Greek could no more have lived in a fraternity located on "the row," than a non-affiliated Negro student could have been sent to a university-approved rooming house other than those operated by several Negro matrons. The Negro fraternity residences and the for-Negro rooming houses, all remotely located from the heart of the campus, were big, old frame structures not in the best of condition, difficult to heat, and lacking sufficient bathing and toilet facilities for the size of the student household.

The forty-odd Negro women lived in a sorority house and several rooming houses down the street from the sorority. Though the state provided dormitories for female students, no Negro woman had ever lived in one of them. More than once I was told convincing stories depicting the settled practice of the Office of the Dean of Women. She referred all Negro girls to the several for-Negro, for-women rooming houses, accompanied by quick, comforting assurances that the homes would be found nice, comfortable, and respectable.

Eating was even a more difficult problem than lodging. By and large, Negro students did not have those three hot meals daily which Negro cooks in the fraternities and sororities, the rooming houses, and the restaurants prepared for the white students. For all their poverty, the Negro Greeks could be and were rather forced to imitate fraternity and sorority rows, but they lacked the incomes for sustaining their own cuisines. The Negro women running the rooming houses sometimes ran dining tables, open to men and women alike, but confined to the evening meal. The restaurants, the confectionaries, and coke 'n' smoke shops along Wright or Green Streets no more would serve a Negro student than would their counterparts in downtown Champaign or Urbana. In 1931 or so, the manager of the biggest private dining place adjoining the campus had threatened to call police on a Negro student couple seeking services; in 1934, its manager refused service of coffee to students who rather sat-in for a while long before Rosa Parks sat in the wrong place on that bus in Montgomery, Alabama; and in 1936, the owner of the establishment was sued by four Negro students for violation of Illinois law against color discrimination in restaurants and other places of public accommodation.

Most colored students simply ate as best they could manage. Except for the few lucky enough to "wait table," as it was put, most men did without a hot breakfast. The hot noon meal, all the more needed, could be had only at one place near the campus. Deal's was a closed-in pop stand, run by a big, burly white man. The place was clean, but the proprietor was scratchy. He clearly conveyed that he felt himself a great benefactor of Negroes in operating his one-horse, Jim Crow hash house, where day in and day out he offered the same choices—navy bean soup, chili, and a thickened to-do which he termed "meat 'n' pertaters," without mention of the onion which made it consumable. Upon occasion one of the patrons would seat himself but decline eating, after suddenly finding himself either simply unable to eat the same old things once more, or able to do without food for a while longer. Thereupon Mr. Deal would crudely indicate that the resulting wound was self-inflicted and not his to bear. He felt entitled to his captive market and that his dull dispensation was to be gratefully, contentedly, and daily received by all Negro students.

Those who did not take the evening meal at one of the rooming houses, after being ill-fed all day, would have to walk either to a little restaurant called "Three Sisters," perched along the railway tracks away out in the North End, or downtown to the Illinois Central depot, whose restaurant would accept Negro patronage.

One evening a very fair-skinned Negro student, after having several beers at a Negro tavern on the edge of downtown, decided to take several friends of darker hue to dinner with him at the restaurant next door, where he had eaten on several occasions. When all were refused service in derogatory language, the white-looking Negro student host, who had previously received "white" treatment, flew into a rage and damaged a few chairs and a table or two.

There was little encouragement of Negro student participation in extracurricular activities, and here and there the racial bar was in effect. The Student YMCA director fostered an interracial club but refused to allow its members to engage in mixed dancing at the Christian premises for which he was responsible. The dancing was permissible, but the color mix was not, and his interracial project soon died a deserved death. The Interfraternity Council regulated all university-recognized fraternities, including the three such Negro groups, but the constitution of the Council barred membership to any fraternity with Negro members. Sachem, a junior men's honor group, was embarrassed when a Negro fraternity was found to have achieved the greatest improvement among all the ninety fraternities on the campus of its scholastic standing the previous semester, a fact entitling the fraternity to an honor cup. The matter was handled by conjuring up an added prerequisite which the Negro fraternity could not meet. Negro men, like all others, were required to take basic ROTC training, but not admitted to the advanced course in military science, so as to avoid the uselessness of producing black second lieutenants, then so little desired or needed by the U.S. Army. Nor were they accepted in the famous Illini Band. As late as 1937, the Illini Band director admitted that during the thirty-two years of his regime, no Negro had ever made his band "because each applicant on the tryout test was discovered to have a jazz tone," the same old thin dodge which my high school band director was using a decade earlier to shut out Negroes. Humdrum from a white musician, and he made it. But let a Negro who could do as much and then some try out for the band, and he was presumably penalized for his artistry.

What a thin veil for one's prejudice.

This was the thirties, when anxious alumni had not seen to it that the doors were completely ajar to the Negro athlete.

Now and then at one of the Big Ten schools, a black performer of such indubitable prowess would come along that barriers enough were removed to enable his play. But generally at Illinois and the other midwestern universities, educators and administrators lagged behind the fight promoters and big-time gamblers. They were slow to learn that football, basketball, and track stars, like prize fighters, are spawned by the poor—Negroes as well as the nationality groups.[1] The kids growing up in the cheap neighborhoods were spirited and physically uninhibited, rough and ready. They had no chance at tennis, swimming, or golf, the country club sports. But just as clenching fists and pounding away at each other was second nature for them, they had legs for running and jumping, could make a stick do as a bat, play pass with anything that would sail, and scrimmage with less than that.

Universities and their graduates had begun to proselytize and deviously pay for the services of athletes whose exploits could build great stadiums and magnetic names for institutions of higher learning. But they were not ready to do much lowering of color bars, even for the sturdi-

---

1. White, European ethnic groups such as Irish, Italians, and Poles.

est, the fleet and agile among Negroes. I never forget that it was physical education students at the University of Illinois who coached the elementary school track teams in Champaign-Urbana. Negro youngsters showed up year after year who could run a hundred yards in 10.5 seconds and less. One evening in the spring of 1926, a fourteen-year-old Negro eighth-grader broad-jumped 23 feet and 7 inches—I was there among the astonished who saw it. But such talent, even for a "contact-free" sport, was allowed to die a-borning; university people showed little interest in all that potential, right there under their noses.

Although a Negro student won several varsity "I's" as a first-string tennis player, when his brother came along a couple of years later and was second-ranked on the freshman tennis squad, he had to put up a fight to get the freshman numerals he had won. Even in "contactless" track events, we suspected the racial foul. During the spring of 1935, a Negro varsity hurdler, predictively conceded a place in the coming Big Ten conference meet by local sportswriters, was not permitted to make the trip to the meet. An admittedly inferior hurdler went instead, with the coach basing his action on the Negro hurdler's having stumbled in the previous meet. His Negro fellow students felt that since a place in the hurdles at the conference meet would have earned him his letter, somebody did not want him to have it.

We also felt that Negroes were not wanted in football and especially in basketball. During the period, Negro students at several midwestern universities commonly spoke of an unwritten agreement among Big Ten coaches against dark-skinned basketball players. This seemed clearly the practice at the University of Illinois, since brilliant Negro players who had made all-city teams in Chicago were in several cases cut from the freshman varsity squad early in the season. This practice persisted until in 1937, when a Negro state legislator charged racial discrimination in basketball at Illinois. The university's director of athletics wrote a letter of denial to the president of the university, stating that, to his knowledge, "there has never been a colored athlete to report for the basketball squad." But as a classmate of mine later said, "Well, maybe he hasn't been in charge very long and anyway by now the boys have quit trying the impossible."

The university was, of course, something more than another unit of the Big Ten conference, with a monstrous memorial stadium and a marvelous marching band to cut capers before the returning alumni. There were courses of instruction, classes to attend, grades to earn, and professors as well as coaches.

Some Negro students made good grades and were duly honored for so doing. No Negroes were elected to Phi Beta Kappa during my years at the university, it being generally felt that the requirement of extracurricular activity in addition to high scholarship was the explanation for it. However, Sigma Xi, national science honorary, and Phi Eta Sigma, freshman honorary, did elect them during the period. A national sociology honorary, an old and revered campus debate society, and Orchesis, a national dance society, also chose Negro members. I recall several times checking the grade records of Negro students and concluding that a dozen or more of the hundred or so Negro students seemed to make B averages or above each semester. This, I suspect, compared favorably with the general scholastic ranking. It also says that, by and large, a Negro who could and did make a good delivery in the classroom and on his examinations received the credit he was due.

One black student, who entered the university as I was leaving its law school, quickly distinguished himself as a scholar. He came from a sleepy town in southern Illinois, where his father was a railroad hand for the Illinois Central. But somehow his proclivity was more in the direction of the abstract than the rhythmic and mechanical.

I first saw him one evening in late September at my fraternity house, where I was startled to find an interesting intellectual contest underway. Each of two graduate students in mathematics was trying to solve college-level algebra problems faster than the other. Freshmen were selecting the problems and supplying the correct answers. Soon it was revealed that the source of the correct answers was not a textbook but the freshman from southern Illinois. He was then asked to join the competition and began working the problems much faster than the grad students, though often cutting corners as he sped along. This awesome performer was one David Blackwell, who stayed at Illinois six years and obtained his AB, MA and PhD degrees in mathematics. He earned his AB in three years and made Phi Beta Kappa. Legend has it that he also earned but received no credit for an MA in English while gaining his in mathematics, since it was done as a benefactor of a girlfriend. Dave studied probability at the Institute for Advanced Studies at Princeton and now serves as professor of statistics at the University of California at Berkeley. He is the author of many articles and coauthor of a book entitled *Theory of Games and Statistical Decisions* and holds membership in the right and proper learned societies for the abstruse, including the Institute of Mathematical Statistics, of which he has been president.

Upon occasion I still feel bitter about the Negro youngsters I knew who, for all their talents, were never to be seen as athletes at the university whose campus they romped as kids. But then I recall that son of a Negro worker in the railway yards in southern Illinois who was a star in mathematics. He carried on while nearby a certain psychology professor was still teaching that Negroes were pretty much chunks of stupidity and absolutely lacking in capacity for the abstract.

Some faculty members did draw color lines among their students or otherwise expose their color prejudices. There occasionally was one who would bother himself to devise a segregated seating arrangement for a class with several Negro students, so as to make of them a neat little patch of darkness. The problem was easily surmounted, however. A quiet, direct complaint or an outright refusal to follow the pattern would serve the purpose, though not without risk of a low mark for the course as punishment for it. There were also teachers who appeared in some instances to serve some confused sense of racial justice in themselves by giving all of their Negro students "C" grades, while a few others appeared firmly convinced that no Negro students could do any better than that middle mark. I must concede that neither of these types was at all representative, as is well illustrated by my own erratic grades, which for my six years of liberal arts and law ran the range from A to F, for failure. (More than twenty years later, I proved myself a consistent scholar, measured by the familiar yardstick of lettered grades, receiving As in seven graduate courses at Harvard University and a B+ in the eighth.) Occasionally also there was an instructor who documented and taught his disbelief of and disrespect for Negroes.

My first personal encounter with a teacher I strongly suspected of color bias was in freshman rhetoric and composition. I sought so tangentially to test her position that I cannot be certain of the meaning of the results.

This is what happened. The lady had somehow made me feel unwanted during the first five or six class meetings. Though I forget the rejective subtleties, I am certain of what followed. When the class was assigned the writing of a long expository theme, the topic for which was left elective,

I determined to employ that medium for revealing my resentment of her racial distastes. Deciding not to engage her head-on, I chose not to write about any aspect of Negro-white relations. Instead I decided to probe and attack "The Mistreatment of the American Jew." The grade I drew is quite forgotten and in any event was inconsequential. What had meaning for me was that the teacher was obviously hypercritical with my theme and proceeded to read aloud to the class several of its passages, following each with critical commentary. She sharply derided the crudeness she saw in one particular sentence, completely overlooking that it was a quotation. What had stung her so was the sentence reading, as nearly as I remember, that "The Jews were an ancient civilization when the Anglo-Saxons were *wolfing* their meat half-cooked." "Wolfing" was crude, and there was no such verb, she complained. I explained to her that the sentence was a quote from an article by no less a writer than Will Durant (whose *Mansions of Philosophy* was then being as widely read on the campus as one could hope for), adding that the article had been published in *Atlantic Monthly*, a publication which the teacher herself had several times commended to the class as a literary model. This left her out on a limb and obviously embarrassed.

After class several students revealed sharing my feeling that it was the substance of my effort rather than its literary quality which had piqued the teacher. I feel more strongly now than then that if she found acceptable booting Jews about, the same, if not in greater degree, would represent her view of the Negro me.

As a junior I "took" a teacher — often a good way to choose a course — who proved to be one of those unable to give a Negro more than a comfortably passing grade. The course was philosophy of education, and the teacher epitomized the college professor. He was properly adorned with the PhD degree, wore tweed suits, smoked a pipe, and sported a neat and handsome beard. He was full to the brim with his subject and lectured with sparkle, seemingly without effort. The course was required for those in training for teaching, hence full of girls who thought the professor "a dream." I liked him immensely also, found him challenging, listened carefully to his every word, diligently read his assignments, carried more than my part of the class discussion, and learned plenty from him. There was no final examination. When the grades came I was flabbergasted to receive a C, especially after discovering that A's and B's had been otherwise liberally awarded. So I went to him for a conference. I told him that he had mistreated me, I knew it, and wanted him to know how I felt. But I added that I begged nothing of him and assured him instead that I would rest on that discounting of the importance of grades. Then I withdrew.

My most serious personal skirmish with a teacher was with a full professor, the head of the department of political science, the subject in which I was majoring. Worse, I struck the first blow by impugning his objectivity in the *Daily Illini*, when I need not have written a letter to the editor at all.

The trouble was rooted in the fact that this professor of international relations and international law had made himself a hero of mine as early as during my high school days. He specialized in Latin-American affairs, and his economic interpretation of American relations with those countries, which seemed to me almost possessions of ours, appealed to me. It was he who, in addressing one of our high school assemblies, had suggested that American troops had landed in Cuba more on account of the sugar plantations Americans owned there than to see to Cuban freedom. I had read an article or two of his before I entered the university and knew no better than to assume that he who stood for freedom for the peons in the southern hemisphere would similarly stand up for native black ones picking cotton in the Southern United States. Suddenly I received a real shock in return for such naïveté.

The professor went to New Orleans during the Christmas holidays in 1930, or perhaps it was 1931, and addressed the Southern Political Science Association. There he presented an address which elaborately justified the disenfranchisement of Negroes in the South, a position which likely fell on welcome ears in the Louisiana parishes but was even at that time unexpected enough from a Northern academician to be picked up by a national press service. What he said jolted me hard, since I had seen him with a halo about his head, and the more so, since his position contrasted with that of a young faculty member from Mississippi whose national government course I had just completed.

This young PhD, in lecturing on disenfranchisement, ahead of the text, had blandly presented the class with the whole complex of the familiar devices restrictive of the Southern Negro vote, running from the grandfather clauses through the poll taxes and literacy tests, and he concluded by asking the class, "What really is the point of all of this?" When I offered to answer the question, he denied me the privilege, observing that I should well know the answer. Then in rich Southern accent he tore the legalistic covering from the whole panoply and exposed the disenfranchisement for what it was — white power serving and perpetuating itself, stamping the black potential underfoot. I had to satisfy myself with volunteering that threats of violence and violence against Negroes who dared vote were also part of the pattern, as years of reading the *Chicago Defender* and the *Crisis* had taught me.

The young Southerner simply mumbled his acceptance of the addendum. After reading excerpts of my hero's speech in the newspapers, I promptly addressed a long letter to the *Daily Illini* in which I took the professor to task, referring to what I saw as the inconsistency of his position. Only a few weeks before the *Illini* had been accorded more latitude in voicing student opinion by the new university president, Harry Woodburn Chase. A student newspaper was to be the students' newspaper. Immediately and without questioning me, the student editors published the letter. It caused a stir in the political science department. Several faculty members discreetly suggested to me that I visit the professor but I declined doing so. Sooner or later, however, he sent for me himself. We talked calmly, but he stuck to his position, and I stood by my criticism of it. There the matter rested for good, I thought. But that it was haunting me I was to learn several semesters later.

The international law courses taught by the professor were offered both as political science in the College of Liberal Arts and as College of Law courses. Hence the professor was a member of the faculty of each college.

Midway during law school, my grade average fell slightly beneath the required minimum, and I was dropped from school. Upon inquiry, I learned that the procedure for a student in my fix was to petition for reentry. Moreover, white classmates assured me that reentry was certain to be granted, pointing to successful petitioning by fellow students of ours whose averages had fallen quite lower than mine. Besides, I could very honestly and convincingly ascribe my difficulties to my long work hours and make a promise to work less when readmitted, as I proceeded to do in my petition. Nevertheless the petition was at first flatly denied and without explanation. A conference which followed with the Dean of the College of Law was to no avail, and fruitless also was a plea in my behalf by the Negro serving as chief clerk in the Office of the university president. The next bit of intervention went right to what seemed the heart of the denial of my plea for reentry. A local Negro minister wrote to the president charging discrimination and threatening an appeal to blacks in the State Legislature. This was productive. I was readmitted; graduated with my class in June 1935; wrote and passed the bar in July 1935; and was admitted to practice as the September term of the Illinois Supreme Court began.

An interesting, and perhaps significant, story was brought to me just before graduation by a Negro neighbor of mine, who worked occasionally for the wife of a certain law school faculty member. The neighbor began by saying, "They tell me you are graduating from law school, and I have come to congratulate you." Then he told me who "they" was and that his lady employer had said this: "Townsend, Professor 'Blank' (her husband) tells me that three Negroes are in the Law School's graduating class this year. Two of them are perfect gentlemen. But one of them is a bad actor, and they are glad to be rid of him. Why he once did the most horrible thing to Professor 'Blinkety-Blank' (my downfallen hero!)" Townsend, of course, had learned that I was the miscreant of which the law school was happy to be relieved but not what I had done to the professor. I had to tell him the story.

It has since often seemed to me, assuming the accuracy of Mr. Townsend's story, that if the College of Law faculty was especially pleased to dispense with me, and awareness of my brush with the professor of international law remained high, perhaps the initial denial of my petition was worse than discrimination; it may have also been retaliatory.

The truth is that during my years at the university, Negroes did not appear welcome in the College of Law. The principal requirement for admission to the college was a 3.5 average. Negroes, of course, had to meet this scholastic standard. Yet, in the period commencing in 1932 and running through 1936, when I left the Champaign-Urbana community, the count I maintained showed thirteen other Negroes to enter and all to have been flunked out in the first or second semester of study. One of them told me that he was advised by his professor of contracts to forget becoming a lawyer and instead to prepare to teach or to become a preacher. Fortunately, he did not allow the contracts professor to select his profession for him. He did become a lawyer and today is a judge in a federal court. It is difficult for me not to believe that something was rotten in the Denmark of the College of Law at the University of Illinois when it came to Negro trainees for the profession.

Nonetheless, the immediately preceding paragraphs are not to say that among the faculty, in the very heart of the university, there was no place for Negro students. There were faculty members, and also one particular member of the university administration, who faced up to color questions. Some did so squirmingly; but others, squarely, especially in response to Negro initiative. For some of those among the handful of unwanted ones did speak up for themselves as Negroes.

One of the most popular lecture courses in liberal arts during the period was "fields of psychology." Each semester the youngish professor who taught the course would hold forth on the native mental inferiority of Negroes, a position also conveyed in his textbook. However, even such a professor easily permitted a student to differ with him on the matter, as I indeed did. At the time, his textbook, published in mimeograph, footnoted references to the emerging and now generally accepted rejection of his view, and I carefully examined several of them. As soon as my class met again, following the several lectures, I was allowed to present the other view as fully as I was able. The professor added a bit more of the case against himself, and, making himself appear ever so detached from it all, concluded by making me appear simply as a shining example of a scholarly student who read beyond the text. He was a nimble and scholarly bigot.

Just as he well knew that my academic exercise was in fact specifically motivated, I was certain on my part that most of my classmates, like myself, were not footnote readers and but for my action would have been exposed only to the professor's view. The professor was not only racially prejudiced and a carrier of anti-Negro bias under the cloak of science—he was a slickster with it all.

Several semesters later, this little history repeated itself for a younger fraternity brother of mine, though not without a bit of encouragement on my part. The professor invited him in for a conference, the two became friendly, my frat brother began to develop an interest in psychology and it became his major. Today he holds a doctorate and is a clinical psychologist.

The psychology professor, whom I remember as a good deal more of a crafty and systematic propagandist of the doctrine of white superiority than as an objective student in the area of race, is now dead, or so I hear. However, his printed words live on, and the other day at Howard University I chanced into a copy of his *Fields of Psychology*, published by Henry Holt and Company in 1931, a few months after my fraternity brother and I used it in mimeographed form.

I examined its chapter on "differential psychology" but could not locate the set of footnotes precisely citing the opposition views which I recall appearing in its earlier, mimeographed version. I did find three paragraphs on race theories, indicating the author's purpose "to set forth certain experimental and investigational findings rather than to form opinions for individuals," attesting to the desirability of an open mind and suspended judgment with the topic, and instructing that "the student should realize the nature of the difficulties in the way of testing racial differences." The professor was still crafty.

The same paragraphs summed up the two conflicting views. The first held that "the white race is superior to all others in achievement and culture because of its superior intelligence." The second was the view of those "who regard differences between the races as being largely due to environment" and to whom "all races . . . are in reality potentially equal in intellectual and emotional traits."

But the professor cited the latter scholars as "aptly named," in his view, "Race Levelers." Moreover, his selection from among the investigations had satisfied him that blacks are by nature mentally inferior to whites chiefly "along the lines of 'abstract' thinking and logical analysis of situations," and also less accurate, on the whole, than the whites. The professor had begun by defining the Negro as "characterized by his black shiny skin, flat nose, large lips and kinky hair" but had later dealt gently with whiter Negroes. "We might say the mulatto is the stepping stone from the black to the white race and admit that some of them do show a marked intellectual ability," he had concluded in service to his own bias. He further had felt certain of the Negro's "heightened excitability" and that he is "less ambitious and more lazy," as compared with whites, though with these matters of emotion and temperament, as distinguished from intelligence, he had conceded that the total cultural and economic setting for the Negro must be considered.

It is three and a half decades later, and the professor is deceased. But I remain satisfied that when he lived, he was full of white supremacy and peddled it to his classes under the sail of science.

Then there was the professor of literature, himself a poet, who could invite Negro students, among others, to his apartment, where he read to them some of what he considered the best of current poetry, including several poems by Negroes. My memory is of one of the most genuinely pleasant and intellectually stimulating evenings at his apartment that I knew during my college days. I do recall being somewhat uncomfortable about the host because none of the six or seven poems by Negroes which he read voiced racial protest. It was not until months later that I realized that, as a teacher of literature, he had selected those who wrote well in the traditional, classical forms, perhaps after the manner of Keats or Shelley.

I had wanted him to read from certain Negro poets who were my favorites. For the time was the early thirties, in the midst of what became known as the "Negro Renaissance" period in literature. It was a time when Negro poets were writing with a bursting of racial pride and protest upon which I fed. As an avid reader of the *Crisis* and *Opportunity* magazines, I had become acquainted with these writers. But as the owner of an anthology of Negro verse, *Caroling Dusk*, published in 1927, I could read, re-read, and relish them as they appeared there.

Countee Cullen, the anthologist, had himself written, "I doubt not God is good, well meaning, kind. . . . Yet do I marvel at this curious thing: To make a poet black, and bid him sing!" Claude McKay had stridently declaimed, "If we must die, let it not be like hogs—Hunted and penned in an inglorious sport—While round us bark the mad and hungry dogs—Making their mock at our accursed lot. . . . What though before us lies the open grave?—Like men we'll face the murderous, cowardly pack—Pressed to the wall, dying, but fighting back!" Jean Toomer had noticed that "black reapers with the sound of steel on stones—Are sharpening scythes." Prank Horne had seen two little Negro boys in a Catholic church, to write, "Look you on yon crucifix—Where He hangs nailed and pierced—With head hung low—And eyes a 'blind with blood that drips—From a thorny crown. . . . Look you well, You shall know this thing." But nothing of this kind was part of the soiree.

The assistant dean of men in charge of student affairs neither saw Negroes as untouchable nor avoided facing the problems they presented.

He once attended a smoker at one of the Negro fraternity houses. This was during prohibition, and the keg of "three-point-two" beer had been liberally spiked with bootleg alcohol, a custom forced upon collegians in those days, if beer was to be worth its froth. The assistant dean drank as much of it, stayed as late, and appeared to have had as much fun as the others there. But it must be said that he enjoyed a warmth of welcome and a degree of acceptance such as possibly no other university figures could have had from Negro students at the time.

The esteem the assistant dean enjoyed among Negro men he had earned. I went to him more than once with color issues, and each time he heard me out, without ducking and dodging, spelled out the university position in fact as well as on paper, and wound up trying to help.

When I protested against the Interfraternity Council's barring Negro fraternities from membership, despite its university-accorded jurisdiction over them, he called for a copy of the council's constitution and by-laws, located the color-exclusionist passage, and showed it to me. He then arranged a meeting between officers of the council and a representative of each of the three Negro fraternities involved at which he gently but carefully nudged forward removal of the prohibition. A few days later the president and secretary of each of the Negro Greek letter groups were invited, with their dates, to an Interfraternity Council dance and shortly thereafter formally tendered membership in the council.

The same young university official was unable immediately to take any corrective action when Sachem welshed out of awarding a cup for scholarship improvement to the Negro fraternity which had really won it. But when another black group appeared the winner, a few semesters later, the award was duly made. We strongly suspected that the assistant dean had effectively advised Sachem against repeating its color-exclusionist artifice.

There was also a young teacher of romance languages from Minnesota who for some reason or other cast his lot with Negro students. He was more than a precursor of the civil rights activists that are today so often found among college faculty members. He was a lone eagle who dared socialize with blacks. He also unhesitatingly supported any effort made to lower an anti-Negro barrier. He not only participated in a conference held in 1933 or thereabouts to expose the discriminatory conditions facing Negro students, he joined in the follow-up meeting with several Negro civic leaders and state legislators held in Chicago. He also was among a small group of faculty members who met in the apartment of a female colleague, following an unsuccessful civil rights suit against a campus restaurant which repeatedly refused to serve Negroes, to plan a continuation effort.

This man must have been courageous with his convictions, to have been so often seen alone among Negroes. I have no doubt that many whites wrote him off as a "nigger lover," and there were Negro students who dismissed him as a fellow who "must be writing himself a book about us." Each of these reactions he likely discerned, but neither deterred him.

Lastly, there was a trio of my faculty acquaintances, each of whose treatment of Negro-white relations in the context of his specialization was distinctly advanced and appreciated by us. One was a sociologist, another a psychologist, and the third the young political science professor I have mentioned. All were Southerners. They exhibited an objective but vigorous facility with the color question I have since often seen in the strong Southerner in a Northern climate, a capacity for treating the matter far more honestly and sharply than the usual Northern white.

CÉNACLE

Faculty members, as more or less a whole, were quite responsive to Cénacle, self-styled as "A University society for those interested in the Negro in art and literature." While thus not confined to Negroes, its membership in fact included only Negroes, and it was essentially an effort to assert pride in Negro identity. We who were overlooked, when not scorned, sought to find ourselves. A scholastic average of B-minus was required, and membership was small and select.

The university readily granted Cénacle official recognition as an honorary society, though the *Daily Illini* drew a rebuke when it described it as "for those Negroes interested in art and literature." Cénacle objected that "a society for Negroes interested in art and literature is an absurdity — not only unnecessary but unwanted as well. . . . There is an abundance of art and literary societies already existing on the campus, to which, let us presume, Negroes are admissible, . . . [and] in addition to this erroneous description leaving a new society without any reason for being, it might in the future expose some albeit deserving colored student to the Negrophobic query, 'Don't you have a society of your own?'"

Cénacle, I must say, was pretty much the creature of my initiative. Its genesis likely stemmed in good part from a book I had received as a prize for winning an essay contest among the eight or nine Negro graduates of Champaign and Urbana high schools the year I entered the university. *Caroling Dusk*, an anthology of Negro-written verse, was just out, and Countee Cullen, the anthologist, had selected not only poems of distinctive literary quality but many of stinging racial protest. I read the book from cover to cover and certain of the selections repeatedly. My fellow Negro students borrowed the book incessantly, and I soon discovered that few of us knew much of anything about ourselves as Negroes, though obviously we were keenly aware of our particularity, tiny, isolated enclave that we were.

Upon election to the presidency of my fraternity and becoming able to influence its "hell week" for initiates, I made a daring little move. I convinced my Negro-Greek brethren that instead of seven days spent beating the backsides of those about to join us, we should send them to the library to carry out assignments in Negro history and require them to report their findings to us. It worked beautifully, this supplanting of sadism with study such as nowhere else called for at the university. A few months later I went to the annual meeting of my fraternity in Cincinnati where I heard my hero, W. E. B. Du Bois, himself, castigate Negro fraternities and sororities for their clannishness and their foolish infatuation with the lightheadedness surrounding them at universities across the country. It was then, I am now certain, that I began to feel that a Negro society on a college campus ought to be one filling a void for Negro students themselves and gaining a truer image of the color group in the eyes of their fellow white students.

Twice during three years, Cénacle presented plays reflective of Negro life which were viewed as creditable and were financial successes. Faculty members packed the audiences, and the African dance drama "Sahdji" had to be repeated because of faculty demand. University instructors of dance and dramatics made these presentations possible. During National Negro History Week in 1934, Cénacle, with the cooperation of university librarians, displayed artistic and literary works of the Negro in the main corridor of the Main Library. When the week was over, and its members approached the library staff to assist with disassembly of the exhibit, as had been agreed, they were told that many faculty members had requested that the exhibit be continued. It was and remained for more than a month.

When James Weldon Johnson came to the university to lecture, he was offered and accepted honorary membership in Cénacle. Several faculty members were guests of Cénacle, along with the Negro writer and former NAACP field secretary, at a dinner following the lecture. I was then president of the group and as such was able to talk at some length with Mr. Johnson, whom I had long admired and several of whose books I read. I remember revealing to him a disappointment I had then recently experienced. Because of my strong interest in Negro history, I had ordered catalogs from a score of Negro colleges, expecting to find that each offered courses in that subject of such manifest importance to their students. Because only two of them offered courses faintly resembling Negro history, I shared the disturbing finding with Mr. Johnson. But he only chuckled and said, "Do not mind so much. In some of those schools there are good teachers who do a good job of teaching Negro history, whether the subject is American history, literature, government, or whatever."

Later he made clear his approval of my excitement about Negro history but also that I should not expect to find courses so labeled and described in the catalogs of Southern Negro colleges. Neither the state officials, nor the trustee boards, nor the presidents of the institutions were ready for so much, he explained.

The Cénacle group and those who made occasional and scattered forays in the direction of civil rights were a minority. Most of the Negro students were ambitious and self-respecting. But they were also quite as W. E. B. Du Bois complained at Howard University in 1931, when he said, "The average Negro undergraduate has swallowed hook, line, and sinker the dead bait of the white undergraduate, who, born in an industrial machine, does not have to think and does not think. Our college man today is, on the average, a man untouched by real culture."

Though their isolation from campus activities left ample time and opportunity for it, most remained blissfully disinterested in discussing social problems, not to speak of action, as is commonplace these days. Month after month, I would get to the Main Library late, still to find, fresh and untouched on its shelves, *Opportunity* and *Crisis*, the official organs of the National Urban League and the NAACP. Lyceum, a twenty-year-old organization, met monthly at one of the local Negro churches for discussion of Negro affairs. However, its principal attraction was neither topic nor speaker, but instead a sort of gossip sheet about black student shenani-

gans called "the Journal" which was read aloud at its meetings. The conservative, university-sponsored lectures were attended by the some five
or six Negro students. When Hillel Jewish Foundation brought in Clarence Darrow and Arthur Garfield Hays as speakers,[2] I looked in vain for
another Negro in the audience, though when Harry Laidler and Senator
[Robert] La Follette [Jr.] came,[3] I saw one other Negro on each occasion.

A liberal, Jewish economics professor, a consultant to Philip Randolph's Brotherhood of Sleeping Car Porters, offered to speak for my
own fraternity on "The Negro Labor Problem," but the offer was declined.
This was at a time when the country was drifting deeper and deeper into
the Great Depression, and Negroes were being those first-fired by the
thousands. In a few months some of us students were to find ourselves
learning the hard way, the jobless way, about the Negro labor problem.

Indeed, within my own fraternity, I discovered that the easy-does-it
drift through college which Du Bois had decried had its defenders.
I was compelled to speak up for several pledges who had taken to reading Shakespeare aloud late at night (an activity in which I joined) and one
of whom was writing a book (that book was never published, but others
of his have since been.) The older fellows insisted that these unorthodox
youngsters were simply making too much noise, should be in bed, and
besides they were guilty of visiting the Negro sorority clad in sweatshirts
instead of dress shirt and tie. They were bad for our good Greek image
with our Grecian sisters of color. As I argued that each of the three Negro fraternities should cease trying to maintain a separate house and live
together instead, it sounded to some of my fraternity brothers like dis-
loyalty, and they strongly advised me to desist. When the president of my
fraternity sought my intervention to assure his attaining a membership in
Cénacle, for which he was scholastically ineligible, I refused him. He then
adamantly opposed conduct of the initiation of James Weldon Johnson

2. Clarence Darrow was prominent lawyer and advocate for civil liberties involved
in some of the most famous legal cases of the 1920s, including the Scopes Monkey Trial
and the defense of Ossian Sweet. Arthur Garfield Hays was an American lawyer who co-
founded the American Civil Liberties Union.

3. Harry Laidler was an American socialist writer and executive director of the League
of Industrial Democracy. Senator Robert La Follette Jr. was a senator from Wisconsin. Part
of the La Follette political family, he served as a senator from 1924 until 1946 and led the
Progressive Party.

into Cénacle in the fraternity house, an objection which I ignored. Afterward he endeavored, almost successfully, to have me banished from the fraternity. Wiser heads decided that it would appear a little ludicrous to support him, since objection to the presence of so distinguished a man in the fraternity house would be so inexplicable.

Years later, after I had at long last found a job that seemed something more than ephemeral, there were moments which threatened to make me regret that I had been among the busybodies at the university who were concerned about people, their rights, and their problems, the world beyond Memorial Stadium and the beautiful Broadwalk with its living canopy of great American elms. For I was in the government career service, and there were lists of organizations to which federal employees must not have belonged. And thus I had interrogatories from loyalty boards and security officers to answer. Had I ever belonged to the National Negro Congress? The National Association for the Advancement of Colored People? Had I ever received the support of a Social Worker's Party bloc for election to local NAACP office? Had I ever belonged to the National Lawyers' Guild? The American Student Union?

The need for these queries I rather accepted, but they were nonetheless irritable. One set of interrogatories invited my adding to my answers anything which I felt pertinent to my loyalty to the government of the United States. In that space I wrote, "I have nothing to hide and little to add. My loyalty to my Government is inevitably of the highest order. All that I am, as the college-bred descendant of slaves, I owe to its ideals and workings. Much of what I am not yet, as a second-class citizen, can be obtained the same way. What I am obliged to count on so heavily, I am committed to preserve."

Town and Gown

THE DIFFICULTY OF NAVIGATING TWO WORLDS

Exclude thyself not from the community.
—Berakot 49; Avot 2:5

Throughout my university going, I remained an active resident of the Negro community in the North End. If there was to be cleavage between town and gown in Champaign-Urbana, it could not escape me, for I was of both.

Negroes have long placed great stock in a college education. In those days a Negro community was immensely proud of each of its members who went to college; he was felt to reflect the best there is to exhibit before the doubting white and larger environment. But as he represented his group's best foot forward, he was watched closely to make certain of both is decorum and his loyalty to the community. Those Negroes seeking to distinguish themselves as college-bred were not to deny the humble and unarrived folk from whom they sprang. This attitude I had seen at work as our little community assessed the behavior of the occasional Champaign-Urbana Negro who attended the university while I was in high school, and I was quite aware of what was expected of me.

Staying very much a townsman while pursuing higher learning was an easy matter in terms of my own feelings, though presenting a clear image of it before the eyes of my fellows sometimes took a little doing. There I was, a janitor's helper at the bookstore located on the hub corner of the campus. Every morning bright and early, I was out in front of that store, clad in coveralls and with broom in hand, greeting and chatting with other townspeople similarly engaged in the university business district or on their way to cook, in the sorority and fraternity houses, as did my mother. Only a foolish self-illusion would have permitted me to see myself apart from the townspeople.

I well remember rebuking a coed from Chicago who found herself either disturbed or amused as she saw me talking to a Negro woman from town. The lady was older, with greying hair which, with her humble and simple garb, left her looking like the stereotype of the colored cook that she was. After our conversation was finished, and my friend walked on, the coed snidely said to me, "And who was your friend?"

"You don't really want to know. But she has known me longer than I've known myself. I've been her paperboy and gone to school with her children. We live on the same street out North, and she and my mother belong to the same church," I replied.

The farther I went in school, as I continued working thirty hours or more weekly, the less time remained for active association with my own age group in the North End. Besides, as was inevitable, our interests and activities began to differ. But my scant presence out North was not to be allowed an interpretation that I was getting too big for my coveralls at the Co-op and the community that was mine. This I had to see to.

It was recreational activity, parties, picnics, and the like, that was the major area in which I had to avoid any appearance of slight, pulling myself above or away from those with whom I had grown up. While a liberal amount of social shyness and plenty of work to do, even as a child, had left me not much of a party-goer and without ever having gone steady until college days, there were situations requiring tact and even diplomacy. I was careful to respond with my awkward presence whenever I was invited to a party in town. The few coeds I dated I took with me to nonuniversity parties as well as to visit older townspeople among my friends. In the other direction, I occasionally took girls from town to campus parties. When a social gathering embraced both town and gown, I sometimes went without a date.

A delightful party given during a university homecoming weekend by a young matron in town put to test my community loyalty. The hostess had invited me to bring along several dateless fraternity brothers, since extra girls would be present. The party, as is hoped for any real one, soon became as lively as it was lovely to begin with. At this stage an imbibing fraternity brother's amorous maneuvers offended one of the girls from town, as she openly and angrily announced to all within hearing, including several fellow townsmen. This event threatened at once to provoke separation of town from gown. There I was in the middle, or rather, a good part of each, and quite anxious to stay that way. It was successfully worked out. I firmly and demonstratively ordered my fellow clansmen to get the inebriated and errant one out of there at once. This, of course, pleased my hostess and the other townspeople. But it was also to the liking of my college brothers. They were sober enough to realize it was far better for themselves to turn upon the rascal among them than to be set upon by the townspeople. So they quickly did just what I had demanded.

More than once it was made clear that those who watched me lest I deny them were willing also to protect one who represented their best foot put forward. One June night, just after my last examination, a town buddy convinced me that I deserved his taking me on a tour of wine, women, and song "down on the line." I was afraid to refuse; I had to prove myself a college *man* and a community one too. So off we went, in and out of one joint after another. Late that night we ran into a girl "gone bad," out of a good family and whom we knew well. Liquored up though she was, she quickly and most soberly appraised my presence. Said she to me, "*What* are *you* doing in *this place*!" Then, before I could answer, she turned to our fellow townsman, who was obviously in charge of me, and ordered "Take him away from here!" We laughed—both of us, I suspect, only feigningly. For shortly afterward, he did just what she suggested and without the slightest objection from me.

A second such occasion took place in the home of a couple who were among my closest friends, town or university.

The husband, an intelligent and affable fellow, portered at a huge barbershop across the street from the big bookstore where I worked, while smilingly accepting my repeated beratings of him for his not taking an examination for the postal service, which I was certain he could have handily passed. His wife was a strikingly handsome woman of shapely, Amazonian figure, neatly chiseled features, and translucent, reddish-brown complexion. Besides being a beauty, she was an immaculate and efficient housekeeper, read good fiction, talked fluently, and was a warm and friendly being. She liked to give parties, and they went off well, not only because she herself was a wonderful center of attraction for them, but she could mix her guests with facility, blend local high school graduates and dropouts with the college people she also entertained.

One night in the home of that couple, I was quite enjoying myself as part of a group of townspeople, most of whom were of my age and old friends who grew up, down, and across the street, and around the corner from me. These people, when relaxed and to themselves, sophisticatedly spoke a complex jargon. It combined the language of the newspaper and the slang spoken by the "cats" about town, with the mixture being also liberally infused with what in other places would be considered profane and obscene. As they drank and talked, while playing dirty hearts or blackjack, the frequent, easy use of "goddamn" was adjectival, merely to particularize its subject. Used alone, it was rarely a dirty oath and more often a joyous expression of triumph. "Bastard" was a term of endearment, completely free of evil allegation. A "goddamn bastard!" meant that its subject was definitely an insider.

It always took a while for me, as socially slow and out of touch as I was, to adjust to the atmosphere. Finally that evening, after four or five hours of kibitzing and conversing with my friends, and having as many drinks or more, I managed to utter a mild obscenity. Thereupon the handsome hostess ruled me out of order, saying, "We'll have no goddamn talk like that from you!"

In one instance I deliberately lied to assure townspeople of my unperturbed sense of community with them. During my presidency of the fraternity, I was allowed to live in a room at the fraternity without payment of rent since unused space was available. This left me time for brotherly behavior as well as being quite close to work and school. But after I moved from home in the North End and away from among townspeople, one of them would occasionally *ask* why I was staying on campus. "The fraternity's rules require it," was an acceptable and protective explanation.

PROJECTS

What really satisfied me that my involvement in the North End and it in me remained intact is more of substance than parties and other pleasures with North Enders.

The assurance lay in my continued concern with the problems that faced the community and my participation in attacks on them. Such an effort I had first made at nine or ten years of age, to counter police discrimination and achieve freer use of the school ground at Lawhead School for play during the summer and other hours when the school was closed. Similar moves were made time after time. The issues were not always so simple, and the moves were not always successful. But I kept making them, easily and spontaneously.

During the latter period of high school, I had twice gone after a place in the North End big enough for its children to play in. The parks and playgrounds I had seen elsewhere I wanted in our end of town, where the children were thicker and had smaller yards of their own. So at sixteen years or so, I addressed a letter to the editor of the *Champaign News-Gazette* asserting the case for a park in the North End. I no longer recall what specifically triggered the four or five paragraphs I submitted. However, I was proud that the newspaper published the piece just as it was written, including my name. The latter had to be provided but upon request could be withheld from print. I made no such request, and so enjoyed the plaudits of my friends and acquaintances as almost to forget that nothing whatsoever beyond the congratulations had been gained.

But I had hold of a real issue and was to make another stroke. This time the move was neither so isolated nor completely devoid of strategy. I stumbled into it.

The gas company manufactured its product at an installation bisected by the unimproved, five hundred block of East Hill Street. As time and the utility's usurpative use of this land dedicated to the purposes of the public went on, its members traveled it less and less except, of course, for youthful pedestrians unmindful of smoke, cinders, and the smell of gas. The gas company then proposed to acquire the street outright. At the same time, a tract of land equivalent in area to two square blocks and located at the end of the street on which I lived remained unimproved except for its crop of field corn each season. Gas company purchase of the area, its trading it to the city for the Hill Street block, and thereafter city development of the ideally situated land for park purposes was a natural.

I now forget whether the idea was mine or merely my adoption. In any event, I advanced it. This time I not only wrote a letter to the editor of the local newspaper urging the logic of the swap, I made my first resort to petition. It was simple to obtain the signatures of "citizens and taxpayers" in the neighborhood; few of them, if any, could have turned back a sixteen- or seventeen-year-old advancing such an easy windfall of an answer to the problem of recreational space. Armed with the petition, I went to the city hall and confronted the mayor. I do not remember seeking an appointment or being in his office. Instead, I strongly recall standing in a corridor looking up at the tall, lanky insurance broker, son of the founder of Champaign's leading florist. As he examined the names borne by the petition, he looked down upon me and smiled. He asked my name and said, "Who had you do this?" I suddenly felt that something of a mysterious, technical nature was wrong with the petition. But politician that he was, he added, "Where are the grown-ups whose names are on here?" calling the names of several petitioners illustratively.

Again I am not certain that I followed up. I remember only that later someone explained to me that the names he called were part of "his bunch" in the North End. Still later, since he made himself appear interested in the idea, I assumed that he wanted and was suggesting a bit of pressure from the right sources. He needed forcing by those who counted and from whom he could get credit for his favors. I had much to learn.

Several years later, the tract did become Frederick Douglass Park, an outcome almost inevitable, so well located was the site and so lacking were alternative sites for a park elsewhere in the North End.

My first recallable effort in the interest of the community during my college days was largely centered in Willard School, at Fifth and Church Streets, which I passed daily on my way to and from the campus. One afternoon as I headed for home, I was hailed by the principal.

Now Willard School was an older but sound brick structure which had for a while been used as a rubber factory but afterward was again used as a school. The principal was also older, sound and sturdy as teacher and disciplinarian, and had formerly taught off and on at Lawhead in the North End. I strongly suspect that the re-use of the sturdiness in each case had common cause. By the early thirties, the North End had become thickly Negro, and there were children enough to justify using the old building again as a school. Besides, this would keep North End kids in their own neighborhood and out of the others. The children themselves, poor, Negro, and increasingly the offspring of parents recently from the rural South, when they were not themselves born there, needed schooling under the direction of a willing and sympathetic but firm hand.

Katherine Frederick was at the time a mature woman and a practiced teacher who had taught in the North End and knew many of its Negro adults. She was a strict disciplinarian and, at least as such, respected by all of the children at Willard, every one of whom she could call by name. She was also an efficient principal who knew she had a real problem on her hands, being in charge of fifth, sixth, and seventh graders who averaged out older and learned matters troublesome to their schoolteachers faster than children who are less deprived. She was able to reach out for help. She had organized herself a PTA, but could also ask for a helping hand from those who had been her pupils years before at Lawhead, such as myself.

As we talked that afternoon, she began by mentioning boys whom I knew as children of my paper customers. Many of these youngsters were headed for trouble unless something was done, was her emphasis. She had something to do in mind: organize a Boy Scout troop. Local Scout headquarters had said it would help, and the troop could meet in the basement of Willard School. She asked me to help, and I agreed to do so.

Within a few months, the troop was organized. A younger World War I veteran, an ex-sergeant and himself the father of boys, accepted the scoutmastership; he was a wonderful choice for the task. I started out as a senior patrol leader and later became assistant scoutmaster of Troop Eleven. It well served the North End community and the youngsters who joined it. It kept many a youngster too busy with meetings, pursuing merit badges, on weekend hikes, practicing for the annual jamborees, and at camp during the summer to drift into trouble. Several youngsters who made wonderful patrol leaders would have otherwise successfully led youngsters on unapprovable missions. It was, of course, a wonderful growth experience for me, too.

I never was enough without need for what work was available during the summers to go to camp with the troop. But I often went with them on weekend hikes and overnight camping trips, one of which I shall never forget.

The county leader of the Ku Klux Klan, then thriving in the Midwest and especially in adjoining Indiana, had invited our troop to camp overnight on his farm. He knew our Negro scoutmaster quite well and, I suspect also, the gesture served to show that the Klansmen were against Karl Marx, the Pope, and the Jews, except for Jesus, but not Negroes. I looked forward to the hospitality but hoped not to have to see the host. (I had not the slightest fear of a Klansman; one evening as a group of robed Klansmen marched into a North End church, I had yelled out the identity of one, or so I thought. So frightened did one of my buddies become that I had to exchange a few blows with him. It was not fear but disgust that made me not want to see the local Kleagle.) The youngsters were not told who he was besides being simply a farmer, with lots of land to explore and a swimming hole on the place besides.

But the Klan leader was a genuine and gracious host. No sooner had we gathered about a campfire than he put in his welcoming appearance. Bereft of hood and sheet, potbellied and smiling, he seemed nothing but a jovial and likeable sort as he warmly welcomed us. However, he stayed to josh a bit.

Suddenly I could hardly believe my ears and contain my disgust with his gall. The man himself was opening up the matter, going straight to the heart of what I held against him. Moreover, he had singled out for conversation Fred Barnes, one of the scouts who had only recently reached Champaign from Mississippi.

Our host was saying, "Do you know anything about the Ku Klux Klan?"

"Plenty," said Fred.

"S'pose you're scared as hell of 'em?" said the Klansman.

"No sir," was the reply.

"Why not?" asked the biggest Klansman in Champaign County.

"Well, I jest figger they are meat men, meat men like all the rest," was the quiet, easy answer. Thereupon the big fat Klansman, himself appearing more of blubber than meat, burst into laughter. Every time he would look at the little refugee from Mississippi, the Klansman would laugh again until his potbelly would shake. The boy would laugh a little, too, and so would the rest of us. Fred Barnes has been a favorite friend of mine ever since.

Another trip taught me that I was not man enough to smoke a cigar. The troop had hiked through a little country settlement and stopped for drinks and candy at its lone store. Shortly after we reached the cabin in which we were to week-end, word reached me that one of the fellows had pilfered a candy bar wrapped in tin foil. I sent for him, got him to admit his guilt, and punitively assigned him to pots and pans after dinner, all before the other fellows who seemed quite impressed, just as I intended. Comfortable with my demonstration that a scout must indeed be honest, I made another step. I sent the thief for the candy bar and confiscated it.

A few minutes later I slipped into the woods for a surreptitious snack of candy, only to discover that what was wrapped in the tinfoil was not sweets but six little black cigars! They were as dry as tinder, the one I tried lighting up like a pine needle. But they were as strong as Samson too and I was no smoker. A few puffs on the cigar and I was awfully sick, with the responsibility of cooking the evening stew still ahead of me. Yet I dared not let out what had happened; after playing judge, jury, prosecutor, and sheriff, I could not appear sick from trying to smoke that cigar. So I kept my lips tight and held my stomach in sheer agony whenever I was out of sight. After the stew was bubbling away in its pot, each time I lifted the lid I would sicken almost to the point of regurgitation and confession. Suddenly it dawned on me that perhaps the thief had himself discovered the candy to be in fact cigars, and that I could not allow the punished one to have the laugh on his punishment. This made me the more determined to carry on, and thus I somehow made it through that night.

In another instance I volunteered an involvement in one of Katherine Frederick's projects at Willard School, not to help execute but to frustrate it. It was in 1932, the day before all of the grade schools in the county were to participate in a pageant at the University of Illinois Memorial Stadium celebrating the two-hundredth anniversary of the birth of George Washington.

As I neared Willard School that afternoon, its fifth-grade class was being dismissed, and I saw that each of the children was carrying a large piece of white cloth. When I inquired about the cloths of a group of three girls, one said, "These are our costumes for the pageant," and held up the garment before me. It was on the order of a "shift," two rectangles sewn together, with a scoop-out for the neck, and the material of plain, white sacking. When I asked what "parts" those were playing who would wear the white costumes, I was told, "It's a pageant. Everybody in our school wears this. We are all the same."

"But," I persisted, "What are you supposed to be, what kind of a person is it that all of you are?" But no one knew. Then I asked the same question of the older children as the sixth- and seventh-graders came along, and still no one could answer it. Simplifying the inquiry, I followed up with, "Well, then, just what have you been told to do?" This, one of the older girls well knew: The Willard children, all Negro and all clad in their white sacks, would be grouped together and seated on the grass. As George Washington's carriage approached, they would take to their knees and bow toward the carriage until it had passed. They would also sing several songs together, spirituals and plantation melodies.

So it became clear. The Negro children at Willard as part of pageantry celebrating the birth of the first president of a democracy would re-enact the root of their troubled presence. They would play slaves. Worse, as their antecedents had been tricked, captured, and forced into slavery, they were being tricked into its dramatization. Still worse, the public school and its teachers were working the ugly fraud for the delight of little white children, who already felt themselves heirs of the white supremacy system.

I decided at once to have a talk with Miss Frederick and walked back to the school. She had gone home, I was told, so I headed for the Women's Town Club where she lived. She was called downstairs to see me and graciously and flatteringly introduced me to the ladies about as a former and favorite pupil of hers, not omitting specific mention of "our Boy Scout troop" which indeed was part hers. But I was not disarmed in the slightest and was very pleased when she ushered me into another room where we could talk privately, for I was full of anger. I affected an air of calm only momentarily, for she readily admitted that her children were to act as slaves. Her story was that she had volunteered the slavery role for them! It was something for which they were so realistically suited, she explained. None of the children had objected; all were cooperating wonderfully. Willard School was certain to perform creditably at the pageant.

But I heatedly pushed my position. Her children were about to do something injurious both to themselves and the white children. Their role implied black inferiority as well as a corresponding right of white superiority. This was all unreal and to be taught against, not dramatized. Certainly little children should not be induced to act out degradation of themselves. None of them was objecting, of course; all of them were being fooled.

Soon Miss Frederick chose to put me in my place, to remind me that

I was a mere youngster, speaking only for himself. Said she, "If the grown-ups in the community shared your views, especially the parents, this would be another matter. As it is, you and I just do not agree." She then repeatedly asked me to view the matter calmly and objectively, and finally brought the conference to an end, with: "You're simply upset because you did not understand. After you've slept on it, you'll feel better about it in the morning, I am sure."

As I walked away from the Women's Town Club, I did begin to calm myself, not for sleeping but for acting on the matter. I was piqued by her suggestion that I spoke for nobody but myself. But I was impressed by her implication that she would respect the views of the larger community were they to coincide with mine. All at once the next step, to be taken swiftly, was plain to me. I would learn that very evening whether the community, no, the parents, stood with Miss Frederick or with me!

I went to a sorority house where I knew a typewriter and typists to be. There I drafted a petition addressed to Miss Frederick which briefly, and with little argument, stated that the petitioners objected to their children's appearing in slave roles at the pageant. While the petition was being typed, I called the patrol leaders of the Scout troop and had them go to Willard School and await me there. I soon joined them and, using the key which I carried as Assistant Scoutmaster of "our troop" (Miss Frederick's and mine), took them into the basement of Miss Frederick's school for a briefing. They got the point of my position quickly and eagerly set forth to solicit the signatures. I went on to the campus for study.

That night when I reached home, the soiled and fingered sheath of pages, bearing the names of one or more of most of the parents of Willard children, was there for me. Several angry parents had made calls to me, but it was too late to return them that night. The next morning, that of the pageant day, I stopped off at Willard before time for its classes and on my way to mine at the university. Miss Frederick smilingly, at least appearingly so, took up where she had stopped the evening before. Said she, "Now that you've slept on it, don't you feel better about it?" My views had not changed, I told her. Nor had hers was, of course, the rejoinder.

At that point I reminded her, "Last night, did you mean to say that you would not override any objections parents might have?"

"Of course," she replied.

"Well, here are their objections," I said, drawing the petition from my coat pocket and placing it in her hands.

Her face became livid with rage. My wrath of the evening before was hers of that morning.

I mumbled something about being in a hurry to reach to campus and withdrew. I did not like seeing her in such a furious and unhappy state.

On the way out of the building, I ran into several petitioners entering the school to follow up face-to-face with Miss Frederick. One of them had several children at the school. I would wager that he had never attended a PTA meeting. But he had read the *Chicago Defender* for years; I know as much because my brothers and I were his paperboys. Calling me by my first name, he said, "I called you last night. Now I want to know, what in the hell is going on out at the stadium?"

"Maybe nothing will, as far as Willard is concerned. Anyway Miss Frederick is the person for you to see, not me. I'm overdue on the campus," I said, rushing away to leave Miss Frederick to learn full well how that one parent felt.

Willard School did not participate in the pageant at all.

That evening when I reached home, I was told that a special meeting of the Willard PTA was to be held a few hours later. The purpose of the meeting, since the pageant was over, and the school had not participated, was to air the naughty deed I had done and, I suppose, to punish me appropriately, as appeared convenient and within capacity. The meeting had been called by a woman who, while fully adult, was no more parent than I was, and who was actually a citizen of Urbana instead of Champaign and hence not a resident of the school district. She did frequently speak for the Negroes in Champaign-Urbana, since, as a Republican political leader, it served her well, and the party she served even better, to assume the posture of Negro civic leader.

I was not invited, but as the principal subject of the meeting, I decided to make my presence first-hand. As it turned out, I did not have to say a word in defense of myself. Not only the neighborhood residents but even the national executive of the NAACP in New York took care of my interest, their own interests, to be accurate about it.

The neighborhood people, the petition signers, charged that the meeting been "stacked" against them (they had not been invited either), made clear that the petition reflected their views, and then put the political lady in her place. She was an outsider, meddling in what was no affair of hers, as she had done before, and should cease to do.

The NAACP had sent a telegram, in response to one of inquiry from the lady politician, indicating that I was head of the provisional NAACP branch in Champaign with full authority to represent that organization. What happened was that when Miss Frederick first observed that I lacked any representative capacity in the community, I passingly referred to a current effort to organize an NAACP branch, of which I was the chairman. I made little of it, since I viewed Miss Frederick's argument as tangential and at most the erection of a straw man she thought she could push over; I had preferred to have Miss Frederick admit that she was wrong in substance and therefore, via dramatics, a sort of teacher of false doctrine. I was trying for too much, of course. But Miss Frederick had passed word about the local NAACP being organized on to the lady politician who—not being really the community leader she pretended to be and allowed the white community to use her as—had not even heard of it. She thought, I am certain, that by wiring the NAACP she could get an answer of usefulness to her. She would learn, she must have figured, that the organizing effort was not really underway, there was no NAACP representative in Champaign, recognized as such by the national office, or other information useful for disparaging my conduct. But she was wrong.

POLICE

That day when I literally stood my ground and failed to join the mass flight of Negro youngsters from Lawhead School ground as the motorcycle policeman pulled in was only the first of my brushes in Champaign with those public functionaries which the older North Enders called "the law."

The *Chicago Defender*, that organ of protest against racial injustice which I read as well as peddled weekly, had given me a primary education in police behavior with Negroes. The teaching may not have been always objective, but it was comprehensive, lively, and repeated, and hence effective. Week in and week out, I read of police action ranging from mere discourtesy and unnecessary pushing around to brutality and murder which the presumed protectors of people and their persons visited upon Negroes, as Negroes.

Moreover, summertime visits with an uncle in Chicago had heightened my distrust of the police. This uncle was a stationary engineer for the Chicago police department and assigned to its Wabash Avenue station, located deep in the South Side racial ghetto. My aunt frequently sent me to the station with lunches and messages for my uncle, and once there I was permitted to linger a bit to see and ask questions about the always colorful and exciting, and sometimes frightening, events which were daily routine at the station.

My uncle, who was Tuskegee-trained and a follower of Marcus Garvey, the Negro nationalist from Jamaica, answered my questions and interpreted what I saw in a fashion not unlike that of the *Defender*. The Black Mariahs [police vans] trucked in loads of victims of raids, all of them Negro. My uncle explained that the police enjoyed raiding Negro parties; they arrested Negroes for gambling, which went on undisturbed among whites elsewhere, and the bigger the whites, the less likely it was anybody would bother them, particularly in the Loop. He spoke to me too of payoffs and the politically privileged, how the police knew whom to arrest and whom not, including even a few favored Negroes. Once when I saw a group of bloodied and bruised Negroes brought in, he explained that they had been fighting among themselves. But he added, "The paddies probably knocked some of 'em around pretty good besides."

One day I was permitted to see the "lock-up," an arrangement which first struck me as much like the cages holding the lions and tigers at Lincoln Park's zoo. There, for the first time in my life, I saw little pink and blue slips, about the size of streetcar transfers, but with numbers on them, littering the floors. My uncle explained that they were "policy" slips. Said I, "Mama has insurance policies on all of us children, but the agent never gives her any papers like these." My uncle laughed and, as we left the lock-up, told what I had said to several of the caged men, whose laughs about it were even louder than his. After we were back down in the boiler room, he told me that policy was a kind of gambling that went on in the big city. Some of the police played policy, and a fellow in the lock-up could still put in his plays! "Collect too, if he wins," he said, "but winning isn't often at policy."

On another day I learned that my uncle's feet as well as those of the policemen were of worse clay. I was sent to join my uncle and help him bring home several packages from the police station. In the packages were bacon from somewhere in the stockyards, a whole slab unfried but "hot," and a bundle of sheets, new and cool white but also "hot." Everybody who was "in" at the station, those in uniform and those not, bought the stolen goods and at added discount. The peddlers got poorer cash prices at the police station, but the customers were concentrated, the sales fast and certain, and the peddlers got protection for themselves as part of the deal.

In Champaign, of course, the police were not so brutal as the *Defender* and my uncle reported them. Nor were they tied in with organized gambling (at least not the policy racket, which had not reached the community, as it later did) or the traffic in stolen goods, I would charitably guess.

Nevertheless, many of the police in Champaign had no knowledge that there were rules protective of the rights of Negroes as of other citizens that a policeman was bound to respect. I early heard and saw enough in Champaign to know that most Negroes were viewed with disapproval by the police much of the time and were likely to be mistreated readily, if lightly, at most any time. They talked disrespectfully and sometimes high-handedly to any Negro they approached. They sometimes made arrests and entered homes without warrants or reference to recency of crime or pursuit of its suspected, perpetrator in the North End. When they confronted and questioned one of us, anything beyond a weak and humble response strictly confined to the question asked was "biggity," or "back" talk, and itself likely to result in arrest. I do not forget, as a town youngster attending law school at the university and one from whom free legal advice was often sought, despite lack of sufficient learning as well as license to provide it, I often had to try to explain the law of arrest. Many of my listeners simply could not grasp that "talking back" to an officer was not a resistance of arrest and, if not that, at least disorderly conduct. They knew too many people to have been in fact thus arrested to find acceptable the principles of law involved. With them it was like the old saw about the fellow who had been jailed and whose solicitous friend advised him, "Why, they can't jail you for that."

"Well, here I am ain't, I?" the fellow replied from inside the lock-up.

My feeling that the police mistreatment was racial was reinforced by the fact that all of the blue-coated were blue-eyed. There sometimes was a Negro deputy sheriff, a choicer political crumb tossed to the Negroes in the county in lieu of the more customary janitor job at the county building. The deputy served mainly to keep troublesome Negroes in line on

North Poplar Street. But the uniformed police were all white until the early thirties or so. To be sure, these men were a notch or two above the dreggy, hostile whites who too often so largely constitute the police force in many cities. The motorcycle cop who enjoyed chasing us off Lawhead School grounds, for example, had been to the university. This degree of exception resulted from lack of work opportunity in industry for poor whites as well as Negroes in a university economy. Still, by and large, Champaign's police were naive and ordinary enough whites who, once uniformed and armed, easily looked upon any Negro as fair game any time and for almost any reason.

The police were especially disturbed by the presence of a Negro male on the West Side or in the university district, if he was not dressed to appear a cook, a porter, or a housecleaner, and the time was not soon before, soon after, or during working hours. If he was not well known by neighborhood whites, he was in trouble sure enough. It was all right for a Negro to look like whatever, at any time whatsoever, and be ever so much a nobody, so long as he stayed out in the North End where most of his kind belonged and into which area the cops made only irregular incursions. But when he was elsewhere, he was off-limits unless he had a "pass," some reason for being there—a black job or a white spokesman—convincing enough to his challenger.

My father was challenged by the police one evening as he left the West Side. He looked familiar enough to his blue-coated accosters. But it was Sunday, no day for yard work or housecleaning.

It had also happened to me when I was a teenager. At the time I was going daily to the back of a fraternity house on Green Street to pick up my mother. One evening the policeman on the beat tailed me all the way into the kitchen. His story was that ice cream had recently been stolen from a back porch nearby, and he was trying to catch the thief. This was likely a lie, since the fraternity house was about the last residence left in a block rapidly changing to commercial use. Certainly it didn't impress my mother, who felt that the cop was so watchful as he worked his beat, he should have seen me regularly enough to judge that I had business to perform in the block. The handout he got in that kitchen was a sharp lecture.

In these ways I was prepared to look upon the police as not to be trusted, just as I am certain they viewed Negroes. A bit of learning at the law school about the law of arrest was sufficient to complete the preparation. My own brushes with the police, "the law" to my elders but only "cops" to me, were inescapable. Two such incidents, in neither of which had anyone committed the alleged wrong, nor had I been personally charged, I well recall. In each I spoke out for others in my community.

During my second year of law school, the Varnado family, whose four girls had grown up as playmates of my brothers and mine, moved from nearby our home to East Washington Street. They moved into a big, two-story, frame house. I suppose the change to a bigger house meant more room and privacy for all those girls, by then young ladies. It also meant residence on a paved street, as Tremont was not, and being the first Negro family in the block, though the street was not otherwise so special. In fact, the new home was backed up against the Big Four railway tracks. Anyway, moving to a new house, even just another house, was a good reason for the party the girls gave. I had heard that the presence of the family was unwanted, and something of how the white neighbors were making this plain to the Varnado family. Still I was as unprepared as the Varnados for what soon happened during the party.

The doorbell rang, and one of the girls hastened to open the door and greet another guest. But instead there stood a big, burly police officer. The girl called out to her mother, "It's a policeman," in tone sufficiently excited to draw me to the door along with Mrs. Varnado, as well as to bring the hum of the party to a hush.

When the mother reached the open door, the officer said, "You're being too noisy here. Your neighbors called in and complained." I glanced first at Mrs. Varnado, who obviously was so scared as to send us all home as soon as the policeman left, and then at the big cop, who seemed about to step into the house. Suddenly I found myself also in the doorway, and somehow in front of Mrs. Varnado, facing the blue-coated intruder. I asked him if he had heard anything noisy as he came up. He said, "Not then." Next, I asked him "Do you have a warrant?" His answer was "No." Thereupon I said, "Then I think you ought to leave us alone," and closed the door in his face.

That was that, except for what I surmise happened with the policeman and know to have followed as the party resumed. The policeman was doubtlessly surprised at what he had heard from me and had allowed to happen. As he walked away, and recovered himself, he may well have been tempted either to return and pick me up, to return with reinforcement and to play it further by ear, or at least to drift back to satisfy himself that the sounds from the unwanted residents were sufficiently subdued. Those alternatives occurred to us youngsters. Mrs. Varnado, born and bred in Mississippi as she was, remained quite disturbed. She was somewhat relieved after several of us went out and checked a bit, finding the policeman nowhere to be seen. The party soon recovered its momentum, though I doubt that it ever regained its noise level.

A bit later, while I was still in law school, I volunteered myself as unlicensed counsel for a friend under police pressure. Hubert Britt, a young teenager who lived next door to us, came in and out of our home at will, as we went in and out of his, belonged to our Scout troop, played baseball on the neighborhood team in the city junior league with my younger brothers, and was indeed like a brother to us. That winter day, with great heaps of snow on the ground, I was plodding my way home from the campus, when the Britt jalopy drove a few feet past me and pulled into the curb. The horn was blown, and I was beckoned over to the car. There was Hubert, his mother, and his father on their way downtown to the police station. I offered to go along and as the journey resumed learned what it was all about.

Hubert began by recalling for me a certain white fellow who daily drove his car down Fifth Street through the North End on his way from the Illinois Central shops and frequently stopped off at a grocery and delicatessen store near our homes. During one such recent stop, he had had words with some of the youngsters who hung about the store, including Hubert and a brother or two of mine. The words were nasty and venomous, you black this and black that, on the part of the I.C. employee, liberally returned in racial reverse by the Negro youngsters. I knew of this.

That afternoon as the fellow returned to his car, following a stop at the store, the name-calling had been repeated. Hubert and several others had tossed snowballs at the car as it pulled off, Hubert admitted. What he vigorously denied, however, was that a car window had been cracked by one of the snowballs, as the man had reported to the police a few minutes later. Hubert insisted that the snowballs were merely that, made on the spot and spur of the moment and without hard filling. He argued the physical impossibility of the alleged window cracking.

But the police had accepted the irate railway employee's story, lock, stock, and barrel. They had phoned Hubert's father to come to the station to pay the replacement cost of the window, if he wanted to avoid arrest of his son. This was the problem.

I bought Hubert's story, and when we reached the station sought to help him sell it to the police. The police chief let me talk all right, but when I finished turned his back on me and his face to the parents, saying, "Well, do you have the money for this gentleman, or must I jail your son?" At this point Mr. Britt started for his wallet, but I interrupted him by figuratively pulling from my pocket the card that was there.

"Wait, just a moment," I began, addressing the chief, "You're finding someone guilty but you aren't a court. Besides even if he were to be charged and found guilty, his parents would owe nobody nothing. A parent is not liable for the tort of a child."

The chief then told me that I was meddling, had done it before, and would one day get myself in trouble in the process. Returning to the issue and becoming specific, he said, "You know we have a city ordinance against snowballing in the streets. I suppose you want this boy charged under the ordinance."

"If you do," I rejoined, "I'll see to it that the ordinance is enforced on the university campus," though I did not have the slightest notion as to how to carry out the threat. I only knew instinctively that the police customarily allowed university students to get away with murder, when it came to spring celebrations, snowballing, and other youthful capers, and would not really single out Hubert Britt for the threatened punishment.

In a little while the discussion waned, and the chief closed it by lecturing Hubert and telling his parents that he still expected them to settle with the complainant. The latter never happened, and I suspect that after we left the station, the chief made the complainant realize that the squeeze they had jointly tried to put on the Britts just hadn't worked.

I had kept the police chief from making Negro parents pay cash for their son's privilege to speak to a white man in the same vein as the white man had spoken to him.

During my college-going, I was an active member of the Frederick Douglass Civic League, surely a reflection of identity with the North End community. The league, like its namesake so many years before it, stood for civil rights, social and economic progress, and, implicitly, the Republicans. But there was less conflict in actuality between its civic purposes and the undeclared political objectives than might be suspected. Obtaining jobs in the public service for Negroes was a major goal of the league. At the same time, all Champaign—the county, the city, and, one might add, the university—was thoroughly Republican, if not rock-ribbed, then cornfed and corn-bound. Those who supported the winning faction's candidate for county office, the mayoralty, and township supervisor could press for the Negro plums, jobs as deputy sheriff, elevator operator, or janitor at the county building or city hall.

The league was effective largely because it enjoyed the leadership of Richard Edwards, who also was simultaneously part of the leadership of other groups in the community, his church, the Masons, and the Elks. But the interlocking was not designed; it merely reflected confidence in the man, wherever he was. Quiet and completely unflamboyant, of moderate views, he could take a position in the North End and press it calmly and steadily with the downtown powers that be until there was a delivery on it. I suspect those who ran things little thought of trying to play off another North Ender against him.

The direct and declared focus of the league leadership was on jobs of civic or racial significance. During my membership, I recall, it won two first appointments, that of a Negro as a policeman and of a Negro woman as a schoolteacher. Each of these jobs was theoretically under a merit system, but it took organized Negro pressure to break the all-white patterns. In the case of the schoolteacher, I was closely involved as the appointed chairman of the league's committee on educational matters. After we had several meetings with a school board committee, and had located ourselves a qualified Negro candidate, the appointment came through. Both the first Negro teacher and the first Negro policeman met every expectation of the appointing officials and as fully the hopes of the Negro community.

After graduation but before leaving Champaign for Chicago, I continued to be deeply involved in community life. I became a staff member of a neighborhood house, where I was permitted to develop my own program. With so much privilege, I tried to teach what I thought was needed. Having learned that the poor pay more as well as earn less, I taught the adults a little law of relevance and family financial management (knowing, of course, not much more than how to use the law books, and never having had family, financial, or management experience). We talked mainly about installment contracts, conditional sales contracts, wage assignments, garnishment of wages, and the like, though I also made certain to pitch in a bit about the legal perimeter within which a policeman was to stay.

However, I received the most enthusiastic response from the young teenagers in my Negro History class, because I probably taught it with vigor and conviction. I told them of the Negro heroes from Crispus Attucks through Fred Douglass and Colonel Charles Young. I had high spots for my students, such as the slave revolts; the Negro participation in the wars, especially that for his own freedom; the free Negroes during slavery; and those in the Congress during the reconstruction period. These offerings the youngsters soaked up as if they were sponges. I became quite pleased with the members of the Negro History Club (for it was not called a class) and arranged parties, picnics, and outings for them.

In the same period I became a member of the local lodge of a certain fraternal order. The invitation to membership impressed me. Some of the most highly respected men in the Negro community belonged to the order and had found me acceptable. Moreover, Christianity is embedded in the order, and by then I was no longer a churchgoer. Indeed there was a rumor that I would not be finally inducted, since I was suspected of a belief somewhat short of adequate belief in God the Father, the Son, and the Holy Ghost. I did not abandon hope, though the rumor burdened me until the final vestment in all the ancient mysticism.

As we candidates neared the transformation, we were completely divested of clothing, blindfolded, and told to kneel in prayer, each in his own way, I suppose, but silently. The kneeling was on a floor that was worn, splintered, and nail ridden. As I settled into position, tightly situated between two fellow candidates, I discovered that each of my bare knees rested on a protruding nail head. Just as I finished saying the Lord's prayer to myself, it occurred to me that it was my behavior in this phase of the ceremony which would be judged. What better way for anyone playing god to judge a fellow than by his prayerfulness. I must not get up too soon, I thought. If I get up now, ahead of all others, I shall be separated as a goat from the sheep. I shall not be admitted to the fellowship. Meanwhile, the nail heads dug deeper into my knees, while in the stillness all about me I could feel the presence of all of the other candidates still kneeling, still praying. 1 shifted slightly and the nail heads dug into my knees so sharply as to force me to leave off my hypocrisy and rise to my feet.

Promptly the fellows next to me and in rapid succession the remainder of them arose, and the ceremony proceeded.

As we newly elected ones went home together that night, I learned that most everyone of us had been waiting for someone else to arise first. Sheep we surely were, and we laughed about it.

After leaving Champaign and settling in Chicago, 1 remained close to my fellow hometowners.

When two young fellows, whose assistant scoutmaster I had been, were arrested without cause in Chicago, I went to their rescue in an effective though indirect fashion. Two policemen in civilian dress had stopped my friends early one Saturday afternoon, as they drifted along Forty-seventh Street, heart of the South Side ghetto and the summit of their weekend trip to the Big City. That weekend, the lively, colorful Forty-seventh was also the subject of a "spot" drive against knife-toting, trouble-making South Side "cats," a fact of which the two country kids from downstate were ignorant. Though they were familiar with the harsh, demeaning ways of "the law" in dealing with Negroes, they knew nothing of the plain-clothed cop. Consequently, seizure by the two white plain-clothed policemen in the midst of a street full of Negroes caused the bolder of two innocent ones to jerk back, demand "Hands off me!" insist on knowing "What the hell do you mean?" and require proof of police authority that neither cop deigned providing. The naive ones became smart alecs, and were quickly "run-in" for "resisting arrest." Once they were booked, they telephoned me and requested my court appearance in their behalf the following Monday morning. I was unable to oblige them and they had no money for employing other counsel.

What I did was less lawyering than stage production by telephone. They were told to abandon their bright, bizarre sport shirts for coat, white shirt, and tie. The costuming thus arranged, the first to speak in court was to do so quickly and politely, saying to the judge something like this, as I recall: "Your Honor, we are up here from Champaign, a little town down-state where all policemen wear uniforms. We have never been on Forty-seventh Street before and did not know what was going on. We didn't resist anybody. We just asked questions. We didn't understand being bothered by strangers in plain suits, especially when we knew we were just walking down the street, looking at everything." The role was played well and the defendants found not guilty.

Another hometowner, again a former Boy Scout, had moved to Chicago and found a job. He was adjusting fast, having learned of the small loan operators and the wonders performable through debt consolidation. He wanted me to co-sign a note, covering three old debts incurred back in Champaign. The lien would settle those debts and free him of his headaches.

Here was a fellow townsman who thought he needed a friend such as I wasn't about to become. So I went to work, to take myself off the spot. I learned from him that his existing debts were interest-free and that nobody back home was threatening to sue him. I then explained that the consolidation loan would bear a high rate of interest and that he would not only be dogged but sued, if he so much as missed a single payment on it. Then I asked about his income and expenses, and invited him to demonstrate his ability to make the payments, something he could not do. Finally, I told him that he was asking for one Big Headache and that I would not share it.

As he left me, he was obviously disappointed, and I envisioned visiting Champaign to be told that I had let him down. But a few days later he was back at my office to thank me for my refusal. He had figured it all out again at home.

"You were right," he said, "and you did me a favor."

Lawyer by Day, Redcap at Night

UNION ORGANIZING AND RABBLE ROUSING

Again I saw that under the sun the race is not to the swift, nor the battle to the strong, nor bread to the wise, nor riches to the intelligent, nor favor to the men of skill; but time and chance happen to them all.
—Ecclesiastes 9:11

The fellow who works his way through college expects to go to work at once when he finishes. He needs at long last to dip into that pot of gold at the end of the rainbow, not to speak of clearing up his debts. Still he is something up on those who merely went to classes, made a fraternity, and a girl or two, the proms and house dances, and the football games. He has learned to labor along with his learning.

All of that I was, in 1935, with my bachelor of arts, a bachelor of laws, and a license to practice law. Work was what I needed. I had a few debts with campus merchants and that special one of five dollars due a younger brother, who had advanced it to me to pay the state for my law license. I had learned to labor, week in and week out at the Co-op, helping to keep it clean, sweeping, dusting, and mopping, before, between, and after classes, whenever I had time to spare and sparing more than was good for my work with the books, especially those latter ones full of *stare decisis.*

AT THIS, THAT, AND THE OTHER

Besides, it seemed to me that I had always worked, beginning at home, with no pay and the certainty of penalty for a shoddy, an untimely, or forgotten performance at garden weeding, cutting kindling, bringing in the coal, or emptying that pan beneath the icebox. I had picked berries, on the Hurd, Smith, and Alagna farms in Urbana and cut yards, trimmed hedges, waxed floors, washed windows and walls, calcamined, white-washed, and painted a bit in the homes of the better-off on the West Side of Champaign. Several times I had cut celery and onions by the bushel and washed mountains of dishes for a Chinese restaurant during university homecoming and other big weekends. I had helped my Uncle George Person, as clerk in his grocery store and to spruce up a big fra-ternity house for a party.

Then there were the summertime jobs. One was for a contractor build-ing a house in Urbana for Professor Schnebly, who later taught me Wills and Trusts. Another was for Gus Dixon and Herman Harris, who ran a taxicab service, a Negro-operated enterprise for which I answered the telephone at night. There were summer jobs also in Chicago. Twice I worked for my Uncle Rob, who for several years managed to operate a tiny little ice-cream factory on South State Street. Here I did everything I was big enough to do and more, ran the ice cracking machine, loaded trucks, washed and sterilized cans, helped make and deliver the ice cream, and ate too much of it. Part of another vacation period I was a "carry" boy in an egg cannery. I carried eggs by the crate to girl workers for candling, breaking, and separation, and eggs away from them as whites or yolks in huge metal cans for refrigeration and shipping to bakeries and hotels whose delicacies are, of course, made only with the freshest eggs.

One day there was a girl working away at breaking eggs who didn't al-ways know a bad egg by its smell, and a huge batch was ruined. A partner-boss was thus upset enough, male though he was, promptly to push into the toilet marked "Female" and send the girls flying out, in his anxiety to push up production enough to overcome the loss. In such a mood and a few minutes later, he yelled a "Hurry it up" at me, accompanied by a push against my back. I had seen this happen to others and pledged myself to quit if it was ever done to me. I kept faith with myself, set the crate of eggs down right then and there, removed my yolk-stained white apron, and walked out.

A few days later, I had a better-paying job at a paper mill. I worked nights, hand-trucking great bales of paper to huge hot vats and tipping them in. One evening during the first week of the new job, a foreman stood and watched me unfasten and tip in a bale. Immediately afterward he tapped me on the shoulder and beckoned me to follow him. I felt certain that I had done something wrong, was jobless again, and so soon. But when we reached a distance out of the way of the activity, he stopped and turned to me saying, "How much d'ya weigh?"

"About a hundred 'n forty," was my answer.

"Thought so, you looked like you were going over into that vat along with the paper," he said and laughed.

He then assigned me to a job station at the end of a long stretch of wide, steel rollers, through which a band of hot cardboard moved until it was cut in uniform pieces by a great blade rhythmically moving up and down. As the pieces of cardboard were spat out and automatically stacked, my job was to watch for those with grease spots and to pull them aside. It is better to watch for the grease spots than to be a part of them, I mused to myself that night.

Along this path, I also had not altogether missed my turn as a servant, that category of humble and often humiliating labor which until recently was the escalator the Negro man rarely failed to take on his way up. He was at some point or other during his college days a bellhop, a table waiter, a redcap, a train or a Pullman porter, and, if he was not bright and rather fortunate besides, he remained a lackey long after he was laden with a degree. I had instinctively recoiled from "hustling for tips," Negroes in Champaign-Urbana being so largely confined to such roles. With the help of my father, who so early made newspaper peddlers of his boys, I happened never to have had to shine shoes on Wright or Green Streets, nor to caddy or wait tables at either of the country clubs. But one summer when I was a junior in high school, I served three weeks as houseman in the home of a prominent lawyer.

Those three weeks presented me with one difficulty after another. I had to learn both to set a table and to serve those about it. The mistress had to buzz for and ask me for an ashtray three times before I placed one within her reach. I could not envision a lady of refinement smoking, and twice provided her husband with ashtrays before I was told the error of my ways. (The year being 1927, mind you.) The mistress spoke "eyether" and "nyether" for "eether" and "neether," and "tomahtoes" for "tomaytoes." Trying so hard to learn so much so fast, I was led once to say "potahtoes for "potaytoes" in her presence and censored for my pains. She thought I was poking fun at her. Her thirteen-year-old daughter was to be called "Miss" by me. This was continually a problem. She was less than my sixteen years, and I disliked the servility implied by that title for one so young, and it seemed too Southern a practice. Besides, outside of the mother's presence and most of the time, I called the daughter by her first name, as she herself insisted. I was, of course, to wear a white jacket, but as soon as all of the family would leave except the lady of thirteen years, she would order me to remove the jacket and shed the posture of servant, to be simply her friend and playmate. She also delightedly introduced me to her visiting friends, using the first names in each direction, and always noting that I attended the same school as did she.

This kind of relationship, hardly of equal status but certainly not as imbalanced as the mother wished, reached the surface and upset things on several occasions. I well remember the stay of a house guest, also thir-teen or so, who bore the odd nickname "Balex" arising out of summer camp experience. Both girls insisted that I use the nickname, though I well knew that at the table and before the parents, I was to call the young guest "Miss Alexander." The latitude allowed me at the junior level of the household slipped out at dinner one evening. I referred to Miss Alexander as "Balex" and literally felt the strong, though silent, disapproval of the adults at each end of the table. That something was amiss still showed on my face as I returned to the kitchen. The colored cook, my guide and monitor said, "Now what did you do wrong?"

"Mrs. Harris," I answered, "I just called 'Balex' just 'Balex.'"

"I told you! I told you to leave those girls be!" she chided, while her frowning face fairly declared that nothing hurts a duck but its bill.

The last summer before my graduation from law school, I had a truer and more extended experience as a table waiter. I waited table all summer at the fancy Lincoln Inn in Lake Geneva, Wisconsin. Here I soon realized that three weeks of waiting table as a houseman left me much to learn about an occupation as artful as it is lowly. Moreover, my entree was harder because I was the first college lad taken in to the crew. More than once I found myself "up a tree," as the other waiters termed it, and a spot in which they were willing to leave me. They would go their own ways, smoothly and quickly, while tauntingly admonishing, "Come on down from there, School!" as I literally sweated out one difficulty after another.

Still more irksome at first was the way in which some of the waiters approached the patronage as they hustled for tips. They grinningly bowed and scraped as they greeted the guests, engaged in various elaborate and excessive gestures, made the routine delivery of a bit more of this and that appear a great and special favor, fawned over the quite ordinary, if not really brattish, children in a party, and the like. The customers, all of them white, consumed all of this black servility with greater relish than the quite delectable food we served. But it was too "Uncle Tommish" for me. I could not get myself in that groove.

Soon however I began to notice that these old hands at tablewaiting were nevertheless discriminating and selective. They knew some of the patrons, tried to "read" the new ones, and sometimes succeeded. As they frankly and easily revealed, "the come on" was "put on" only when it appeared worth the trouble. They did not worship the guests. They beguiled them. The "Tomming" was an act, and for a price, an artful obsequiousness added to the tray toting for those known or appearing able and willing to tip well. It was an anointing with sweet oil reserved for those expected to grease the palm in return.

Before the end of the summer, I had sensed more of what was really happening as the older waiters fawned and fussed over the whites they served. The feigning and chicanery worked because the patrons were gullible. They so much needed and enjoyed the showy semblance of subservience that they were willing to buy it, in small and fleeting chunks. And the need was for a superior status, obviously lacking, else it would not be sought in such fashion. The servant seemed to be really more in mastery of those he served than merely fawning, hopping, and skipping for them. I learned to let it all amuse me.

In a certain respect, the Lincoln Inn was distinguished for more than the high quality of its cuisine, its smooth service, and the beautiful view of Lake Geneva it afforded. The place was owned and operated by a Negro, though many of its occasional patrons doubtlessly never suspected as much. Bill Long, the owner, was of strongly Negroid features, very dark skin, and his hair completely gray. Donned in a white jacket and apron, he looked as though he had stepped from that familiar whiskey advertisement done in color. As he busily and firmly directed the busy personnel, he looked for all the world like the head waiter. Moreover, the image was backgrounded by the presence at the cash register of Mrs. Thompson, a mature, but quite attractive white woman who appeared to be the proprietress of the place, or at least the wife of the proprietor. This effective reversal of the Negro clerk "fronting" as the owner, for the true white owner *in absentia,* as is so widely practiced in the racial ghettos, was most entertaining, even intriguing to me.

But all of this preparedness for work was of little avail. Work, a real job, week in and week out, was hard to come by in 1935, midway in the Great Depression. I was to make one courageous job start after another and find nothing that would stick and satisfy me until 1942. And just as the adhesive began to take, a long, strong arm pulled the job and me apart. Theoreticians of the dismal science had traced the patterns of the business cycle and were teaching them to college students. But the depressed phase of the economy which began in 1930 was of four or five times the depth called for by the studies and lasted a decade. It was far more dismal than expected. Whites were unemployed and reduced to part-time employment by the millions. Only government relief through make-work programs and food distribution kept people going. Negroes, of course, were the worst off: every other Negro family in the big cities was on relief.

So all my shining armor meant little or nothing. I was starting at the wrong time and with the worst-off skin color. Chicago was absorbing, as usual, thousands upon thousands of Negroes from the rural south but had nothing but bread-lines and relief for them. Going there after graduation would have simply added wrong place to wrong time and color.

I decided to stay in Champaign to live on my folks more so than I had as a student. After admission to the bar, I scrubbed and waxed a few floors in good lawyer-like fashion, was a worker in a neighborhood center for a few months, and went to court sporadically, twice worth noting.

The first time, I was before the county court, which handled juvenile offenders. The judge was more accustomed to youthful Negro delinquents than young Negro lawyers. He at first looked upon me as a delinquent and asked me if I had a lawyer. He was profusely apologetic after learning that I myself was one.

The second matter was in a forum of even humbler level, before a justice of the peace. I was defending an old paper customer of mine against a plea for his eviction incident to foreclosure of mortgage on his property. We never went to trial. As soon as counsel for the plaintiff bank saw me, he was plainly most eager to settle. It was not because either the plea or the youthful counsel appeared so formidable. The counsel for the bank was simply that lawyer in whose home I had been houseboy several years before. He would have been as bothered to win his case against me as to have lost it to me.

LAW CLERK AND REDCAP

The next year, I dared to head for Chicago, armed with that law license for aspirational comfort and perhaps utility. But I was also equipped with two more realistic issuances. These were letters requesting employment for me, written by the leading furniture dealer in Champaign, who also was an active and influential alumnus of the university. One commended me to an executive at the huge Chicago Furniture Mart on Lake Shore Drive, where there was floor after floor of furniture to be dusted, a task for which my skills and experience were unquestionable. The other went to the General Counsel for the Illinois Central railway, located in its central offices and terminal station at Twelfth and Michigan, where there were junior legal positions to be filled but also, as intended in my case, bags to be carried for passengers by Negro redcaps.

Affiliation with a Negro law office was no problem in Chicago, where several law schools turned out young Negro lawyers in considerable number, and illusions about the advantages of life in the big city kept them there, to service swelling needs for legal help on the part of people less able to pay fees than ever in that mid-depression period. The rent-paying lawyers simply moved in another second-hand desk for the youngster wherever sufficient space remained and took him on without salary, or at most a most nominal one. The Furniture Mart fellow gave me an interview, but the fact soon showing through the bush-beating was that only whites were permitted to wipe all that furniture. However, the General Counsel at the I.C. congratulated me on passing the bar and took me at once to the chief usher. I immediately became a redcap. I was to "hustle bags," as the redcaps put it, for tips.

FIGURE 1. Lucian Belvey Nesbitt, father of the five brothers, b. Pulaski, TN, 1886.

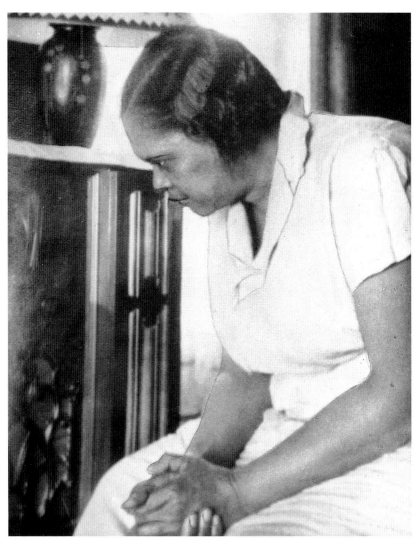

FIGURE 2. Christine Barker Nesbitt, mother of the five boys, listening to the radio, a favorite pastime of hers.

FIGURE 3. George Nesbitt when he finished Champaign High School, 1926.

FIGURE 4. Members of George Nesbitt's all-black fraternity, Alpha Phi Alpha, Tau Chapter, including Joel Adams (second row, second from left), William "Bill" Attaway (second row, third from left), Ed Mouzon (first row, first from left), Edward "Red" Toles (first row, second from left), and George Nesbitt (first row, fourth from left). Edward "Red" Toles became a famous lawyer and later a judge in Chicago. William "Bill" Attaway became a well-known novelist and wrote the lyrics for many of Harry Belafonte's songs, most notably "Day-O!" Photograph courtesy of Lea Adams.

FIGURE 5. George Nesbitt during World War II.

FIGURE 6. George Nesbitt and his wife, Josephine, when he was in the service.

FIGURE 7. Group opening the new Mayfair Mansions black housing development in Washington, DC. George Nesbitt is at bottom left, and his wife, Josephine Ball Nesbitt, is at bottom, fourth from left. The picture was published in the October 6, 1951, *Courier*, an African American newspaper.

FIGURE 8. George Nesbitt circa 1946.

FIGURE 9. The five Nesbitt brothers. Left to right: George Nesbitt, Rozell Nesbitt, Lendor Nesbitt, Russell Nesbitt, and Robert Nesbitt.

FIGURE 10. Left to right: Prexy Nesbitt, his sister Roanne, and two cousins.

FIGURE 11. Four of the wives of the five brothers: Doris Turner Nesbitt, Josephine Ball Nesbitt, Peggy Reese Nesbitt, and Marilyn Overton Nesbitt.

FIGURE 12. Sadie Crain Nesbitt, wife of Rozell Nesbitt.

FIGURE 13. George Nesbitt circa 1946.

As a law clerk, I drew an old desk at which to sit, without any obligation to pay rent. In addition, I was to have my typing done by the lone stenographer, serving the four older men, whenever there was nothing more to be done for any one of them. The latter was an arrangement requiring of me not only plenty of patience but the preservation of an amicable relationship with the overworked, underpaid girl. There was no salary whatsoever, though one of the lawyers saw to it that I was provided fourteen cents each evening for the next day's round-trip fare on the streetcar. (One evening I let all of my associates leave me alone in the office, to find that I was penniless. I quickly visited about nearby in the Loop in search of a lender or a ride, but without success. I had been a hobo but wouldn't be a street beggar. So that night I walked from Randolph Street to my home near Sixty-sixth and Vernon Streets, well over seventy long blocks).

Besides the opportunity for experience, as I commenced drawing simple complaints, helping prepare briefs, answering court calls, and arguing motions of lesser moment for the lawyers, another and related route to reward was early outlined for me. Many a Negro lawyer was making his way up in the organization, whether Republican or Democrat. I was already under compulsion to help such a lawyer at my office, a member of the state legislature, to serve the near-indigent, rank-and-file members of his ward organization. I should also commence speaking at ward meetings, I was told. I consented, my speaking debut was arranged, and the date was kept.

As I listened to the preceding speakers, the shallowness and false fervor of it all, the blazing oratory and the nothing specific said about anything specific, made me want to flee. But there I was that night, sealed to the platform as the last of a half-dozen speakers, and already having been paid excessive tribute by the presiding officer as the meeting opened. It was too late to duck out. At last it was my turn to speak, my turn "to shovel some of *it*," as the fellows in the street put it. I gave a lively little talk, by no means a rouser, and fitting only to help the long meeting come to a close. Still there was handclapping afterwards, because those on the platform always quickly and liberally applauded each other, with the crowded followers from the rural South following suit. I was glad to get out of there and never went back. Once was too much for me.

Law clerking in an office that served the racial ghetto known as Chicago's South Side confused my innocent image of the profession of law, leaving me little taste for the practice as I saw it. The sorry creatures I had to see in such large numbers as I visited the Eleventh Street and Forty-eighth and Wabash police stations on office missions left me sickened. They were poor, folk Negroes, the same as those who were so much a part of my nurturing in Champaign, and often hailing from the same towns in Mississippi, Louisiana, Tennessee, and Alabama. But something awful had somehow happened to them. I knew, of course, that they were in immediate trouble, for drunkenness, disorderly conduct, assault and battery. But the trouble seemed deeper, and the people looked bewildered and lost, mean and bitter.

As I made my appointed rounds in the huge municipal court, at the clerk's and the bailiff's offices, I chafed to have to pass on the cigars I was provided to keep their personnel cooperative. I felt uncomfortable whenever I faced a handsome bronze name plate with which a certain Negro lawyer reportedly had graced the bench of a judge before whom he frequently appeared. "That's peanuts!" I was told by someone older, and he laughed. I felt unhappy, too, whenever I was in the presence of a fellow who was a very versatile handyman attached to one of our lawyers. This fellow was an actor and often used his talents to brow-beat the poor and ignorant. He would, for example, serve tenants with notices to vacate, while acting quite as if he were a bailiff or other court officer. This theatrical skill would cause the naive, fearful poor, behind with the rent, to flee the premises before legal action was even commenced.

The municipal courts themselves, the lawyer-politicians seated there, were no less disturbing. Many times I was first angered and then sickened as I saw a certain judge, himself the son of an Italian immigrant, shout at and name-call Negro defendants, tongue-lash and poke fun at them, playing to an audience of followers and political cohorts hanging about his court. Once I lost a case before him simply because he took over the prosecution and decided in favor of his own side.

A policeman was "smart-talked" by two Negroes in an automobile. The policeman's resentment of what he considered uppitiness, and not any reason to suspect them of any crime, had prompted his search of the car, without a warrant. Some innocent item, not a gun but usable as a weapon (I have forgotten what it was) turned up in the back of the car and was seized. The driver was charged with carrying a concealed weapon. I pled illegal search and seizure and moved for suppression of the evidence but without success. Said the judge, "Now, counsel, you don't expect me to take the words of these fellows of yours against that of this fine officer?" The "fine" officer had concocted some tale stabbing at a reason for stopping and searching the car. No, I should not have expected the judge to accept my clients' word against that of a policeman, the more experienced lawyers explained. "Look at the names of the defendants in the cases you were prepared to cite," one said. Those names were often those of Chicago gangsters, people affluent enough to get due process of law by taking appeals.

I also lost a civil case in the municipal court, not so much to the other side as to the political system for choosing its judges.

The Negro janitor I represented had sued his employer, a Negro woman who was the owner-occupant of a small apartment building, for back wages. The woman had not paid him for months. She had been forced suddenly to finance major repairs, and her building and was thereafter unable to retain a regular janitor. She then hired my client, a widower and an elderly man without the remotest prospects of employment as a black during the depression days of 1937. He orally agreed to accept in return for his janitorial services a room in the basement, two meals daily, and a small monthly payment in cash. But it was further agreed that the latter was to accumulate until the employer's note for repairs was paid off, when she would then be able to start payments on the accumulated back wages. When that time was reached, the woman had denied the indebtedness to her janitor. She contended that the payments in board and lodging were all she had promised to pay, no cash wage had been included, and the court accepted her story. Moreover, the judge pronounced himself impressed that no rational man would really conclude such a preposterous arrangement.

The judge, an exceptionally bright young lawyer just out of law school, was from a family not only affluent but with "good connections," it was said. This latter circumstance had won him a place on the Democratic machine's ticket, resulting in the young lawyer's becoming a judge while still wet behind the ears as a lawyer.

I accepted, of course, that he could fairly believe the defendant rather than the plaintiff, but it was his observation that no rational man would wait for part of his wages until the employer could pay which embittered me. Here was a smart fellow, blessed with a head start and a political boost, but who came along too easily, moved too fast, and had lived too little to see the plausibility of our case. He was not aware of what was growing fairly common and did not know the time of day—the depression had not touched him. He was Jewish but no Brandeis, and the socio-economics of it all were beyond his grasp, I thought.

Still there were some matters of pleasure in the fledgling practice of law among the black and poor. I helped people discover and collect payments due them under lapsed insurance policies and sent them home looking for others and spreading the wonderful word. I stopped collection under a wage assignment against a stockyards worker. He had paid exorbitant prices for shoddy clothing, but the merchant had not adapted his contract forms to new statutory requirements. I obtained divorces for immigrants from the rural South so that they could get married, not have to live "common-law" with their spouses, and behave instead in the new way expected of them. I also helped with several minor anti-discrimination cases, inevitably a self-fulfilling kind of involvement for me.

But most of what I saw and felt all around me as a law clerk left me uneasy. It was not at all as I had expected and wanted it to be, and it left me feeling out of place. In 1940, I left the beginnings of a practice, against the advice of my colleagues, to take a job. I could use the job all right, but also I needed the fresher air.

Being a Negro redcap (railroads call it "station porter" or "station attendant") was no more to my liking than law clerking, though it did provide a relatively handsome livelihood, amidst so much employment and underemployment.

Station portering was more of the business of being menial, like waiting tables at the Lincoln Inn but a lot worse. It was putting one's body out to hire by whomsoever for a price fixed at whatsoever by the purchaser of the services. Those calling the tune were not the elite and those other patrons making as if they were, as at Lake Geneva. They were instead the run-of-the-mill and mostly poor-to-middling whites, the better-off having gone to the airlines. Besides they were heavily Southern.

Most of the I.C. executives, occupying offices above the passenger station, which we dubbed "upstairs," were also Southern whites. The vice presidents among them, as they rode the I.C.'s private cars, employed the services of "private car men," who cleaned, cooked their meals, made their drinks, and kept them preened and properly fawned over. All of these lackeys were Negroes, as were the redcaps. But the private car men were paid modest wages, whether they were on travel or not, and were privileged to redcap in addition. They were a favored few, the company's men among the redcaps. They absorbed and reflected the views of the men they served, and felt themselves responsible for keeping their fellow redcaps "in line," as the vice presidents would draw it and whatever the subject.

Altogether, we were a bunch of black flunkies in red caps, at the beck and call of the plainest, most ordinary whites, who often knew little of how to tip and sometimes hardly had its wherewithal but found white comfort for themselves in the short-term servants we were to them. Whenever such a passenger felt he had been shorted on deference, no matter how well the services themselves were performed, his complaint would mean real trouble for the redcap. The Negro ushers at the I.C. depot were expected always to be "good Negroes," no matter what was said or done to them.

The chief usher, himself a former private car man, remained a good Negro as he bossed us. A redcap who let himself get out of place with a passenger would be promptly "sent across Michigan Avenue"—fired— unless, of course, he chanced to have an "in" with a man "upstairs," the fateful decision then having to be made from on high. The chief usher had help with his overseeing, much more than from his assistant chiefs. Everybody had his notion of what a redcap should and shouldn't do and could back it up—anybody from "upstairs," the stationmaster, the conductors and trainmen, the passenger and ticket agents, the gate attendants, the cab starters, the city's cop, and the passengers, be they ever so demanding, drunk, disorderly or discourteous.

Besides all this, the work was hard and its conditions unpleasant. A station porter was a doorman in a dozen different places daily, opening, holding, and closing doors of cabs and autos, doors to coaches and sleeping cars, and doors here and there throughout the station. He lifted, carried, loaded and unloaded, pushed and pulled bags and baggage all over the place. He hustled himself up and down great stretches of stairways and to and from the cabs and trains over and over again. He endlessly ushered people, telling them where to find and, if need be, leading them to, ticket windows, phone booths, the baggage stand, the restaurant, the news stand, the traveler's aid, the sanitary ones, too, the right gate at the

right time, and the other redcaps who had their bags. And he hourly answered scores of questions, often repeatedly and for the same passenger,
though never in the slightest with the surliness of a bus driver, and most
of which would have been unnecessary, if the passengers had but read
the schedules, their tickets, and the signs everywhere, or simply allowed
the loudspeaker to penetrate their ears. No, they preferred the word of
a lackey, for all of his simpleness and ignorance, rather than trusting the
many other media for their guidance.

The redcap carried on within the din and commotion inside the depot and out, hustle and bustle, train calls, whistles, clang clangs, steam
releases, and cabs blowing and screeching. The work went on in whatever weather, the hot made stickier and the bitter cold more cutting at a
location so near Lake Michigan. The atmosphere was always smoky, gas-
eous, and grimy. For the redcaps, the depot was a place to "watch your
step" for certain, as they ducked and dodged the cabs, rushed up and
down car steps, jumped off and on cars still moving, and cut through
and in front of trains. There were, of course, dull moments between trains,
during which they could sit and blow to themselves. But the crumby
and cramped locker room was for lockers, not people. There was not
enough space in it for a full crew, nor were washbowls and toilets available. The locker room was dirty, smoky, and greasy, too close and smelly,
and always hot and damp.

This was redcapping at the Illinois Central depot, at no salary, for tips
only.

Still, when my first week at Illinois Central was over, the accounting
made plain that I had a good job. That first weekend made it clear that
my tips would average out a comparatively handsome figure, about twice
the salary of a white-collar man on the WPA! Moreover the chief counsel
for the I.C., my fellow alumnus of the university, had made an arrangement for me which fitted my needs as neatly as hand in glove. I was to
carry bags only at night and to be permitted to report each evening at any
hour conveniently related to the work flow at the law office. Moreover,
as I soon learned, the lawyer by day and redcap by night was entitled to
round-trip passes, free passage to and from home in Champaign, whenever he pleased.

But during the week also I had sensed something strange and be-
fuddling on the part of several redcaps. These were younger men, sev-

eral of them college graduates, including two from law school, one in chemistry, and another in psychology. (Luggage carriers who also bore college degrees were nothing shocking. Many a fellow carried bags to get his college training or until he found a chance to use it. The older redcaps at the I.C. at first often called me by a name similar to mine but of a red-cap previously their fellow worker, who went on to become a well-known civil rights lawyer, president of the nation's leading Negro university, and a U.S. delegate to the United Nations). These men had been quick to make friends with me, but occasionally as I approached them they would lower their voices enough to make plain that I wasn't to hear them. They once or twice invited me to accompany them across the street and down into "The Hole," we called it, for dinner. But it seemed that the once or twice was to be the extent of the hospitality. I could not fathom it. They seemed to want to take me "in" but also they would shut me out.

A few days later, I caught on, not from the college crowd but from a couple of the older men. The younger fellows were talking-up and orga-nizing a union! I had heard one old redcap say to another, "These young upstarts have been around this place fifteen minutes and wanna run things. They'll fool around and get us all run away from here. Whites are pushing out the colored everywhere these days, and them smart alecs are asking for it here. Lots of whites would be glad to hustle these bags."

One of the men I had overheard was only too pleased to follow up his discourse on labor economics with me. He knew that the chief counsel had gotten my job for me and assumed that I would be skittish about, if not against, the union-talking troublemakers. They were for the most part the very fellows who could not make up their minds about me. Later I was to learn that what made the older men count me with them and against those flirting with unionization also had made my new friends suspicious of me. They too assumed that I would be afraid to make a move of which the chief counsel might disapprove. In fact, as one revealed to me months later, they figured that maybe I had been hired the "upstairs" route to do a special job, to "rat" on those with whom I would work.

I was in fact most eager to see the union established and to have a hand in its activity. Perhaps it was the influence of *Defender* again, driving me to help get a union at the I.C., because, as it had told me, so many unions would not have had me. Or perhaps I had a subconscious desire to pay a debt to Professor Berman back at the university. I had been unable to get him a hearing before Negro students on the Negro and organized labor, so I would make it up by helping to set up a union. Or maybe it was determination not to miss another chance to help organize the workers where they were pushed around as I had been at the egg factory, where the boss himself had pushed me, literally pushed me. But again maybe it was contagion that caught me. "Organizing the unorganized" was all about me in Chicago — even the teachers, the newspaper writers, and the artists were unionizing.

Before long I was let in on the details of what was afoot. A fellow named Willard S. Townsend, "Bill" Townsend, a college-bred redcap over at Northwestern depot, seemed to be the leader. Northwestern was shaping up fast. The ushers at Dearborn Street station and the Greyhound bus depot were talking union too. Even the white bag-toters at La Salle Street station were in touch with Townsend, as also were fellows in other big cities, including the I.C. depot in Memphis. And we would have a tougher row to hoe in Chicago than the fellows in Memphis; we would have to overcome the vice presidents "upstairs," the private car men, the I.C. Boosters Club ("It's a company union, that's what it is," said my informants), and the older redcaps among us, with their visions of pensions, not a union to upset the apple cart.

I joined up.

One day soon afterward, as I headed for the locker room to climb into my uniform and start after the shekels, the chief usher called me to a halt. The chief counsel, "Judge" Craig was his name, wanted me upstairs. "Maybe you're done for here," the chief usher said, and it was plain that he hoped so.

Maybe I am done for sure enough, I said to myself as I headed for a meeting with the man who was my maker at the I.C.

The judge shook my hand, sat me down, smiled, and explained that he simply wanted to know how I was getting along. "Do you like the job?" "How are they treating you?" "Any troubles of any kind?" After a series of such questions, followed by easy and unrevealing answers from me, he moved to his point.

He had heard that there was "a funny kind of business" going on among the redcaps but was confident I had nothing to do with it. I professed not understanding what was meant by "funny business," having sensed the ambivalence he was suffering, even as he prepared to pressure me. He was a seasoned and skillful lawyer, and of course quite familiar with the Railway Labor Act. While his intervention in my behalf was to get me a job as a menial and not as a junior on his legal staff, he wasn't about to overlook the possibility that the minion before him might at least have heard of that law—a law guaranteeing certain rights to railway labor which the judge, as an I.C. official, was about to ignore. So, mouse that I was, I teased the big fat cat a bit. I continued feigning not to have any idea of what he meant, while he persisted with his vague "funny business" reference to the beginning efforts of redcaps to exercise their rights to organize themselves and bargain with the powerful railways. After having had enough of my act, he moved to dismiss me.

"I think you know what I mean," he said. "I have tried to help you, and I am entitled to your cooperation. I want you to promise me you'll have nothing to do with that business."

"Well, judge, you are talking about the union we are starting," I replied, "While I do appreciate what you've done for me, I also owe something to the men with whom I work."

The rejoinder was to the effect that the men would get along; they had been managing to do so before my arrival on the scene, and they would get along also after my departure. My job was to tend to my own affairs. He concluded by repeating his request that I pull away from the drive for a union.

For some reason or other, I decided to appear responsive. "Well, sir, I can't promise all of that," I ventured, "But I shall think it over."

"You do that," he said, and I departed.

A few weeks later, I had been elected president of Local 602 of the International Brotherhood of Redcaps, an A.F. of L. affiliate. Letterheads carrying my name as president were struck, and one bearing an announcement of a meeting was posted in the locker room. Some anti-union busybody, and at that stage there were many more redcaps against than with us, removed the letterhead from the wall and saw to its reaching the judge. I was promptly summoned for the second confrontation with him.

This conference was quite unlike the first. There was no warm-up, for it wasn't needed. As I entered his office, Judge Craig grabbed a paper from his desk and pushed it across the desk at me, all but into my face, and heatedly demanded, "What in the name of hell is this?"

"It looks like something on our union letterhead," I said, reaching for the paper. It was the announcement of the meeting which had last been seen tacked on the locker room wall.

"I thought you were going to quit this damned business," he exclaimed.

"No sir," I corrected him, "I promised you that I'd think it over."

"And a hell of a job of thinking you've done!" he declared.

Then he calmed himself and proceeded to go to work on me. What I was doing had not only disappointed but hurt him deeply. "You have been a snake in the bosom to me. You are not being fair with me and my railroad. You aren't playing fair either with Charlie Kiler, my friend and yours, too, or he wouldn't have asked me to get you on here," he pled. He would certainly let Mr. Kiler know what I was doing. He wasn't sure he would ever again get a job for another fellow alumnus from the university, so deeply had I wounded him.

When my turn to talk came, I used it carefully. I was sorry that he felt as he did and wanted to assure him that I appreciated the favor he had done me, and always would. But I was compelled to say that I felt guilty of no wrong. Indeed, I was exercising a right, as he well knew it to be. The redcaps were doing nothing different from what others had done: the engineers, the conductors, and the Pullman porters. The judge's railroad would deal with us one day as it did with them, I freely predicted.

As I left the office of my embittered benefactor, I saw two men in the hall, both of whom had heard the dialogue through an open door. As the one, another lawyer, walked away and into another office, I heard him say to someone, "Well! The judge sure had a hot little African on his hands." The second eavesdropper was a redcap who, it turned out, had followed me as I went for the conference and stationed himself just outside the judge's door to see what would happen.

Upon walking into the locker room, I was greeted with expressions of approval, pleasure, and pride. The redcap listener had made it there ahead of me and had quickly delivered his report. This gave a fellow unionist an idea, and he promptly executed it. All of the redcaps on duty, those with us, the fence-sitters, and those against us as well, were invited to meet in an empty coach as soon as the next dull period came. At the meeting, my eavesdropping co-worker told what he had heard, in detail. Then one after another of the redcaps gave his acclaim. One of them, a holdout, said, "He sure stood up like a man. I'm one too, and I'm ready for a union card right now." We picked up seven or eight more union members, and as "Bill" Townsend, by then the international president, later said, "That did it at Twelfth Street station."

The judge kept his word. When I visited home in Champaign again, my mother told me that the judge's furniture-dealer friend, who had asked him to look out for me, had called her. The furniture man had told Mama that I had gone wrong in the city. He had also bemoaned my behavior with at least one of the Negro waiters at the Champaign Country Club. That one had let it be known out in North End of town that I had gone wrong indeed—I had gone communist!

When my encounter with the judge was reported to Townsend, he sent for me and carefully instructed what was required of me in the days immediately ahead.

"Maybe they'll bounce you. If they do, the real reason for it must be left clear," he emphasized.

The union must now work openly and with me up front. No more moving on the quiet. Ask anybody who wears a redcap to join, collect dues, deplore what's to be deplored, "give 'em hell," any time, any place, and before anybody was to be the strategy. Then if the I.C. fired me, the fledgling international union would see if the Railway Labor Act meant what it says for redcaps as other for railway workers at Twelfth Street depot.

I was not fired, but I wasn't favored at the I.C. anymore either. At first the chief usher instructed me that I was to start work at the same time set for reporting by all on the evening shift. A few days later, I was transferred to another shift, a two-man shift—the "dog-watch" it was called—from midnight to 7:30 a.m., when few trains departed and arrived and "the pickin's," the tips, were thin indeed. In addition my pass to Champaign was withdrawn. In these ways the railroad sought to punish me, though not without quiet countervailing on the part of fellow union members. As they started work at seven in the morning, their time overlapping the last hour of mine, they would "throw a few loads" my way—passing off passengers arriving after 7:30 a.m. as having arrived before then and during my duty period. More often than not the tips from such passengers during the early morning rush far outweighed the gleanings made during the long, lonely hours preceding the rush. When I wanted to go to Champaign, an older union member would intercede with the conductor of my train, and the conductor would make certain to overlook me as he took up the tickets. As one of my intercessors said, "This'll show whether the conductors stand with us redcaps, whether they really believe in unions with Negroes in them."

Before I stopped redcapping, the local was a going concern, and the I.C. station porters were under contract. The private car men were reined in, and all redcaps were paid wages at long last. The grievance committee had handled several cases and won them. In one of its earliest cases, a surly, Southern passenger "niggered" a redcap, who promptly knocked him to the floor. After the grievance committee saved the redcap's job, Townsend sent word, "Now, let's not overdo things."

I quit redcapping to have more time for the union and all the ancillary activity. Reversing the course of many people I knew who were trying to get off the WPA and into a real job, I abandoned one that had become real to get on the WPA, first on the writer's project and later to become a teacher in its labor education unit. Frequently in the evenings and on Saturdays, I would go to International's modest office at Thirty-fifth and Michigan, there volunteering assistance with anything afoot, from addressing envelopes to dipping in and out of skull sessions engaged in by the foundling union's national leadership; Townsend, its president; John Yancey, its secretary-treasurer; and Ernest Calloway. Calloway, most seasoned of all, was the son of a John L. Lewis coal miner, a Negro, born, bred, and educated as a trade unionist and editor of the union publication, *Bags and Baggage.*

Three special events I carry in memory from those days.

One Saturday Townsend took me home with him to dinner, at which the principal guest was no less a person than A. Philip Randolph, president of the Brotherhood of Sleeping Car Porters, a man for whom I held awesome respect. The man had long seemed to me a blend of racial, labor, and democratic leadership, honest, fearless, and devoted. He seemed to me stirring but self-effacing and committed to all working people, the unorganized as well as the organized, blacks but whites too. But his broad and clipped speech, coming from one neither a son of the British West Indies nor of Harvard, had left him suspect with me. Thus, I completely forget the topic of conversation. I simply remember watching Randolph and listening to his every word. When dinner was over, the blemish I thought I had seen was gone. Randolph is real! Randolph is real! I knew it.

Another of the events took hours of my time.

The general counsel for the union invited me to assist him as he prepared to go before the Railway Labor Board to remove a great cloud hanging over the union and the men it was organizing. The position of the railroads wherever the union activated was the same: "We are not compelled to bargain with you, for you do not represent employees of ours. Redcaps are not railway workers. Perhaps they are 'independent contractors,' each with his passengers. But with us, redcaps are mere privileged trespassers, allowed to solicit and carry bags as newsboys are permitted to peddle newspapers and the blind to beg on our premises." It was exciting to help document the case against this sophistry: The detailed work instructions issued by the various railroads; how they hired and fired us; uniformed and numbered us; instructed, supervised, and reprimanded us; the scope of our duties beyond services to individual passengers, such as those of custodial nature; the tipping system, the deprecations inherent in it, and its economic insufficiency. How much more than the servant in the redcap's situation and the master in the railroads' rigorous surveillance over us could have even been conceived?

The third memory is of a contribution made to *Bags and Baggage*, in which I ventured a prediction of such radical and solitary position that it was published only on condition that I use a pseudonym. Hugo L. Black had been nominated for the United States Supreme Court, and Negroes across the country were vehemently opposed to his confirmation. He was not only an Alabaman but had been named an honorary member of the Ku Klux Klan. He had been a New Dealer in the Senate, as everyone knew. But somewhere I had read that he also had represented striking unions in the courts and, as a minor court judge, had often ruled for the little man, black as well as white. So I read whatever else I could find about the man. I began to feel that here was a true liberal, big enough to speak and act for the rights of the people, Negroes too, once he was no longer beholden to Alabama voters. The Ku Klux Klan card I saw as a symbol of a "connection" as useful to Black, the politician, with his poor white constituency in Alabama, as being a Knight of Pythias would be to a Negro politician on the South Side of Chicago. I argued thusly and went out on a lonely limb to predict that Black would behave toward race issues as he has.

My work in labor education for the WPA for $90 monthly, I believe it was, coupled with helping out the redcaps' union, led me from one gathering to another of those with causes to espouse. I served on a YWCA committee concerned with adult education; recruited members for the Chicago teachers' union during a city-wide conference of WPA teachers; and did picket-line duty during the newly organized Newspaper Guild's strike against the Hearst papers in Chicago. I went to this mass meeting one week and that one the next; paraded with labor groups in the Loop; and joined in a mass memorialization of those who died in the massacre at Tom Girdler's Republic Steel. I went to lectures, leftish plays, art exhibits, book sales, and parties, too.

At the parties, the boogie and the blues were well done and the conversation bright, but almost always the parties wound up in lengthy debates. More often than not, everybody present exhibited informed concerns and voiced strong protests, especially respecting racial injustices. But the what to do right off and the long-range, grand strategy split us apart. I talked little, but listened and stayed late. Then I began to see what Townsend had tried to flag for me. There were people at the parties who knew too clearly just what should be done, and that only that should be done. They said so in the same language. They talked of self-determination for Negroes, set off in some Southern state or states, as if they were a separate people; in fact, they had a way of saying "the Negro people," and it would irritate me, like the "you people" whites so often used. I suppose I appeared tractable and easy pickings because I said so little, beyond a nod or grunt, as the discussion went on. Whatever the reason, one night I was offered a certain card to sign. I could belong to "the party" I was told, either under my real name or an assumed one; I could wear a figurative hood. It was no go for me; I knew it was all no good. I like to think that I would have known as much, even without the warnings I had received.

In 1940, and this time in pure service of my own interests, I left the WPA to take a real, though temporary, position. I was appointed assistant supervisor of census for the First Congressional District, a responsibility of substance that paid well and had a fine-sounding title.

This new job was to be satisfying in several other ways. Like thousands upon thousands of other college-educated people during the Great Depression, I had successfully written Federal Civil Service examinations one after the other but had never succeeded in securing an appointment. I recall at one time being on the register of eligibles for eleven different positions. The fact is that in those days, an applicant was required to declare his race and provide a picture of himself. But the general odds against one, among the too many applicants, being picked for one of the too few openings were formidable indeed. They were so great that a Negro hesitated to ascribe his failures to color prejudice on the part of appointing officials, though he might strongly feel that it lurked in the background. Thus it would be good to get started in the federal service through a side door. Moreover, the sanctioning official (or indeed, as such matters actually went, the appointing official) was Congressman Arthur W. Mitchell, the Negro congressman who had a few months previously refused to approve my placement in a junior attorneyship with a federal agency. Mr. Mitchell, himself an immigrant to Chicago all the way from Alabama, had cold-shouldered me, saying, "What did you ever do for me?" While I was born and reared in Illinois, I had moved to Chicago several months behind him and had no answer to the question, save that he had never asked me for a favor, nor had I ever been in a position to volunteer it. Mr. Mitchell had picked the supervisor who in turn picked me to do the work. So I would show the congressman my wares. Especially would I see to a quality of enumeration that wouldn't require a good bit of redoing, as was rumored to have been necessary when the Republican Oscar De Priest was congressman of the district a decade before.

But I lost the chance to put an able foot forward for the Negro district, while also showing Mr. Mitchell a thing or two. Fate dealt me a hand which all but took me out of the game of life. I had no more than finished selecting and training the nearly two hundred census-takers, when a cold seized me. The cold was followed by pneumonia, pleurisy, emphysema, and a lung infection, one after another. My weight went from 162 to 120 pounds. I lived in a bed for nearly nine months and on the way back upon my feet learned to drink cod liver oil in the raw as if it were fine wine.

Once I was able to work again, it was for the sales tax division of the Illinois State Department of Finance in Springfield. Here I worked as a lawyer, preparing legal memoranda and appeal briefs, reviewing records, and making recommendations for disposition of contested cases. But I was not permitted the title of "attorney." Nor was it felt that businessmen would appear before a Negro "hearing officer." I was simply an "investigator." I was the first Negro in a white-collar position in the Springfield office of the division, and upon reporting for duty as an "investigator" was handed the standard form for completion by messengers. The secretary who thus ushered me into service had not read the letter of instruction; she had simply seen my color and attempted to classify me in accordance with prevailing custom. After I finished my first week of work, buried in the books in the library of the State Supreme Court, my supervisor told me to call any one of the stenographers to take my dictation. One of the girls who heard this immediately and cavalierly declared, "Well! I draw the line on that!"—a position in which the others appeared about to join. The secretary to the supervisor then volunteered herself to take the dictation and to save her boss a problem for the moment. The hearing officers themselves were friendly until the noon hour approached, when they would back away and join up for lunch without me. They ate where I could not in Springfield; there were few places in the state capital which obeyed the state law against racial discrimination in places of public accommodation.

The Republicans wrested the capital from the Democrats in November of 1940 and by mid-1941 supplanted me with one of their own.

THE MAN FOR IT

I was back in Chicago for only a few days when I ran into an officer in the state office of the National Youth Administration [NYA] who called and asked me to drop in to see him at my convenience. I did so, and he offhandedly asked me if I would like to work for the NYA.[1] For two weeks I performed a series of assignments, casually made and easily carried out, when I was called in again by the same official. He explained that there was a vacancy downstate in East St. Louis, and what I had been doing in the state office had not been a permanent position. I could have the East St. Louis job, if I wished it.

He had done a clever job of combined orientation and observation on me, without my awareness of it, and had concluded that I was fit to take on troubles in East St. Louis. Continuing his guile, he told me little more than the title of the vacant position and not that it was a hot spot. Several times he did muse aloud, "I think you're the man for it." Young, eager,

---

1. The NYA was a New Deal agency created to help find work and educational opportunities for people between the ages of sixteen and twenty-five. It operated from 1935 until 1943 and was under the purview of different agencies in that time.

and job-hungry as I was, it did not occur to me that "it" was something special and to ask him precisely what "it" meant. I rushed off to East St. Louis, blind and in the dark.

The heavy Negro population in East St. Louis lived in what was rather a part of the back yards for St. Louis, a squalid stretch of railroad tracks crossed by roads filled with cinders and lined with nondescript frame houses, many of them of makeshift construction and having never known paint. In the houses were people either drawn, or a generation or two removed, from the black belt of the south, especially Arkansas and Mississippi. They had been pulled from the cotton fields to railroading, meat packing, steel foundries, oil refining, and chemicals. But in 1940 many an East St. Louis plant closed. When a Negro managed to have a job, most often in was at Monsanto Chemical, "Aluminum Ore," or on the NYA. To the Negroes in town, the NYA was a major industry.

There was an average of seven or eight hundred Negro youngsters, eighteen to twenty-five years of age, on the NYA program. They were paid wages for a forty-hour week of work-training, some of them in such pedestrian occupations as laundry helper and baking (for women), and woodworking for men, but mostly they were in defense-related skills such as welding, sheet-metal working, forge machine operation for the men, as well as power sewing machine training for women. It was my job as personnel manager to interview, hire, discipline, and counsel these young people.

A few days in town, and I had repeatedly heard a story that brought to mind the expression which several times had slipped out as I was being sent to East St. Louis, "I think you're the man for it." The story, in brief, though relayed in more entertaining detail, was that my predecessor had been released because of his inability to remain the personnel manager, and that alone, in his relations with several attractive young women on the program. Let it be a lesson for me, I thought, and I promised myself to avoid the delightful but errant paths taken by the man who had gone before me.

But a few days more, and I was to learn that the "it" was a serious matter indeed.

The training operation looked good. Seven to eight hundred young black people were "off the streets," and working in three eight-hour shifts, around the clock. They were "measuring up," most of them coming from and taking pay home to families certified to be in need of relief. They enjoyed instruction and work supervision from competent, well-trained Negro teachers, and administration by highly respected young men from town, who had gone off to college, "made good," and returned home to serve the community. They were about to break a vicious circle—Negroes would not train for skilled jobs because they could not have them, and they could not have the jobs because they had not trained themselves for them. Someone who was somebody, someone to put some stock in, had said that the vicious circle could and must be broken. Mary McLeod Bethune, "large, black, full-bosomed, and strong-limbed" with "jutting jaw and mighty stride" had been to town and spoken her piece. "You get the training, we'll see to the jobs," was the message from the inspiring head of the NYA's Division of Negro Affairs. And it had fallen on open ears.

But, as I arrived, the program's pulse beat weakly. In those very shops of greatest potential, power sewing for the women and machine operation for the men, trouble was plain to see. Women who had once reached daily production rates of twenty-five or thirty garments (pajamas, as I recall) were finishing only ten or fifteen each day. Youths who had mastered each of the several types of installations in the machine shop had lost interest also. The trouble at surface level, in both cases, was that too many of the trainees were repeating the courses of instruction just to remain on the job; they had absorbed everything that was offered; the learning challenge for them was gone. They were as bored as they could be. They were putting in time only to be able to draw a check and help feed the folks at home.

Besides, I was told, the machine shop trainees had never had but half the loaf: the practice but not the theory. White trainees in machine shop were being taught "blueprints" but the Machinists' Union local had successfully said, "Not the Negroes." This I protested and was properly joined and supported all the way up, I suppose. Word soon came back from Washington to schedule the theory: the government was mightier than the Machinists' local.

Still the larger and common problem remained and seemed to me itself to point to the answer. Get some of those trained for skilled jobs into the jobs, and the program would also become meaningful for those still in training. The time had come to deliver on the job placement, or else the training itself could not deliver.

So I did the next natural thing to do. I went to the local office of the state employment service to talk to the manager about jobs for Negro NYA trainees. The answer was blunt, straight and hard: there were no such jobs, and there was nothing he could do about it. Then I learned that white NYA trainees were being placed. When job orders came in marked "for whites" or unmarked, whites only were referred to the employers. So back I went to see the manager and asked that black trainees be sent at least when the employer had not ruled out blacks. But he would only say that if and when an order came in for Negroes, he would call us. I protested the acceptance of "for whites" orders; objected to the assumption that whites only were acceptable when an order came in "color blind"; and again suggested employment office responsibility for initiative on behalf of the Negro trainees. The protest was of no avail; indeed, the manager was operating according to Hoyle, though at the time Hoyle and Uncle Sam were one and the same, the federal government having assumed jurisdiction over all state employment offices. Soon I had won sympathizers on the employment service staff, one white as well as several Negroes. In this way, I was alerted several times that job orders bearing no color label had come in, and each time I had sent youngsters from my program to show up at the same time as those white youngsters officially called in. This tactic, designed to make it highly convenient for the manager to himself give racial equity a trial run, was beyond his capacity for a constructive response. It upset him so much that he decided to put a stop to it.

He wrote to the state NYA office complaining, as he had with me, that my responsibility was with training, not placement. He demanded that the NYA order me to stay in my own backyard—backyard indeed. A memorandum followed from the state director of NYA personnel confirming the employment service's position and ordering me to stay out of its office.

Not having been forbidden to canvass the "employees wanted" section in the classified ad pages of the newspapers, I continued with this practice and one day saw an item of interest. A big laundry over in St. Louis needed girls as shirt menders and preferred those who could handle power sewing machines. Color presented no problem, its laundering employees were Negroes, and I placed two girls. The manager explained, "Our white girls at power sewing had learned how to use these machines at our expense, but kept taking off for the garment makers. Guess I can't blame 'em. This was enough of a tip to send me in two directions, the other big laundries and the garment manufacturers. Several more laundry visits turned up openings at one of them for two more trainees. Moreover, they were starting as its first Negro employees and they succeeded without any racial repercussions.

Once across the river, poking around in the laundries, I went other places. Among them was the Missouri state employment office, whose threshold I had not been forbidden to cross by the Illinois NYA office, at least not explicitly. There I stumbled into an interesting piece of intelligence. As nearly as I remember its details, this was it. A huge plant was under construction somewhere in the St. Louis area for Winchester Arms, itself armed with government contracts for small weapons manufacture. It had been expected that as soon as the building was completed and the work lines made ready, they would be manned by personnel from three government-run defense training programs, including the NYA. But someone had let slip that it was Winchester's intention to train its own operators and not to use people of any color from any of the three government programs!

I was shocked by the horrendous illogic of what I had been told and promptly sent forward in NYA channels a memorandum passing the information on. Not many days later I received a commendatory note. That same state director of NYA personnel who was keeping me out of an employment office in Illinois found it wonderful that I had gone into one over in Missouri and picked up such significant information.

But since my conferences with the manager of the employment office out in East St. Louis remained forbidden, while our male NYA trainees continued without promise of work, I was forced into a bit of deviousness. I stayed out of the manager's office; he was instead visited by members of the East St. Louis Urban League Organizing Committee, who exerted the same pressures upon them as I had previously. The committee was bona fide. East St. Louis certainly needed a local affiliate of that national organization concerned with conditions of urban Negroes and devoted to the objective of "opportunity not alms" in their behalf. The National Urban League office was in communication with the committee, made up of several Negro businessmen and professionals, and backed up by younger people compelled to remain behind-the-scene since they were schoolteachers as well as employment office and NYA employees. The office manager was soon either suspicious or penetrating enough to sense my hand in the committee and informed the state office that I was in violation of the injunction he had won.

On this occasion, however, the complaint provoked no formal censure. The NYA would hamstring a Negro personnel man bent on racially equal opportunity but would not tackle the Urban League. What happened instead was that my behavior became a subject of discussion at a meeting at the local administrative center for the NYA. The office chief and his deputy were both white. My own supervisor, a projects manager, was Negro, as also was a third official in the administrative center. Several particulars of the discussion impressed me. My two Negro superiors said little or nothing, in that passive way signifying at least that they were not against me (as I well knew). But the chief made plain that I was "pressing things too hard for this kind of community." This was, of course, to avoid appearing strongly to oppose the efforts at job-placement as well as to avoid squaring to the issue himself. But his deputy followed me out into the hall after the meeting and made for himself quite a point, an observation designed to appear beneficial to Negro as well as white interests in the community.

"If you are not careful, you'll bring about another race riot in this town," he warned.

East St. Louis had once had a race riot, a terrible one, which left a hundred Negroes dead and six thousand homeless, so the books say. Moreover, the rioting had grown out of the Negro search for employment in war work in 1916. I knew, of course, that history could repeat itself, and the point that I, a stranger, was urging on the repetition did shake me, as it was intended to. But it did not dissuade me from my course. One of the Negroes to whom I talked and who knew the NYA deputy chief as a former school official, as I recall, said, "If you quit, you'll be doing what he's after. He's against our race, not race riots." This, of course, was not quite to the issue. Strangely enough, though perhaps not for a newspaper man worth his salt, an editorial man for the local newspaper called me in for a talk and went straight to the question with me. He volunteered an interest in my effort and got me to promise to talk with him again should a race issue arise about which he wished to question me. This encouraged me to tell him about the riot flag that had been raised. He laughed and then said, "I have heard about it. But the more of those kids that get work, the less likelihood of racial trouble. Forget it. Keep on doing what you're doing." And I did.

At long last one day, an exciting possibility appeared. Jobs, jobs made-to-order for the folks in the machine shop! There was no word from the sources of long hoping, not from within the NYA, nor the employment office, nor Winchester Arms. But there hope was. It jumped upon me as I started out of the post office, where I had gone to drop a letter, and walked by a bulletin board. Post office bulletin boards had come off my reading list. Hadn't I culled from their postings announcement of eleven civil service examinations and successfully written each but all to no avail? But when the sensitivity is there, the corner of the eye will perform wonders. I glanced at the board, cluttered with photos of wanted men, the postmaster's pronouncements and all, when from it leaped two words—MACHINE OPERATORS. The Rock Island Arsenal wanted them badly and in a hurry.

My heart beat hard and fast, my head fairly spun. The call indicated that *beginning* machine operators would be welcomed. The jobs were under civil service, but the examination was unassembled [test takers did not have to appear at a set time]. Qualified applicants were asked to come to Rock Island prepared to commence work. And the arsenal, of course, was part of the government, Uncle Sam himself!

Then came the sobering thoughts. Civil Service had not done anything for me; why should it for my kids in the machine shop? The Machinists were the Machinists, and if they had tried to block the blueprint reading in East St. Louis, they'd be standing across the doorway at the arsenal. The Negro newspapers were saying that in Chicago, Detroit, and other big cities, Negroes were being denied defense jobs, and why expect it not to happen in little Rock Island? And worst of all, I had read or heard tell that an arsenal as well as the Navy Yard in Philadelphia were giving the runaround to Negroes who wanted to train or had somehow managed to train and qualify for machine work.

Still there was a straw to reach for. Only a few weeks before, after a threatened Negro march on Washington under the leadership of A. Philip Randolph, President Roosevelt had issued an executive order establishing the Fair Employment Practices Commission. The FEPC was to see to it that there would be no discrimination in the employment of workers in defense industries or government. Work at the Rock Island Arsenal is decidedly both, I felt, so I decided to give that announcement a try. If and when my applicant for an arsenal job is turned away on some pretext or other, as I deeply feared would happen, I would see to it that the arsenal had the FEPC on its hands. For the purpose of this test, I knew I must use the best-qualified youngster I had to offer.

I was already certain as to who was the best trainee in the machine shop. I had just reviewed the entire payroll for eligibility against maximum age and other requirements. One of the other requirements was that a youth could not remain on the NYA program while attending high school full time. This was exactly what David Lamphrey, not long in East St. Louis from Mississippi, was doing and doing well, as both the high school principal and his NYA supervisor attested. The former had said that David was quite a little scholar, and the latter had said that he was far and away the best machine operator in the shop. And I had decided not to let red tape rob either program of so much talent! Besides David was a hard worker and got along well with everyone. I picked David to pioneer for our program at the arsenal for the same reasons of substance that had prompted me to overlook his technical ineligibility for continued training.

David's supervisor accompanied us to Rock Island, not to coach David—he didn't need any last-minute prompting—but at my request. I wanted the instructor to be present so that when David was rejected, there would be three of us, one an expert, able to complain to the FEPC and swear to the story of the discrimination as he had seen it. But the examiner at the arsenal excused himself, took David away with him, and, behind a closed door, put him to trial. I then thought that I was in the midst of a losing cause and without the expert witness-to-be. But a few minutes later the examiner and David emerged with the face of each blank. Calling me aside, the examiner then quietly announced his judgment.

"How many more do you have back there who are as nearly ready to go to work as this lad? We want 'em here as fast as you can get 'em here," he said.

Good news, the chariot had come!

Bright and early the next morning, David and I were over in St. Louis to purchase the calipers and the micrometer he had been told to bring with him as he reported for duty at the arsenal. The hardware store which carried machinists' tools was located on Market Street near the Union Depot, a skid row area that included many Negroes among its habitués. We walked into the store and began sifting around. We looked about and kept looking about, while the two clerks in the rear of the store continued their conversation, seemingly oblivious of our presence. Always expectant of slight and still fearful that I was in the middle of a dream, I was about to wonder if the Machinists allowed Negroes to buy their tools. Barring the half-thought, I walked away from David, addressed the two clerks and said, "This young man wants to make a purchase here. He wants to buy machinists' tools!"

The older man replied apologetically, "Oh, I thought you fellows were just looking around. Lots of fellows do, you know."

After learning that David was bound for the arsenal, and as he completed the sale, he added to his apology: "Well I've been right here for twenty years, and this is the first time I've ever sold a micrometer and calipers to colored."

As we drove back to East St. Louis, I said to that little machinist beginner from Mississippi, "That guy in the store thought we were a couple of more bums off the street, colored bums. But he found out that we were in there for business. That's something!" The quiet, modest one at my side gave a little grunt and grinned.

The next evening, our NYA Defense Training Center in East St. Louis closed its entire, around-the-clock activity for a couple of hours. The trainees on all three shifts, the staff, and some of our friends in the community assembled in a church auditorium to hear what had happened at the arsenal and on Market Street, to get the full story of how little David Lamphrey was about to slay himself a Goliath. Mary McCleod Bethune was being borne out. Others would soon go to Rock Island to join David, to start at salaries higher than anybody on the staff! Still others from all of the shops would sooner or later have jobs. As the kids listened and cheered that night, I could feel the morale rising.

In the days that followed, those NYA youngsters worked harder than ever, and the shops began to hum. One group after another went off to Rock Island. One by one clerical trainees began to depart, headed as far away as Washington, D.C., and some of them later sent for others to take jobs they had discovered. Now and then a trainee was leaving another shop—welding or forge or woodworking.

Nine or ten months of trying to be "the man for it" in East St. Louis and a telegram came to me at my rooming place. State headquarters for the Illinois State Employment Service was willing to take me off one of those eleven lists of eligibles for a civil service job. "Waiting lists" we children of the Great Depression called them. I was offered a position as employment interviewer and I was interested. But the telegram included what I was certain would prove a joker. I was to report for an interview to the manager of the local employment office, the same official with whom I had bickered repeatedly and who had successfully asked that his office be "off limits" to me. He would do me in for sure, I felt.

I had waited long for a civil service job offer. The position was permanent, as the NYA job was not. It would take me back to Chicago, where by then there were two brothers living. There was a girlfriend there, too, and it was she who was to become the girlfriend for keeps. So despite my fear, I went for the interview.

And it happened that I could go with a certain card up my sleeve. The Urban League Organizing Committee had learned of the job offer, and one of its officers had worked up its offer to me. If I would remain in the community, doing as I had done, several Negro businessmen and doctors would raise fifty dollars monthly to supplement my NYA salary. This would mean an income better than that the employment interviewer job paid. Besides maybe they could turn the Organizing Committee into a full-fledged local Urban League and have me made its executive secretary. If the employment office manager kept me out of the employment service, I would simply stay in East St. Louis, one day perhaps to "watchdog" him for a local Urban League.

The interview was short and pleasant. No questions were asked; the interviewer knew of me firsthand. He would write to his state office immediately, he said. Yes, I thought, and I know what the letter will spell.

But in a few days I was back in Chicago in the midst of weeklong orientation for employment interviewing. As the week ended, each of the initiates was handed his personnel file to take with him to the office of initial assignment, I pulled from my file the letter written by the East St. Louis office manager. It was distinctly and completely complimentary. His working relations with me were expressly referred to, and the ways in which I had pressed him seemed to him to assure that the employment service was getting a new interviewer of capacity and larger promise.

Three months later I was invited off another of those civil service "waiting" lists, to accept a position as wage-hour inspector for the Labor Department in its Chicago regional office. It had not happened without the intervention of an Illinois senator to whom I had complained that, time after time, persons I had outranked as a result of the written examination had been employed. The regional director had himself conferred with me, offering a thin excuse for passing over me that was then a familiar one of bitter taste to job-seeking Negroes. The job had not been offered because the applicant was "over-prepared"; he would be "unhappy" in the job. Altogether ignored was the fact that either the excessive training was deliberate or the lesser job was sought in an effort to surmount the color barrier. One was further and personally penalized, either for the extra effort or the humility exercised, in the face of racial reality.

The Labor Department job lasted one day, a Friday. For that evening I found at home a telegram offering me a position in Washington at an annual salary a thousand dollars more than that paid a wage-hour inspector.

Once the long-awaited rain started, it had begun to pour.

The following week, I reported to the United States Housing Authority to commence work as an associate race relations advisor. Here was the promise of an adventure, challenging and satisfying.

In 1942 the separate-but-equal doctrine, blessed by the U.S. Supreme Court, continued rock hard. The low-rent public housing program used its racial relations service not against discrimination but to achieve equality within separation. The service sought what it called "equitable participation" for nonwhites in the occupancy of the housing but also in its construction and management. Even this limited mission was carried forward against the opposition of operating officials who either feared it, saw it as a sheer nuisance, or sought to use it as mere window dressing. But the service itself, I soon saw, was superbly businesslike, as it doggedly worked its way into participation in the formulation of policy and procedure; skillfully developed means for the measurement of "equity" results; carefully selected, trained, and deployed its personnel; and sought to cultivate the decision-makers.

Indeed I admired it for more than its craftsmanship. What intrigued and excited me was the way it looked ahead. It sought equality within separation as a floor only. For it also supported and urged experiment with and the example of housing equally available to all and without separation. It was beginning in addition to catalogue the social and economic costs of racially separate housing, to suggest to all who would listen techniques for undoing segregated patterns and better ways of achieving open occupancy for housing when newly built and initially tenanted. That long ago, its people were seeing and bringing others to realize that segregated housing serves as the basic mechanism for racial separation, de facto segregation, and discrimination.

So, there I was, apprenticed to Frank S. Horne, B. T. McGraw, and Constance Robinson Morrow, people who were at once creative craftsmen, superb teachers, and social visionaries.

It was too good to last more than three months, when still another job came my way. This time I had not tried to make the "waiting" list, but somehow it bore my name, and the offer was not to be denied.

The new position was as Private First Class in the United States Army.

The Army and Its Apartheid

THE RACIAL SYSTEM IN THE WAR YEARS

The policy of the War Department is not to intermingle colored and white enlisted personnel in the same regimental organizations. This policy has proven satisfactory over a long period of years and to make changes would produce situations destructive to morale and detrimental to the preparation for national defense.
—U.S. War Department, 1940

I suppose that I was predestined to be a misfit in the army. "Soldier" is a game I had not played as a child. As a man, I saw the military as a business of which I wanted no part.

In the months immediately following the Pearl Harbor disaster, whenever young men gathered to themselves, the conversation sooner or later grew serious indeed. They discussed the war, their draft classifications, and their prospects for call. One spring evening in 1942, I sat engaged in such a discussion with friends of mine, college mates, all of us Negro and in the early thirties. Nobody was interested in weaseling out; each sought the service alternative most to his liking. Two were inclined to volunteer for the army, with the privilege of going on into training to become administrative officers. A third would mark time but watch for opportunities to his liking as he waited. A fourth said little but we knew that he hoped for an assignment as a newspaper correspondent. I had little to say also. Only two years before I had run a gauntlet of respiratory disorders and knew that a tell-tale scar remained on my lung. Perhaps I would not be acceptable for service.

In June I was in Washington at work for a civilian agency, where I observed an interesting phenomenon on several occasions. A white co-worker last seen in a business suit would take off and in a day or so return in officer's attire, especially the Navy's. Getting a direct commission was not so simple, I knew, and the wangling would be far more complicated for me, not only a stranger in the capital but a Negro, for whom not many openings so labeled would exist. One possible approach would be a deliberate search for Negro-tagged spots and to pick up from there. But I made no move of any kind.

The truth is that I was fully convinced that any position anywhere in the services would be miserable. I abhorred the idea so much that I was unable to consider the options. The whole appeared so evil, I sought no less evil part within it.

I was thirty-one years old and too mature to be looking for fun, comradeship, adventure, or glory. I didn't believe they were really to be found in the military service anyway. While I held no systematic religious or philosophical view against war, worthy to be called conscientious objection, I strongly felt that all war was costly, wasteful, useless, contrived by a greedy few, and a reflection of a variety of social shortcomings. The military system was also hard on my democratic impulses, though I was not so naive as to expect the army to function as a democratic society, even when appended to it. The functions of the rank and command systems and all the trappings, the uniforms, the insignia, the salute, and the like, I could understand. I had seen them at work as I had reluctantly undergone basic ROTC at the university, as well as in slight degree and awkward though effective fashion in the Boy Scouts, where I gave the commands and received the salutes. Still I disliked them. I preferred being a part of action which proceeds from consensus arrived at by those I had helped choose and in which people participate because they agree upon and seek its objectives.

Most of all I was racially reluctant. I was dead sure that as a Negro and wherever I landed, I would be as unwelcome as I was certain to be subjugated. I would be dually disadvantaged, and for a net result greater than the sum of the two. In teaching those youngsters in my Negro History Club, I had stopped to stress how the Negro had fought, bled, and died for his country, to defend her and, most important, even to bring her into being and to help secure his own freedom. But he never had been wanted in uniform; his service was accepted mostly when and after it had become clear that his help could not be done without, if victory was to be had; and yet he had always acquitted himself well, only to find when it was over how despised he remained. The thanklessness in it had been amply illustrated in the wake of World War I, when returning soldiers were lynched in uniform. I had told them, too, the story of how Colonel Charles Young, a West Pointer and the army's highest-ranking Negro officer, had been retired for disability as World War I started to avoid the promotion and the active command due him. He had exposed the lie by riding a horse from Wilberforce College in Ohio to Washington, only to be retained but soon afterward shipped off to black Haiti as a military attaché, there to die of tropical fever.

Now the trouble was that the lesson so taught had stayed with its teacher. So I did not relish what I knew had to be faced, unless that lung proved bad. Still I wanted no side door out. There were people who were saying it was "a white man's war"—white against yellow—and "let the white man fight it." But that I could not swallow. I had always protested the white man's putting me aside and was not about to put myself there.

Poor soldier as I was certain to be, if soldier at all, I remained a good civilian waiting to hear from his draft board.

In October, the call came, and my induction was in motion. The physical exam was held in Washington, where the white doctors found my feet "planus" in the third degree, in accordance with their prejudices. They also found my lungs good enough for Uncle. The doctor I politely queried about the lung I knew to be damaged laughed and said, "Oh, that. Well, there's a scar there about the size of a quarter. It looks like a good one. We take lots like it."

I had chosen not to change draft boards as I moved from job to job, duly notifying the Champaign board of each new residence. In this way I had hoped to land outside of the South, an objective toward which I seemed safely moving, as I was sent to a reception center at Fort Custer in Battle Creek, Michigan.

But my reception was not to be like eating cornflakes, even in Battle Creek. We were at the fort only a few hours; Uncle Sam was in a big hurry.

During the accelerated processing, I bumped into what was either the cold, callousness of the army or its color crudity, as I took the classification test. As a huge group of us inductees were being led to the culling, like sheep to slaughter, I properly tightened up. For I had determined to become an officer candidate and had been told that the first step was to score a minimum of 110 on the AGC (Army General Classification) test. I suddenly recalled having taken such a general intelligence test, the grading system for which included a reduction in the positive score as a penalty for skipping questions. Specifically, I became most anxious to know whether I could afford initially to skip the questions in mathematics (forever a weak area for me in which I tended to flounder and even panic) and leave them for answering after I had completed the others. This would be my strategy, provided there would be no penalty for leaving altogether untouched those math questions that time would not permit my attempting to handle.

During the test, the choices in the mathematics area seemed more puzzling and time-consuming than ever. I was afraid to skip them and probably missed nine out of ten as I proceeded in a nervous sweat.

The brief stay at Custer was nevertheless long enough for an unhappy encounter with a couple of "ninety-day wonders." I passed by the two quickly fabricated second lieutenants, hungry for obeisance, and failed to salute them. I was still in civilian dress and obviously a novitiate. Nevertheless, one of them sharply called out, "Soldier!" and beckoned me to him. The two then marched me ahead of them to their battery area and before one of their superior officers. There I was "dressed down but good," as it is said, for my discourtesy.

Those who had accosted me were Negro officers of a Negro field artillery outfit, converted from an infantry outfit of the Illinois state guard. They had demanded from me what they were not getting and were less free to force from white enlistees, I felt. I was part of their special province; they were privileged to trespass against me by those who withheld from them support in getting salutes from white soldiers. I would have wagered that not many white soldiers were saluting Negro officers at Custer.

TWO OF EVERYTHING

That was but a mild introduction for what was to come at Camp Stewart, near Savannah, Georgia, where I was soon shipped. As we left Custer, we were a trainload of enlistees without the slightest idea of where we were going, but we were going for sure. We knew for certain that we were in the South, even the sleepy-heads and those who had been oblivious to the changing vegetation, once we left the train and were herded through the railway depot. For it was laden with two of everything, ticket windows, waiting rooms, restaurants, and toilets. The one was marked "white," the other "colored"; in each instance neither was much, but the "colored" was invariably sloppier and smaller. It made me feel sick in the pit of my stomach. Systematic Jim Crow, color labels everywhere, struck me hard. I was more accustomed to the sneakier, Northern type.

Savannah, Georgia, was my gateway into the army, and the apartheid with which its railway depot confronted and sickened me was the army's racial system too. For this was not 1963, when President Kennedy could say that "the military services lead almost every other segment of our society in establishing equality for all Americans," nor a year later, when the Department of Defense could safely boast that "in fact, the military base or post is probably the most integrated environment to be found in America." Instead it was 1942, when the military services in matters of race followed the most racially retrograde segments of our society and they and their bases were tightly and systematically segregated.

Camp Stewart was an anti-aircraft training center. All Negro personnel served with Negro units. The units were all-Negro except for white line officers. No Negroes commanded white troops at any level, nor did Negroes even officially pray for other than their own. Negro chaplains and other specialists served only Negroes.

The automatic weapons battalion in which I received basic training was no exception. All of its officers, in both its headquarters and line batteries, were white. In my own battery, one of them, a first lieutenant from Alabama, soon showed himself to be a racial brute and sadist of first rank. In that battery, as I suspect in many another Negro outfit at Stewart, there were men of no usefulness to the army. I remember well the charity two such men received at the hands of the lieutenant. One of them was so mentally limited that when he talked the saliva flew from his mouth and he simply could not learn right, left, and about face. But the lieutenant more than once summoned the hapless and pitiful creature before the formation, there to make a spectacle of him for no one's enjoyment save his sadistic self.

The second soldier of limited intelligence came from the back swamps of Florida and once told me that until the army issued shoes to him, he had never worn any new ones. This soldier was continuously refitted with shoes but his feet remained sore-ridden. Morning after morning, he could not make reveille, not because he was unable to stand in the latest pair of shoes but because he could not get them on his sensitive, swollen feet. One morning, after finding the soldier again on sick call, the lieutenant flew into a rage and, after cursing and charging the sore-footed absentee with "gold-bricking," called for volunteers.

"I want four men to go in that hut and bring him, his god-damn cot and all, and dump him here in front of us," he proclaimed.

Nobody volunteered to join him in his inhumanity, though he loudly repeated the call, "All right, who'll volunteer?"

I stood directly in front of the bellowing brute, drawing comfort and strength from the resentment I could feel running like electricity through the black ranks about me. Yet I was afraid, too, afraid that I was headed for trouble for a direct command, certain to take me in, was next in order, and I was determined not to move. But the order did not come; the lieutenant yielded up his sadism to the indignation he also felt exuding from the men.

During the first few weeks of basic training, there was little or none of an active color problem. We were Negroes, completely off to ourselves, except for our white officers. Besides, we were pretty much confined to the battalion area.

I was in stride with much of the "breaking in." Reveille was no problem, my father having taught his boys when they were six or seven years old to hit the floor shortly after he had drunk his first coffee at five or so. The bedmaking and other housekeeping duties were easily done; Mama had seen to that, since there were five boys and no girls among us. An early bit of K.P. duty was a sop; I had washed many more dishes at that Chinese restaurant back in Champaign, not to speak of my share at home. Helping to police the area about my hut came naturally, too. Papa had conducted my brothers and me in that kind of operation on our yard at home "front, back, and all around," whenever the notion struck him.

But there were aspects of the routine and training which chafed me. For these, my past had left me unfitted. It was not so much that strawberry jello plopped in the middle of that cold lamb gravy (I had tried to decline) but the day-in and day-out flatness of the food. Besides, it was served family style, though eaten in the manner of hogs, as the men pushed, shoved, grabbed, and gulped. As unexciting as the food was, I had to eat, and several times my inhibitions left me eating more lightly than I would have chosen. Worse yet was another conflict with my style of living, it was permissible, even expected, that missing gear be stolen to enable passing hut inspection—a sort of "white" theft—which I never learned. It was easier to say, "Sir, I don't know where it is" and to be told, "Soldier, you'll never make it."

Several other strains were more serious; they involved matters closer to substance in the making of a soldier. The salute had always bothered me, either to give it or receive it (as I had as an assistant scoutmaster). One day during a quiz session on military courtesy, after I had come to know the "first louie" from Alabama, and he had learned that I was among the several more literate men in his platoon, he turned to me for an explanation of the salutes in line with that provided in the *Soldier's Handbook.*

"Sir," I said, "It's this way. A salute recognizes the rank and uniform of the officer, not his personality. No matter what a soldier might think of an officer—he might really think he is a s.o.b.—he gives him the salute to which he's entitled."

"That's correct but a little overdone," he said, cutting his eyes sharply at me, as the snickering I had sought quickly died away.

Marching was plentiful but hard on me. While my feet were not as planus as the doctor had classified them, I was indeed overweight, out of condition, and had only twenty-eight inches of inseam to my trousers, so short-legged am I. The longer the conditioning marches were stretched, with a wind-up at "double-time," the more of a laggard I became.

The guns were also a bother, both the carbine for personal use and the big, forty-millimeter gun, mounted on wheels. I never really learned much about either. Indeed, I was in all honesty much in the position of a battery mate of mine during the wrap-up inspection following basic training. A major on the inspection team had asked him several specific questions about the forty-millimeter gun, none of which he could even attempt answering. Finally, in trying to avoid further embarrassment for all concerned, one of our officers turned to him saying, "Private Childs, why don't you just tell the major anything you do know about this gun?"

"Well, sir," said Childs, "It has tires on it, tires just like my automobile back in Chicago."

I not only was weak on nomenclature and without mechanical aptitude, I had not the slightest interest in the firing of either gun. When we got around to practice-firing the M-1 rifle on the range, it turned out that I was a pretty fair shot. My aptitude likely resulted from my being so unanxious about firing it as naturally to squeeze instead of pull the trigger, a procedure precisely the secret of rifle marksmanship.

Then one evening, after a trip to the rifle range, I suddenly recalled the one time I'd ever gone hunting. I had nipped a rabbit with a bullet fired from a .22 rifle, making him sort of flip-flop in the air before he hobbled away. I was left worrying whether he would die or be crippled for life. I realized that deep down in me, shooting another human being wasn't there. Could I get angry enough to shoot from skin? No. Who's to make me boil? The enemy, a bunch of fellows caught in a trap, like myself? Why, I had never even felt like shooting the second lieutenant who does upset me one time after another, and acts as—is—my enemy, and wants to be my master to boot. Would I shoot in self-defense? What self-defense? It's self-exposure I've let myself in for, the trap, again. That night was a rough one for me, talking to myself like that.

Meanwhile I grew close to the men in my unit, especially those in my platoon, performing a variety of services for them. There was one who wanted no more than for me to keep his money for him after payday until, bit by bit, the other gamblers had taken it. There were the fellows over thirty-eight years old, each of whom could be discharged if he could satisfy the army that he had a job to which to return. I guided and wrote letters for several of them toward that happy end and not without a good bit of envy.

Our black top sergeant was as tough as one in the movies. He could drill and bellow and threaten with the worst of them. He had had little use for me after I exposed the weakness of a threat of his to make a soldier "go dig a stump." This was a repeated threat and had its intended effect, because the surrounding woods did contain so many huge pine stumps. But one day, I cited language in the *Soldier's Handbook* to the effect that only a battery commander could administer battery punishment. Shortly afterward, he assigned me to K.P. duty and added, "Now, see if you can find anything in the handbook to help you in that kitchen!" Still, when the sergeant came to me to help with his correspondence school problems, I did, and we became friends.

Even one of the lieutenants, a big, blonde ninety-day wonder from Detroit, asked for help.

"Why is it that so many of these men won't look me in the eye when I talk to them? They kind of hang their heads," he said to me.

"It's easy, sir," I said, "You're white and an officer and they're black and from the South. Down here a Negro is uppity and out of line if he looks a white man in the eye."

The officer from Detroit would talk with some of us a bit; as a result, several of us soon became presumptuous enough to ask him about going to Officer Candidate School (OCS). He then clammed up, and it is easy now to understand why. He likely was simply avoiding an arousing of false hopes, so restricted were the officer training opportunities for Negroes. At first each battery officer approached by one of us would ask what AGC test score his inquirer had made. If the score left the soldier eligible, the officer would know nothing, even though he had himself just finished OCS. Some liberalization—some increased need—must have occurred, for later we were told to try for artillery training. Two of my buddies chose that route. As for me, of course, I had no interest in shooting a carbine, much less becoming a big-gun officer.

A few weeks later, I knew noncoms in headquarters battery. They provided me the guidelines on applications for OCS, and I began submitting them to the schools for "desk men," those for the adjutant general, the judge advocate general, and one or two others. It was like applying for civil service jobs, I felt. I also wrote to the civilian aide to the secretary of war, a racial affairs specialization. I knew the fellow and asked his intervention and support on behalf of my applications. This was not so much looking for a drag as facing the racial realities I understood to obtain. I had heard that a quota, a limited and token number of Negroes, was being accepted at this and that school, class by class, and the Civilian Aide's office likely had a hand in filling the quota. However, I heard nothing at first from my acquaintance and soon was receiving rejections. It wasn't so much like civil service applications after all. I could not even get on a waiting list.

In the meantime, I began to learn my way about the base and to feel the press of its racial practices. All about my battalion were other all-black battalions; we were a "racial ghetto," at the back of the base, and the white units were up front, nearer base command and its service units. The service clubs were separate, Number 1 for the whites and Number 2 for those not white. Negro officers were seen at our service club; they were not welcomed at the Officers' Club, which was for whites. The post exchanges and theaters were separate, an easy following of "the neighborhood color pattern." All personnel going to and from the base by public transportation rode the same decrepit buses, but the whites were up front, and blacks were in the back.

Once off the base, there was no question but that the rule of Jim Crow by state law and hallowed custom prevailed. Moreover, the army and its patriotic backers went along. What was done in Savannah and for the soldiers was done separately and unequally. The U.S. Army seemed beholden to Georgia, not the separate-but-equal doctrine of Plessy vs. Ferguson. The USO was downtown and for whites only; the SSSS Club, whatever each "S" stood for, was not united with the others, for it was located on the outskirts of town and strictly for Negroes. There was a post exchange in Savannah serving the others and closed against us. We traded in the "shoestring" grocery shops and ate in the "greasy spoons" along West Broad Street, near the railway depot. There was a "ferry system," an army-owned truck with an elongated trailer bearing bleacher seats attached to it, for free transport of enlisted men to and from their gathering places, provided they were not of the wrong color. The Negro GIs instead rode Negro-owned jalopies, mis-called "jitney cabs," for the charge was whatever the traffic would bear, and all too often the drivers were thuggish and threatened their GI riders, dared they question the amount of the unmetered fare.

For white soldiers on pass in Savannah from Camp Stewart and Camp Gordon, there were scores of beds (government-provided military cots and linen) in the Georgia state armory for twenty-five cents a night. Their Negro counterparts had no such central and handy facility of even faint resemblance. There were rooming houses, makeshift rooming establishments, which crowded them in for two dollars a head, and at many of the places, the toilet facilities were of granite ware, movable to and from the back porch.

All of this is not to say that Savannah was unbearable. It was enjoyable enough for me to go every time I could get a pass. The SSSS Club was Jim Crow, but all of the ladies there, the lovely girls and the matrons who watched over them, were wonderfully warm and hospitable, as if bent upon wiping away the rejections elsewhere. Even that landlady whose place was a poor excuse for a rooming house treated her soldiers with understanding, sometimes of an almost maternal quality. The first woman from whom I rented a room was just such a person. She ate Sunday morning breakfast with us soldiers, after one of us had said grace. The breakfast of fresh fish and grits she served was something I did write home about. Later I found a more modern home, clean, well appointed, and full of friendliness, at which to stay. I went there whenever I drew a pass and was welcomed there to celebrate my wedding. Indeed, I made friends to keep of two Savannah ladies, neighbors on a quiet, well-kept block of East Henry Street and senior hostesses at the SSSS Club. In their homes, I ate Sunday dinners and spent pleasant hours with their families, hours which were protective and recomposing. In one of these homes, I railed long and loudly enough about the color system at Camp Stewart to cause another guest, the highest-ranking Negro officer at Camp Stewart, firmly to observe that I should never have been made the warrant officer I had then become.

I shall never forget that in the other home I was once ordered to sit and accept the graciousness of the home for a while before proceeding further. I had rung the bell and been admitted to hear my friend immediately say, "You look upset. What is wrong?"

I was indeed still out of order, for something quite "wrong" had almost happened.

I had just left a bus loaded with Negroes and on which I sat near the front. As it traversed a white area and picked up more "up front" people, I moved my seat toward the rear twice, though not far enough. Still more whites came on the bus until only one empty double-seat separated the two kinds of people. There I was frontmost of all the Negroes, all dressed up in my army khakis, clean and neatly pressed, which said to the people of Savannah "I am getting fixed to fight for your way of life." Suddenly I was struck with a notion that I would not move again! Not one more time! The crazy impulse and the adjustment being carefully made were pulling one against the other, leaving me taut inside, sweating outside. There were six or seven blocks to go. A blue-eyed, thin-lipped old man boarded the bus and took half of the seat in front of me. The bus rolled on. Two more whites aboard and I must move again, or else! It started stopping again, and I could see whites outside waiting to get on, and they were mostly women. But fearing the worst, I had not noticed that whites were also leaving the bus. It turned out an even exchange, as many whites off as new whites on. The next stop was mine, and I breathed more easily; it was a close shave, but I had made it. I got off, walked a few steps, rang the bell, and was admitted to that place of refuge.

The answer I made to "What is wrong?" I well remember.

"Nothing, nothing now," I had said. Then I told my story.

But the periodic relief that was mine in Savannah was only for the few and more fortunate. For most Negro soldiers, there was no escape from Georgia's Jim Crow and the army's apartheid, not even passingly.

"Shorty," a laughing, lovable sprite of a fellow, was a favorite hut mate of mine who chose to use his first pass to visit his uncle in a small town near Georgia. He had talked incessantly of finding his uncle. The sergeant had lined up those holding passes and given us a last impressive word: "Show me you're making real soldiers. No AWOLs, no showing up late. I'll be checking every hut."

He checked our hut that Sunday night and Shorty was missing. All of us turned in, by the book, and still there was no Shorty. Near daybreak, the MPs brought him in. We couldn't see his laughing face, for his head was swathed in bandages. When the MPs left, we heard his story. He had found his uncle all right, and the weekend had been wonderful. But on his way to the bus for the return trip, he had stopped in a little park, spotted a water fountain, and taken a drink from it. Then from out of nowhere a bunch of whites had shown up and brutally beaten him. Later he was told that the park and the fountain were the "wrong ones."

Shorty was not by himself either. We began to hear many stories of insults, threats, and beatings. It did seem better to stay away from small towns and safer to circulate in groups whenever off-base, though this was no absolute guarantee against trouble. It was plain to see and easy to feel that the whites had no use for a Negro in uniform; such a Negro had automatically gotten himself out of place. The white men we met on the street looked upon us with rancor riding their hard faces. They looked through the khaki. Though their thin lips stayed tight, they had something to say that could be understood: "You're still niggers, and you better know it!"

The soldiers began writing to the newspapers, the Negro newspapers, about their troubles. Then word was passed that soldiers should not be reading the *Chicago Defender* and the *Pittsburgh Courier*; a record was being kept of those who were subscribers, it was rumored. Some GIs wrote to the National Association for the Advancement of Colored People. This must have included me, though I have no recollection of it; I only know that Walter White, the NAACP executive secretary, visited Stewart and asked for me. I did not see him; I was on pass. We heard that a Negro brigadier general, the highest-ranking Negro in the army, who was assigned to the inspector general, was scheduled to visit Camp Stewart, as he had other installations. Some of us looked forward to the visit, though others were cynical about it. Their view was that the general was a piece of window dressing; his inspections would be duly announced for the black press, but fruitless for the black GIs. One fellow warned the rest of us, "Sound off, if you want to. I have my doubts as to what the general can do. But what you do will get in your records."

Meanwhile an exciting and morale-boosting event occurred. A new gun battalion, with Negro officers, not just chaplains and warrant officers but line officers, real officers, and some of them even battery commanders, was to move in. It was an experienced outfit, real soldiers, drawn from a deactivated anti-aircraft regiment that had been guarding the locks at Sault Ste. Marie, Michigan, along the Canadian border. This battalion was, of course, assigned an area adjoining the other Negro outfits. As soon as the battalion arrived and began to settle, I was among several GIs to hasten that way. We went not so much to welcome the rank and file as to salute and receive salutes from Negro officers. The several salutes I exchanged, including a couple with white officers, that evening, were the most meaningful I had ever experienced.

At the same time, I grew increasingly unhappy in my battalion. The more I went through the motions as a "telephone man" on a team training to fire a 40 mm gun, the less I cared for the role. Every one of my several applications to attend an OCS school had been denied. An enlisted man in headquarters battery had tipped me about clerical openings at headquarters, but I could not get permission from my officers to go to headquarters to see about the jobs. However, one day I was sent there to see the adjutant on a mission for my sergeant. The adjutant was not in his office, and I was leaving when the executive officer noticed me and pleasantly inquired if he could help me. He was a tall, clean-cut Southerner, a schoolteacher, whose inquiry somehow seemed so sincere that I at once replied in all honesty, "Yes, sir, I hope you can." I forgot what the sergeant wanted and took up with him my own problem.

I told him something of my civilian background and that I felt fitted for and was interested in work at headquarters. He listened carefully, asked a few questions and, turning to a noncommissioned officer, ordered my "Form 20." He then intently examined that big yellow card bearing entries summarizing all of my presumed talents and potentials, looked up and exclaimed, "By golly! You're just the man we've been looking for!"

In a few hours, I was transferred from a line battery to headquarters battery and promoted to T-5, which is to say a general clerk of corporal rank. The next day the adjutant offered to make me battalion sergeant major within a few weeks, if I would agree to give up the idea of going to OCS. I would not agree; as bleak as the outlook for OCS was, I would not trade it away. Two weeks later I was advanced to T-4, a sergeancy. As I began to read and use army regulations a bit, I started toying with an idea. Perhaps I should forget OCS and take a "warrant" in personnel, become a warrant officer. So I began to study army regulations on personnel.

Headquarters was adding up nicely for me. I was freed from the gun business, at a desk again, moving along, and working on another step up the ladder.

But, of course, on weekends I still went to Savannah, and it remained segregated. What kept bothering me most was the color differentials in what had been arranged for soldiers on pass in Savannah. So when I got wind that the Negro general was indeed coming to Camp Stewart, I decided to make certain that he would hear of the inequality in the racially separate system for GIs on pass in Savannah. By then I was adjusted enough to know that the general could do nothing about the separation. But I hoped, if not thought, he could do something with the glaring inequality. Otherwise, what is the point of the heaviest Negro brass in the assignment? I asked myself. So I would see that the complaint was made, in writing, made a matter of record.

I prepared a petition setting forth the availability of the ferry, the post exchange, and those beds in the state armory at twenty-five cents each, all for white GIs only and without any comparable facilities whatsoever for Negroes. The first sergeants of all batteries eagerly signed it, each on behalf of the men in his unit. Word about the petition, got around, and when the general, his aide, who was a white colonel, and the sergeant-reporter arrived at battalion headquarters, they were met by a host of men far larger than the several individual complainants. The little building serving as headquarters for the battalion was quite crowded.

The general stood to receive the complaints. It all moved quite fast, like traffic court in a big city. The complaining soldier would sharply salute the general, get his gripe off his chest, and answer any questions asked him, though usually the general stood stone-faced and silent. In a few minutes, six or seven complaints had been heard, and it was almost over. The general was about to close the shop that had just opened, when his aide asked if there were any additional complaints. I looked up, felt myself looked upon by several soldiers near me, then quickly moved out and in front of the general and saluted him.

"Sir, may I ask if you have received a written statement signed by all of our first sergeants?" I began.

"I have," he said, and nothing more.

"Well, sir, we would be pleased to hear any comment you may care to make now, if we may," I said.

It was so quiet that a pin could have been heard to fall on a carpet, and I could see the stern-looking old gentleman bristle.

"I'll comment for you," he declared in a gruff and summary tone, "You are a sergeant. As such, you ought to know that a pass is merely a privilege. You need not be permitted to go to Savannah at all." It sounded like a final and dismissing judgment. There was a slight stir among the enlisted men. I caught it and was not to be so easily and curtly choked off.

"I understand that, sir," I continued, "But it seems to me that the purpose of a pass is the maintenance of morale. The morale of Negro troops has to be maintained as well as of whites. If anything special is to be done for soldiers—"

"Sergeant, that's enough!" he interruptingly commanded.

"Within a racial separation system—" I started again, but again the General angrily stopped me.

"Sergeant, I said that's enough!" he raised his voice and hand as well, and turned away. I scrambled to salute him as he began turning his back to me, while his return of my salute was itself a scramble, sliced to the rear and the right as he completed his turn.

He moved on into the office of the battalion commander, who must have tried smoothing the old gentleman's feathers and apologized for the renegade. Meanwhile, the colonel who was the general's aide beckoned me into another office. He said to me, in a calm and considerate fashion, "Sergeant, you have a responsibility, for I can tell that these men look upon you as a leader. You'll have to be careful and not be talking the army downhill."

"Sir, that is the question, whether the army is going uphill or downhill in this matter, whether the army runs its camps or lets the State of Georgia do it," I replied.

The general's performance left the men filled with disappointment and disgust. They felt him to be weak and evasive. We had put before him a problem burdening every Negro soldier at Stewart; the discrimination we charged was manifest; it required no proof, and the solution was in the hands of the army. Moreover, the greater army obligation was that of providing adequate services for Negroes among soldiers on pass, in view of the exclusion of Negroes from places of public accommodation in the South. It was such an observation that I sought to make to the general but which he would not permit me to complete. The General had obviously wanted none of the issue.

In the days that immediately followed, many of the Negro men at Camp Stewart referred to the general as "Uncle Ben," with decided emphasis on the "Uncle."

But I had no part in this verbal vengeance. My instinct told me that the old gentleman, for indeed he was a gentleman, was a helpless creature, part and parcel of the army's color system, who was by then doing what came naturally as well as what he was told. Later I was to feel all the more that the general's performance was to be understood and overlooked, at least in comparison with that of younger brass of his kind, college-bred Negro draftees who became officers and "hustlers," bucking always for the next higher rank. These men "made it" not only because they had good heads on their shoulders but also because they could turn deaf ears to their own hearts and keep their mouths shut as the race system trampled the Negro GIs they commanded.

A few weeks later saw my departure by railway for Chicago, on furlough. Several other Northbound buddies and I behaved in proper keeping with the Southern prescription for us, whether using the benches, restaurants, and toilets marked "colored" or avoiding altogether the dubious comfort they offered at both the Savannah station and that in Atlanta. I might add for the sake of accuracy that I do not recall the facilities at the Atlanta station being so blatantly labeled as those in the Savannah depot. The labels were lacking, an illusion of "advance" possibly pleasing alike to certain white as well as Negro Atlantans, though the unmarked Jim Crow path surely remained strictly to be followed by all strange and statusless Negroes, such as soldiers. The redcaps and other local Negroes in and about the station anxiously guided aright those black and unknowing of their ways in that depot.

We ran into no trouble either in Savannah or in Atlanta. It came instead in between the two cities, and we bore it all night long. We had to ride across the state of Georgia that night, not sleeping nor even sitting, but standing up, as if we were dumb beasts, in the baggage end of a car whose other end contained the only seats for Negroes. We had taken seats to begin with, but as the full complement of Negro passengers climbed aboard, almost all of them women with little children, we had given up our seats to them. The conductor welcomed us to ride with the baggage, a passage which was at first passingly to be tolerated. After all, the Jim Crow system of travel aside, we had elected ourselves to treat Negro women as ladies, a courtesy likely a treat indeed for them. However, one of us made the mistake of going back and peeking into the coach for whites. Then one by one each of us repeated the observation for himself.

What we saw was that less than half of the seats in the white coach were occupied. Often a single passenger lay stretched the full length of a seat!

Shortly after returning to camp, I discovered that my march through Georgia in a baggage car had been more straining on my guts than my legs. Nobody had done anything to me. The trouble was simply something officers in my battalion had to say about another battalion.

The recent arrival of the new gun battalion had excited as much distaste on the part of some of our white officers as it had pride on the part of Camp Stewart's Negro GIs—the hundreds of others as well as those of my battalion. As a noncom in my own battalion's headquarters, I had more than once heard disparaging remarks from my officers about the new battalion. But since the nasty remarks were made among officers, I had kept my place and my peace, as an enlisted man and one not in on the conversation.

One hot afternoon soon to follow, my battalion was on a long march deep in the backwoods and had broken for rest. I lay sprawled on the ground among a group of noncoms and near a group of our officers. Soon several platoons of the new gun battalion approached. They had hardly gone past us when I heard one of our officers say, "Yeh, it's sure a goddam goldbrickin' outfit."

This time the defamation was too much for me. My verbal counter-attack was quick, though at first indirect. I said nothing to the officer but spoke to a comrade loudly enough to make certain the officer would hear me.

"What he means is that it has Negro officers. We've got white officers who can't take Negro officers even in another outfit, so they call it a 'goddam goldbrickin' outfit,'" I said.

My words found their mark. The officer who had made the nasty remark got to his feet and walked toward us, forcing me to my feet. I had asked for it and was about to get it, I well knew. The angry officer began by sharply informing me of the obvious. Nobody had said anything to me. I offered no apology, re-asserted my charge of prejudice, and added that he was not alone in it. He properly reddened as he ordered, "I don't want to hear any more from you, Sergeant." By that time the other officers had gathered around him, as the noncoms had about me. We stood, black noncoms pitched against white officers. The heated debate remained a dialogue, my battery commander having declined a request to intervene. I was unable to recall much of what was said, even soon afterwards, so furious was the exchange. However, I shall never forget one remark of mine. As soon as it was made, and despite my heatedness, I realized at once that I had gone pretty far. I am no longer certain of its precise context but it ran: "Lieutenant, I don't know what I have to go overseas to fight for anyway. The other day I rode standing on my feet all the way across Georgia and stuck in a baggage car, so white folks could have their Jim Crow. And it's Jim Crow I have to fight. I'm ready to fight it, here and now!"

The next day I had gone to noon mess, and it was the noncom who manned the switchboard who told me what took place in the battalion office while I was at chow. Another young lieutenant, Northern-born and a graduate of the University of Michigan's Law School, came in and, as the prosecutor for the special court martial board, approached a captain and the presiding officer of the board, Southern-born and the son of a professor at the University of Alabama.

"Captain, did you hear about Sergeant Nesbitt telling us off out at the bivouac yesterday?" the Northerner began.

"Yes, Lieutenant," said the Southerner, "I heard all about it."

"Well, under what article shall I charge him?" followed up the Michigander, so certain was he that I was to be prosecuted.

But the Alabaman said, "Charge him? Humph! The Sergeant may be about half right, Lieutenant. Why don't we forget it?" And officially they did.

FROM FRYING PAN TO FIRE

Almost immediately upon being made "Mister" again, I was transferred from my battalion to the new gun battalion to serve as its personnel officer. To the officers of my old outfit, this move doubtless spelled both a good riddance for themselves and something "good enough for them!" the "goldbrickin'" outfit on which I was inflicted and the presence of whose Negro officers had catalyzed my most recent and violent protestation.

The transfer to the new outfit kept me still in the same army and the same South. Several incidents, one upon the heels of the other, were enough to leave no mistake about it.

The first was for me the most odious expression of the segregation system I had encountered in the army. It was a published document entitled "Educational Program for Colored Troops," accompanied by several supporting attachments. Here were formal, printed instructions issued by the base commander and addressed to all officers with colored troops. They ordered us, in sum, to brainwash them of democracy and to make them like Southern separation. They made plain that not only was segregation official army policy but so also was the Southern race system. Moreover, the program was to be carried out through troop indoctrination. Its details were nauseating in the groveling to the South which each officer was to teach his platoon. Two canned speeches were in the kit, saying the Southern race system was old and hallowed, and had to be respected by Negroes, especially when it came to the Southern white women. A Negro must be ever so careful in addressing one! (And I remembered the sultry "come on" from a slightly inebriated and very flippant woman with a southern drawl whose bags I carried as a redcap late one night). Worst of all, in each platoon there was to be a man who could be counted upon to

reveal those of his platoon mates who failed to follow the prescription—
a spying, snitching Tom!

Almost to a man, the Negro officers fiercely resented this "Educational
Program." It was offensive in at least three ways. Its contents were so
much "Ned in the first primer" to any Negro old enough to be in the army;
that the army and the South were deep in wedlock was plain to see. But
worse, it was a bitter insult to have to tell men preparing to wage war for
world freedom how they must make certain not to expect some of it for
themselves. And an internal spy system among Negro soldiers was the
gimmick for making the ugly thing work! Small wonder that, out of self-
respect, at least a half-dozen of us promptly dispatched our kits of the
program to the leading Negro newspapers, hoping to evoke their protests
and condemnation, as did occur in several instances.

Returning to Camp Stewart from leave, I found Negro-white tensions
at the camp heightening. Racial clashes were occurring with more frequency, on and off the base. A base command which had issued an "Educational Program for Colored Troops" could hardly be expected to understand the deteriorating situation and make helpful adjustments. A young
Negro officer went to the commanding general and offered a constructive suggestion to prevent fights between whites and Negro soldiers while
they were on pass. He proposed simply extending the system of racial duality to the pass privilege, by allowing passes to whites on certain days of
the week and to Negroes only on the others. The general seemed somewhat interested but slipped into both racial stereotyping and slurring as
the conference moved on to a consideration of which days would best be
assigned to what color of troops. When Saturday was under discussion
and the young Negro officer did not rush in to claim it for use by Negro
GIs, the general crudely observed, "Come now, Lieutenant, you know
that Saturday night is niggers' night."

I wrote to a friend of the trouble in the air. My feeling was that "the tensions here are so heavy, they can be cut with a knife." In early June of 1943,
the tensions broke. I remember the date, for I was in Savannah on special
leave, to finish keeping a date which, once kept, a man is not permitted
to forget. I had been married in Savannah on the very day whose evening
saw race rioting at Camp Stewart. My wife often says that I nearly escaped
"the hook," so deeply had I resented the behavior of the clerk as she issued
the marriage license. She treated us as the children the Southerner finds

useful to tell himself all Negroes are. After reading our names on the application for a license and in handling the completion of the certificate, she not only called my wife by her first name, she also all but held her by the hand to guide the writing on the certificate. Nor was this enough. When my turn came to sign in, the maternalistic process was repeated. Both times, my wife often says, I appeared disgustedly on the verge of giving up, leaving me to add, "That I didn't shows how much I loved you."

We were married in Savannah, and the next morning boarded a bus headed for the camp. As we properly sat behind all the whites on our side of the aisle, the two white girls immediately in front were feverishly whispering away. We paid this no attention, until one of them said something which could be heard and was meaningful to us. It was this: "And the Negras were just sumpthin' awful!" Her friend agreed.

As soon as we left the bus at Service Club No. 2 and began to meet people of my acquaintance, the overheard remark was given its context. The race riot had come, as I had felt it would. In the days that followed, there were rumors of what happened, how, how much, and to whom. There were questions, investigations, and a hearing. It was said that base tended to blame certain Negro chaplains and other officers who had protested against discriminatory conditions at the camp. But nobody official said anything to me, and I said nothing much about it all to anybody. When I would hear that this officer was being shipped and that noncom "busted down," I would let the details go past and ask no questions. Fate had dealt me a fine time to have been away from Stewart on pass, and I cooperated.

Then came an occurrence providing me a closer view of the kind of brutalization which my buddy Shorty had suffered in a little Georgia town. This time it was in a big one, Savannah.

A Negro private was walking along West Broad, a main drag and a stop street, when a white motorist who was preparing to pull across the street could not stomach having to wait a moment or two for a Negro in uniform to pass by. The white civilian cursed and racially abused the Negro soldier. The latter failed to take low in keeping with Southern expectations, as well as to take to his heels when threatened. The infuriated white man then curbed and left his car, pulled out a heavy stick and with it clubbed the soldier across and about his head until he bled profusely. A few minutes later, as three other Negro officers and I pulled up in a jeep, the soldier ran up to us and begged protection and help. His assailant stood by, master of all he surveyed. "The police are acomin' and I'm awaitin'," he said, glowering at his victim and us alike.

As soon as a squad car with three white policemen arrived, it became clear why the soldier's assailant had waited so calmly for the police—he had nothing whatsoever to fear and a duty to perform. Two of the policemen went to him to get *the story* of what happened. The third officer said nothing to the Negro soldier, leaving him standing there half crying and bleeding until the MPs came, but busied himself by keeping people from congregating. The inquisitive whites were entreated not to linger, while the curious Negroes were ordered to keep moving, as he pointed the way and prodded them lightly with his nightstick. Meanwhile, I walked over to the two policemen and the Negro-beater, turned to the policemen and asked, "Aren't you going to arrest this man?" Thereupon one of our group jerked me from behind, took me by the arm and walked me across the street to our jeep, explaining that the question I had asked would get a second Negro battered in worse fashion. I would be next up, next down.

As I sat alone in the jeep, while the other officers did as much as they dared—listened, observed, and kept their mouths shut—it occurred to me that three Negro women who were standing twenty or thirty feet ahead of me at a bus stop might have witnessed the beating. "No, no!" each quietly but firmly said in reply to my inquiry, while shaking her head to make doubly sure of no involvement. One, however, followed me back to the jeep and whispered the name of a Negro man who had seen it and where to find him. I found him a few doors around the corner. He had seen it all, yes, but so had the three women. He did not want to be "in it," owned property, something to lose, as they didn't, he explained.

It was a half-hour, bird's-eye view of the southern race system.

A month or so after the episode on West Broad Street, my battalion was at the port of embarkation in San Francisco, headed for somewhere in the Pacific.

We crossed the Pacific on a Dutch ocean liner converted to a troop ship, and without battleship escort, plying instead an irregular course to avoid discovery by enemy ships. We were but a few days at sea and into dangerous water when an evening which was at first amusing to me, though bitterly, turned into a decidedly uncomfortable night.

The various units jam-packed aboard the ships were assigned mysterious and meaningless numbers in lieu of the usual designations. However, the ship's command was well aware of the color of the personnel of each company or battery, for the GIs were as neatly segregated on the ship as at the camps from which they had come. Still a funny thing happened to the segregation system. *It fell apart because the white enlisted men could not take it on the ship.*

All of the men who had been paid at the port of embarkation had had no chance to spend their money in San Francisco for various and sundry items and services hardly procurable in the jungle. So there they were on that ship with nothing better to do than people who are crazy about Las Vegas, and they promptly began shooting craps all over the place. Cluster after cluster of men as color-mixed as salt and pepper spent long hours on their knees rolling the spotted cubes. When they would get up and move about the color mixing persisted. The men were paying little or no attention to the black and white sections into which the decks had been divided. It seemed as if Jim Crow was being left behind with the States. The most amusing feature of it all was the makeshift urinal, an elongated stretch of roof gutters. This had been sectioned off for use, half by the men in units bearing certain numbers and half by men in units bearing other numbers, the former being all white GIs and the latter all black GIs. Signs bearing the two groups of numbers hung over the urinal. But as the men left their desegregated gambling, they paid no attention to the signs. The latrine logistics were lousy anyway, the white GIs having the farthest to go to reach what was to be their end of the gutter. Indeed they tore down the sign several times, and the GIs could be seen standing wherever along the gutter, as intermixed as folks buying stamps at the post office.

Finally all that leveling in the latrine disturbed someone able either to use the ship's amplifying system himself or to influence someone else to do so in a stupid fashion. Following a "Hear this! Hear this!" the men were berated for tearing down the signs and ordered thereafter to urinate by the numbers, as posted, so to speak. The men kept on with their craps but everywhere began grumbling about the stupid order. Soon the speaker blared forth again with the same voice now ordering all men to their respective areas. This seemed officious meddling. The grumbling spread throughout the GIs, rising to an audible, angry hum. Only a few men headed for their areas and hundreds of crapshooters kept rolling the dice. It was then that the officers had to circulate among the men, break up the dice games, and sternly order the men to go at once to their areas. It had taken many direct commands, really some importuning, to get the response that the amplified voice of authority should have promptly received.

Later we learned that that second command over the loudspeaker had not been a petty backing up of the petty command which had first issued. No, what had happened was a sighting of another vessel in the distance. Our ship had signaled the other without getting the desired return flashes. So our ship had suddenly picked up speed, turned aside or about, and commenced bee-lining in a new direction instead of the leisurely zigzagging. I had recalled feeling the change in course and the acceleration. No wonder that second command!

That night I awakened time after time to feel the ship still pulling hard and fast, and wondered if we were being chased by the Japanese and would be fired on.

A little while later, as we were temporarily billeted in Townsville, Australia, one of our men was one of four Negro soldiers accused of the most serious offense with which a Negro, civilian or soldier, can possibly be charged: carnal knowledge of a white woman. The soldier from our battalion denied the charge, admitting the act but contending that it was with consent. Several of the Negro officers believed his story. I believed it mainly because two weeks before the act occurred, I had overheard noncoms on my staff call the name of the woman and tell of the freedom with which she was dispensing her favors among Negro men. The soldier's battery commander, a Negro, and I immediately retained an Australian lawyer as defense counsel, though not without some difficulty. His fee had been raised easily, by "passing the hat" among the men. But the Aussie lawyer himself at first explained that his services were not needed; they would be superfluous, because the American military would provide defense counsel. Besides, he emphasized, the accused would be deemed innocent until proven guilty. We were hard put to disabuse him of such a theory when it came to the matter of a Negro charged with raping a white woman. However, he soon saw the light for himself, as he repeatedly met resistance in trying to see his client and heard the "guilt findings" all about him that had been made even before he could see his client and hear his story.

The general court martial board found the four soldiers guilty and sentenced them each to hang by the neck until dead, so the cablegram from Negro Red Cross workers in Townsville unsurprisedly informed us in New Guinea. We promptly cablegrammed Walter White, executive secretary of the NAACP, and asked his intervention. A few hours later, the colonel had official word of the judgment and passed it on to his officers. Said the colonel, as casually as though making conversation about an occurrence back in the States, of previous mention and no connection with his command whatsoever, "They were all found guilty and all are to hang."

Then, looking my way, he added, "They were undoubtedly guilty, and I do not want the men agitated with this."

The men, as the colonel did not know, had already been informed. Moreover, they were neither disturbed nor disturbable. They were old enough to have expected what still is so altogether likely when a white woman fingers a Negro, and they knew of our prompt appeal to the NAACP. They also could look with hope and comfort to the NAACP, for they had identified their battalion with the NAACP months before, again by passing the hat on a payday, and sending the NAACP a substantial, battalion-wide contribution.

A third en masse collection for a cause drew express condemnation from the colonel. I was the cause and considered by the colonel a most undeserving one. A large sum of money, paid into "Soldier's Deposits" (a savings account system), had been stolen from my desktop, and the men had collected a sum to replace that stolen. The sum was quite large, because it was my practice as personnel officer to press the men to save their money for the rainy days that many an economist was predicting would follow the end of the war, as well as to encourage conversion of their term-type insurance policies into ordinary life policies. The latter was also a savings program as well as a bargain for a Negro, I had emphasized. "You get real insurance at the same prices charged whites, something you can't get outside of the service," I said as I talked to the men of each battery. This I suspect the colonel viewed as inflammatory, though he once expressed pride to an officer from the Inspector General's in the impressive extent of both the savings and the insurance conversions which the I.G. officer had noted as the service records were examined. Moreover, the colonel conceded that the more money the men saved, the less they had with which to gamble.

The colonel informed me that the theft was the result of my negligence and observed that the men should not have been permitted to pass the hat to make, in effect, a gift to me. I explained that I had at first written home for money with which to replace that stolen but that the men of the battalion had volunteered to protect me against the loss and insisted on carrying through. He then credited me, or rather discredited me, as he chose to see it, with being "too close to the men, anyway."

The executive officer, a major, was the colonel's true right arm, the index finger on the end of which was at least twice pointed at my presumed shortcomings. Late one afternoon, the major walked into the personnel tent just in time to hear me say to my sergeant-major and clerks, "Men, don't you think we had better start on the payroll in the morning?" This remark, despite its question form was, of course, an order. The polite and suggestive format was as effective as it was familiar, accepted and heeded month after month by my crew. It was not intended to stimulate discussion and a vote; the men were on their way to wash up and from thence to mess. But the remark provoked the major to say as soon as the men had left, "That was a hell of a way to give an order! They should have been told, 'Men, tomorrow morning you *will* start on the payroll.'"

I got the message but disagreed. I argued the workability of my approach. The men knew the time of the month, they only needed a bit of prompting, and the "we" passed responsibility on to them. If I had a crew of men digging a ditch under my supervision, I would "we" them and convey to them something of the importance of the task, any timing involved, and the like. With a small staff, sharing responsibilities makes more sense than foremanship or straw bossing. "But, it's unmilitary; it's sloppy; it's not command," the major explained. The next day the colonel took up where the major had left off. I wondered, Is it the commissioned officer poking at the warrant officer, a mere "Mister?" A worshipping of form and ritualistic language? A rationalizing of distaste for me personally? A result of belief that Negroes can produce only when ordered and driven? And, it takes a white man to handle them anyway?

The next time the little major poked his big nose in our tent, the issue which resulted was less complicated. What he heard from me, he did not challenge but quietly passed on word of it to the colonel, who brought it to the surface months later.

It was near the close of the day's work, and several of the men were discussing what they had read in the papers, so to speak, though the news was likely weeks old. Some Southerner in the Congress had flexed his muscles, and one of my clerks turned and asked me, in the current vernacular,

"How come them ole people got so much to say anyhow?" Just as I began to develop an answer to the question, the major stepped in, to stop, look, and listen, saying nothing to anyone, as was his snooping custom. I refused to choke myself and kept talking, in a backward process, touching on the conservative coalition, committee chairmanships, seniority, the consequent parliamentary skill, and Negro disenfranchisement. The truth is that the uninvited and hostile presence in our tent had made me talk longer than I would have otherwise. The major had discovered me "out there," and I would not "go under" before those who were both my men and my racial fellows. When it was over, the silent and red-faced Major walked out. Later I was to know that this was another item for the colonel's book on me and had been placed under the heading "agitator."

Meanwhile, I began to feel not only out of place with the colonel and his white officers, but as unwanted by them as I doubtless was. What began really to hurt was that the rejection spilled over on my personnel crew. The humidity of New Guinea was hard on portable typewriters; the cases fell apart, and the mechanisms rusted rapidly. But the supply officer repeatedly rejected my replacement requisitions on grounds of economy. My several recommendations for promotions of my men fell on deaf ears, though other noncoms in headquarters were routinely receiving theirs. My clerks grumbled only slightly; indeed, they and others in headquarters battery showed me favors in their own robust ways. Somebody made a strong potion—from canned corn and sugar, I believe it was—and slipped me a drink on a highly selective basis. When some enlisted men from Louisiana caught fish, fried them, and invited me to have a sandwich, I thankfully accepted the favor, though not without trepidation. We had been instructed that some of the tropical fish thereabouts were poisonous, and I doubted that our fishermen were sufficiently knowing with the strange seafood.

Returning from a brief leave, I found a turn for the worse in my status with the battalion. "The squeeze is on," said one of my men. It was apparent, too, that the men were its victims quite as much as myself.

During my absence, the whole battalion had been moved from one locale to another nearby. The several tents in which the units of headquarters operated had been set up in a cluster as usual, and this time on a ridge, except for that used by the personnel unit: myself, the sergeant major, and clerks from each of the batteries. Ours was instead set apart from the rest, pitched several hundred feet away and down at the foot of the slope leading from the ridge. The disparity was in obedience to a clear and explicit order from the colonel. Those who acted "sore thumb" were being treated accordingly.

My men were, of course, angry and distressed. No one had offered them any explanation of the discrimination, but they well understood what lay behind it. They knew that it was I who was being punished; they themselves had been caught between the colonel and his target.

I promptly went to the colonel to lodge my complaint. The isolated position for our personnel unit served no useful purpose, I contended. It burdened physical communication between our unit and the others; the mosquitoes, and malaria risk, were worse in our low-lying area; and worst of all, the ostracism was hard on the morale of my men. The colonel, despite his usual cold manner, obviously enjoyed getting at once to the major point—how the men of personnel felt. In so many words, his view was that they were getting just what they had asked for. The arrangement was convenient for all concerned, the personnel people could now sit to themselves and discuss Southern Congressmen, "poll taxes," and other such questions as much as they pleased, without bothering others. I returned to the men and revealed the fruitlessness of my complaint.

It weighed heavily on me that the men were being forced to share the impact of animus meant for me, though they professed being able and willing to take it. I commenced living on edge, and a day or so later, one of the white officers chose to bait me as we sat down for midday mess.

As the expression goes among Negroes, "He took the problem and jumped in the bed with it," as white men most often do with the color problem sooner than later. The captain asked me whether I believed in interracial marriage, after a quick and vague reference to something related which he presumably had just read.

"Well, captain," I laughed and began, "Races don't marry. It's people, two individuals, that do." Then I hurried nicely but pointedly to answer his question.

"You know marriage is perhaps the most intimate social relationship there can be and difficult at best. I would never have tried a mixed one for myself. But whenever people do, I figure it's nobody's damn business but theirs. I leave them alone."

This was not sufficient unto the day. The captain followed with an observation that a Negro captain who formerly was with our battalion had said he was against intermarriage. Naturally, I reminded the captain that he had asked for my opinion, not the Negro captain's, and then said, "It's all right with me, but really neither any of my business nor yours." His pulling in the Negro captain had added fuel to the fire. My adversary, for that he was, like too many whites, wanted all Negroes to think alike and as they would have them think. What were purportedly the Negro captain's opinions on race relations had been cited to me more than once by white officers of the battalion. I had concluded that, again as so many whites tend to do, they had selected him as *their* colored leader of convenience, though they likely also misrepresented him whenever it suited their needs.

The captain continued with his questions, one after another, almost as if employed by Gallup, to each of which I made unbridled, if not sharp answers, so angry had I become. Meanwhile, the other officers, black and white, seated about the several tables pushed together, remained silent. Soon the colonel entered, taking his place at the head of the tables. Catching the drift of the dialogue, he sought to end it by introducing a new topic, as I supposed was his right as a matter of military custom. But he overshot his prerogative, I quickly felt. He first made reference to news about a major league baseball game, or something of similar innocuousness. He then added, anent the heated discussion of race relations and with a glance at the captain and me, "Forget it. The race problem will solve itself in a hundred years, through amalgamation."

"Maybe so, sir," I said, "But meanwhile the captain and I have to have a way of getting along," and turned back to talking with the captain.

This was too much for the colonel. He took up the discussion, the captain grew silent, and the colonel became his own spokesman for the military and segregation systems. I remember little of the exchange that followed, save his critique of me as an officer and my rejoining note. I was, he indicated, no good as an officer, too close to the enlisted men, unable to give orders in a military manner, really nothing more than "a labor agitator," and he had therefore ordered his intelligence officer to keep check and report on me. The label of labor agitator immediately threw me, since

I had never talked with anyone about my sympathies for organized labor. His deprecations of my capacities as an officer, I dealt with on the spot in a light but bitter fashion. Sure I was not much of an officer by the military book, I conceded, though I felt my personnel work well done and that my men respected and followed me. Perhaps he spoke as the career officer, he was, I stressed. But I had neither aspired to nor could ever have aspired to a military career, I added. Then I made plain that I saw no especial honor in a military career. Career soldiers were to me rather parasitical, waiting their day of glory when the host body, the body politic, could not manage itself. This combination of pacifist leanings and lightly veiled *argumentum ad hominem* had plainly cut him to the quick. His face was flushed with inner rage. The meal was quickly finished, and soundless, save for the quiet chewing and an occasional clink of tableware.

The next morning there were more words between us, sharp and bitter ones. What triggered them I do not remember. The colonel was emerging naked from beneath the "white" shower, makeshifted of an oil drum with a perforated bottom, and I was in similar state underneath one quite the same, separate-but-equal, for his colored officers. What the colonel said at the height of the exchange was nakedly plain. If I was not careful, he would have me court-martialed. My unasked answer to that was, "When I get to your court martial, I'll have things to say also."

"Are you threatening me?" he asked. "No, sir," I took low and replied, "I'm just saying what I'll do at your court martial."

Meanwhile, I was saying little, even to the other Negro officers, and kept pretty much to myself. I could sense that the festering had about run its course, and when it broke, I did not want to see them in trouble with me.

A few days later, an officer from the Inspector General's came through. After he had examined my personnel records and complimented their condition, I asked leave of him to present my personal troubles. He agreed and heard me with seeming objectivity and understanding. However, when I made bold to suggest that he recommend the colonel's having me transferred, he declined. He would simply go over my situation with the colonel. Before leaving the battalion, he summarized for me that the colonel impressed him as feeling obliged "to make or break" me.

Soon afterward, the colonel refused my direct request of him for a transfer. It was then that I began to feel that he was indeed bent on "breaking" me, whatever that meant. The alternative of "*making*" me, making me over or a re-creation, as it were, seemed out of the question. But that "breaking" me. What did it mean? I had to talk to someone and related the word from the I.G. to my tentmate.

The "labor agitator" label worried me and as well the realization that the battalion intelligence officer was "casing" me. My personnel record would show that I had belonged to a union and briefly led one of its locals. Moreover, an FBI agent in Springfield, Illinois, had once questioned me about membership in several organizations. In those days, it was but a short step with the aid of guilt-by-association techniques, to smear a person who spoke and acted from democratic convictions, as I well knew. I instinctively felt that the step could be even shorter in the army. Though guiltless, as I certainly was, of subversive alliance or sympathy in the slightest, I was fearful. I wanted no smear and no cloud of suspicion as to my loyalty.

Soon I was being eaten by fear and worry. I had difficulty sleeping and spent long, lonely hours awake at night, tossing and turning. Such sleeping as I did was broken by nightmares, full of suspense, terror, and struggle. I would come out of these horrible dreams talking, if not screaming, and tired, and sweat-laden. There also was a night during which I walked in my sleep, my nocturnal wandering taking me through a tent in which the colonel and his white staff officers sat talking and drinking, as they told me the next morning.

One night, shortly afterward, I had quite a series of screaming nightmares. As I was getting up the following morning, my tent mate came and joined me where I sat on the edge of my bed, tired and worn as if I had worked at heavy labor the night through. He was as tired and sleep-broken as I was, for he had been awakened time after time and had finally decided to stay awake so as to shake me out of my struggling and before my screamings. He said to me, "Something is tearing you up for sure. The colonel will see you broken sure enough. You'd better do something for yourself."

Soon after washing up, dressing, and coffee, I was at the base hospital and in a bed. That morning there was a physical examination and there were questions about gas formation, urination pressure, and night sweats. That afternoon a psychiatrist questioned and talked with me for several hours. Among other things, he asked me when and under what circumstances I had first become sharply conscious of the color problem. In this context, and as soon as I mentioned the *Chicago Defender*, he raised his head sharply. He was familiar with that newspaper and wanted to know how early I began reading it, how often I read it, and what I thought of its position.

Finally, he said, "Listen to me and try hard to understand what I mean. You and the army don't fit. You're a round peg in a square hole. What do you want to do? Be released? Go home?"

I thought that I understood his quick analysis. It was indeed quite plain. But I was both suspicious and resentful of his questions.

"Sir," I said, "I am not asking to go home. I want no favor beyond a transfer. I would like an assignment to another outfit where I can get along better."

"You don't really understand," he said, "The square hole you don't fit is not just your organization. It's the army. It's the whole army and its way that you're up against."

Then shifting to another analogy, he added, "You're one guy, beating his head against a stone wall. You're beating up yourself. And it isn't necessary. You've tried and you're not indispensable. There's a man somewhere to take your place. You should go home, while you're still hung together."

During the next couple of days, several of the men from the battalion stuck their heads in to see me. They just wanted to know, "How you're feeling?"

On the third day, I was ordered to pack up. That day I boarded a hospital ship, headed for San Francisco, bearing a shipping tag around my neck on which was scrawled two words, "Adult Maladjusted."

CHAPTER 9

The Ugly Specter of Race Discrimination

*As time passed, some of the small test groups would be seated after a considerable
wait, only to be served meat with egg shells scattered on it, or a plate of food salted
so heavily that it could not be eaten, or a sandwich composed of tomato and lettuce
cores picked out of the garbage in the kitchen (so the group was told by Negro bus
girls who witnessed the making of the sandwiches).*
—"Dinner at Stovers," Chicago, 1942, from a CORE pamphlet by George Houser

Now I must tell here some of what has happened to me as I have sought
service in places of public accommodation. No Negro, readily seen as
such, and who moved about as I did in the Midwest during the twenties, thirties, and forties can have escaped racial mistreatment in restaurants, theaters, hotels, and like places. The discrimination was not always a bluntly applied bar. It was often veiled or rationalized, but the
veil was usually easy to penetrate, and the rationalization as weak as
water.

I have purposefully withheld this telling until now. The rejections, as
I have known them from time to time, so deeply offended me that revealing them in place would, I fear, have made difficult telling the larger story

as thus far I have related it. Besides these stories are of trauma in repetition, a pattern in themselves for separate recounting. Few of the wrongs done to me as a Negro have been as upsetting, as rasping within my very guts, as to encounter discrimination in a restaurant, a theater, or a hotel, even a bank. In this kind of encounter I often have had much to do to control myself. Once I quite failed.

I think that I somewhat understand why it was this way with me. Reading so much of the *Defender* had made me acquainted with the existence of Illinois law against discrimination in public places, and I was quite aware of the complete disregard for it in Champaign-Urbana, even as a youngster. A bit of Negro history, in addition, soon allowed me to understand also that Illinois was among these Northern states which made shining banners of such laws, adopted after the Supreme Court held unconstitutional federal prohibition of the kind under the national civil rights act, but that they were little used—and little believed in. It was all so much hypocrisy, uglier in Lincoln's state than others and most shameful in Champaign-Urbana, seat of the state university.

Besides early knowledge of my rights in restaurants and other public establishments, growing up in a neighborhood whose adults almost altogether were restaurant, hotel, and household servants, cooks, and janitors saved me from any illusion that hotels, restaurants, and theaters are so wonderful, and their habitués so uniformly refined, that such places should be off-limits to Negroes. The older I grew, and the more jobs I had taking me in and out of places of public accommodations and white homes, the stronger the conviction became. After all, those who prepare and serve the food, or wash the dishes and scrub the floors, well know the back parts and hidden places, the seamy sides and the nooks and crannies, of restaurant, tearoom, cafeteria, and hotel dining room. They know the guts of the place, no matter how distinguished, clever, or corny its name, exotic-seeming its menu, soft-lightedly beautiful its decor, well-padded its carpeting, and beguilingly gracious the doorman, hostess, or head waiter. The servant knows too those he serves, for the striving and pretenseful can relax with the subjugated, lay aside the cloak, let the hair down, and leave evidences of true self behind. If the servant is also a Negro, he is twice removed from those upon whom he waits and after whom he cleans, and they can be twice as relaxed and revealing in his presence. The black bellhop in a hotel and the Negro janitor at a theater know what really goes on in these places and what those who patronize them are really like, for all their vaunted whiteness.

Thus I early knew that I was unwanted in these places but also that I wanted nothing special of them and nothing in particular to do with those who patronized them. All I ever wanted from a restaurant was decent food, from a hotel a good place to sleep, and from a theater a movie good enough to see. When I have sought these services I have often known that, if they are provided, they will come to me with a surcharge—the reserve and resentment of the white patrons, the gaping and gawking, and maybe the hostile stare or loud-whispered racial rebuke from among them—an added price I must pay. In consequence, and in all honesty, I have most often approached the usual place of public accommodation of decent quality—those which many Negroes still quite accurately call white hotels, restaurants, and theaters—only when quite needful of their essential services, needful enough to put up with the whites who are there. Under these circumstances, denial of service grossly misinterprets my mission, deprives me of right, and withholds what I want and need, as a human, all in a single stroke. Moreover, the denial usually takes the form of a dodge, to add insult to the injury.

COLOR BARS IN "LINCOLN COUNTRY"

When I was a child, it was the custom throughout my home state to keep Negroes outside of places of public accommodation, to refuse them service altogether if possible. If this was not manageable, then the custom was to make the service fast, get them out as soon as practicable.

The racial bar was maintained even in Springfield, where school children went to visit the home and the tomb of the Great Emancipator who, an Illinois poet has said, still walks its streets at night. There was no room for Negroes in the Springfield hotel proudly bearing the name "The Lincoln," not even for the several from Chicago who sat in the state legislature and from time to time updated the civil rights law so long on the books. These lawmakers, like other Negroes in the state capitol overnight, were forced to find shelter with Negro landladies.

In Chicago things were somewhat, but only somewhat, different. Now and then a colored man of distinction was kept in a Loop hotel, or several of them—a benign token—scattered among a convention there, events notable enough for recording somewhere in the *Chicago Defender*, though without revelation of the delicate negotiations rendering the lodging feasible. Rarely was a Negro guest discovered in a hotel outside of the Loop. The large, Loop theaters were open and so were many, perhaps most, of its larger restaurants. But those movie houses listing their offerings under the heading "Neighborhood Theaters" and the restaurants nearby, except for those in the Thompson chain, were of another category. Negroes neither used nor attempted to use them freely. The most that those few Negroes who did approach these places were certain to obtain was a set of facts sufficient for filing a complaint of violation of their civil rights. Enough of such complaints were successfully lodged in the civil courts of Chicago and Cook County to result in a difference in racial practice from that prevailing in the rest of the state. It was not that the rule of the legislature became the practice in the twenties in Chicago, it was simply broken less directly. Instead of "we don't serve colored here" or "you will have to take it out," as was more the system downstate, the Chicago restaurants dealt with nervy Negroes by marking-up to offensive levels the prices of them, serving them cold food or warm butter, filling their food with salt, breaking the dishes from which they had eaten, and the like.

Champaign-Urbana was the center of light and learning for the state. It was a great place for agricultural experimentation, and farmers could go there and learn how to increase corn yields and raise bigger hogs. But neither the university nor the community was innovative with human relations. Unlike a southern Chapel Hill with its relatively liberal University of North Carolina, Champaign-Urbana was no oasis for Negroes in the civil rights area. Its Negro residents and the black students there stayed away from its restaurants and hotels altogether, and little ventured with its movie houses. Theirs was the view that "blessed is he who expects nothing, for he shall not be disappointed."

As a younger man, I went to town and "across town" on many missions: as newspaper carrier, to pick up and deliver laundry, to the A&P supermarket and the butcher's, to the Main library because it had more books than the branch on my side of town, and to eighth grade. Then high school took me across town twice daily. Besides, as a high schooler, I began working after school and on weekends, washing windows for Rosen, the haberdasher; cleaning-up for Doc Simpson, a chiropodist; and sweeping and dusting every evening at Brown's Business College. So I knew where all of the service establishments were downtown: poolrooms, drug stores, confectioners, eating places, and theaters.

Indeed, just underneath Brown's Business College was Swannell's, drug store and soda fountain, favorite haunt of my high school class-mates. No matter how neat and schoolish I might have appeared before work at Brown's and how hungry I might have been after the dusting chores and washing-up, a banana split downstairs at Swannell's was decid-edly forbidden. I knew this and accepted it. Candy or fruit for taking out, I forbade myself, in self-respect. I kept to the custom, breach of which I never heard tell. At Swannell's and the other soda fountains, restaurants, lunch counters, and hamburger joints, no matter how greasy, it was all the same. I never saw a Negro in one of them without pot, dishcloth, or broom in hand.

The theaters were of the same cloth, with minor variation in pattern. The newer and largest one was the Virginia, aptly named, for it readily ad-mitted Negroes only so long as they knew and kept to their place, as high and far back as possible in a corner upstairs. The older Rialto felt itself and its patronage also too good to do any better by Negroes. The Varsity, lo-cated near those railway tracks on the wrong side of which I lived, was a cheap little dump, featuring worn out westerns and corny comedies. Oc-casionally, as a youngster, I headed for town with white buddies but usu-ally to part abruptly as we crossed the tracks and neared the Varsity, for the Varsity barred such as me altogether and absolutely.

There was a certain shade of difference between color practice on the part of the local hotels, The Inman and the Beardsley, and that of the Abraham Lincoln at the state capitol. For now and then, with a long stretch in between, we local Negroes would hear of a colored man stay-ing at one or the other. Such a guest was usually of lonesome presence among a group of professionals conferring at the hotel, and the successful result of intervention by someone really somebody over at the university.

I remember being singularly present myself as a person of color at an ever so special luncheon held at the Beardsley in the late fall of 1940. Those dining were nothing more than Champaign county politicians. Worse, they were just Democrats, a decided political minority themselves in what was then still strong, rock-ribbed, corn-belt Republican terri-tory. But the honored guest and principal speaker was the candidate for the vice presidency on the Democratic ticket, Secretary of Agriculture

Henry A. Wallace. So every local Democrat worth his salt to the party as well as those of possible particular usefulness in the campaign then underway was there. I was present, neatly fitted in the latter category, for it was hoped that I could perform a wonder of wonders by getting some of the Negroes, staunchest of Republicans in the county, to vote New Deal, the deal which was keeping them going, as the Great Depression of the thirties still clung to them. I sat near the end of the head table, not in a place which I had earned but as a bit of window-dressing, heartening for Mr. Wallace to look upon.

After the vice presidential candidate was properly applauded and cheered into his seat, and before the program began, he suddenly ceased his conversation with the county chairman and rose to do something which excited the entire assembly. He came down the table to me, the lone Negro present, and drew me aside for a whispered huddle. All eyes were doubtless doing their very best.

The subject of our conversation was information Wallace had just received. The *Pittsburgh Courier,* largest of Negro news weeklies and of national circulation, had just declared itself for Wendell Wilkie and the G.O.P. Mr. Wallace wanted my predictive opinion on the effects of the declaration. It was, for him, a case of any port in a storm, and a large order indeed for the novice at politics that I was. Nevertheless I tried hard enough so that the lengthy whispering built up curiosity throughout the dining room.

I am certain that what next happened was far more astute, for all of its pure instinctiveness, than my assessment for Mr. Wallace. After his return to his seat, a local party leader who could no longer contain his curiosity came over and politely asked what the huddle was all about. I told him what I wanted him to believe, not at all what Wallace wanted from me.

"He wanted me to know that they need all the Negro votes downstate that they can get. He asked what we are doing to get them," I tactically lied.

My first brush with movie house Jim Crow came when I was no more than nine in years and found me at first completely unwitting of what I was up against. I had learned to join several white youngsters in "slipping-in" at the Virginia theater. It was as easy as pie and as tasty. We would wait outside until the rush-in for the first show was over and then under cover of darkness would quietly gather beneath the weighted iron fire

escape. The tallest of us would lift-up an agile buddy against the wall until he could get a good hold on the weighted end of the stairway for lowering it to the sidewalk as noiselessly as possible. We would then ascend
the stairway while carefully slowing its return to position behind us. After cracking open the door and peeking to assure that the usher was not
in the immediate area, we would slip-in one by one, beneath the lighted
exit sign, little savages and head for the nearest vacant seats.

The trouble was that the emergency exit we entered led directly to the
several rows of seats set aside for Negro patrons (a thoughtless bit of priority of protection for the unwelcome). Once, soon after we had settled in
our seats, the usher lighted the way for the next Negro couple and discovered my three little blue-eyed friends obviously out of place. His "What
are you fellows doing here?" sounded like we were caught. But he quickly
followed with, "You don't belong here. Come with me." As my friends got
up to follow him and I to bring up the rear, he waved me back with his
flashlight saying, "Not you, you stay where you are."

A few minutes later a Negro patron, who had seen us make our way in
and what the usher had done, explained the bi-racial arrangement, as the
usher doubtless did also, for the edification of my buddies.

I never tried slipping in the Virginia with my friends again. The color
line is kind of cumbersome for little trespassers.

The Rialto provided no such handy entrance made-to-order for penny-
short youngsters off the streets. Here I paid my way in and knew what
I was asking for.

I had been there once or twice on Saturday afternoon as a little fellow, when the serial was more of an attraction than the feature for school
kids. But between odd jobs and my father's frowning on movies, I never
became a regular like many other youngsters. Mostly I would merely
hear Negro moviegoers talk of the movies, what they had seen, sometimes twice, what was coming, and occasionally what went on during the
movie. I was in high school and not only knew of the "crow rows," as the
colored section was often called, but also that the segregation was strictly,
even ruthlessly, enforced.

Early one evening when something good was featured, I tried the
Rialto. I was ushered to the very last rows upstairs to become their lone
occupant. But it was so early that many seats closer to the screen were
available. Shortly after the usher left I moved forward completely to the
front of the upstairs section. Soon the returning usher missed me from

the back of the section and made certain to locate me where I sat. He bluntly informed me that I could not remain there and I asked him why not. There was no ducking. He gave me his answer plainly and firmly "Because colored can't sit in these rows and you're colored! You belong where I put you in the first place." But I continued in my seat.

I had heard about the particular usher. He dealt roughly and was equipped to do so. He was a university student and an athlete, wearing a sweater with freshmen numerals on it. As he stood over me, twice my size, I was quite scared. There was a long moment of silence and he suddenly reached toward me, causing me to say, as quickly and strongly but as quietly as I could, "Don't put your hands on me!" For some reason or other, he drew back his arm, choosing not to add assault and battery to the violation of civil rights law he was doing his best to commit. I could feel the heat of his glaring rebuke as he sharply whispered, "I'll get the manager!" As he walked away, my fear went too. The manager would come but he could not possibly be as foreboding. And again for some reason unrevealed, it did not happen; the manager never came. I suppose I sat through the movie waiting for him. Certainly it was one sat through but little seen.

Though I was downtown in Champaign so frequently as a child, I was never so hungry as to have to try to force the issue of color exclusion in its restaurants. I never sought so much as a sandwich in one of them and certainly would not have bought one to carry out, which I suppose would have been possible. I was well fed at home, never too far from there, carried sandwiches whenever I wished, and could purchase fruit or candy in grocery stores where I would at least be treated with cool civility. So I was able always to turn away from the restaurants that stood ready to turn me away.

Besides there were several places where a Negro lad away from home could get a bite to eat. At the edge of downtown and on the "colored side" of the Illinois Central tracks, there were "colored places" to eat. When the new I.C. depot was built, it included something new indeed for Champaign, a counter and dining room open to all. Moreover, though the high school was by no means free of color prejudice and practice, its cafeteria operated nondiscriminatorily, as also did a makeshift lunch counter across the street in a part of a private residence.

But once I was big enough for occasions away from the hometown, I had to face racial patterns as I found them in strange locales.

Forty or so miles west of Champaign is Decatur, which boasts of being the first Illinois home of Lincoln and the seat of the first home of the
Grand Army of the Republic. One Saturday in the fall of 1927, this Decatur seemed little different to me from the cities of the same historic label in Alabama and Georgia. A friend and neighbor of mine and I were
the Negro members of a Champaign high school's scrub football squad
in Decatur for a game with St. John's Academy. There were four or five
carloads of hungry youngsters in our entourage, breakfasts at home having been skipped. Filling our voids should have been a welcome windfall
for a restaurant, for easy handling, especially between the breakfast and
lunch rush periods, since we arrived at eleven or so that morning. Nevertheless, the thin streak of dark ones, two out of perhaps twenty-five players, almost forced our team to take to the field in hunger-weak condition.
We shopped Decatur restaurants unsuccessfully until almost too close to
game time for eating, finally managing to eat institutionally. Y.M.C.A. or
Y.W.C.A., I forget which it was, but the place proved sufficiently Christian
for that moment. Perhaps our coach phoned the St. John's coach, who
called his principal, board chairman, or an active and influential alumnus, who got hold of the executive director of the council of social agencies, who contacted the power-that-was among the Y officers, who told
the Y director to tell the lady manager to "Go ahead and serve 'em." In any
event, I saw our coach putting in a plea with someone at a phone booth,
and I am fairly certain that our eating at the Y was something more than
business as usual. The Negro kitchen help peeked at the two of us Negroes
too many times for believing otherwise.

For youngsters, the squad members ate lightly, it should be added, and
not because of the watchful eye of the coach. At the last of the "exclusive"
hash houses, the question of to serve or not had been debated a bit before
the decision to violate the law was reached. Meanwhile, the bread and
butter had been served and consumed. When a waitress announced that
she would have to pack food for two of its members, the whole squad decided to walk out.

In Danville, Illinois, where the Great Emancipator maintained a law
office for seven years, I received the customary due of a Negro in a "Lincoln country" restaurant in 1937, while practicing law myself. After a court
appearance and while awaiting a train for the return trip to Champaign,
I sought coffee at Thompson's, the local unit of a Chicago-based chain

of cafeterias of that name. The counterman quickly drew and handed me a cup of coffee. I then went directly to a front table and seated myself. Looking up, I saw the counterman hurriedly and agitatedly bearing down on me. His mission was to inform me that I could not sit at a table up front but instead must remove myself to one of several armchairs at the rear of the place, near the doors to the toilets. I refused to move and informed the counter fellow that I could sit wherever I wished in the place. I explained that the Illinois state legislature had so arranged the matter, adding that the Thompson restaurants that I had patronized in Chicago seemed well aware of the fact. "But not in Danville!" was his reply, in firm enough fashion to imply that neither his state nor his employer had any voice of the kind in Danville. He kept insisting that I move, and I kept explaining the law, until several customers stood waiting for service. He then seemed to give up, angrily assuring me, as he walked away, that the next time I came in I would be remembered and refused service altogether. Before I finished my coffee, he had served the waiting customers, and had come from behind his counter and all the way to the front, again to pass judgment on the errant that I was to him. "You'll never get another cup of coffee in here," he said.

I am sure that I became a case in point for a thesis of his subscription, "give 'em an inch and they'll take a mile!"

Thirty years later and I have not once been back to Danville, Thompson's, and the counterman for another cup of coffee.

During the same period, the meaninglessness of the Illinois statute prohibiting racial discrimination in restaurants and other places of public accommodation was made plain to me, its meaninglessness not for a mere hash handler but to a state university community. For in the Circuit Court of Champaign County a civil jury, "twelve men good and true" and in the last analysis reflecting community opinion, virtually said as much.

It all began neither in downtown Champaign nor downtown Urbana, but almost on the corner of Wright and Green streets, in the heart of the university area. For the little business district serving university faculty and students offered no relaxation of the color bar in places of public accommodations which prevailed throughout Champaign-Urbana. It did not matter that all of that enlightenment abounded thereabouts, the business proprietors being mostly university alumni; their clerks and other attendants, university students; and their patrons, august men of learning and scientific objectivity, not to speak of the thousands of young people who sat at their feet. The presence of Negro students was unwanted in rooming house, barber shop and beauty parlor, tea room, cafeteria, restaurant, hamburger joint, and soda fountain. A small university cafeteria would serve them, and there were a couple of third-rate, for-colored spots, one on each side of the dirty, debris-laden creek known as "the Boneyard." But none of these places was open late in the evening.

So it was that near nine o'clock of a late spring night in 1934, as time for semester examinations approached, two Negro law students stepped just across Wright Street from the School of Law for coffee at a place called Hanley's. As they crossed Hanley's threshold, they were suddenly and for once among dozens of their classmates for whom coffee there was as standard practice day in and day out as turning the pages of Illinois Supreme Court reports. Hanley's confectionery and restaurant was not only a highly convenient accessory of the Law School, it was the biggest and most popular coke n' smoke spot along Wright Street, main stem of campus life. It was a huge maze of many booths which daily saw changing hordes of students eating, drinking, and smoking; chortling, conversing, and caucusing; "bulling" and seemingly studying, on occasion; dating and just plain hanging out there. It was forever busy and filled with free-wheeling, youthful motion, as much a part of the university as its classrooms.

But the two Negro students were promptly denied service. The waitress had gotten the cashier, and the cashier had called the man-in-charge, or, at least, who took charge, delivering the rejection in the nicest way he knew, "Now, you fellows know we can't serve you."

"Why not?" one of them asked.

"We don't serve colored students here. Nobody around here does. You know that," was the answer. All of which was to say, in effect, "We don't obey the law. The other restaurants about don't either. We follow the practice and you know what is."

The two Negroes sat quietly in their seats. Meanwhile, other law students took notice and several spoke to the Negroes but only that. These white students went on past, hurriedly past the booth contaminated by the presence of two fellow students of color. For this was in "thirty-four" not "sixty-four." While study of the law gave these white students an awareness of the injustice being done, they had no sense of commitment against it. It was none of their business.

The man-in-charge periodically stopped by the strangely occupied booth, quietly to tell its occupants that they were embarrassing to him, which to be sure had become the point. He somehow never raised his voice, nor strongly invited them to leave, nor made the slightest threat. So the Negroes sat and sat, and he fidgeted and proclaimed his embarrassment.

Finally, after an hour or so, the two intruders left. Their short-lived stay, gentle harbinger of student sit-ins to come years later in many places across the country, was that night a dismal failure. It had followed no plan and enjoyed no organized support. Its participants were law students who knew they had suffered a grievance for which Illinois law provided a remedy. But they also knew that it was unthinkable to pursue it, if they were successfully to pursue law degrees. For at the time Negroes were unwanted in the Law School at the university.

What they did was to delay the action they could have then taken and mutually to make a vow. If Hanley's persisted with its practice and either ever finished his law studies and was admitted to the bar in Illinois, he would bring suit against the place.

Hanley's kept to the color bar, and the two law students surmounted the "ifs" and kept their vow. In 1938 both became attorneys for four Negro students who were refused the food they ordered at Hanley's and filed a civil suit alleging its violation of the Illinois law forbidding racial discrimination by restaurants among other places of public accommodation in the state.

I had been one of the law students mistreated by Hanley's in 1934 and was one of the two attorneys for the plaintiffs. Edward B. Toles of Chicago, now a federal referee in bankruptcy, was my fellow student and the other lawyer.

The complaint was filed in March and immediately became a local cause celebre. Discriminatory patterns affecting Negro students were occasionally discussed and mentioned in the local press. But never before had such a lawsuit been instituted. The Circuit Court of Champaign County viewed the complaint as marked "Handle with Care," if it had to be handled. For on more than one occasion, it found the complaint faulty, though it had been in fact initially prepared with that exceeding care typical of young lawyers who prepare their pleadings painstakingly, being so uncertain of the road and with plenty of time for studying the maps. Moreover, the complaint the young lawyers had drafted, as well as each of its revisions required by the court, had been reviewed in their Chicago offices by older counsel skilled in civil rights matters. I vividly recall that when I asked the older lawyer of counsel to me to review the third version of our complaint, he said, "It looks to me like they are trying to beat you on the pleadings. This must be a real hot potato for them, down there."

"Down there" it was freely predicted that the case would never reach trial. This the restaurant owners in Champaign-Urbana would see to, it was whispered in the Negro community, as well as that they were jointly financing the defense. On the other hand some whites about the campus thought that the NAACP branch in Chicago had raised funds to finance the plaintiffs, a logical but most erroneous assumption. The true character of the retainer we could not afford to reveal. Nobody was financing the suit. There was no written contract, and no understanding whatsoever respecting fees, not even for fees contingent upon recovery of damages. The four plaintiffs could have paid for their meals had Hanley's served them, but they had no money for lawyers. Their fraternity brothers raised the fees for filing the complaint and paying the sheriff to serve the summons, a total of $13.50. Beyond that, not another penny was spent; it was fee-less litigation on the side of the plaintiffs. This was not an altogether uncommon occurrence in those days among younger Negro lawyers when it came to civil rights. The compensation was in the experience gained against bitter and artful opposition, the goodwill garnered in the Negro community, and surely the inner satisfaction which returned, win or lose.

We feared revelation of the fee-less character of the retainer, a recognition which, when added to the more obviously limited finances of counsel themselves, might indeed tempt the defendants to dispose of the suit through protracted pretrial maneuvering. For we were always hard put getting money for gas for the old Ford in which we drove down to Champaign for hearings. Besides we had no spare tire. If we had had a blowout between Chicago and Champaign, a successful motion to dismiss the complaint might have meant other hearings, hard to make, or the end of the matter, so discouraging was what we felt to be the Court's picayunishness toward our pleadings.

Finally, at one of the several hearings on a motion to dismiss our complaint for technical inadequacy, I could no longer contain my suspicion of prejudice on the part of the judge, a very popular local resident, born and bred in Champaign and a University of Illinois graduate. As counsel for the defense concluded his argument, and the judge appeared responsive, my feeling that the court was inclined against breach of local custom expressed itself before I myself realized what I was saying. I asserted inability to understand the alleged weaknesses in our complaints; advised the court that our pleadings carefully followed the format of similar anti-discrimination complaints which were found satisfactory, and upon which Negroes were recovering damages regularly in Cook County courts. "And yet down here —" I began, when the judge interrupted me.

His honor was a redhead, and the implication of my remarks had embarrassed him enough so that he seemed ablaze with fire. He most sternly reminded me that it was his duty to rule on the validity of the complaint and threatened to rule me in contempt of court if ever again I made such a hint of impropriety on his part.

But no such hint was again necessary. At the next hearing the complaint was found acceptable, and the case set for trial. A Chicago newspaper carried an article with a lead paragraph reading "Champaign, Ill., Oct 15, 1937, A major preliminary skirmish in the fight against race discrimination at the University of Illinois was won Friday when Judge John H. Armstrong ruled the Hanley-Lewis Confectionery on the campus would have to face trial in a suit brought by four students for violation of the state civil rights law."

Meanwhile, as the trial date approached, some people took the side of the student plaintiffs, while others played the tangents available to them. Without solicitation, the *Daily Illini*, the student newspaper, editorialized on behalf of nondiscrimination in local public accommodations of all kinds serving students, and the student senate published a resolution of similar import. A rumor ran through the Negro community to the effect that if the suit were not withdrawn, Negro cooks and porters would lose their jobs at the fraternities and sororities abounding on the University of Illinois campus. At first this disturbed me, since Champaign-Urbana was still my home; my family and most of all others I cherished and whose affections meant so much to me were there and so largely dependent on those jobs.

But upon reflection and after a little inquiry, the rumor proved strengthening. The *Daily Illini*'s editorial and the student senate's resolution showed that in fact the white students at least leaned our way, not against us. The rumor was likely without foundation, nasty skullduggery on the part of the opposition. Besides, even the several local Negroes whom I consulted, and who were themselves cooks and porters, seemed unafraid, not about to panic, and in sympathy with our cause—their cause.

But another maneuver was direct, plain as day, and intended to bring leverage on me personally. A prominent, young campus businessman who had always been friendly, generous, and democratic in his relations with me, startled me with a proposition. I owed him a sum of money—a small but appreciable amount, as measured against the poverty-stricken state of my affairs. After explaining that the suit was troublesome to the university business community, he offered to forgive me my indebtedness if somehow the case never went to trial. I am unable to remember the words of my refusal. I only know that it was done without anger, for I was a bit stunned when his proposal finally came out, and he had made it with obvious difficulty. Instead of accepting his offer to forgive the debt, I was able to forgive him his trespass.

The novelty of the suit in Champaign-Urbana, its challenge of racial practice in the community, its history of pretrial contest, and the cleverness of counsel for the defense, a young white lawyer skilled at jury trial, combined to attract a crowd as its hearing commenced. The courtroom was packed with an interesting assortment of people. Among the Negroes, there were most of the student body and many such local residents, young and adult. Among the whites, there were the courtroom habitués who knew a "hot" case from a humdrum one, a liberal sprinkling of university students and younger faculty members, what must have been at least half of the members of the local bar, and several of the professors who had taught us something of the law and its trial practice. The local newspaper reporters were there to cover a true news event, a striking version of man biting the dog, at least giving it a try.

One expected party of central importance was not present. The resident, red-haired judge was missing, if not to get out from under a monkey on his back, then to allow the contending parties an atmosphere of more apparent neutrality. An imported judge was to hear the case.

Just before the judge took the bench and jury selection was to start, a young Negro lad approached the railing near us and our clients, and beckoned for me. I had known him since he was a child, the youngest son of a paper customer of mine, who owned several parcels of near downtown real estate. The youngster had a long, white envelope in his hand and, thrusting it into mine, quickly whispered what it was. His father's lawyer, who was in the back of the courtroom, had instructed him to hand it to me but also that neither I nor my associate was to be seen in contact with him. He felt that the information enclosed in the envelope would be helpful to us. We asked the lad to thank the lawyer for the mysterious missive and hastened to our table to examine it.

That white lawyer had taken the list of veniremen and pencil-checked the name of each he viewed as racially prejudiced and unfit for service on a jury to hear a civil rights matter. Here perhaps was a gift indeed, the judgment of a white lawyer about fellow whites in a color-divided community. He could well know what we as Negroes could not possibly know about persons on the list. On the other hand, we were wary of the Greeks bearing gifts. We put the list to test at once in this manner: we would question a venireman, without referring to the list, and if we elected to reject him, would then examine the list for his status. We soon found that those we feared, based on our interrogation, were consistently under the lawyer's disapproval. It was uncanny and a gift indeed. We began gratefully to use and count upon it.

During the trial, that same lawyer, a complete stranger to us but somehow friend of our cause, had additional notes passed forward to us that were helpful with our interrogation of defense witnesses.

The evidence for the defense was, of course, the high point of the hearing. It beautifully complemented a line pursued in the cross-examination of one of the plaintiff-witnesses, questions designed to suggest his membership in left-wing youth groups. The key defense witness was the white waitress, who admitted refusing to serve the Negro students but went on to ascribe her action to the one of the four students having pulled her skirt and called her "Baby," as she related it. The immateriality and irrelevancy of the red-baiting questions were objected to and may have been stricken. The testimony of the waitress, suggesting a sex play, was objected to also but ruled admissible. Moreover, the waitress stood by the fabrication, for such it was, as she was cross-examined. Thus the plaintiffs were doubly-smeared, made to appear communist-led and sex-bent, in the direction of a white woman.

The four Negro students had been, of course, witting of the delicacy of their venture and on their best behavior as they dared enter Hanley's for the first time and sought the service they would have been astonished to receive. Theirs was a hunger more than of body, more than for food, and surely not carnal: they had wanted simply a taste of fair play. All of the four are today successful and highly respected: the owner of a thriving business enterprise; the principal of a high school; an administrative official in one of the nation's largest public school systems, with a PhD from Harvard; and a physician.

Despite the red herring, and the smellier sex-herring, dragged across the nostrils of an all-white, midwestern jury, hope for a favorable verdict rose as it remained out for nearly three hours. Somebody on that jury was not taken in by the lie and believed that in Champaign-Urbana it would have been legal, or morally right, or Christian, or becoming in a community whose chief business was that of enlightenment—maybe a soul big enough to grasp them all—for Hanley's to have served the four Negro students. That person or the several of the kind held fast for those few minutes and then joined the majority for return of the verdict of not guilty. This judgment of mine enjoyed the concurrence of the professor who had taught my associate and myself pleading and trial procedure. He wrote us a letter, soon after the trial, complimenting the quality of our work as young lawyers and ascribing the verdict of the jury to community rejection of that civil rights policy so long established by the state legislature. Years later a young man who had sat through the trial as an undergraduate at the university and the son of one of its professors told my associate that what he saw and heard at that trial enhanced his inclination to study law and his concern for civil rights. Today he is an excellent lawyer and, as a member of the board of education operating one of the most segregated of Northern school systems, has made valiant efforts to secure its revamping toward equalization of educational opportunity.

More immediately, the readiness of whites in the community to help continue a struggle so spontaneously commenced and poorly organized became known to us. We were invited to meet with a group of younger members of the university faculty to discuss formulating a campaign to open up to Negro patronage all places of public accommodation about the university caucus. The effort never got underway. But a few months later, a newly built theater a block or so around the corner from Hanley's opened its doors to Negroes and whites alike. Straining for some measurable return from our venture, we ascribed the phenomenon to the unsuccessful lawsuit, well knowing that our law professors would say that the first event was not necessarily the proximate cause of the second and that those who taught us logic would raise for us the risk in reasoning *post hoc, ergo propter hoc.*

In Cairo, Illinois, I knew the state law forbidding racial discrimination in places of public accommodation to be less impressive than elsewhere in the state and expected nothing more. But when my white traveling companion was refused admittance to a "colored theater," he found the new shoe a real pincher.

The "capital" of Southern Illinois, "Little Egypt," at the lower tip of the state, is in the midst of what was once cotton country and as late as the early forties was still deeply bowed in a southerly direction. A white colleague and I were dispatched to Cairo by our government agency. Our mission included inquiry into problems of a racial nature to start with, and we therefore expected to abide by customs in Cairo in order not to compound our difficulties there. My colleague registered at the white hotel, and I at what passed as one for colored. When the hot summer day's work ended, he returned to his hotel and ate, while I found a place to satisfy my hunger and returned to my place of abode. (The word "hotel" is withheld in all accuracy. Late that hot night, when I sought to escape further blood-letting to droves of mosquitoes freely entering the lone and screenless little window in my room, the night attendant told me where he thought I might find myself a screen in a vacant room down the hall. The screen was there all right, full of holes.)

A half hour or so later my friend showed up where I had checked in, something I would have felt less free to do where he was registered, and we sat out front in his car for a review of the day's activities. The movie notion struck him, I agreed, and we headed for the colored theater. Its feature we knew would be older, its seats harder, and its atmosphere hotter and stuffier than at the white theater, but we would be admitted.

He would be welcomed with me, as we knew I would not be with him at his movie house. The sole attendant—at once ticket seller, ticket taker, and bouncer, if not also janitor and owner besides—refused me two tickets. He could admit me, he stated, but not my friend. My friend then quietly spoke of the civil rights law and offered the opinion that racially reversed exclusion was as much in violation of it as the common anti-Negro variety. But the attendant was not the least impressed. He shook his head slowly but surely. When finally he spoke, it was to tell of a bi-lateral arrangement for what would at least appear separate but equal mistreatment. "Over there, they shuts out the colored and over here we shuts out the white. That's the way it is," he said. And that is the way it was.

As my friend and I walked away, he suddenly grunted aloud, "It should have been done to a real bastard."

"How's he gonna know one of you from another?" I pretended to ask.

"Okay," he laughed, "I've heard something like that before."

On another occasion I refused, I am certain, to allow myself to be discriminated against by declining an invitation to have a drink in Waukegan, almost at the other end of the state from Cairo but with its near northern-mostness serving to provide little by way of more decent racial practice. Forty or fifty of us, a group of civic leaders and professional intergroup relations workers, were midway in a two-day discussion of racial problems at Bowen Country Club located near Waukegan. Bowen was a sort of retreat for social actionists and a summer camp for poor children. Though located in a beautiful, wooded setting befitting its "country club" label, it neither included a facility for drinking, nor was any such relaxation expected on its premises. This shortcoming, if it was that, plus some observations made during the discussion about the plentitude of segregation all about us, tempted a conference member immediately to undertake a challenge of one of the reported racial barriers. The after-dinner, evening session had just concluded, when the conferee turned to me and suggested that the two of us drive into Waukegan for a drink at a public bar. That was all that was said, an easy, natural, and logical expression of sociality, and I could have done with a good drink.

Nevertheless, I quickly said, "No thank you." And lied, "I have some reading I must do before tomorrow morning."

The invitation had come from a young white lady, an attractive and lively one, and it was near eleven on a Saturday night. What she was suggesting was the wrong couple, on the worst night, and in the worst kind of place for an abiding with the law of the state, in Waukegan as most anywhere else within its boundaries.

IN OTHER STATES TOO

All that is within my experience with unequal treatment in places of public accommodation was not confined to my home state.

One cold, snowy night in Racine, Wisconsin, after a long, tiring day examining housing and related living conditions for war workers in the community, my colleague and I decided on a good, hot dinner before driving back to Chicago. Since many of the war workers were West Indian blacks and Negroes, and they were meeting with community hostility, we knew that finding a place where I could eat would not be easy. My colleague insisted on clearing the way, a tactic with which I soon agreed for several reasons.

He's a decent sort of white with a certain measure of guilt feelings about racial discrimination in restaurants; let him do something about them, I thought. Racine is very German, so is he, so let him find the sauerbraten, I felt. Besides Racine is within his assigned territory, he goes in and out of it regularly, he should have fixed it by now in the restaurants for the black war workers and his black co-worker too, I laughed to myself. Finally, and rather seriously, I thought, he knows and is known in a few places and thinks he can drag his black sheep behind him; if he can, I'll eat and certainly behave as my own man; if he can't, good enough for him, and we'll both go home hungry.

My friend, Schultz, was doing the driving. Twice he pulled his car up in front of restaurants, told me to wait a moment, climbed out and made his soundings. Twice he climbed back into the car, greeting me with, "They won't have us."

Suddenly it struck me. Schultz was perhaps as much of the problem as the restaurants. Whatever and however he was saying it, he was worried less about me than the feelings in the restaurants, explaining how nice a Negro I was and maybe how different from the rest, all that togetherness of ours and how long it had been. He was going in those places "hat in hand," as Negroes say, when I wouldn't have done so myself. He was so sorry to have to ask that I be fed, that the restaurants turned him down to keep him from so much suffering.

We pulled up in front of another restaurant, and he began his routine, this time with the words, "One more try," while reaching for the door. But I laid a restraining hand on his shoulder.

"Nope, not you, I go first this time. Follow me," I ordered.

I climbed out of the car and marched into the place. Then I seated myself at the counter and picked up a menu in a single, continuous motion. The waitress looked up and I started talking fast.

"I'll start with some of that hot coffee," I said, pointing at the big urn beside her, and then began looking at the menu.

As Schultz joined me, he called, "And another here!"

And that was the way the two of us finally had dinner in Racine.

IN UNEXPECTED PLACES AND THE NATION'S CAPITAL

The most blatant discrimination in a place of a public accommodation ever inflicted on me occurred in the forties and in the most unseeming of places for it. I had come to accept the risk of discrimination in restaurants in Chicago — mean and ugly, though subtle and indirect, especially in outlying neighborhoods. The people in some of such neighborhoods were unable to have Negro servants but so adamantly careful about keeping them exclusively white that Negro presence at any point other than a bus transfer was risky. One day during that period, a Negro youngster standing at a bus transfer point in such a neighborhood was seized by four youths and beaten to death with a hammer, simply for the hell of it, as the youths explained. Indeed, during the same period, I was given the reservations-required runaround by a fancy tearoom with a ye olde English name upstairs on Michigan Avenue in the heart of Chicago's Loop.

But I did not expect a racial blow in a great Loop banking institution. Its total unexpectedness was a good part of the hard jar of its striking.

Banks, along with other moneylenders and their brokers, are sometimes charged with discriminatory refusal of loans to Negroes or refusing to make them on the same terms as to whites, especially real estate loans. They were also long reluctant to allow Negroes behind their cages and sometimes even to wield the mop, don the doorman's uniform, or run messages for them, though their bigger and better customers themselves are quite plainly of other notions. But when taking in money to make money, moneylenders usually are pretty democratic. The green in the black hand remains the almighty dollar; it is black as well as white power. The great moneylenders will accept a Negro's money, even the widow's mite, like a white's, and pay for its use at the same rate. Their Christmas savings clubs are open to all without regard to color, and all alike are paid no interest. The mechanics of it all are cold and efficient and uniform with all. Most often the banking people don't say, "We don't serve colored here"; or "This is a club, and you don't have a membership"; or

"That window is for you people." Desk pens, like currency and coin, are dirtied by the dirty hands of dirty Negroes, and it does not seem to matter. The customers, black and white, line up salt-and pepper-like and are dealt with first-come, first-served.

But not invariably. I was the first at the window, but the white lady was the first served that day at the First National Bank in Chicago.

The larger banks in Chicago occupy great expanses of space, branch banks being prohibited in Illinois. The First National is the biggest in Chicago, and is not only in a high-rise structure but on a site a block long and perhaps half as wide. Its huge stretch of first-floor space was rimmed with scores of savings windows, a stretch of iron cages such as those of a great zoo, if it is imagined that all of the captive creatures are quite meek and making much the same motions, never including frolicsome ones.

I was in a hurry, and it was during the noon hour, when many of the savings windows were closed and each of the fewer windows in operation was serving a long line of customers. As I hurried in, I spotted a window without a queue before it and behind which its returning clerk seemed obviously preparing to open up. As I turned in the direction of his window, he raised its shutter and beckoned his way the people in the rear of the long queue at the adjoining window. Several people left that line and hurried toward his window, reaching it a split second behind me. Giving me a hard but quick glance as dark as my presence before him, he suddenly stuck his arm out and completely around me to pull a passbook from the hand of the woman just behind me and offer his service. His brazen discourtesy jolted me as though he had struck me with all of his strength.

"What in the hell do you mean by that?" I demanded.

"I called this lady from the other line," he rejoined.

"So what! You were asking for customers, and I was the first to reach here. You are to treat people first come, first served, and you know it. You've no damned business picking them out," I argued, loudly and angrily. As I paused for breath, I could hear the stillness about me and feel the line of white patrons behind me coming apart.

Meanwhile, the clerk from the adjoining cage entered that before which I stood and moved to the support of his fellow worker. The latter had begun to tremble and stammer as he groped for a line with which to defend injustice, while likely also fearing that the president of the bank himself would show up at any moment along with those of its customers gathering around. I got the jump on this would-be second adversary, as he moved to the window and started to speak.

"This is none of your business! Get on back where you belong!" I shouted in his face, and he immediately obliged.

I then turned and headed for the nearest desk man and related my story. He said nothing but quickly arose and asked me to accompany him back to the scene of my difficulty. There he obtained a statement from my clerk, delivered haltingly and apologetically (to his superior, not me). Then we returned to the desk of the quite minor official of First National who, having heard both sides, sat me down and endeavored to calm me by assuring me that the First National tried to treat all of its customers alike, expected such behavior from its employees, of whom the clerk was one of the best as well as one of the fairest, and that what had happened was the kind of thing that could happen to anyone. When his artfulness reached that point, I started to interrupt. He had gone beyond feather-soothing and was denying that the discrimination was racial. Before I could speak, he added, "Sometimes you people are a little too sensitive."

I left my chair as fast as I could and, looking down on him, said, "You're no good either. To hell with you and your damned bank!"

I walked away and out of the bank, so filled with anger that I could feel it surging throughout my body. I knew I was in no condition to return to my office and began to walk aimlessly until I chanced to pass a drugstore. After turning in at the drugstore and seating myself at the luncheon counter, I glanced up and saw my countenance in a big wall-mirror. What I saw about my face I could not believe. There on my left temple seemed to be a bulge bigger than an AA hen's egg. I felt it, and it still seemed there, though I could not yet believe it. Turning to the stranger on the stool next to me, I asked him if he could see the knot.

"Sure," he said, "it's as plain as day and as big too. What's the matter?"

"Thanks," I replied, and thoroughly frightened, returned to the streets and my walking, this time in the direction of my office building. Upon reaching the building I went directly to a lavatory to confirm by sight what frequent feeling was telling, the knot on my temple was shrinking. Looking in the mirror, I could see that it was gone.

I had indeed been "popping mad" and I promised myself never again to let it happen.

Meanwhile, many new office buildings were going up in the city, in which operators of eating facilities had to decide whether the old custom of exclusion would be followed. In several instances, an easy way out was to seat no one, by providing a take-out service only. But the government agency for which I worked had leased space in a new building, in which the restaurateur would provide a counter and table. I had seen them under installation and knew that here was a restaurant which would not decide not to decide but would either shut me out or allow me in.

The little restaurant opened before my agency moved into the building and had begun to serve the building's Negro car hikers on a take-out basis before the issue was raised. A young lady co-worker of mine, one every bit in the tradition of Mary Church Terrell, joined me in stopping in for coffee at "The Huddle." We had beforehand huddled ourselves and decided to reserve for later resort, if need be, the particular character of the owner of the building, a Jewish civic leader and philanthropist whose wife was then the supreme socialite in the capital, rather an auxiliary of government itself. We would first ask for coffee and see what would happen.

The proprietor himself handled us, frankly indicating his reluctance to breach the custom, though he finally served the coffee. As happens so often with so many whites, he wanted to be selective when it came to Negroes, though they would still all look alike to him. He could accept the patronage of people such as the young lady and myself, he explained, but was worried that the car hikers, in their uniforms, would expect to sit among the white, white-collared coffee drinkers, were the place open to Negroes. We suggested that such fears were not realistic; the car hikers were already trading with him on a take-out basis and should be privileged thus to continue on other than a racial basis. Most of the people in the new building would be government employees, accustomed to working together, white and black, and they could do with coffee breaks in the same manner. We also explained that the court decision in the Thompson case was only a few months away and was generally expected to result in a legal requirement of non-discrimination in all restaurants throughout the city. Were he to establish an open pattern for his restaurant at once, such a decision would find him already in order and without adjustment to make, we emphasized.

Our position seemed to impress him, but he suddenly asked for a day or so for further weighing the issue, during which he would also like to see our supervisor. We knew that any white wearing a white collar could serve as our "boss" but decided to use our chief personnel officer for the purpose. After all, he should be concerned that agency employees are able to eat and find shelter with convenience, we felt. So we asked him to drop by the coffee shop, after briefing him on our argument and making certain he would support it.

The result of it all was that we did not have to try wangling our way to see the powerful and wealthy real estate entrepreneur and learn whether his Jewishness would bring him to suggest to his lessee that he treat Negroes as people. Nor did The Huddle have to change its way of doing business when on June 8, 1953, the Supreme Court found the lost ordinance still effective.

Then there is a kind of discrimination which is most peculiar that I still frequently experience in Washington. It is anti-Negro but comes from other Negroes. It is not a shutting out and is rarely ever verbalized in the presence of its victims. It is more a slighting, quite plainly manifested. This kind of discrimination occurs in dining and other public places, and is directed by some Negro waiters and waitresses, bus boys, doormen, and bellhops, and other such employees against the Negro patrons they must serve. The *some* is important here. For indeed, there are Negroes in service occupations in hotels, restaurants, and other places of public accommodation who see the Negro patron with pride and in racial self-esteem. They say as much when it comes to working in Negro homes. They display the feeling in the way they treat Negro patrons, as they work in hotels, restaurants, and other settings where they cannot refuse altogether to wait upon them.

Take the Negro girl I've long known and observed behind the steam table and serving its meats in a government cafeteria in Washington. Hers are invariably quick, sloppy helpings, and she smirks and grunts if a particular piece of meat is requested when it comes to her Negro customers. Yet I have frequently seen her patiently and smilingly await the choice from a delaying and dubious diner, voluntarily suggest what is "good" among the day's dishes, and inquire as to whether this piece of a particular meat dish or that is wanted. These excesses, actually making for inefficiency in a hurried, mass-type dining operation, are favors reserved for her white patrons. One day she told one just in front of me that she had this and that, classifying the meats there before the man's eyes, but also that she had saved for him a portion of something of his liking! The fellow simply had to take it.

A certain bus-boy in a private cafeteria I frequent repeatedly clears the dishes left by one or two diners on tables for four when a white person approaches it, while allowing groups of Negro patrons to stand about a table completely loaded with dishes until he has done what he considers "first things first." Once I started and finished a meal, seated at a table otherwise completely loaded with dishes, while he passed by me time after time, doing what comes so naturally to him: ignoring the Negro patron.

This is a nasty kind of mistreatment on two levels. It is not delivered easily, unconsciously, or guiltily, as increasingly characterizes discrimination practiced by whites in similar situations. Instead it is done boldly and callously, sometimes with a surly air that betrays its deliberateness. But what is worse is what is behind the malice aforethought. The unspoken message seems clear indeed to me: "You've been busy trying to cut off yourself from me, us. But you haven't, and I'm showing you as much. You're still nobody and nothing, like the rest of us." The enveloping self-deprecation deeply disturbs me.

Still, it is our problem within the big problem, this crabbiness within the bucket, and it is hard to handle. A complaint to white management is beyond reach, the mistreatment would hardly be believable or understandable. Display of resentment or direct challenge with the Negro servant is dangerous. The action would but appear to bear out the suspicion of escapism which gave rise to the offense in the first place. The slight is made to "try" the Negro patron. If he loses his "cool," he fails the trial. So the Negro patron best meets with such Negro servants with understanding, patience, and sufferance, in friendliness and relaxation, passing the time of day. If the brother must be criticized, it is best to do so when it can be done with deftness. Sometimes I let them know that I've done what they do, and I find that it helps.

But the most despicable discrimination I have suffered in Washington is of the customary type. It has been the work of the taxicab company enjoying a franchise for passenger pickups at the Union Depot.

For years this company's white-only drivers not only refused to pick up Negroes on the streets, its starters and drivers studiously shunted them aside as they departed Union Depot, where the company had a franchise.

Though there is some hangover, the practice has now been substantially abandoned, a circumstance likely less attributable to intervention at long last by the Public Utilities Commission than the company's finally realizing that its lily whiteness in a city increasingly Negro left it cutting off its nose to spite its face.

I learned, of course, to skirt the blow, often to use a bus instead of cab when the hour was not too late, or to walk on to a "Negro cab." I could climb into the latter, which picked up whites as well as Negroes and was free of racial tit-for-tat, and tell myself that I was simply using a service operated as it should be. Besides, the driver was a Negro in business for himself, moving himself up, often in fact a student at Howard University or a "moonlighter," who was "hacking" on the side to buy himself a nice home in a good neighborhood for the convenience of his wife and the advancement of his children. But I could not listen to this comforting voice alone, for that of ugly reality would insistently tell me over and over again before I reached home that I had been Jim Crowed in the nation's capital still another time. It was sometimes worse, for all too often I would have left standing and still waiting at the depot, first bewildered and then hurt, Negro women, sometimes utter strangers, with children at the side and little ones in their arms.

Several times I bucked it all. Once, I literally pushed a woman and children in front of me into a cab. On another occasion, I simply remained among white fellows with whom I had walked away from the train in conversation. But it bothered me to beat Jim Crow in this way. I felt that the driver saw me as part of the baggage of whites who knew no better than to pull me along, or saw them as "nigger lovers." His ire was against them, not me, and I had won no battle.

My memory is vivid of walking from the depot one night alone and just ahead of a party of two white couples—gay, sparkling, and well-dressed. The cab driver, next out, stood with his cab door wide open, looking beyond me and to the party behind me, fully expecting me to walk on past him, in keeping with the custom. Instead I all but walked into his unwelcome arms, slipping into the back seat of the cab as quickly and deftly as Maury Wills ever stole second. A mixture of consternation and anger was plain upon the cabbie's face as he turned and peered in at me for a moment. He pulled back, slammed my door, walked around his cab, and took the driver's seat, slammed its door, and sat in stony silence. He never asked my destination, but as a horn behind us blew, I blew at him my address, just as loudly and sharply, coldly and mechanically. He jerked the vehicle into motion, and thereafter, for block after block, he sped, stopped and started jerkily, and sped again, keeping his mouth shut, containing his spleen behind gritted teeth and lips tightly shut all of the way.

I sat just as silently behind in the dark, broken occasionally by a street-light allowing me to see his dirty red neck.

I was never so glad to walk away from another human being. Perhaps never so close to choking one.

This has been, I must note, a story only partly told of my troubles in places of public accommodation. The rebuffs have been many, many more then the several recounted, and occasionally gross, but more often subtle. More often than not, differences made with me have been not accepted but ignored, in an effort to lessen the inner disturbance. The longer wait for service in a restaurant, even the too frequent assignment to a room adjoining one used for service, next to the elevators, or in a corner of a hotel, I have tried to overlook. One likes to feed a stomach at ease and to sleep unperturbed.

Mistreatment of Negroes in places open to the public is much more common than appears on the surface, and I speak of the North as I know it. The increasing frequency with which they are seen in hotels, restaurants, and theaters in larger cities contrasts with the rarity of such presence in the smaller ones. In neither category of cities are they welcomed in bowling alleys and skating rinks. These Negroes, seen as members of a garrulous and "integrated" convention party, are sometimes barred as individuals in the same places. Negroes may be viewed freely circulating in the chain hotels in many a city whose older hotels, locally owned pride and joys, absolutely exclude them. They can stay in the big city hotels but are forbidden at the big-time resort hotels. They can drink at first-rate downtown bars but not in the second- and third-raters in the same city's neighborhoods. They are not expected in beauty parlors and barber shops, even including those in the hotels whose guests they may be. In some places they can be seen only when the season is dull or because the management has been alerted that the convention will include some of them but assured that there will not be too many, and that those will be respectable, if not also rather prominent.

This discrimination takes a thousand shapes and forms. It ranges from

shutting Negroes out altogether and making no bones about it, to admitting them, but thereafter "letting them have it" in ways expected to keep
them from trying again. In hotel and motel, reservations are often said
always to be required; they are made but not honored ("There simply are
no more rooms available"), or only the highest priced ones are; or "Try
down the street or around the corner"; or, "Come back later," if you'd like.
In restaurants, Negroes can be admitted but ignored by the hostess; hidden away in the back, near the kitchen, the far corner, the private booths,
or the small private dining room upstairs; assigned to the busboy, not
a waitress; served in a such a hurry that they are certain to get the message; or served slowly, indifferently, or sloppily, so as to make the same
point; served warm butter or water, or cold food, or hot food but with an
extra dash of salt, or provided the food on cracked dishes. In the bar or
tavern, the ugly ways with Negroes are many too. They can be told that the
place is a membership club, they are too drunk for another drink, or they
look like minors. Once they are in and seated, they can be overlooked, the
brands they prefer are said not to be carried, the service can be slowed,
and the drinks for them poorly mixed, or the prices for them raised beyond reason. Plainest of punishment is to break the glasses they've used
before they leave and to make the crash a loud one.

Still the "stop signs" against Negroes in places of public accommodation are coming down. Many did as a result of the federal Civil Rights Act
of 1964. More will follow, as the Negro vote in the South tempts state legislators to supplant requirement of race separation in places of public accommodation with a "same and equal" standard of service for all in various types of establishments, or thus to substitute explicit state policy for
the present silence on the subject, a posture inviting racial custom to hold
its sway. Indeed, as my experience in restaurants in Northern Virginia at-
tests, barriers dropped in Southern communities may well prove more
cleanly and definitively lowered than ever in Midwestern states such as
my own Illinois. More important, mounting Negro use of facilities which
are legally open is to be expected, as the incomes of Negroes increase,
their expectations rise, more leisure time becomes theirs, and they are
permitted to behave with the mobility that is such a striking feature—
almost a requirement—of life in our society. Enough of them will seek
and obtain service repeatedly enough in most places of public accommodation to wear out through discouragement those who have made an art

of discrimination against Negroes, once they were admitted, by mistreating them in various and sundry ways.

Yet a certain irreducible minimum of mistreatment of Negroes will remain so long as people have their color prejudices, and automation fails to replace altogether those who make the sales and provide the services in places of public accommodation. If prejudice is in people, it will make its way out, especially when they must treat with those they would prefer to scorn. With or without instruction, the discomfort will make the slip.

But perhaps this much happens not only in places of public accommodation but simply as white chances to rub against black or vice versa. And this is itself another story.

Poking at the Good, White Liberals

DISCRIMINATION VEILED AND RATIONALIZED

Some speak with their eyes, some with their hands, some with the shaking of their head, some with the movement of their body, and some with their feet.
—Tikkune Zohar, T. 70, 1776

In 1948 or so, I chanced to reveal to a white friend and associate a certain daily discomfiture of mine as I went in and out of the huge office building where I worked. As I recurrently held open a heavy door to the building to simplify entry or exit for women, white women working in the same building, I had felt forced to group them into three classes in terms of attitude toward black persons. Many, of course, saw me as merely a courteous male. But there were too many of two other types. The first appeared to view me as black subjugated servant as she breezed through the door seemingly oblivious of my mannerliness. The second, and worse, appeared to suspect me of black beastliness, hurrying through the doorway lest my courtesy prove in fact a prelude to a pass, perhaps a pat on the posterior.

Now my friend was more than a liberal white. He was also a young minister, years ahead of his church in concern with Negro-white relations; a professional intergroup relations worker, and thus by definition equipped with an understanding of the subject; and a sophisticated student and practitioner of the art of facilitating racial harmony, since he was the executive director of an official agency assigned that task in what was then the second largest city in the country, one remaining rife with racial tensions. Nevertheless my friend and associate was astounded by my observation. He wrote it off as unreal and the product of excessive sensitivity. My casual response, as I recall it was, "Well, you're liberal and a racial relations specialist, but you're white. Maybe one has to be a Negro to understand what I'm saying."

The fact was that, in 1949, little revelation—black to white—of the character and extent of such feelings as I had disclosed took place, even among those holding themselves out as experts in Negro-white relations.

Two decades later, decades including the disorder of the latter sixties, it ought to be painfully clear that the revelation, in terms of personal relations between blacks and whites, is overdue. For as Kenneth Clark has said, "the psychological distance, the hostility, the wariness and the ignorance that keep the Negro and the white apart are overwhelming. . . . Though the expression of these feelings is proving painful to both Negro and white, there can be no healthy relationship between them without the present pain."

My own bit of black experience in this context, how I perceive and respond to the behavior of individual whites as I have met and mingled with them, is entitled to a place of its own in this book. For that experience is largely Northern, occurring in what passed as racially integrated settings in which I brushed with whites on equal status level. It thus will suggest what is to be expected as the walls of segregation come tumbling down (and if they are not re-erected.) My experience predicts that in a future of lowered color barriers across the country, a Negro's feelings will square with these conveyed by a sixteen-year-old lad to a *New York Times* reporter in 1966. "Take me, I was born down South, Savannah. They tell you, man, right away, you're a nigger. I mean, they let you know. Here they won't tell it to your face, but you can feel it. Down there you can tell a guy, 'I hate you, too.' Here it's all behind your back," he said.

I have been called *nigger* or something of the kind—from "Anthracite" to "Zulu"—many times by "nobody" whites. But still more often, I am called *nigger* when the word, or its substitute, is not directly aimed at me, nor uttered at all, save through tell-tale gestures or greater subtlety. I can feel it out and get the message in many, many ways. And it comes from so many kinds of whites—including "somebody" whites—whenever and wherever I move among them *with the color fences down*, that I would be less than honest to withhold its revelation. The black who asks, and works for, and endeavors to live in an integrated society, must expect soon to know that he has been "'buked, 'bused, and scorned."

In desegregated settings, North and South, for years to come, tricky lines to restrain and trip, spun finer than a spider's web and not always seen, will remain in the wake of the fallen barriers. People will still live in a way that says white is good and black is bad. They will not tell it to the face, but they will make it felt. The more equalized the setting for black and white as they meet and the more absent the visible dividers, the fences fixed between them, the more certainly present will be the slippery and subtle lines. Negroes may circulate freely, and they must, but they will not be able to escape the drawing of these lines. They will be rejected day by day, sometimes directly but more often indirectly, now and then crudely, but mostly with subtlety. The shunning will sometimes be spoken but more often unspoken, through gesture and slip, the long, hard stare or the quick furtive look, the ugly frown or the sly grin—who can count or tell the ways? Negroes must live to be hurt time and time again and continuously to bear the burden of its expectation. They will have to shoulder, too, the burdensomeness of its deflection and their reflections upon it when it has happened. And they must come back for more of it, again and again, while it learns to lessen.

LADIES AND GENTLEMEN DO IT

Ladies and gentlemen with whom I was compelled to treat have done me dirt, cut through my heart calling me "nigger" in the abstract, calling me by my first name when they better knew my last, "boy" when I was a proven man, and "George" for white kicks, not knowing that so my first name is.

In Flint, Michigan, in 1945, I walked into a men's haberdashery while in the company of DeHart Hubbard, once the world's champion broad jumper. I was then almost thirty-five years old, and Hubbard was closer to forty. But the young sales clerk who greeted us as we entered the store wanted to know, "What can I do for you *boys*?"

"Well, I said, "the first thing you might do is recognize men as *men*."

Moving closer to him, while he colored-up, I pushed the lapel of my coat up under his nose and added, "Maybe I was a boy before this, but now I think I'm a man." In the lapel of my coat was the tiny, bronze "ruptured duck," symbol of World War II service, as I had just returned from the South Pacific theater.

The sales clerk hastened, if haltingly, to explain that no disrespect had been meant. He called "all the fellows who come in here boys." The latter note was about to worsen the situation, for it sounded too much like *fellows* meant Negroes, and they were still all *boys* in Flint. But dismissing the thought, I said, "We want to see some shirts—men's shirts." He then obliged us, and we left after indicating that we were shopping around and might possibly return.

An hour or so later, and after having examined shirts at several other stores, we went back to the haberdashery. Its shirts appeared the best buys in town, and we wanted them. As we walked into the store, the sales clerk smiled and said, "Oh, you *gentlemen* are back."

Hubbard and I often have chuckled together over how that day we so swiftly leapt from boyhood to manhood. I tell him that it was the best jump he ever made.

But, of course, the racial slur is more often unspoken; it simply slips to the surface and is so plainly there.

At the Illinois Central depot, where I was a station porter that morning, the well-dressed, urbane-appearing fellow whose bag I had picked up could have called me "Redcap" or "Porter." But no, he had to have me for his own, and for all of twenty-five cents, during a journey of a couple hundred feet to his train. So he called me "George," hitting my true name on the head, winding me up tight, but also inspiring a counterplay, all in a single stroke. I set his bag down, grasped and began pumping his hand, with a great show of warmth to conceal my anger. "Glad to see you again. But I've forgotten your name. Were we down at the university (of Illinois) together?" I said.

"I don't know you. I never went to the university," the embarrassed one replied.

"Oh, I did and thought you knew me there," I lied, finally releasing his burning hand, and adding, "George *is* my name."

"I meant no harm," he lied in return.

But his companion spoke in a whisper I overheard, what may well have been the truth. "You'll know the next time you call *one* 'George,'" he offered.

IN TRAFFIC AND ON THE BUS

I have also been party to a common kind of traffic encounter. It is the case in which the traffic cop arrests a Negro because he does not approve of the way the Negro chooses to spend his money. He particularly objects to a Negro driving a shiny, new automobile, especially if it is a flashy, high-powered job. In this case, the car was all that, a spanking new Oldsmobile 98, and more. It was a roadster, two-toned in color, and we were driving it with the top down, sun beaming down on us, as we headed for Baltimore on a beautiful Saturday morning.

The motorcycle policeman blew us on to the shoulder and after checking the driver's license and other papers, seemed satisfied that the car was not stolen. But suddenly he informed us that we had been speeding. This was news indeed to us. Car after car had passed us as we rolled toward Baltimore, as we explained to the officer. His rejoinder was to the effect that he had chosen to favor us. He was taking us "in" and we must follow him.

"In" was down the highway toward Baltimore a mile or so and onto a rundown farm property. There, in a patch of woods, was an old, two-story frame house which had doubtless known better days, though never a drop of paint. Its living room, with plaster departing its walls despite layers of torn and tattered wallpaper, dirty bare floor, tin cans filled with sand and each topped with a mound of cigarette butts, an old, chipped spittoon, a rickety old table and several chairs to match, was nevertheless seeing its grandest days. For it was the courtroom of the justice of the peace.

As the policeman marched us in, the fat, unkempt old man seated behind his table looked up and sharply eyed us. I carefully turned my back on a huge calendar with a big, half-naked blonde at its top and looked back at him easily so as neither to ignore nor buck his eyeing, both gestures being instinctive defense against any compounding of the trouble we were in. But this wasn't enough, for our driver had his hat on, as did also a crony of the justice's sitting over against the wall.

"Take that hat off! This is a courtroom!", the J.P. declared.

My friend quickly doffed his hat, with the justice's crony following suit, though in such leisurely manner as clearly to convey that he was not really under the same compulsion. There followed the pretense of a hearing and the inevitable finding of guilt, with exaction of a fine.

I often tell my friend that the fine foisted on him that day was an addition to the high price he paid for his conspicuous consumption. Had the policeman known that besides that Oldsmobile 98 my friend possessed a PhD in economics from Harvard, he would have been also fined for such disorderly conduct.

Now the typical crowded city bus, behind schedule, jerking, bucking, and rocking, and manned by an irritable and discourteous driver, is only the beginning of discomfort for the Negro passenger who boards its local versions plying Sixteenth Street in the District of Columbia. Most of the buses there are left-over, narrow-aisled, with motors noisy, springs worn out, and windows jammed. Moreover, both heating and cooling systems are out of order. Before a passenger like myself boards one of those wrecks, he must stand at his stop and see bypass him suburban-bound express buses that are filled with whites and are newer, faster, bigger, and cooler in the summer and warmer in the winter than the ones marked "Local." These express buses slap him in the face, for though his taxes and the displacement of Negro homes make possible the broadened streets on which they roll, Negroes cannot freely live in the communities those buses serve.

If that Negro passenger-to-be stands at the front of a waiting group otherwise made up of whites, the white driver is all too apt to stop either short of or beyond him so that the paler people can board first. Or, should he stand waiting alone, or as one of a group altogether Negro, and the driver already has anything faintly resembling a loaded bus, he might be passed by altogether. Or, let the bus be loaded but the driver feel generous, he may stop and squeeze in a few more passengers from the folks at the stop, especially if their front edge is white. His charity often ceases precisely as the first Negro foot is about to fall on the doorstep.

Still more irksome to him than those decrepit, local buses—those symbolizing his exclusion from suburbia, whose way he underwrites—and their surly, racially abusive drivers, are the passengers he must join aboard the bus, especially the white women among them. Yes, the whites who are most upsetting are older and female, clinging harder to yesteryear's color separation practices and the super-super status said to be theirs.

First there is that kind who approaches the only vacant spot left in the bus, the aisle-side of the seat I am in. Instead of sitting at once, she stands over me, quite obviously making another survey of the place, then gingerly seats herself by backing into the seat, perhaps to remain seated in such side-saddle fashion until one of us departs. All of this is to display that sitting in that place was a matter of the very last resort, "I was just so very tired!" Many a time I have had such an old woman hardly get herself seated and all her packages in her lap, when suddenly it became her move again. A vacancy next to another white passenger develops, and as old and worn (perhaps fat, too) as she is, she has to pop up and take to the aisle fast, before that safer seat gets away.

Then there are the white lady shoppers who board buses in the central business district that are destined to take on and discharge many Negro passengers before the ladies reach their stops, but as they board, the bus is fairly white and empty. Often such a lady prepares her defense by staking claim to a whole seat, aisle and window side both, sitting in one part and using the other for her baggage, so that it says in effect, "No Negroes Allowed." The lady simply sits and feigns not noticing the Negro arrivals (a book or magazine in which to bury the face is a good, added prop for the nasty act). Then as soon as a white person approaches she lifts her packages over into her lap and smilingly makes the seat available. Her face is adorned with a look combining the benign and the immensely self-satisfied. It says, "This day 1 have done this for you, myself, and our Caucasianness!"

Not long ago, during the evening rush hour, I boarded a quite crowded bus, its aisle filled with passengers forced to stand. I was hanging over a seat occupied by two white women when the one seated next to the aisle and nearest me arose and began pushing her way out. Though my hand remained on the rail along the back of the vacant half of the seat, I was not permitted to enter it. For the lady seated by the window had also risen, backed herself out into the aisle in a manner to leave, her ample bottom a completely effective blockade against all save those meeting her approval. Then she called aloud and toward the front of the bus, "Mary! Mary! Here's one," Mary was a third white woman standing in the aisle at least a half-dozen seats ahead, who had to push and pull her way past a half-dozen Negroes to reach the seat thus commandeered. During that same trip, and as I continued standing on the very same bus, a white fellow stole a seat for a girl of his acquaintance under similar circumstances, gallantly professing to give her the seat which was by no means his in the first place. Indeed, I would label as common practice a certain procedure employed by many white women leaving the Sixteenth Street buses for their homes in the many apartment houses along the way. It is to catch the eye of a lady who is still standing, a passenger of her own choosing, one a stranger but invariably white, and beckon her to come and have the seat about to be vacated. I have seen this ignobility done dozens of times, as Negro women, workers who have stood all day long in elevators and behind food counters, stand nearest those seats preempted for white "ladies" by white "ladies."

I became most fed up with the antics of a white lady passenger on a Sixteenth Street bus, not during the evening hours, when tension on the buses is inevitably high, what with the long waits, the scramble to get aboard, the surly drivers in charge, and the crowdedness that all passengers in common must suffer. Instead it was early one sunny morning, when I was ahead of schedule and all was right with the world. Boarding a white-sprinkled bus from a suburban direction, a Negro most often looks for a completely vacant seat. If it is not readily seen, a vacant half will do. That one nearest the front is preferred and taken with complete disregard of the white occupant to be joined, lest he or she gets the slightest notion that leave to sit there is sought, or that any value save the seating is to be served. This is at least an honest revelation of my own perspective, and it was the way I sought a seat that morning. It led to me to sit between a Negro woman and a white woman, each at an end of a three-passenger seat placed lengthwise and across from the driver's seat.

Pulling myself in and together as much as possible so as to avoid sitting against either lady, I sank into the open space. As soon as I did so, it became evident that the white lady to my right, and next to the entrance, was in a high state of discomfiture. She stirred, squirmed, shifted, and shrugged, as if suffering some sort of malady. I turned casually and gently in her direction expecting to see a sickly looking soul. But I was met with such a hard scowl and burning stare as to cause me to abandon my concern. The lady wasn't sick, she was mad, mad as the proverbial wet hen, that I would sit next to her. I turned away from the sight of her and tried to put her presence out of mind, taking a section of the morning's newspaper and folding it lengthwise to half its width in the best of big city transit-riding tradition. But the fidgeting continued, I could fairly feel her fuming. Suddenly, near surprising myself, my resentment of hers spilled out.

I folded up my paper, stuck it under my arm, and turned toward the woman, saying, "Lady, I have this seat, and I am staying in it. This is a public bus, and I'm part of the public. If you think you're so wonderful that I mustn't sit by you, it is you who doesn't belong here, not me."

She did not appear moved in the slightest, replying simply, but in a rockhard tone, "I said nothing to you."

It was the white bus driver I had angered. He gave me a lynching look but said nothing and stuck to his appointed task.

WHITE EXPECTATIONS OF BLACKS

My realization that whites expect me to behave as they fancy most Negroes act (which is to say short of the standards they set and presumably themselves meet) first came quite early in my life.

The introduction was at the county fair. Somebody staged a watermelon eating contest, and I was among the contestants, largely a group of eight- and nine-year-old white and Negro youngsters. We were the near penniless and hungry ones taking in the fair without our parents but missing little, because we would work our way in to this show and that, and if not permitted, "worm-it" in. There were three of us who were colored, stuck together at one end of the line of contestants. None of us was among the winners. But I remember that almost all of the people who watched the contest gathered at our end, laughing and yelling. They stayed around us and kept laughing even after the man running the contest had picked the winners. (Years later I gained for myself an explanation of why a Negro is viewed as inordinately fond of watermelon. It is because the white man is ashamed of himself, especially of some of the more gluttonous areas of his appetite, that he seeks to share his misery, even to pass the buck. For this reason Negroes love watermelon, fried chicken—and sex.)

The rhythm business—"all of them have it"—was bothersome early also. There I would be on the streets in downtown Champaign, eight or nine years old, a hard-working old man of a little boy, most always with a mission. At first it was merely taking laundry across town, but soon, shopping and paying bills for Mama, delivering my Negro papers to Negroes employed downtown, getting a money order at the post office, or picking up examination questions from the central office of the public schools for the principal at mine. I knew my way about downtown and was responsible. But I was Negro, too. So the white trash who hung about town would call me whatever they wished and ask me to sing or dance; I had to have rhythm and was to play simple and happy for them. I fancy that this expectation left me one who rarely sings and who dances like an elephant. For I never smiled for them, only seethed inside and glummed up outside.

This having to grin and have rhythm had something to do with a little event on the Boardwalk in Atlantic City one Sunday morning. My six-year-old nephew and I had stopped to look at a window filled with toys. The Shriners were in convention at Atlantic City, and two of them joined our window-looking. Before I could intervene, one of them had asked my nephew to "cut a step for us," and he was cutting it. I never reached a boil quite so fast in all my life, though my wits remained with me. When the lad finished his jig, the Shriner started to hand him a quarter.

But I pushed my nephew back, saying, "No, Buzzy, no. Now you can ask them to do something funny for you. See the little red monkey-caps on their heads. That means they are monkey-shiners. They do lots of crazy things."

My nephew stood watching and waiting and finally turned to that one for whom he had jigged, saying "Wel', wacha gonna do?"

By this time, faces were, of course, as red as fezzes. The blunderer offered an apology, and the two soon slipped away, leaving me to try explaining to Buzzy why they did not seem to want to do anything funny. It was a hard job, partly because Buzzy was so young and unknowing of white expectations of him. But it was difficult also, because what had been done was so galling and had left me so angry.

That "they just will steal" is an abiding notion. Today it still slaps me, and more often when I am in the public presence of older white women. It is the more noticeable, as women carry those huge handbags big enough to contain all of their makeup material and most of their other treasured trappings. Despite the bulk and weight of these luggage pieces, many older white women, when bus riding, quickly move them from one hand to another, or from shoulder to shoulder, or when in restaurants and cafeterias, from one chair or corner of a table to another to get them beyond my presumedly larcenous reach. Once when I stood in the aisle of a packed bus next to such a lady with such a bag that was wide-open, I momentarily hesitated to advise her of the fact. She might soon afterwards dig among all of the many, many items and fail immediately to locate the object of search, and I would be a thief for sure.

FROM MERE BLUR TO MIGHTY BIG PROBLEM

Worse, of course, than being seen indistinctly and expected to fit the mythological uniformity is hardly being seen at all, being at most a blackish blur, near nothing much at all. This is an offense which cuts hard, because it strikes in unguarded moments, and the offender seems so unconscious of what he is doing. The prejudice is so deep that its expression is unwilled. It is automatic.

This often occurs as I stand in a queue. One citizen after another, all colors, all classes, occupations, sexes, sizes, unceasingly line up in public places these days, caught in what passes as most plainly a hit of democracy, surpassable only by the "take-a-number" system. I have often been frontmost in line waiting for a bus, and if the bus driver does not pull up short or go past me, whites, one or even two of them—more often women but also men—step around and board first. Then there is the cafeteria line at an institution I frequent, which each noon hour grows long enough to shut off access to the newspaper stand and the elevators. Newspaper readers and riders to the upper floors must cut through the line. Most of these people forced to break the waiting line are white. Too many of them too often pick the space in front of me as the place to cross, frequently doing so without an "excuse me" or a "beg pardon," a smile, or even a grunt. Notice of the presence of my kind seems lacking altogether.

Consider the department stores and the lines that sprout in them more profusely and grow longer than ever. As I have stood in them, at the counter and next up, the white from behind has often made his or her inquiry or hanged-in from the side, seemingly oblivious of the priority of my Negro presence. If any account of me is taken, the excuse is offered not to me but to the clerk. "I'm in an awful hurry," it may run, which I must suppose also is to say "as, of course, this Negro is not." Or, when I am next in line, as happens to me most often at the bank, the white person in front of me chooses the occasion to relax with the clerk across the counter, to comment upon the weather, get acquainted, tell the latest story heard, and maybe hear another in exchange.

I feel most definitively pushed from the realm of humanity and rendered nobody whatsoever in a certain cafeteria situation. It came on me one day in a government cafeteria where I stopped for coffee. The hour was quite early, and most of the dining tables were unoccupied. Leaving the cashier, I chose an unoccupied table near a rack for empty trays. I had just removed my cup of coffee from the tray, placed it on the rack, and seated myself, when a white girl chose the table next to mine. After placing her cup of coffee on her table, she turned and disposed of her tray, not on the rack, which was as near to her table as mine, nor on an empty table to her right. No, what she did was to drop her tray on my table! As she turned and sat, I pushed her tray forward and off my table, from which it fell at her feet with a loud bang. The few people scattered in the cafeteria looked up, as the girl rose to pick up the tray. She was as embarrassed and flustered as she offered an explanation as I was angry and unforgiving.

Another cafeteria encounter occurs more often and with my being and its blackness taken into careful account. The annoyance is initially slight but sometimes slips into vexation.

The lady with a loaded tray looks for a seat in a hostessless, crowded cafeteria. It is one whose patronage is largely office workers from nearby buildings, who eat in groups — "our crowd" — often four each, a neat adjustment to the tables with that many chairs about each. During the rush hour, tables with empty chairs, and much less anything like a welcome aura, are few and far between. But deep in the crowded room there is a table with a lone occupant, a Negro fellow.

The lady spots the potential and commences a hesitation waltz in the direction of the three empty chairs and the lone Negro male. She is hesitant because she is ambivalent; the chair she needs is there, but so is a man near whom she feels she cannot afford to sit. He sees her half-hearted approach, her continued search for a place to squeeze in. She stops and surveys the place, once, twice, maybe three times. It is more than a survey she repeatedly makes; it is also a pantomimed soliloquy conveying a "social" message to all who see the act. "If some of *you* don't make room for me, I shall have to sit with one of *them*," it says. But the message is missed; those of her kind are too busy making the most of the noon hour respite to get it. Reaching the table with empty chairs, needed and wanted but unwanted too, she may not immediately sit. One more look about is often made, even after the tray has been released to the table, thus to portray her absolute helplessness and claim mercy from her kind. Then she grimly drops into the shadowed seat.

I am often the Negro fellow at that table.

I can accept that kind of maneuvering and have grown accustomed to it.

But what occasionally happens cuts through my acceptance and irritates me. This is when the "some lady" suddenly switches off all the disdain displayed for the benefit of those in the white world, but which I have read better than they, by staging a big smile and in faked graciousness asking, "Do you mind?" That inquiry, I do mind. For in truth what had obsessed and then still obsesses her is that her world would and does mind her sitting across the table from me. The "minding" has not been left to me, and she knows it. Moreover, she and her world comfortably assume that I would not mind her presence and would inevitably be pleased and flattered by it. In their blighted view, if any question remains, it is that I may prove overly and presumptuously pleased.

There also are the cases of relationships across the color line in which I am seen too precisely for my comfort as a Negro, seen as a servant. For example, I frequently ride railway sleeping cars and more than once have been assigned the role of porter. I do have the coloring and features of the typical porter. But 1 have never gone about a sleeping car in porter's cap, white jacket with silver-colored badge, navy blue trousers, and black shoes. Still, on more trips than fingers on my hands, other passengers have stopped to ask of me questions that are for the porter.

It happens also on automatic elevators. The sign outside makes plain that the elevator is automatic and the one inside above the buttons tells one to push the number of his floor. But as "push button" as our culture is becoming, it remains nice to have a Negro at one's call, even briefly and fleetingly. So when one of them stands too near the panel, he's sometimes asked to push the button. Several times an older woman has called her floor to me as she stood with her face to that panel on her side of the car.

On the other hand, some white people are excessively considerate with Negroes. They treat us like children, and we are not permitted to do for ourselves. The caring is custodial; control goes along with it, and I never liked it. It mistreats me because it calls me "Boy!"

These people, for example, hand me the simplest kind of an informational piece but stop to draw word pictures of its meaning, with an air which reads, "See how nice I am to colored people." They hand me the standard application for this or that only after marking on it a huge *X* wherever the form plainly says in heavy type *Applicant's Signature*. Or, as the marriage clerk seemed about to do for me in Georgia, they stand ready to place a hand on mine and guide me aright with the laborious event.

PANIC POINTS

Jesus Christ was thrice denied by Simon Peter, a well-known episode. Negroes are denied daily, not by their followers, but by those whites who profess to practice integration with them, especially on the job. Thus scorning of a black colleague or fellow employee can occur at the office or in the plant, but more often takes place beyond the workplace, wherever the twain might meet—were they not white and black. It's done snidely, subtly, sometimes gently. The individual white is its perpetrator. Sometimes he or she is shameful of the stooping, though hardly able to avoid it. It takes more strength to stand tall and straight in this situation than most whites have.

I know something about it, because I was a Negro employee of the federal government in a professional job for nearly thirty years. Uncle Sam may not yet be the fairest employer of all, but he has been moving along for many years, and I have always worked for him with and among whites. I have been a member of what at least looks like an "integrated" work force, at the desk, in and out of the lavatories and cafeterias, and, yes, sometimes at those Christmas parties.

Now this was the funny thing about those whites and me as we "integrated." Most of them recognized and communicated with me as freely in the hallway, the elevator, and the building lobby as they did when I had business with them in their cubbyholes, or they had a mission in mine. But beyond those more familiar haunts, the oil of our togetherness often ran awfully thin. Some of the men had a hard time seeing and knowing me, for all my visibility, once the encounter was beyond the building and occurred in the neighborhood cafeterias, downtown, or out in their suburbs, particularly when they were in the presence of other whites. When the two of us suddenly and unexpectedly saw each other, all too often that inadvertent collision of eyesights was followed by a swift and subtle exchange of recognition—and nothing more. That light flash of recognition took place quickly and warily, his for the sake of white conformity and mine out of empathy for him and his weakness. And this only begins to suggest the care which must be exercised when the white co-worker who becomes caught in a similar off-beat setting is female.

Indeed the color-weak and -wary among those associates of mine could have been distributed along a continuum of distance stretching beyond that floor of the building that served as our sanctuary as far as we traveled. For some of them, the "recognition-reach," it might be called, extended no farther than the lobby.

But the hardier dared openly to greet their Negro co-workers farther and farther away from the offices they shared as their paths crossed in neighborhood shops and cafeterias, in the downtown district, on buses destined for the suburbs, and in the suburban shopping centers. The panic points for them varied ever so widely. The numbers of those so courageous diminished in proportion to the distance of the outermost point for recognition from the workplace. There were, of course, factors of happenstance to strengthen the spine of the white worker. If, when he meet his Negro fellow employee, he was alone, or with other employees of his agency, or with his children, an open salutation was understandable, explainable, excusable. (A Negro girl of my acquaintance was once amused by the young white fellow who worked the desk adjoining hers in an employment service office in East St. Louis. He lunched wherever he willed in downtown East St. Louis, and she in the one or two places where she could. He daily met her on the street, and the two greeted each other as pleasantly as when they were together in the office, he being on his way back, from lunch and she on her way to get it. But one day he saw her and did not speak; he only flushed a deep red instead, for he was not alone but in the company of other men — "businessmen I just met," he later explained, flushing again.)

When this kind of silly circumspection involved a lady encountered by a Negro male hundreds of miles away from their common ground and cohorts, social reciprocity was fairly to be strangled.

But take my encounter with Betty, to start with. She is a young white girl from West Virginia who several years ago began her probationary period as a clerk-typist in government in an office which I shared with several other men. She was a slow typist and error-prone to a high degree. A bright, young, white associate of mine wrote her off as "too dumb to bother with." But she seemed friendly and secure with me despite my color. So I tried to be helpful to her, interpreting for her government instructions for stenographers, showing her how to use the organization manual, helping her with spelling, and the like. After six months of such association, I chanced one evening to find a vacant bus seat beside that in which she sat. She recognized me immediately but at once deigned not to appear to do so on that crowded bus. We rode for at least thirty blocks, seated next to each other, as each of us feigned not knowing the other.

Now take the strangulation.

Not long ago, on a train headed for Washington, I encountered a certain lady who has known me for at least fifteen years. We not only knew each other as fellow public servants in the same agency, but we had once spent a long, pleasant evening at a party as guests of a mutual Negro friend. Moreover, for several years preceding our meeting on the train, each of us had filled a position requiring occasional telephone conversations and office visits between us. At the particular time we were stationed in the same building, a small one in which we saw and greeted each other frequently and easily, each calling the other by the first name.

But the train was necessarily another kind of meeting place, as it would have been for any white woman, save the extraordinary one. The train was altogether first-class, and its several hundred passengers as near that level as they come. Still, amidst all of those people, urbane though strange to her, passingly involved with her, and generally never to be seen again, it was I who had so long known her who was to be alien, indeed less than alien. Within the steel walls of the speeding enclosure that is a train, strangers often make rapid acquaintance, recognizing instinctively, though unspokenly, that they are in the hands of fate and an engineer, both unseen. The phenomenon sometimes enables an easy and quick relating of two even across the color line. But friends, at least acquaintances, as my co-worker and I were back in the familiar haunt of our agency, on that train we studiously denied each other.

During the eighteen-hour trip, we saw and unspokenly recognized each other twice in the crowded diner and once in the club car. As we sat across from each other in the club car, each of us swiftly and silently acknowledged the presence and being of the other, time after time, upon looking up from our magazines. It was I who fled the car after an hour of the farce. As I left, I first told myself that I was allowing my co-worker the convenience and peace of my absence. But, more deeply, I admitted to myself that the relief was mine too. I was abandoning the discomfort of the forced restraint which was fast converting the innocence of our relationship into one so needlessly felt surreptitious. I had fled before yielding to a temptation to break all the hypocrisy asunder by speaking to her by name. If she suffered embarrassment, let her, for she was the weak one. The etiquette book, and the common practice of race relations, as well, privileged her to take the initiative to speak to someone she had long known as nothing other than a gentleman. She should have done so and been done with it all.

I fled to avoid being so radical and making any sort of an ado about it all.

It was my intention, upon returning to the sanctum of our salt mine, forever to play my part in the silly game of "it-never-happened." As I saw my colleague in the corridor and on the elevators we shared back in Washington I would accept her greeting as in the past, should she offer it.

Soon after returning to work, I saw my friend in a hallway. On such safe ground, she rushed to restore our relationship, in language making plain that I had not misinterpreted her behavior.

"Wasn't it you I saw on that train? You know as soon as 1 left it, I had the feeling it was you I had seen in the club car. Wasn't it you?" she said.

"Yes, it was I," I replied, and moved on.

I think that I understand the box in which my co-worker found herself. It was not one of her own making, though it is one which all white females, past puberty, are expected to neatly fit. The strength of the taboo against sex relations between the Negro male and the white female dictates against even the faintest appearance of its violation before the eyes of whomsoever. Whenever there is an open association between the two who are never to meet in the dark, all others put themselves on inquiry. Especially does the white male searchingly view the sight with scurrilous bend. Thus the white woman of sufficient maturity and sensitivity to be witting of her social ways painstakingly avoids the risk save for some truly pressing reason.

BEAST AND REBEL

The most horrible nigger conceivable in America is that black male who dares transgress the taboo against his consort with a white female. He is thereby a black beast and a black rebel. Once the two are seen together in the light of day, they are envisioned together in the dark, and they constitute an ugly and scornful spectacle.

One evening during my junior year in high school, one of the loveliest and brightest girls in my class and I found ourselves walking together East on Green Street in Champaign, she toward home and myself toward the University of Illinois Armory and Indoor track practice. I was burdened with books, mine under one arm and hers under the other, a circumstance precluding handholding, I should perhaps add. As we neared a big rooming house, a coed sitting in a great wide window seat glanced at us and quickly ran away from the window. In a moment, and before we were completely past the house, the girl was back in the window; not only was she back, but what seemed twenty other girls had joined her. They looked at us, some gaping, some laughing, several pointing. I looked at them out of the corner of my eye, while my companion kept on with her merry chatter. I resented being a spectacle, while she seemed not to notice. I was, of course, no special cause of hers, not even much of an occasion, only a bit of happenstance.

Since that day, on a number of occasions and as employee of the federal government, I have gone to lunch with a white female, a professional colleague, a visiting "firelady" seeking services from my agency which were within my responsibility, or a local citizen volunteer concerned with the problems to which the programs of my agency were addressed. Such a luncheon date, the trips on the way to and from it as well as its duration, becomes an adventure in race relations for its immediate parties. The white eyes are upon them gawkishly, inquiringly, disapprovingly. Whenever my engagement has been with a lady wearing flat heels and tweed suits, and especially when she was older or without striking appearance, the stupid staring has let up some as time passed. But when her heels were spiked and her appearance attractive, there was no subsiding of curious concern, particularly that both white and masculine.

I remember too having to decline the services of an excellent stenographer, despite her competence, because she was also quite the most attractive and personable such employee in the lot. When she had learned that I was to have full-time stenographic assistance in lieu of part-time help of the kind, she let it be known that she would be pleased to have the job. She had enough seniority to entitle her to a priority of opportunity to fill it and had no competition. Nevertheless, I hastened to the ghetto to locate a Negro stenographer. The crux of the responsibilities of my position involved persuasive efforts with others of a staff virtually all of whom were white males. I well knew that having that girl for a secretary, despite her efficiency, would inevitably and unnecessarily complicate my winning friends and influencing people.

SKIRMISHES WITH SPECIAL KINDS

Now take the people who invite me to join them in their bigotry against other minority groups, non-Negro people, low on the totem pole, though not at the very bottom with me. Negroes know, of course, that they are the most despised of all the disparaged. This means too that many who detest Negroes also dislike other groups. When John Rankin of Mississippi really spilt his spleen in the Congress, he lumped the "wops" and the "kikes" with the "niggers." So a bigot is a bigot, and I know it. To ask me, he is the worst-off of all the victims, and to join in the victimizing insults both my intelligence and my humanity. To expect me to do unto others, or to bless being done to others, what I would not have done to me assumes that I am a moral fraud. It always angers me.

Once in a Pixley and Ehlers cafeteria in Chicago, during the noon rush, I was one of three young men who all reached an unused table at about the same time. The other two were black-haired and dark-skinned but whites. One of them suddenly re-loaded his tray and left the table to find space for himself at the next one. The remaining one ate hurriedly and was soon gone, whereupon the fellow who had first departed at once returned.

"The god-damned kikes! They push in on you everywhere," he explained his plight.

"Oh?" I said, "Was that why you left?"

"Yeah," he replied.

"Well," I began, "Do you know him, know that he's Jewish?"

"I wouldn't let him know me, but you can always tell 'em," he replied.

"I can't," I said, "and the truth is that you and he looked something alike to me."

"Well, we sure 'n hell aren't. I'm Italian," he angrily advised me, as he flushed a bit.

It was then that I chose to say what had begun rushing through my mind, as I recalled the Italian families I had known as I grew up.

"You know," I said, "down in Champaign, where I grew up, the Italians I knew were mostly truck farmers, grocers, fruit peddlers, and cab drivers. I thought that was about all there was to them as I played with their children. But the more I went to school, the more I read of Rome, Florence, and Venice, and Italian statesmen, painters, musicians, sculptors, and such. And I don't think that really you know anything much about Jews."

I stopped for breath, and I could tell that he was ready for the one more thing I had to say.

"Besides, you really would as soon run from me as from that Jewish fellow, if not sooner," I finished and walked out.

For a while afterward, we remained passingly familiar with each other.

I would see him in the Loop, and he would say, "Hello there," in a friendly manner.

One day a little later, it was the Chinese I was to join in scorning. I was expected to join an Aryan, or someone who thought himself somehow higher on the totem pole, in snickering at a couple of them. The Chinese consul's office and that of my government agency employer were both in the General Finance Corporation building at Lake and Wells in Chicago.

Two people at once appearing to me an affluent and distinguished Chinese couple, she in native dress, stood in the lobby waiting for an elevator, as a white fellow, of rather nondescript appearance, and I joined them. They seemed happily busy with themselves as they conversed in a strange and musical tongue, broken occasionally by a brief exchange in very good English. As all of us boarded the elevator, the white one of us Americans took one of its back corners, and I the other, while the Asian two stood in front of us, continuing their chatter now steadily in Chinese, or whichever of its many dialects, punctuated by bursts of gay laughter.

The speed of the express elevator was not so great as not to allow time for me to feel humble as I heard but could not understand the two strange people who also spoke my language impeccably, and laughingly left me all the more on the outside. As they were leaving the elevator, my fellow citizen from his corner, lost in his pseudo-superiority, slyly winked and grinned at me. In response, I tried as hard as I could to freeze my face precisely as it was, totally to reject his silent and stupid message. Later my disgust with him was followed by amusement. But still later I pitied his confused being.

One night a poor, white woman, so naive as a sleeping car passenger as to be near frightened, nevertheless looked deeply down her nose at Asians who were to ride in the same Pullman car, easily assuming that I, as her redcap, would share her concern. A relative had given her a trip to Canada, but she had never before ridden a train, not to speak of a sleeping car such as she was boarding. She asked me dozens of questions, having another for me whenever she saw me during her stay in the waiting room. At last her sleeping car was ready for its passengers. I deposited her and her humble luggage in the seat that would become her berth, answering each of her last batch of questions by passing the buck. "Lady, the Pullman porter will take care of you now. He'll answer any questions you may have," I told her.

But little did I know that she would ask me still another. For in a few minutes I was back at her car, this time with a party of Japanese gentlemen. They appeared elegant in their Western dress, several of them speaking fluent English, and all bearing camera cases, brief bags, and luxurious luggage of heavy cowhide leather. The central figure was an envoy plenipotentiary of His Imperial Majesty, the Emperor of Japan, and headed an entourage on the way for discussions with the Canadian Government. The lady watched me bring them in and settle them in their bedrooms. However, she was not at all impressed by them as I was.

As I started from the car, she summoned me and this time whispered, her query. "Do I have to ride in this car with *them*?"

"Lady," I said, "see your porter."

I must also tell of a kind of personal rubbing with whites, usually on the street, which never ceases to leave me with mixed feelings. This white is the down-and-out fellow who begs me for a quarter, money for a sandwich, a bowl of soup, or a cup of coffee. I speak only of those who pick me, a Negro, or my one or two companions and me, all of us being Negroes, from among all those passing his way, who are in great majority white, to ask for charity. The problem, for problem it is to me, first presented itself late one night long ago on the platform of an elevated train station as I stood there with my date. The young lady and I were leaving the theater and but for that visibility of ours would have been lost in the crowd of people leaving the place. We were the only Negroes in an assemblage waiting for an elevated train that numbered fifty or sixty persons at least, all of them neatly dressed, laughing and talking after the relaxation handed them across the footlights. I looked up and noticed a fellow, sticking out like a sore thumb, wending his way through the crowd. He was what Chicagoans call a "Madison Avenue bum," an older man, dirty and unshaven, beaten and bedraggled looking. I had momentarily forgotten him and was facing my companion, when I felt a nudge in my side. Turning in its direction, I faced the poor fellow and his plea, first for a cigarette, and next for coffee money. I gave him the cigarette, struck a match and successfully held its flame for him until he managed a puff or two. A quarter for his coffee was provided also.

Now I am a fairly easy mark for the fellow who needs a friend. I was early made that way, and it includes a deep belief that I am not to be concerned with the color of the man who needs me nor to go far in judging either the reality of his need or the honesty of his declaration as to how he will use what is mine to give. What bothered me on the elevated platform, and bothers me in similar situations, is the white singling out of a Negro, for behind it is the idea of white superiority. What this white man's picking of a Negro to beg says is that no matter how unfortunate his circumstances have become, how low his fortunes have sunk, his whiteness leaves him free to beg a Negro. Though he is so ashamed of his sorry plight as a member of his group that he must avoid them, he need not hesitate to beg me. Yet, I rebel against the strong temptation to weigh the color factor, even as I sense its presence.

Insult carries added injury for me when it comes from one whose antecedents were drawn into the welcome arms of the lady in the New York City harbor long after mine were brought in shackles to Jamestown or some other southern port. I began to understand what makes these people run from me, when they don't also stop to slap me one, long before I had a good course in sociology. When I was a little fellow, my Uncle Rob had taken me riding on a Halsted streetcar in Chicago and explained why its white passengers reeking with the smell of garlic hated to sit by us blacks, while the other white riders disliked sitting by *them* as well as *us*. Many have been my brushes with these people so anxious to be melted and especially their younger ones, who use less garlic and speak better English, though they still struggle furiously.

But it is the brush from a special group of folks who feel compelled to win their way by frowning hard upon me that bothers me most. It happens infrequently, but whenever it does it stings me like hell.

At first the hurt was hard simply because it was so unexpected. As I grew up in Champaign, the Jewish children with whom I interacted had mostly been reserved but civil, and several were bold and strong enough to be downright friendly anywhere. As my reading extended, I learned more of the Jewish people as an ancient civilization and, ever since, as a strong people contributing good to other peoples around the world, even in the midst of persecution. I learned to wince from "kike" as from "nigger" and to rebuke the anti-Semitic among *us*. Still later, I came especially to appreciate the grasp of Jewish leaders and scholars upon the importance of keeping intact civil liberties in our country and sensed that without this effort, civil rights are not to be won. By the time I reached Washington in 1950, the sum of it was that a Jew had less business mistreating me than any of all of the others who do. He had had centuries, in so many places and in so many ways, to know better, from the Torah through wholesale terror, time after time.

In the mid-fifties I bought and moved into a house in a neighborhood in Washington heavily occupied by Jewish people. I was immediately faced with many milder manifestations of objections to the black influx (Jewish people in neighborhoods of changing color do not behave violently, as do whites and the less secure ethnic groups). Down at the end of the block, a Jewish lady had said to my wife, "I am afraid the niggers are taking this neighborhood." This, despite my wife being rather plainly one of them. Next door, the elderly Jewish lady had invariably called her seven-year-old grandson away from his play with a Negro girl of the same age who often visited us, as if miscegenation would get ahead of his Bar Mitzvah. When she received by telephone a message that her husband had been felled by a stroke and was dying, it was my wife to whom she turned in her screaming and pitifully emotional state.

What deeply angered me was an occurrence soon thereafter. I had started into a neighborhood Kosher delicatessen, when I was suddenly interrupted, almost accosted, by a well-dressed, comfortable-looking Jewish fellow leaving the place.

Said he, "Wait a moment. You look like a friendly fellow. I want to ask you something." I pulled up and stood facing him, ready to be the friendly one.

"Tell me," he continued, "why do so many of *you people* come in here?"

"I'll speak for myself. I happen to like the pastry and Posin's is selling to the public. It's not the dietary laws. Now, why did you have to know so much?" I said, sharply.

He had no answer for me. He merely protested, that he had meant no harm. I had slapped his face, as he deserved, and he could only lie and slink away.

I must not omit the skirmishes with two groups of people that are especially disturbing to me. The first brings me close to hate. It is a brush with a fellow who is plentifully and systematically present. There are enough of them about to make every day for Negroes a time to try their souls.

These whites are in every community of any size across the country, North and South. They are unavoidable by any Negro who is mobile, plays on sidewalks, walks the street, or drives a car. If he stays behind closed doors, these whites come for him. Moreover, as they abuse Negroes, society looks the other way. The newspapers too often profess not to believe that the mistreatment occurs, or they explain it away. The lawmakers prefer more to strengthen the hands of these abusers than to tie them. They provide loose and ill-defined standards of conduct which become at once handy cudgels and easy outs for these prejudiced ones. The analysts of human behavior, even those of misbehavior, are reluctant to study their inhumanity. It is evident that these people are the sickest, sorriest whites in the society and can little be helped. But even those who are specialists in human relations profess that they can be trained into decency, and try it.

Lastly and worst, of all, the community, in effect, especially privileges and equips these whites to mistreat Negroes.

If you have not skipped ahead or are not big and unbiased enough to have guessed it, I write of white policemen.

By and large, the police job falls to left-over, misfit whites. They are often sick and authoritarian besides. They carry an animus for Negroes in their hearts, and their heads are filled with anti-Negro myths. They are next blessed with uniform, star, club, and gun and then proceed to push Negroes about. And the range of their persecution is wide, running from the studied withholding of courtesy and making common language of the racial slur to mayhem and murder, upon less than the drop of a hat. Police officials and the minor courts vie with each other for the honor of protecting this blue-coated edition of the white supremacy system at its rawest, save for the white-robed. And it is said that some men wear blue coats by day and sheets by night.

Let me simply say that I have been law-abiding all my life and cop-pushed just as long and all the same, beginning when I was six or seven years of age.

I have previously mentioned some of my early encounters with policemen. They do not cease.

I had lived in the nation's capital only two days when a policeman threatened me. "You're a smart *one*, I oughta lock you up," he said.

I said no more. He might have exceeded his threat; he might have beaten me up.

What had I done wrong? I had failed to take low and had spoken up for myself like a free being and a citizen, entitled to reason and considerateness. As a stranger in the city, I had parked a car in the wrong direction on a one-way street and was leisurely removing my bags from it. No sign was nearby. The policeman had jumped from a squad car and immediately jumped me.

"Who in the hell do you think you are?" he bellowed. I told him who I was and asked him what was wrong.

"You're asking me!" he again yelled, with inscrutable sarcasm.

By then a stream of vehicles, completely spanning the street, approached and I could figure for myself the mistake I had made. I then pled myself the stranger I in fact was, offering to prove it. I had just come to Washington to take a government job and offered to show him my appointment papers. But he was not interested in the slightest, and I was to follow him to the precinct station. At the station, 1 asserted that his was a fine way to treat a newcomer, and therein I was a "smart *one*."

Shortly afterward, I received and paid for a parking ticket under shadow of an odious racial differential. My car was among those in a long string parked along one side of an alley during a commencement exercise at Howard University, "a nigger school." But such parking nearby and, during ball games, at the adjoining Griffith's Stadium throughout the season drew no such penalties.

A year or so later, I was ticketed for entering a parking space two minutes before the permitted hour, by the say of the white policeman. The "scene of the crime" was Fourteenth Street, North of U Street. I was aware that the time for permitted parking was very close and had rounded the block twice to allow the remaining few minutes of prohibition to expire.

Each time I passed the white officer standing on the corner. He had noticed me, watched me, and walked down the street to draw the fine line.

He told me as much. He had checked his watch as he saw me pull ahead in and park. My watch was two minutes ahead of his, and he and his time piece were the law.

Stories of this kind need telling. For too many people find it comfortable and convenient to assume that it is only the criminal and delinquent, the Negro poor and misguided, who are always with us, that are troubled by the police. But the truth is that many white policemen pick out, pick on, pick up, and persecute Negroes, as they will, and without rhyme or reason. The context need not be crime, nor delinquency, nor street misbehavior, nor improper driving. Parking makes plenty of room for the prejudice and persecution of the police.

If you're a Negro, and a white cop is about, then read the parking sign and understand what thou readest. Make no mistake with the lines painted on the street. Watch that meter that the Man watches, because it's watching you for him. Fool you are to expect reason and the benefit of doubt, for these are the handmaidens of justice, and yours is a confrontation with one who has none for you.

The last of the special encounters is difficult to depict, for here I concede the thinness of my skin. I know that a lot of subjectivity is involved; for to me there is no greater wonder on earth than a child. There is nothing dearer to me than to have or to be able to win the acceptance of a little one. If there be a hereafter, as the Galilean spoke of it, of such indeed should be those to live there.

Yet in this Christian land we warp the measure of man. Children are not permitted to be children in all the pristine pureness meant to be theirs. They too often look upon me with reserve and sometimes with trepidation. There are those who, caught in nearness to me, are brought near whimpering, even in the arms of their mothers. And still, upon occasion, one does the best he can with the slur: "nidder" can be managed. In other instances the child remains half-taught, ventures my way, but is pulled back.

Once on a bus in Milwaukee, a little girl stared at me in shyness and curiosity until she could contain herself no longer.

"Mama," she piped aloud, "What kind of man is that over there?"

The guilty young mother drew her close and whispered something to her. But either the gap was too great for quick closing or the postponement of explanation was not acceptable.

"I know," the child rejoined, "but what kind of man is he?"

239

Several years ago on a Sunday afternoon in Chicago, a little boy scrambled into a bus seat beside me before his mother could prevent his faux pas. She promptly pulled her little son out of the seat saying, "Oh no, Son. You know, we don't sit next to colored in Texas."

"You and your mother are a long way from Texas," came from my lips as he was dragged away.

A moment or so later, all of those aboard the bus could hear his still unsullied innocence. "Mommy," he protestingly piped out, "the man says we're a long way from Texas."

In these situations, there is little place for deep anger, none toward the child, and rarely room for verbal rebuke of the parent. What is left to me instead is a mixture of feeling and musing which altogether is bitter frustration. I can do nothing relieving of the initial hurt and resentment and must leave them to pass slowly.

The child is faultless; he but reflects the misguidance that has become his misfortune. He deserves sympathy, for he has been mistreated; the sweetness of his nature has been confused and blighted by early nurture. Moreover, what is happening to him is not merely emissive, it is commissive in any case, given the permeation of the society by color prejudice. His curiosity, like his love, is being ill-served, to leave him ill-prepared for the years ahead and the world about him. But then the parents who fail him are likely not witting of their way. Indeed, they do not merely withhold the guidance which seems to me right and the child's entitlement, they more often than not teach wrongly, believing their instruction to be quite right. Lastly, the society surrounds the parents with evil practice and has taught them ugly precepts; they are but unknowing carriers of the virus.

What can I do of immediacy to serve my own spirit?

Finally, I suppose I should speak to a likely lingering concern of some readers of the preceding paragraphs.

I would now say this to them: To be sure, who can honestly claim that he has learned infallibly to live by the golden rule? Negroes quite aside, whites are only people, and some of them are discourteous, ill-mannered, inconsiderate, mean and evil, left to themselves. Moreover, few whites daily and deliberately make it their business to mistreat Negroes. Indeed fewer whites than ever do so these days, and instead more and more of them consciously, even penitently and demonstratively, succeed in treating Negroes decently. Besides, what one person does to another in a personal encounter with him can be awfully complicated. Plausible, alternative explanations can be made for many of the incidents I have just related, and I have ascribed racist motivations to unspoken and subtle actions which are hardly provable.

But the devil's due and the difficulty of proof are beside the point the personal encounters related in this chapter would make. The purpose has been to describe *perception*, to tell what has happened and how it struck me. For thousands upon thousands of Negroes have felt slighted in such ways as I have described here.

Find yourself a Negro who respects himself as such, has circulated for a few years in places free of strong fencing between black and white, and can tell it like it is. Get him to do so, and he can tell you stories similar to those above. Swapping such experiences is a familiar pastime among older Negroes. "Now I'll tell you how it was done to me" runs the refrain.

The same informant ought to be questioned carefully. For the fact likely is that he is not only aware of the risk that he may mistakenly attribute mistreatment to color prejudice, he feels constrained and endeavors not to do so. Especially does this burdensome mental and emotional process take place when the apparent deprecation—the racial slight he thinks occurs and knows he felt as such—is unspoken and subtle. For in this context he is caught between his *twoness*: the duality of his being in his own country, as Du Bois long ago conceived it. On the one hand, as a strong and secure Negro, his first impulse is to defend and insist upon the respect to which he is entitled. But on the other, demand and will to be a good and deserving American, according to the creed, tells him that he must himself avoid committing color-based misjudgment, akin to that against which he forever complains. He also senses added challenge in the indirection and the surreptitiousness inhering in the unspoken slur; he will be determined not to let the culprit get away with it, if he in fact is a culprit.

Let me try a description of how a Negro of gentility tries rationally to deal with the suspected irrationality that the unspoken racist slight represents. Suppose that as he walks along a busy street downtown and passes several white men walking abreast of each other in the opposite direction, he receives a sudden swiping, almost a jarring bump from the shoulder of the one nearest him. This fellow turns swiftly, momentarily catches the eye of the Negro who also has glanced back, but The Negro says nothing and proceeds down the street with his companions.

The Negro takes himself in hand quickly, checking the swift surge of anger. He pushes aside the skin-felt finding almost made and at once considers the possible innocence of the suspected one. The Negro mind is crossed by several of a series of explanations of the bump, any one of which may clear the suspect. The white fellow had been merely careless, indifferent, absorbed in thought, or in discussion with his friends. Or perhaps the fellow's eyesight is poor, his movement clumsy, his kinesthetic sense out of order, and so on. Still, he said nothing after the bump. Even so it could be that no racial animus was involved. Perhaps the fellow was generally ill-mannered or so accustomed to bumping and being bumped as not to bother with apologies, or too busy with his friends to stop to offer one.

The Negro must next quickly look and probe for relevant facts, mainly through recall, to support the possibility of innocence. Was the sidewalk crowded? Was it too crowded to expect yielding, without stopping? Had the trio seemed in too big a hurry for that? Is it possible that I was an unnoticing and careless walker myself? Was the trio in conversation? When the fellow turned my way, what did the look on his face say? Did he have on glasses? Look old? And thus a silent finding is made along one of three lines: I am perhaps wrong, and I can forget it. Or I am indeed wrong, and I'm glad I said nothing. Or I am right, and I must not let him get away with it. When the finding is that "I am right!" the silent judgment must receive a prompt follow-up. In the case of the illustration, as terribly swift as the mind can race, it obviously is too late to act once the "bumper" is down the street. But in whatever event, appropriate action is difficult. Propriety rules out tempting approaches: An unspoken remonstrance is generally not possible, for the resentment must be clear and certain. Physical rebuke, cursing and name-calling are beyond usefulness; either of them would lower the mistreated to the level of the wrongdoer. The punishment must no more than fit the crime, for its objective is not vengeance but exposure and deterrence. The Negro is forced simply to speak out, to shame or upbraid, and thus provide a clear rebuke.

The burdensome process need not necessarily have run its course, once the reprimand (if one is deemed necessary) has been administered. It may deliver poorly, leaving the offended Negro frustrated and plagued by thought of the better mouthful he might have spoken. Or worse, on third thought, he may have a lingering suspicion that his finding of guilt was wrong after all. But the very worst of the aftermath of the slight and its rebuke is what occurs however aptly the racial motivation for the slight was discerned and the rebuke administered. In the wake of the episode, the active, personal, and emotional confrontation with the reality of racism reinforces awareness of its pervasiveness. The offended Negro is brought *up-tight*, as it is said, toward all whites among whom he circulates. For a while he may pull back from them with an excessive reserve. He might also carry himself coiled-up, prepared to strike out upon slightest provocation, and without the painstaking rationality characterizing his normal reaction when he feels racially slurred. The provocation might too soon occur, and his behavior leave people wondering what really happened, while little realizing that so much had. The chain of emotional events leading to the unhappy result will likely remain as secluded as those of the same kind producing many an auto accident.

Indeed, there is a wider risk that the Negro of gentility runs, as he suffers the racist slur and slight. Consider that the stings are recurrent. The misdeeds perceived are less and less crude and gross and more often subtle. They are not the work of a few whites who are plainly marked "bigot" but of the legions who are simply condescending and disdainful, easily and unwittingly so. And they take place not in isolated, special circumstances but in a public place and place of public accommodation passing as *integrated* and to which employment, shopping, and the like take one regularly.

This is somewhat the nature of what happens and is risked, it seems to me, when polite and politic blacks demand respect, and whites, even urbane whites, are unable to yield it as the two encounter each other in the presumed absence of the color line. The wide risk is doubting the wisdom, workability, and worth of real integration, losing heart from the long road, and wandering away!

An Exceptional Family in the Lawndale Ghetto

O, yes
I say it plain,
America never was America to me,
And yet I swear this oath—America will be!
—Langston Hughes

In 1966 Martin Luther King of Atlanta, Georgia, made for himself a second home in the slum-ridden Lawndale section of the West Side of Chicago. From there he would wage war against the "slum-lords" and the housing segregation upon which they feed.

There he would dive as much as need be among the poorest and most non-urbanized of Chicago's immigrant Negro masses, lost and hapless in her second-rate ghetto, and scorned by all other Chicagoans. For not only do whites abhor this great black heap of people, their ugly presence in that lake-shored, skyscraper-studded city, but so also do those Negroes in the bigger and better ghetto, the first-class one on the South Side. After all, many of the South Side Negroes reached the city in the twenties, thirties, and forties and have forgotten the fields of Mississippi and Louisiana. They have the better of the jobs that Negroes may have in Chicago and boast of addresses in the shined up, high-rise sections of the number one ghetto and its bigger, run-down apartments left by fleeing whites. As they look toward the West Side and down their noses at their kinsmen there who arrived only yesterday, they can have grand illusions about themselves.

These certified Negro Chicagoans like to feel that they have made it. They go in and out of the Loop daily, live along the Lake, and can pay higher rents, drive longer cars, have bigger parties, and drink better liquor than those country Negroes on the West Side. Though the fact may be that the great racial ghetto in which they live and the white racism which binds them there are both the worst in the nation, the truth was too ugly for their facing. They were in Chicago because the *Defender* had said that freedom was to be found in Chicago, and they had long since learned to act as if it really were. They had built themselves an image and had a face to save. So their habit was to ignore ghettoization and its frightfulness, much as Mayor [Richard] Daley once assured the NAACP's national convention meeting in Chicago that the phenomenon does not exist there. Indeed, they had learned to play blind better than the mayor, bragging of having long ago won black power, playing up as political precocity their election of black aldermen, legislators, and a Congressman from districts virtually lacking white residents. They really know better; they are still short of the freedom they sought. But they cover their failing by faking that segregation has been productive, and all is well. Most of them could afford no admission of need for King; they wanted him left to Montgomery, Selma, and Albany.

There is little wonder, then, that the apostle of nonviolence chose to symbolize his identity with the worst-off, those who are nobody much to anybody in Chicago and who played no make-believe with themselves, by pitching his tent on the West Side, where rioting was to occur that summer.

In that West Side ghetto, a few blocks from King's second home and closer to the scene of the 1966 rioting, stands an apartment building of aging and nondescript appearance, much like that of its sagging companions, teeming with black tenants and crowded along Albany Avenue, as it overlooks the western edge of Douglas Park.

But a closer look will set the building somewhat apart from the others.

Grass adorns its front. Its windows are all unbroken and screened, some containing air conditioners. The window sashing is freshly painted. The terrazo tiling in the entrance hall is intact and clean, the stairway carpeting is complete and in good condition, and the stairway bannisters remain strongly fixed in place. All of this is of far cry from the conditions of its neighboring structures. Most distinctive is the single family name beneath each of its mail slots, for its ten apartments serve ten families, no more. Far fewer people are seen going in and out of this building than of its companions, and occasionally among them are whites, not insurance men and bill collectors either, but whites who are welcomed visitors, and a few of whom even live there. Its Negro occupants are clean, neat, and better dressed than their neighbors, and all of them, grown-ups and children alike, carry books and briefcases. One carries a small leather bag and gets in or out of a black sedan with license tags bearing the prefix "M.D." He is the lone doctor, black or white, with a residence in the Lawndale ghetto.

The Nesbitt brothers, along with their wives and children, are the people who go in and out of the Albany Avenue building laden with books and briefcases. They have been anchored there for twenty-odd years, living caught-up in the tentacles of a great growing octopus, the ghettoed slum surrounding the building that is their home. But they have stuck it out.

These Nesbitts have had the wherewithal for staying on the move, to keep close behind the fleeing whites and ahead of the poorer blacks, as is the practice of many Negroes of their economic level in our ever-blackening central cities. They have not gone on to the comfortable and modern, even luxurious, rental apartments in the redeveloped areas of Chicago's near South Side and near North Side sections. They have occasionally talked of replacing their jointly owned building with a more comfortable one in a safer neighborhood on the far South Side of the city, but they have not so much as examined an offering. Nor have they sought to become what fair housing committee workers call "pioneering" Negro families, those daring first to breach the racial barriers against their presence in suburbia. My brothers have turned deaf ears to the importuning of friends, "tips" on opportunities to get out and get a "good deal" in the process. They spurned too my own counsel that values in the Lawndale section had obviously slidden to the point of no return, and we should all sell out, as I pulled out my share of the ownership.

My brothers somehow found it possible to sit tight there in the losing Lawndale neighborhood. It is time then to tell more of them, what they were like that stays with them and allowed them to stay in Lawndale.

My brothers, of course, came much the same route as was mine, at play and growth, led by Mama, disciplined by Papa and the neighbors, and protesting the racial slur, while struggling to be somebody and cope with color problems. Yet each was and is himself, different enough from the others, because of influences which reached him but not the others, or did so in different degree, or in other ways altogether. Besides, there was all that stress of Mama's on "every tub resting on its own bottom."

BIG BROTHER

Russell Aaron Lovell was the firstborn and bears an official label no lengthier than that borne by any of the rest of us. Mama doubtless contrived those long, given names, each in three parts, so that we would strive to deserve so much, though by the same token, she inadvertently allowed us choice, and each of us has eliminated that one of his names found in some way distasteful.

Russell was a bright and daring child, a wonderful big brother to me, two years his junior. He knew and taught me how to make cart, wagon, and skate mobile, using castaway items of Papa's salvaging; how to put together and take apart a bicycle and ride it swiftly, dangerously, deviously; and how to play the neighborhood games, from shinny and "rounders" to "playing the dozens." Once a kid dared play "the dozens" (alleging incestuous, promiscuous or other improper activity on the part of his playmate's kinspeople, especially his mother), he needed to know how to fight. Russell knew, tried to teach me and, failing, fended for me.

His brains and nerve were also used constructively. At eight or nine years of age, Russ led me back and forth to town, by way of the "shortcuts," across fields, the drainage ditch, and railroad tracks. He showed me the paper route and the locations of the A&P, the wholesale butcher shop, the ice plant, and the dairy—places distant from home to which Mama sent us, saving pennies.

He had fun tutoring his slower, shyer brother. I remember the fig bars like yesterday; he went alone into a little store along our paper route Saturday after Saturday, to buy those cookies, telling me that they sold "four for a nickel." He would always pull two from the sack and hand them to me. "Your half," he would say. It was months before I discovered that the fig bars really were priced at six for five cents and demanded to no avail all those cookies due me. Perhaps a dozen times Russell found a fascinating window for us to look in, then quietly slipped away while I gazed and gazed upon its wonders, only to become "lost" from big brother, who sooner or later came out from his nearby hiding place, full of laughter and teasing. Once he slipped underneath a circus tent, grew disgusted that I lacked nerve enough to follow suit, came back and jerked me in, with a "Gee whiz, how long you gonna stay there, half-in and half-out?"

But his boldness was to lead to long suffering and the learning of real courage. For he hopped one fast-moving truck too many, and the leg that he simply bruised developed osteomyelitis, a crippler which had yet to meet its match in a wonder drug. So the first nine years of Russell's life were followed by nine at Outlook Sanitarium, Champaign County's home for the tubercular and others facing either the last of life or a long struggle to reach mobility again. There he lived much of the time as a lone Negro among whites, and one of a handful of children among adults. He learned to live in bed around the clock, month after month, to accept the periodic cutting of his limbs and scrapings of bone, to endure the lagging healing, and to hang on. At long last and eighteen years of age, he returned to us, first on crutches, then with cane, and finally walking without the aid of artifact save a built-up shoe at the end of a shortened leg.

Russell brought home with him, to share with all of us, knowledge of how to use a thermometer, clean and dress a wound, and take tablets, always easily and only as needed and prescribed. He also came back teaching us a disdain for pain. He still snorts his disapproval of whimpering about hurts and writes off as hypochondriacs all those who complain of pain openly and frequently.

His long years at Outlook Sanitarium included no formal schooling. But he read greedily and beyond his age, whatever fell into his hands, the literary magazines, the social commentaries, some of the classics, and lots of poetry. (Several times he slipped to me collections of verse of his own writing, to read myself and keep hidden from other eyes.) When he came home, he spoke to me about people like George Santayana, H. L. Mencken, John Dewey, and the Webbs, all news to me, though I could tell him about Du Bois, Carter Woodson, A. Philip Randolph, and other black figures of note of whom he then knew little.

That first summer of Russell's at home again, and for good, the super-intendent of schools agreed to give him a test to determine whether he should be permitted to skip the seventh and eighth grades and enter high school. But the two chatted before the test, and Russell's kind of talking led the superintendent to forget the test. Russ graduated in three years and as valedictorian of his class. In the meantime he had become a volunteer neighborhood worker, providing a miscellany of services: reading, writing, and interpreting letters; filling out forms for folks; making complaints downtown for them, by phone; now and then tutoring a child, especially in algebra or geometry; explaining how a medicine works and that it had better be taken; and the like.

Russell works as a quality reviewer for the payment center in the Chicago regional office of the Social Security Administration and also helps train its new employees.

SLIDE RULE AND SIDE LINE

Rozell R. is the third of the five brothers. He abandoned his third name and would have dropped Rufus, his second name, had it been at all possible to do so. For when we were children "Rufus" was linked with "Rastus" to provide white pleasure at black expense. But Rufus was also the name of a warm and generous uncle of ours, of a grandfather, and a great-grandfather as well. The name was too distinct an element of a hazy heritage to drop.

Even the "Rozell" was troublesome, since it appeared feminine to our rough and ready companions. Fortunately it became "Ro" for those in a hurry, and my brother helped make it stick by becoming the biggest, the toughest, the thinnest-skinned, and the most vocal of the Nesbitt lot. Ro's temper flares most swiftly in the face of racial rebuke and no matter the odds against him.

One summer morning, only four or five years ago, Ro again displayed this mix of acute color sensitivity and questionable judgment. He and I were rolling leisurely along a Wisconsin highway, headed for a long weekend of fishing and loafing at a summer home his family shares with several others in the little town of Fox Lake, when a highway patrolman, who seemed at first to be pulling around us, suddenly signaled us to pull to the shoulder. After checking Ro's driver's license and finding it satisfactory, he busily and naively displayed his bias. He admitted there was no speeding, he was acting on a hunch. He admitted he had no probable cause for acting but insisted none was needed. Then he decided that the car seemed a stolen one and wanted to know Ro's occupation and destination. Rozell showed him his identification card as a teacher in the public schools of Chicago, adding that as such he would hardly steal an auto and certainly not a jalopy. Ro's revelation that he was headed for Fox Lake and fishing prompted inquiry as to why he had no fishing tackle along.

Thereupon Ro asserted himself to own property in Fox Lake, where he kept boat and fishing gear. As the young cop gave up and before he took off, Ro dressed him down in language as loud and angry as right. He was plainly prejudiced, had not learned when he could stop and check out a motorist and when he could not, had wasted a lot of his time as well as ours, and maybe missed the chance to catch someone really a thief. He then told the officer that he must not stop every Negro moving because he was in Wisconsin, not Mississippi. He walked away from us in obvious shame, while I found much comfort in knowing that the scene was indeed Wisconsin and not ol' Miss.

For all of his brashness, like many another, Ro keeps a warm and soft interior. He was always a loyal one of his bunch, barefooted along road and street, as Boy Scout, and baseball player, sticking up especially for the lowest on the totem pole. His B.S. in electrical engineering was just that, B.S., to personnel managers as he finished college in 1938. He was ready, but neither industry nor government was prepared for his kind. So initially he made a living from his liking for people, first as youth worker in Champaign and next as a case worker for the Emergency Relief Administration in Chicago.

World War II caused industry to need engineers by the thousands. A firm under contract to make war goods for Uncle Sam was expected to hire even black engineers, as a bit of quid pro quo for its profits. So in 1942 Sperry Gyroscope sent for Ro by name and from a civil service roster. When he showed up in the flesh at Sperry's Brooklyn installation, there was "some mistake." That there wasn't another Negro in the place Rozell could see. The shocked officials soon recovered to scurry about in whispered consultations. They finally explained that the project to which Ro was to have been assigned—the manufacture of anti-aircraft searchlights—was finished. Ro's quick retort was a good one, "Is the war over?"

Then he commenced a fight, insisting on having the job that had been offered him. The liberal newspaper, *P.M.*, took up his cause. Lester Granger of the National Urban League, Adam Clayton Powell, Hope Stevens, Mayor Fiorello LaGuardia, and Eleanor Roosevelt gave him backing. Calls went back and forth between bigger government people in Washington and the smaller ones in Brooklyn. But a great government at war could not help itself nor Ro. Rozell was assigned a locker and a towel, but he was not sworn in nor permitted to hit a lick for Uncle Sam as an engineer. Sperry passed the buck to the army, and the army raised a white flag.

Back my brother went to emergency relief administration in Chicago, where a few months later Western Electric called him and was not bowled over when he arrived in the black. It put him to work repairing and later inspecting the rebuilt transformers, the lone Negro employee at its big Forty-seventh Street plant. But the work lasted only three months.

From Western Electric, he went to Chanute Air Field in Illinois, where he was trained to help train (in electrical systems for aircraft) black mechanics to service the Ninety-ninth Pursuit Squadron and other all-black air units. Ro was part of what was to be the core staff for an all-black training school, expected to parallel — resemble sufficiently — those already in operation and assumedly best reserved for whites only, at Chanute, Shepherd, and Paterson Fields. But the project failed because the army could not persuade any community suitably situated to serve as its base, to accept the nearness of all the black soldiers that would be a part of the package.

Later, International Harvester, said to accept and fairly treat Negroes on its assembly lines, offered Ro an engineering assignment at one of its newer plants. However, by then he had begun teaching math, mechanical drawing, and electrical shop for the Board of Education in Chicago, and so he declined the Harvester offer. Teachers of skills, it is sometimes snidely said, show others how to do what they really never managed to do well themselves. But, in this case, teaching had extended Ro the opportunity he wanted, and he went to work at the Wendell Phillips High School on Thirty-Ninth Street, where his colleagues made him the dean of students. Several years later, he went to Crane High School on Chicago's West Side. Everywhere he went, students embraced and believed in him.

Nine months of the year with troubled and troublesome youngsters pay a teacher no bonus, and like many another one, Ro has had to supplement his salary by working during the summers. He has worked at come whatever but usually with people: summer camp director or trades school instructor, but also as a railway redcap and bus driver.

TWO DOCTOR-BROTHERS

Lendor C., the *C* for Conrad, is the fourth one of us. He is even-tempered, slow, and quiet, and was a scholar at the start. It was he who cried to go to school when he was too young for admission to the first grade and finished high school as salutatorian of his class. I first discovered that he was a fast learner as I prepared to enter the Boy Scouts. Rozell and I repeated aloud the Scout laws and oath to each other, but in Lendor's presence before taking off for our first troop meeting, while he corrected our mistakes, not from the manual but from his quick and apt memory of what he had heard.

Self-discipline and concentration are also among his strong points. It took extraordinary amounts of both to see him through the Medical College of the University of Illinois in Chicago, more for coping with what he had as a home and study place than for mastering anatomy and physiology. For his home was the kitchenette apartment he shared with Rozell and me. It lacked space enough for privacy and quiet, a bad matter made worse because the place was so often busy. Ro and I were bachelors and as such had plenty of noisy friends to welcome at any time, any night of the week, for as long as spirit or spirits moved us. But for four long years, Lendor sat and dug through his big, thick, Latiny books in whatever vacant corner he could command, night after night, mentally insulating himself against the confusion, the capering, and the dissuasive temptations abounding there.

Lendor's capacity for work saw him through medical school as it had carried him through college. During his first year as a med student, he was also a member of the yard gang at nearby Illinois State Research Hospital, picking up litter and slinging garbage cans. The next year, he moved over to his own campus and up the ladder a rung or two, becoming a technician in chemistry for the Medical College. The third year, he worked as a research project technician in chemistry, a position he held until he commenced interning.

But it had taken some doing to get into med school and to get work.

As Lendor and one other black entered med school in 1938, they were the first two students of the kind in a freshman class in a decade. This break in the "only-one-of-them"-per-class pattern was purely accidental. Lendor had pre-registered but withdrawn because he had not located an absolutely necessary job, and a second black registrant was in hand, when suddenly a job fell to Lendor, and he bounced back, requesting restoration of his status. The registrar granted the request, finding it more expedient to have two instead of one of the black kind than to turn back the second one or refuse restoring Lendor, just as the term was to start. The injustice would be manifest; in the case of the second fellow, his rejection would open up the quota issue, and Negro legislators would take it up. But cold-shouldering Lendor was really risky for the registrar of a state med school. He knew that some big state official had dictated a job for Len at the Research Hospital and that the same leverage could be applied to the Medical College.

Len's job should have been that of orderly or male nurse, as was routine for white med students able to wangle State Hospital work. But Len decided to deal in litter and garbage, and hold his tongue; he might have to use his political pull to get in school. One thing at a time, and the first thing first is good enough, he told himself.

On the other hand, he had grateful memories of white orderlies, fellow students who slipped him a timely word so that he could change clothes and sit in on the surgery staged in the amphitheater, after they had learned that the colored yard boy was bent on becoming a doctor. Lendor similarly remembers the Medical School librarian who took reference books off the shelves for his use as the textbooks he was unable to buy.

But he recalls his professor of obstetrics and gynecology with blemished gratitude. The professor once both complimented Lendor's recitation and predicted a successful future for him, before the entire class, of which Lendor was the sole Negro member. Still, the professor easily declined intervening on Lendor's behalf to help get him laboratory space in which to study pathology, thus to help bring about the prediction. He felt that Lender had asked too much; it was within his power to intervene, but the color barrier was there and not to be broken by him.

Lendor began taking his chosen career seriously months before he swore after Hippocrates and surmounted the state medical board. One evening while he was still a student, I came home to the apartment to find him busy examining the little hunchbacked youngster who played in our neighborhood. As Lendor sought the syndrome and to make a somewhat educated guess, on his very own, the youngster gloried in all the attention, something possibly the closest to expert study of his disability that ghettoed child had ever experienced. Soon afterward, Lendor came home to report, with what was considerable excitement for him, that a woman had been transferred from the streetcar he was riding to an ambulance and rushed to a hospital. She was merely about to deliver her baby, an advent which my brother modestly but confidently announced he could have performed, if necessary, then and there on that streetcar. The "ob" and "gyn" bug had deeply bitten him.

After he began his internship, he would regale us with stories of hospital happenings as he served in the emergency room. Some were of gore, such as the one in which the fellow who lost his fight with a knifer rode up in a Yellow Cab with his own severed ear safely in hand. Another one I remember was more a matter of gall. A white policeman had refused at first to budge from the examination room in which Lendor, a very Negro-appearing doctor, was to examine and treat a very drunken white prostitute. Only after Lendor laid down the law for the law man, told him the woman would not be helped until he removed himself, did the blue-coated one leave the blue-though-bleary-eyed woman behind closed doors with the Negro doctor.

Robert Douglas Donnell was the mouthful hung upon the youngest of the Nesbitt quintet. The Donnell was dropped.

As Lendor was the only one of the boys to demonstratively display his affection for Mama, occasionally kissing her and gently patting her fat brown arms and neck, Bob was the only brother ever so much as somewhat of a little buddy to Papa. Our authoritarian father perhaps allowed Bob more leeway, knowing that he was the last man child Mama could provide. Or maybe Papa felt that the last little one would need fending from the crude surveillance of four older boys. For having been taught so sternly to obey anyone older, each and all together would in turn require obedience, when they could get away with it, from their little brother. In any case, I recall hearing Papa say to us on more than one occasion, "I am his father. You leave him alone. I'll tell him what to do and what not."

As the affinity between Papa and his youngest grew, one thing Bob was to do for his father's sake stood out. He was to accompany Papa to his church on Saturdays for a longer period, more regularly and more willingly, than had any of his brothers. As my father and the captive, little Bob, walked past the neighbors on Saturday morning, Papa in his somber brown suit with swallow-tailed coat and Bob in what would have otherwise been his Sunday best, Papa marched proudly and assertively. He was showing all of those Sunday-worshiping Methodists and Baptists, still errant followers of the Pope, that he and at least one other Nesbitt were keeping the true Sabbath. Bob would stay with Papa amidst the little flock of self-raised saints all day, learned to call its preacher Elder instead of Reverend, reverence being due only to God, and loved to greet its members with "Peace," and to salute them with the holy kiss. Returning home, Bob would play Elder, lengthily declaiming after the manner of the preaching heard in Papa's church.

A more lasting attribute early manifested was Bob's distaste for simply being of the mold, the last of the Nesbitt boys. Independence became his mark. I remember his returning from high school one evening and vigorously voicing his disgust that still another of the older teachers had held up his brothers before him as a model. As a university student, he declined an invitation to pledge with Alpha Phi Alpha fraternity which each of us had joined, one after the other, in the fashion of sheep. He did choose medicine for a career but doubtlessly on his own and not following after his brother Lendor. Moreover, at Camp Grant in 1943 Bob was inducted into the army and at once sent along with other black medical trainees, not to the barracks for ASTP's doctors-in-the-making but to live with Jim Crowed black enlistees, an order recanted only after he and several others vigorously complained to the commanding officer of all the physicians-to-be. The awarding of residencies continued largely to turn on the right skin color and a sufficiency of political clout at both the Illinois State and Cook County hospitals, even for Reserve Officers in the Medical Corps. Bob had neither the first nor the second—at first, though, he yearned to intern in pediatrics at County, a massive operation forced to serve Negro children by the hundreds week in and week out by the walls against them in other Chicago hospitals. But County nevertheless had never broken in a black pediatrician. The need was for lever enough to impress the politician-doctor heading the hospital to appoint and break the pattern, or vice versa. The biggest black cog in the ruling party failed us, but the next highest did the job.

Bob made some return to the government for its investment in him by serving on the staff of an army hospital in Germany for two years and, after his homecoming, successfully "took his board" for a specialty in pediatrics. But he made better reimbursement and received a sense of self-fulfillment in his career twenty years later, as head of the pediatrics section of a family multipurpose center in the Watts area of Los Angeles for a while, giving little blacks medical attention, love, recognition, and a bit of the sense of black worth of which they had been deprived.

MORE OF MYSELF

I was the second child and called Lucian George Belvey, the first and third names coming from Papa and flattering him more than I knew. I early dropped the Lucian without disturbing him but when I came home bearing a high school diploma from which it was missing and which carried only "B" to stand for Belvey, he discounted me as "A graduate that doesn't know his name!"

After the U. S. Army made a good riddance of me in 1945, I resumed work as a race relations specialist for government in the housing field, and I remain so. The label's modifier has changed, periodically, from "race relations" to "intergroup relations" to "equal opportunity," but the functioning continues essentially the same. It is to travel the street between the nonwhite community and government in both directions, explaining to each that the segregated housing system is the last bastion of apartheid American-styled, pointing up the perils for all in leaving it intact, and trying to help whoever is interested and willing to act to discover the places at which intervention for change was possible and the ways for getting it done.

The task has never been easy and is usually a thankless sort of endeavor. The work is advisory, staff-most of all staff, in which the major recommendation too rarely finds its way into larger decisions. In the earlier days, the forties and fifties, the engineers, the project planners, the real estate professionals and, of course, the administrators ran the show. The slide-rule men were simply that and could not get our particular message. The project planners sometimes understood it but were always too afraid of the administrators to dare cooperation with our specialization. The administrators were concerned with little more than production and especially that the boat not be rocked, even ever so gently, the captain of the ship being the southern Congressman heading the committees that were housing's lifeblood. And the real estate operator was all over the lot, guiding the administrative people — no, administering the administrators, ever the guardian of homogeneity in housing, as he still would be.

The administrative people wanted only a "go along" from the race relations staff, not to have from them what policymakers needed to hear. We race specialists were frequently overlooked or remembered as an afterthought. The usual unspoken intent was to confine us to troubleshooting and firefighting, or to use us as window dressing and, at best, to settle upon us as little more than a nuisance that had to be tolerated. Meanwhile, at the other end of the street, the Negro community looked upon Negro race relations specialists with reservations. It sensed that they exercised no real power and made no decisions, had no real policy weapons, and enjoyed little support in government. Little real change in the race system occurred; housing was especially separate and far less than equal. Besides, the Negro race functionary in government could not even vigorously and openly voice the protest, as did the Negro civic leader. Whatever he did was done behind closed doors, unseen within the labyrinth of government. So the Negro community tended to write us off as blacks used by the whites to face the other blacks when confrontation could not be escaped.

Nevertheless, I found the job fulfilling. As I have earlier stated, my colleagues and tutors were committed people, clearheaded and resourceful. They sensed and brought me to sense that segregated housing is the basic mechanism for race separation and Negro subjugation. It was excessively complicated, the last big barrier against equality that would be the toughest of all to topple, but someone had to help build and apply the pressures against it.

So I learned to stick and stay at it, to keep pitching, and to live off my small part in an occasional step forward, or simply in its devising against great odds: a minor policy or procedural advance, now and then a project winding up with a biracial occupancy pattern, a local housing authority adopting a nondiscrimination policy, the publication of guidelines on how to develop and manage housing open to all, assists to scholars bent upon exposing the color myths in housing, the nurturing and nursing of a private developer somehow willing to build new housing for Negroes, counselling a lawyer preparing to attack discrimination in housing, convincing a national minority organization and its local affiliates to employ housing professionals, or bringing into being a national organization of organizations, whose sole purpose would be waging war against discrimination in housing.

Sometimes the frustrations were so great as to nearly snuff out the little satisfactions gleaned. I could see nothing resulting; it all seemed too much a pushing against a mountain. Or the supervision and the decisions came from one who less than tolerated the function. He would be rid of the function, if possible, and the functionary for sure (one called me an "agitator," a firebrand," who spoke for that "Negro advancement outfit, not the government"). But, of course, I could not run. So I learned now and then to write and publish an article, to put a case in print that had no better way of being. Perhaps a score of such efforts—exercises in self-therapy, palmed off as "analyses"—bear my name. When I glance at them now and then, none is the last word on its subject, but several spill early words of the kind, and I find that satisfying. These pieces have been published in *The Crisis*, *Phylon*, *Land Economics*, *The Journal of Housing*, *The Journal of Intergroup Relations*, *The Journal of Negro Education*, and *Interracial Review*.

I also found it stimulating and refreshing to prepare for and speak to students and professors at such universities and colleges as Fisk, Prairie View, Tennessee A. and I., Southern, Miami (at Coral Gables in Florida), Atlanta, Howard, Northwestern, North Carolina State, and the University of Chicago. For most such occasions, I carefully prepared statements in anticipation of editing and official clearance, and occasionally was edited into innocuousness. But the prepared statement was but a point of departure. After its delivery, bright young minds often asked good, honest, questions, entitling me to cover the gaps in the statement. Occasionally, too, I have presented a paper before a national professional body, and often I have advised undergraduate and graduate students with their papers and theses on various aspects of the problem of color in housing.

In 1956 I was reporting to an engineer who quaked in his high boots at mention of the initials NAACP and sought to freeze out the intergroup relations function. It was a good time—a better time than any—I decided, to go off and learn more of the mystiques of those with whom I worked: real estate economists, planners, and decision makers. Upon the advice of carefully courted men of Harvard, I received a Littauer fellowship, and I became a student again after two decades outside the classroom. A year later, I returned to the Housing and Home Finance Agency bearing a Master's in Public Administration. The new boss I found seemed not to fear me and my mission nearly as much as his predecessor. Still he suggested that as an MPA, I should consider abandoning the race relations specialization and become "more of a generalist." It sounded good. But I had become more broadly knowledgeable to better perform as a specialist, and I stayed in the groove.

Still, in 1961 I was beguiled into generalization of a particular sort. The new, and Negro, Housing Administrator offered me a new and better-paying position, after other and better people had turned it down. Congress had created the low-income housing demonstration program to start in July, and in November Robert Weaver ordered that I become its director, commissioned to handle demonstration of "new and improved means for housing low-income persons and families."

In seven or eight months, I put the program together and had it rolling, wrote its policies, procedures, and guidebook for applicants, hired a tiny staff, assembled an advisory committee four times as large, processed four or five projects, and defended them before the Senate Banking and Currency Committee's subcommittee on housing.

We had lessons to learn fast. Fresh ideas are not a business to wait for; they had to be drummed up. Our door had to stay open to all, from seeming "nuts" to reputed "nutcrackers," to make certain not to overlook a Fulton whose boat might actually sail. The bureaucrats preferred projects to check out, not to try out the new. Once a novel project was underway, it would come apart without close watching, and maybe anyway. Those new approaches that worked successfully were claimed by the operating bureaucracy, too often without mention of our little demonstration staff. They ignored that we had helped conceive and refine them, packaged and sold them to the decision-makers, put them under way, and nursed them until they could hold together and move along well enough for showing off.

Despite all, the results were gratifying, as we saw the program heads embrace and advance the ideas tested, such as "rent supplements," the leasing of private dwellings by public housing authorities, the so-called "instant" housing-rehabilitation process, "financial counselling" to support liberalized standards for assessing credit worthiness on the part of low-income borrowers, and the first public housing project designed for occupancy by the physically handicapped.

After six years, I slipped nominally back into race relations service for the new Department of Housing and Urban Development. I had really never lost hold on my commitment. Several of the low-income housing experiments staged had lifted the fog of economic and cultural differences to leave clearer the ugly specter of race discrimination in housing. Meanwhile, I wrote additional articles on race and housing, portraying misconceptions on the part of the movement for its equalizing, poking at the good, white liberals running the fair-housing committees for helping only handfuls of respectable, middle-class Negroes, while ignoring the lower-income mass, and advising nonprofit housing enthusiasts on how better to organize themselves to achieve housing for racially open occupancy.

As I write these lines, I await the appearance of my most recent piece in a planning journal. This time I contend that national industry should go ahead with pilot undertakings, cracking the color barriers in suburbia in its own self-interest. I demonstrate, I think, that our great industrial corporations have what it takes for the task: the public image; the power and leverages; the financial, organizational, and personnel resources; and strategic opportunities for the demonstrations.

THE WOMEN WE MARRIED

All of the Nesbitt brothers are married. The wife of each is the only one the husband has known. The first of the marriages saw its silver anniversary (without intake of the precious metal) two years ago, and the youngest alliance has survived almost twenty years. Strains and spats, fussing and fuming, take place, of course, but they rarely are severe enough to surface before the whole clan of us, and in no case has there been a separation, in the open.

Our marriages have run so far, so good, perhaps because they were late undertakings for the male partners. The two oldest ones of us were past thirty years old, the next two beyond twenty-five, and the youngest almost that old, before the venture was dared. Each of us was old enough to look for the lady with care and to recognize her among the others. Nor were the chosen girls immature, it might be gingerly and briefly noted, only for the record. It has nothing to do with their ages now.

It is more important to record that all of the wives seem somewhat like Mama, only somewhat being expectable. It isn't that they could cook much to start with, but all were unafraid of work, and each proved quite able to exercise the larger voice to which her labor entitled her. Four are college women, and all are well-bred. Four are the daughters of hard-working fathers—yardman, huckster, preacher, and railway clerk. The fifth's father was a hard worker too, but his father had learned how to manage money, his and other people's. Thus she is a granddaughter of a Negro banker, a distinction indeed, even though his bank went the way of many others during the Great Depression.

My sisters-in-law and my wife, like their husbands, worked hard and personally achieved such status as they have. They are sure of it and wear it easily, free of anxiety. None could have been too much of a climber to begin, considering the poor, simple, old-shoe types they married. There isn't a club woman, a continuous card player, or a dresser in the lot. They wear clothes to suit their ages and subdue their assertive figures, shoes to fit their feet, and white gloves only for special occasions. Altogether our women are an unsophisticated, sturdy, comfortable, and, of course, gabby group. They busy themselves on their jobs, out in the world, and at home, seeing after their husbands and "the children"—their own and the nephews and nieces.

The wives of the three brothers living on Albany Avenue are school-teachers, two of them for the public school system and assigned in the immediate area of their home. One of these, Doris, teaches at Howland, an elementary school at Sixteenth and Spaulding Streets, within easy but unsafe walking distance from home. There she is a master teacher, responsible for the improvement of instructional quality on the part of the entire faculty and also for serving as its representative to and a vice president of the P.T.A.

The second wife teaching in the public school system, Sadie, is also a master teacher at James Weldon Johnson, only a block away from home, where she keeps an eye on beginning teachers, experiments with team teaching, and handles disciplinary problems and liaisons with parents. She had previously taught in other ghettoed schools, including Dante, in the area of famed Hull House, where she taught special classes for Mexican-American children. Careful to advance herself on the theory side, she holds a certificate in child care from the Chicago Institute of Psychoanalysis, which she now serves as a part-time staff member. In October of 1962 she was the first teacher to be cited by the Citizens Schools Committee of Chicago to receive the Kate Maremont Foundation's Dedicated Teacher Award. She was recognized "for significant contribution to inter-cultural understanding and leadership in meeting the challenges of a community in change, and for dedicated service to her school and community far beyond the call of duty."

The third teacher, Peggy, is the nurse-trained wife of that one of my doctor-brothers living on Albany Avenue. She goes forth daily from the building, where all of the children are taught to call all adults "Mister," "Missus," and "Miss," to teach kindergarten at a private school attended by the Nesbitt children and which is of a kind permitting and encouraging its pupils to call teachers by their first names and their nicknames. (This is a great leap forward, I suppose, though I find it pleasant that the little Nesbitts never become confused and have always called grownups by title, including the ladies who come to the building to do cleaning and ironing).

Peggy went back to school for training as a teacher after she and her husband found themselves paying fees for three boys at the school and she had learned that, as a member of its faculty, she could keep them there tuition-free.

A fourth and younger sister-in-law, Marilyn, no longer works but busies herself at housekeeping and for the community. Her husband practices medicine in nearby Pasadena, where she has been treasurer of the Lincoln Avenue Methodist Church, as well as the Women's Association for the Pasadena Boys Club. She regularly engages in door-to-door solicitation for such causes as the United Crusade and the local heart and tuberculosis associations.

My own wife, Josephine, grew up in the town of Evanston, Illinois, boasting a great university, which she never attended. The university missed a good student, and I drew a wonderful wife, trained in wealthy homes and fancy dress shops instead of the college classroom. Her hand is skilled and thorough at any and every household task, from the drudgery level to plants raised from seeds and slips, dress and drapery making from patterns, and without, keeping the family books, minor electrical and plumbing repairs, painting the bathroom, and the like. She refinishes furniture like a professional, cans peaches and makes cherry pies with fruit right from the trees, does a bit of ceramics, and can make from weeds a potpourri for the mantelpiece, a centerpiece for the dining table, or a pot of greens or a salad fit to serve a gourmet.

Still, all of my wife's artfulness as a housekeeper is only the second part of the strength in her that serves her husband. She scourges me with her tongue or shores up my sagging spirits, whichever appears needed. She also serves the community upon occasion, ringing doorbells for this or that social agency or giving someone at the Urban League a hand. She is, in sum, a good fortune I'm challenged to try to deserve.

The Future of Our People

The simple believeth every word; but the prudent man looketh well to his going.
—Proverbs 14:15

Staying put in their building was not easy for my brothers and their families. Defensive measures had to be taken. But participation in the community, living with one's neighbors, was also part of the sticking. And the three family units learned to work together; they cooperated like a good clan should. Now and then some bright young visitor termed their way of living "like the extended family" he had read about in his studies.

When the Nesbitt children were small, they stood out among their public schoolmates as middle-class youngsters, were picked on and pushed about, and were perhaps awarded better grades for the same reasons (it was several times felt), though they certainly were getting inferior schooling in buildings that were old and outmoded, classrooms that were overcrowded, and from teachers that were at once poorly qualified, over-burdened, and indifferent, if not sometimes racially hostile. The answer was to turn to private schools. The wives have been chased by male marauders, and they have had repeatedly to ask for more police in the area. Apartments in the building have been broken into time after time, with the steel guards for some of the windows and doors, and extra lighting outside of the building having proved only partially effective. The Negro dentist who bought next door soon sold, and now that building is a makeshift kitchenette operation in which people are packed like sardines. The Jewish Convalescent Home, adjoining the other side of the Nesbitt building, sold its property, and it is now occupied by an assortment of decrepit and disabled wards of the State of Illinois. Worst of all, the block on which the Nesbitts live is well within the territory of an organized youth gang and within easy reach of the doped, drunken, and bellicose derelicts from nearby Kedzie Street, a string of greasy spoons, pool rooms, dirty laundromats, and other places more "hangouts" than business establishments.

Still, the Nesbitts remained in their building. They stay put there in Lawndale. Moreover, they have always associated themselves with those few others in such a community who try to serve and even to save it.

In the mid-forties a little Nesbitt in the Sunday school was the lone Negro attendant at Warren Avenue Congregational Church in the midst of tension occasioned by an extension of Negro residence on Chicago's West Side along either side of Lake Street. The Nesbitts, then living at 2752 West Warren Boulevard, invited to their home for a meeting members of several neighborhood white churches who were more and more talking brotherhood at Loop gatherings. At this meeting Julian Keiser, thirtyish in age, raised in the suburb of Aurora and minister of Warren Avenue Congregational Church, made plain that he meant what he was saying. He was ready to act and right there in the neighborhood. Three adult Nesbitts, a brother, his wife, and another brother's wife then became the pioneer Negro members of that church, which served as the command post for the Martin Luther King forces during their campaign in the summer of 1966 against segregated housing in the Chicago area. The same brother has subsequently served as a treasurer and chairman of the board of trustees of the church and as a member of its board of deacons, along with another brother. The wives of both have been members of the board of deaconesses.

Two of the Nesbitt wives teach in the neighborhood's schools and serve it beyond their instructional duties. One of them carries her concern for people out of the neighborhood, serves them whenever she meets with them and whoever they may be. She is the sister-in-law with an open heart and home in which it is always "open house," who likes to do things for people and does not hesitate to entreat and enjoin, and inveigle, if need be, those nearest about her into joining her causes. It is she who received the award, as she had earned it, for "dedicated service beyond her school and community and far beyond the call of duty." In 1953, the National Conference of Christians and Jews had also cited her "daily devotion to the ideals of brotherhood and for outstanding service to neighbors of every color, religion, and national origin." She now serves on the Woman's Board of International Hospitality Center of Chicago, a position which more recognizes her weakness for strangers in the United States than occasions her activity in their interest.

Two of the brothers also find time to work in the community. One of them is the engineer-turned-teacher who finds so satisfying helping to manage those youngsters who seem unmanageable, the tough, troubled, and troublesome ones spawned by weakened and hapless families.

He has been a working member of the Mayor of Chicago's special project for "dropouts" and served as a counsellor for the city's Upward Bound program, a program of special tutoring and remedial instruction for disadvantaged children conducted by Roosevelt University. He is also an active member of the Lawndale Community Conservation Council, an organization incessantly engaged in a search for consensus between the planners downtown and the people in the area, neither of whom is able to understand and believe much in the other. Meanwhile, he must also move out on his own from time to time, trying to get the police first to fulfill and then not to exceed their missions in the area, importuning bunches of youngsters to "break it up," keeping an eye on the little ones playing in the park across the street or trying to cross it when "the rush" is on, and the like. One hot summer evening, I saw him take a drawn knife from a young woman, engaged in a shouting, cursing clash with her boyfriend. The street fight was inevitable and did follow, but there was no mayhem or murder, that time.

The doctoring brother manages to do more than serve his fee-paying patients. He early pulled back from his private practice enough to serve as a clinical physician for the Planned Parenthood Association, handling twenty such clinics monthly at six different locations in the city. Several of the locations are in depressed areas, and once again, as he first experi-

enced as a resident physician at Cook County Hospital, it became necessary to allow certain whites to learn that a Negro gynecologist who has
white females as his patients does so simply as their gynecologist and no
more. As I briefly visited with this busy brother during a recent summer
day, he suddenly excused himself. He was due several blocks away at the
Marcy Center, a Methodist settlement house, where he was to examine
a batch of youngsters before their departure for summer camp, a service
for which he has volunteered for several years. He was recently appointed
a Chicago Medical Society representative on the State Advisory Committee on Public Aid.

THE CO-CHAIRED COMMITTEE FAMILY

Each brother's family is run as many middle-class families are these days,
it seems to me. They operate on what might be called "the co-chaired
committee plan," with father and mother co-chairing the operation, especially when the mother works, and the rank-and-file committee members include all of the children. Each of the latter has a voice in family
affairs, a loud one, and casts a vote whether or not the question has been
put. Like most committee members, after each speaks his piece, the children let the co-chairmen do the job. Like too many committee chairmen,
their parents let it become a habit and do the shopping, the cleaning, the
dishes, and other family chores themselves.

Co-chairmanship for a committee has, of course, at least two possible
weaknesses. Neither of the two heads may be any good, to leave the committee headless. Or, one of them may be quite strong and take over the
leadership despite some county official's and the preacher's having named
them co-chairmen. The first risk has not materialized in any one of the
three families, I can report. The second may well have occurred, though
I am not inclined to be specific about it.

The advantages potentially inherent in the two-headed committee
have worked beautifully for the Nesbitts. Since one co-chairman is father
and male, while the other is mother and female, and neither places a sex
tag on a responsibility, the total of their capacities and resourcefulness is
employed. I saw, for example, the biggest and most rugged of my brothers
washing the diapers of his first child on many occasions but never once
saw his wife so engaged. On the other hand, his wife has never had to turn

to him with disciplinary problems, as many mothers do. While my brothers' families have tended to follow the prescription of love and security always and discipline only now and then, this sister-in-law has substituted "when and as needed" for the "now and then." I once saw her spank her six year-old son for name-calling, with her first blow landing almost before the nasty sound died away. Fifteen years later, I notice that her six-foot-three son listens respectfully and seems to find her advice worth taking, even when it is a matter of his not doing what, if done, would be certain to impress a young lady of his choice.

Co-equality for family responsibilities, irrespective of what more traditionally is assigned to one sex or the other, has been a boon for all of our wives, especially with household chores. Since my mother had no daughters, her boys shamelessly learned to cook, wash, iron, sew, and clean house. None of our wives fails to enjoy this windfall. Most of my brothers taught their wives to cook and themselves remain good cooks. I have one sister-in-law who can become furious if her husband declines to cook dinner when she invited guests.

The male need not unduly suffer in this situation. In my own case, for example, my wife does make flattering remarks about my cookery and can easily get an assist from me by way of a pot of stew, chile, spaghetti, a casserole of leftovers, or even a pound cake. On the other hand, I am careful occasionally to praise her skill with a paint brush (the wide kind, for walls) and her mechanical aptitudes. In this way I get lots of help too, charity returneth severalfold. In fact, when she turns to me with a painting, an electrical, or a plumbing problem, it is likely serious enough to force my resorting in turn to the craftsman.

The three committees, along with Papa's family, live too closely together for any one of them to escape being part of a single organization. Certainly the mailman does not bother to distinguish one Nesbitt family from another. Most of the time the three do pull together. Even upon those rare but inevitable occasions of slight strain, say between a couple of sisters-in-law, the tension can hardly persist. Each does have her own kitchen out of which to keep the other, and neither can for long remain put out with someone she has to see sooner than later in the hallway, if not to borrow from her a cup of sugar, then to beg a lift to the Loop, or a ride to school for one of her children. The husband-brothers are certain to remain brothers in any case. Besides, the children are like children everywhere, paying little attention to any fuming and fussing among the adults and being quick to forget it all if they ever shared in it. They simply keep going in and out of each other's apartment, quite as freely as their own, come what may between the grown-ups. Indeed they are one thick little mess of cousins, including twin girls whose mother married my oldest brother after divorcing her first husband, and a girl adopted by another of my brothers and his wife, already her "blood aunt," as it is said.

Once two of the first cousins, a boy and girl then five or six years old, began such a screaming and fighting in the back of my car as I sped down a boulevard that I was forced to pull to the curb and engage in peacemaking. The little girl charged the little boy with the first blows, which he manfully admitted. Thereupon I firmly promised to spank him "good" if he repeated the offense, only to have the little lady suddenly stop her sniffling and tell her uncle, "Don' you hit him! Don' you hit him! Tause he's my li'l cousin."

The concentration of the several closely related families has worked to their mutual advantage. Babysitting, the cooperative nursery, the teenage recreation spot, a jointly owned deep freeze, and the buying club, familiar features of suburban life, have also been practiced by our amalgam of families in the racial ghetto. Each of these arrangements for saving time and money was of utterly simple format. It developed easily, almost inevitably in such a strong and natural setting, and without either an organizing effort to speak of, by-laws, or an election.

But the greater immediate conveniences, if not also long-run benefits, of the self-colonization on Albany Avenue run to the children. Since they were quite small, for example, they have eaten all over the building. I remember when my wife and I lived there, and a little nephew took to showing up in our place at dinner time for a piece of pie more to his liking than that he had left, or simply for "seconds," if not "thirds." One evening he appeared a minute or two after my wife had seen him finishing dinner at his home. She reminded him of the fact, but his rejoinder was, "Yes, but I didn't eat yet at your house!"

The children, of course, have never hesitated to play their handily present uncles and aunts against mama and papa. This one would want to do, or feel that he should not have to do, this or that, because his aunt or uncle permitted it, or did not make his little cousins do it. If the family prepared to make a trip in which a child was disinterested, he went to his aunt and uncle and arranged to stay with them, presenting this advance accomplishment as added reason for his being allowed to stay. (Yet these representations had to be honest, for they were easily checked, and I have seen them turned back with the explanation that the decision was parental, not the uncle's or aunt's).

Naturally also this batch of youthful cousins living in such close proximity have sometimes organized themselves and reached unanimous decisions before the parent in any one of the families raised an issue. In one family the children would say, "May we go to the basketball game? May we? A and B and W, X, Y, and Z (the other cousins all) are going." This would be rather a misrepresentation, all three sets of children having conspired to take the same approach with their respective parents and none, of course, really knowing that the others could go. However, the parents, also living in close proximity and able to organize, consult among themselves, and anticipate such maneuvers, learned to take care of themselves.

One other advantage in having aunts and uncles as well as mamas and papas so close at hand is that each child has had a variety of resources from which to pick and choose help with this problem or that, how to make pie crust hold together, make a dress, drive an auto, do an algebra problem, or what not. There was no small bit of luck in being able to turn to someone for help without expecting too much too fast and getting impatient with something kind of tricky, say like driving an auto. It has been a big help to have a teacher who is not one's father or mother but is one's uncle or aunt.

ONE WORLD AND ECUMENICITY

That clan I claim in Chicago knows that today's is a shrinking world — and it welcomes her people. My wife and I are rarely able to be in Chicago for several days without finding strange people moving from one Nesbitt apartment to another.

As most of the family members gathered with us one afternoon in the summer of 1966, I urged them to try naming the countries from which their neighbors from afar have come. From Africa, which fourth grade geography had led me to believe was rather a country than a continent, all of whose people were of jet-black and primitive sameness, they listed Chad, Cameroon, Sierra Leone, the United Arab Republic, the Central

African Republic, Ghana, Nigeria, Liberia, Tanzania, the Congo, Kenya, Ethiopia, Upper Volta, Mozambique, Buganda, Guinea, and Uganda. Lest it be thought that my family is some active cell of "black power internationale," I hasten to add that people from Madagascar, Sweden, Germany, Israel, Saudi Arabia, Jordan, Turkey, Poland, France, the U.S.S.R., Japan, and India had also visited the Nesbitts. Interestingly the family made no mention of countries in this hemisphere until after specifically asked about them. Several such countries had been overlooked, though I like to think that it was because of a sense of their so much belonging with than to the United States. Haiti, Columbia, Nicaragua, Guyana, Jamaica, Trinidad, and Brazil were the omitted ones. At this point the youngest of the children spoke up for "the Borreros" from Puerto Rico, only to draw an admonitory reminder that Puerto Ricans are Americans and besides "the Borreros" had been paying tenants in the building, not mere visitors.

Some of the foreign visitors show up by pre-arrangement, at the request of the International Hospitality Center, or a similar organization, which in turn, or once or twice removed, acts for the government. They stay only briefly. Others come more informally, stay longer, visit several times, and become family friends, especially younger people in the Chicago area for schooling or extended tours. The latter are taken over by the youthful Nesbitts, dated and provided dates, taken to parties, and entertained in other ways common among the young around the world and carrying across language and nationality barriers. Several times the Chicago Nesbitts have called my wife and me, with too little notice, to look out for foreign visitors on their way to Washington. One such visitor was from the Congo and married to a white girl from South Carolina. I had a friend of mine who spoke fluent French to come and join us at dinner for Pierre Maloka and his wife Fran, who lived in the building. Pierre was Congolese, and Fran was a white Southerner who had gone to the Congo as a missionary. They met there, fell in love, and were married by Ed Hawley at Warren Avenue Congregational Church. During the evening, the big joke with Maloka had to do with our professed fear that those bitterly anti-miscegenationist among his wife's representatives in the Congress might have us under watch. We were once suddenly sent a half-dozen students, including three my wife described as the "beautiful girl from India," the "handsome Brazilian," and the "big, friendly German student." I was disappointed not to be able to see them, since they visited during the day and I could not leave my office and go home.

More often than not, when my family's visitors from here and there return to their homelands, they send gifts, write to repeat their thanks for the hospitality shown them, and urge our families to visit their lands and homes.

So much of this experience has encouraged the Nesbitts to travel out of the country and has especially been stimulative with the younger ones. Four of youngers have made trips beyond the borders of the States. The twin girls have gone many times to Stratford, Ontario, in Canada, for tastes of the annual Shakespearian festival there. Their parents have also taken them into Mexico, at points deeper and more meaningful than the souvenir-laden communities baiting the Yankee suckers just beyond the California line, and in 1960 took them on a ten-week tour of Europe. The oldest nephew, when in high school, spent a rich and exciting summer in Solna, Sweden, near Stockholm, as a participant in the Experiment for International Living program. The beautiful color slides of his trip and his accompanying lecture as he shows them at one point clearly suggest that the experiment in Swedish living was indeed of significance for him. As the first picture of a big, blonde, and rather striking looking woman comes upon the screen, my nephew proudly and with obvious affection announces, "And this is Mother Ingrid Holmgren. She was my mother in Sweden." As an Antioch College student, the same nephew completed a year of study in Tanzania, at the University College in Dar Es Salaam.

His sister spent five weeks in the summer of 1964 in Mexico as the guest of a family of a Chicago schoolmate. Summer before last, she also tried Experiment for International Living in Japan, where she lived with the Okuyamasan family near Osaska. She reports the venture a delight, and I suspect it was more meaningful than she realizes. For in Japan, the tall and willowy figure and the good looks of this mahogany-colored girl with her great, soft, brown eyes drew a degree of admiration which the color system in her own country still withholds from darker-hued people. The Japanese camera bugs politely asked and were allowed to take many pictures of her. One of them, especially adept with his camera, made a series of beautiful pictures of my niece, blew them into large portrait-like reproductions and offered her a set. She accepted only one and explained protestingly to her family: "What would I seem like, bringing back all of those big pictures of myself?"

* * *

Some of the young strangers I find at home on Albany Avenue are not from foreign lands. Sometimes too they are there long enough to become my friends, despite long intervals between my visits, and to dub me "Uncle," as they do my brothers, whom they see daily. Most frequently they stay with that one of my sisters-in-law known to all as "Aunt Sadie," who cannot forego "fostering" people, wherever and whenever, though from her apartment they learn to roam as freely among all of the Nesbitts as they themselves do from one of their apartments to the other.

The grown-ups in the family remain close to the people back in Champaign-Urbana, which is only a hundred and thirty miles or so from Chicago. Several times each year, my brothers drive or take the I.C. train down there, especially to see elderly folk who are ill, or to look upon them, as they are to be seen for the last time. These were the people who were our neighbors, members of Papa's and Mama's churches, and paper customers. They were the ones who kept an eye and were privileged literally to lay a restraining hand on us, if need be, and as occasionally occurred. When death comes to one, and no one of my brothers is able to go home—the real home from which the start was made—flowers are sent. Now and then money to help with medicine or the doctor for a sick one has been left in the hands of a neighbor. Summer before last summer, my wife and I were in Chicago and able to join three of my brothers and their wives to be a part of a happy occasion, the golden wedding anniversary of a couple who had lived first across the street and later next door to us. She had chastened us and been our mother's friend; he had been on a committee for our Scout troop; and their son had been buddy and boon companion, especially to my younger brother, whom he called "Shorty" and to whom he was "Spinach," as still they are to each other. It was a wonderful summer afternoon of quiet and strength-giving goodness, as I saw one after another of the older people of my first knowing, people of strong and simple faith who had worked hard, lived quietly and so long.

Some of the Champaign-Urbana folk my brothers see more often. My doctor-brother treats a few who come to him in Chicago for attention and has delivered a number of babies whose fathers or mothers were his play-mates. Others simply come to visit the Nesbitts when they are in the city. Several summers have seen a picnic in Douglas Park, just across the street from the Albany Avenue building, where those Chicagoans with whom we grew up in Champaign, their children, and, in some cases, grand-children gather with the Nesbitts and their children. A few elderly folk, some coming up from Champaign for the day and others living in Chi-cago, also attend. Two of our old neighborhood buddies have visited for several days to help patch up the building. One is a painter and the other a plasterer, building trades not easy for Negroes to come by back home.

Last February one of my brothers celebrated his birthday by having eight of his childhood pals up from Champaign for a party. A few weeks later my brothers were told that St. Luke's C. M. E. Church in Champaign had been gutted by fire. Now we must stop talking and act, make that fam-ily donation to the church in memory of Mama and gratitude for what it taught us that we have often talked about.

THE NEW GENERATION

The seven Nesbitt children in Chicago are as thick as pea soup, includ-ing a girl who was adopted soon after the sudden death of her mother, and identical twin girls bearing their father's name, the mother of whom married my brother when the twins were quite young. The adopted girl came aboard, an only and recently shocked child, at eight or nine years of age. She was badly in need of the warmth and attention which she at once received not only from her foster parents but the three "ready-made" brothers, and a bunch of uncles, aunts, and cousins besides.

One summer morning after a stretch of three weeks in the company of the whole collection of nieces and nephews, when they ranged in age from eight to eighteen, they were bidding my wife and myself good-bye and a safe trip by auto back to Washington, when I said, "Now I've been with my nieces and long enough to know what makes them so won-derful."

The bigger ones were wary and avoided the bait. But the little and sev-eral demanded, "What is it? What is it?"

"Well, I said," "That's it. It's only that you're *my* nieces and nephews."

There is in truth much more to the story of the children. Each is quite different from the other, even the two who came from the same cell and look so much alike. Occasionally there has been a problem with one child or another, but fortunately the parents seldom ascribed it to "he's just that way" or "it's the phase she's in." Several times outside professional help has been needed and obtained. For all of their relative isolation from the families of professional Negroes on the South Side and the nonconforming, simple behavior of their own, they are nevertheless middle-class children. They have had it easy enough and enough of things they wanted mainly because others had them to be a little spoiled. They have had to perform few of the household chores as responsibilities—not mere duties—that were their parents' when they were young—the dishes, dusting, mopping, help with the washing, cutting and cleaning the yard, odd jobs, and the like. Not until quite recently did my nieces begin to run the risk of "dishwater hands," and each learned to handle a car before a vacuum cleaner. With the exception of the oldest one, who has long had adult responsibilities, the nephews know little of how to make a dollar and nothing of how to make one stretch. More than once I was unable to get the children to pick rhubarb and crab apples in the country, theirs for the taking. They were not interested in the slightest and would add that neither were their mothers. Both nieces and nephews couldn't have cared less, as that phrase somehow so comforting to their generations puts it.

It is now dawning on me that perhaps I have been using outmoded measuring sticks—unrealistic standards both for these days and for the children of more comfortably situated parents—in judging my nieces and nephews. Besides, I had had a certain misguided anxiety with them all along, hoping to see them more as replicas of their fathers and uncles, for whom early life was no crystal stair, than chips off the old block, for whom things were supposed to be made much easier.

Now that the children are older, and I may as well put aside my anxieties, the water being pretty well under the bridge in any case, I tell myself that they are a pretty fair lot. They exhibit a good run of morals and manners, though mostly they have dispensed with Sunday School. They actually seem to share the morality system which is their parents' and do not seem to be hell-bent on trying to erect their own. Even at the college level, there is only one cigarette smoker out of the five. The two boys in college have had beer, they admit, though I suspect that all five at college have hid a bit of aided Kool-Aid at some place or other. All have heard of LSD, though none has partaken, I am confident. They accept and are quick to defend the "way out" in their generation but they seem not to be completely out there with them. They speak a language I can understand. Only one has tried a guitar, though all like the ballads and 'billy songs as much as I do the blues. The girls use their cosmetics sparingly and wear their Levis less than daily and skintight. Neither of the two older boys has yet tried a beard. The coarseness of their hair saves them altogether from its covering ears and eyebrows. One does wear his hair "au naturel," after the manner of Belafonte and Makeba rather than Sammy Davis, though this is for him something more than a passing rebuke of those Negroes he deems white-submerged. It happened after he spent a year in Africa, which caused him now to spurn even a hard rubber comb and a stiff brush. Instead he uses what is rather a hand-sized rake, cut from an African hardwood.

In addition to the five nieces and nephews in college, there are two nephews in high school and a niece in junior high; so far there has not been a dropout in the entire batch. Each one seems more socially flexible and outgoing than either of his parents and any of his uncles and aunts, except the outgoing sister-in-law of mine. They have learned to share, to give, and to at least accept a modicum of social responsibility at home as well as "in the streets," a bright and shining phenomenon which is perhaps a windfall reaped from life in the Nesbitt colony. They are fairly cause-conscious and easily engage in direct social action projects, without losing themselves in a vagary of cosmic disenchantment and showing it off by antagonizing and agonizing their elders with way-out cosmetics, coiffures, beards, and dress.

My nieces and nephews have learned to do a few things with their hands and can be cajoled into physical exertion—beyond qualifying for a driver's license or doing the watusi, the frug, and whatever comes next. All four of the girls passably play the piano; one can make a dress, two get by at it, and the fourth and youngest shows real aptitude and interest at sewing; the dressmaker is also acceptable as an interpretive dancer, as well as a "fisherman"; one of the twin nieces does well enough with water colors; and the other makes a blueberry pie worthy of a red ribbon, or at least did on one occasion. The youngest niece has the keenest ear for music and a considerable aptitude for art, her cousins concede.

On the other hand, none of the nephews pursues a handicraft, an art form, or a hobby of any sort. My offers to pay for their music or voice lessons fell on deaf ears, and none has been able to believe that the "fun and profits" advertised for stamp and coin collection are really there. Except for the oldest, they are absolute duds at beginning investment. "Ten dollars will get you $18.75 and later $25," I told them over and over again with my Class E savings bond plan, but to no avail.

Nevertheless, each and every one of the boys can be an able and willing worker, if unengaged otherwise and fed well. They have demonstrated as much in the country at Fox Lake, Wisconsin, as they have helped with digging, planting, harvesting, a bit of haying, fence-posting and other chores. I saw the biggest and oldest wield a sledgehammer with neatness and force, driving the piles for a pier which his father now says he built. Four years ago, one summer day, it was all I could do to get one of the younger boys simply to help plant a sapling on his father's big, bare lot in the country. It was necessary to paint for him a picture of how giant and magnificent that measly little maple sapling would become and to explain that it would then be a living monument to his vision and a mark of his devotion to his father, before he would turn a spade. But country trips during the last two summers have seen that same teen-age nephew willingly and manfully digging holes, carrying water, mulching and staking, as we planted one tree after another, not on his father's but his uncle's place—my own five, mule-less acres—just down the road.

Each of the girls also grows and develops, of course, and in ways other than dramatic transition from what might be called a mere "giggle-stick" one summer to a buxomish young lady the very next. I well remember, for example, that one of them when five or six was a real irritant to her father as the children played "follow-the leader." She would boldly join the bunch taking off across the countryside, but as soon as the first barb-wire fence was to be crossed, she would call for her daddy to come and lift her over or stick her through. A summer or two later, she showed herself the most adept of all, children and grown-ups alike, at gathering crayfish, "craw-dads" we call them, grabbing them up in seeming complete disregard of their sharp claws. There was no shyness either as she joined the men before daybreak to put out fishing lines, quite oblivious of the snakes that kept the other girls away from the best fishing "holes" even in the daytime and able to cover her hooks with the fat, wriggly night crawlers more neatly than any of the others on the pier.

I recently updated myself on all of the youngsters in the colony, and the information I gathered seems to say that they are moving along in uncle-approvable fashion. Everyone had a job this summer. All were in school the preceding months and are headed back this fall.

Now to be spoken of is that nephew who seems to be reaching hardest for a newer day. As this is written, the parents of this twenty-two year-old are living in fear of what might happen to him. It is not a matter of induction into the military service and a place for him in Vietnam, though that may lie a few months ahead. It is an immediate risk of real enough analogy to the danger in Vietnam that is now upon them. For this lad is at home in Chicago this hot summer, where time after time he is in the ranks of the young freedom marchers for equal rights in housing, as they make their nonviolent forays into the bitterly hostile white neighborhoods, where they are awaited by white youths who have equipped themselves and were long ago prepared by their elders to meet my nephew and his likes with violence. He does not deny when the danger is pictured for him, after he has been reminded of the more recent acts of violence, like the killing of Emmet Till, as well as the long and ugly history of housing-bred, anti-Negro mob behavior in Chicago, as happened in Trumbull Park. He simply looks up, and looks the last voicer of fear for him in the eye, saying "Yes, sure. So I have to go."

All of the Nesbitt children at college level have been "in the streets" on occasion. They have marched in Chicago's Loop, headed for a giant civil rights rally at the Chicago Stadium, and participated on their campuses in marches in memory and re-dedicated support of the cause of Jim Reeb, the young Unitarian minister slain by Alabama racists.

But this oldest one of them seems to think that a civil rights demonstration is not bona fide if his presence is lacking. Or perhaps more accurately, he himself does not feel bona fide unless he is there, if at all manageable.

He is a student at Antioch College, a fact which, it is only fair to add, is not so much to be blamed for what he is, as credited with an image which made it his choice. Beginning with a grievance directly his, his first participation in a demonstration was on the picket line thrown up about that little barber shop in little Yellow Springs which never kept the civil rights law in Ohio nor yielded to the protestations of the Antioch students. No Negro among them ever got a hair trim in that place. His fledgling part in that losing venture, including his introduction to mob terror (when young white hoodlums maimed a Negro child being ridden on the bike of a young white demonstrator) gave him something upon which to build.

A few months later, while he was in New York, working as an Antioch-placed hospital orderly, he found a place among the freedom demonstrators at the World's Fair.

More recently, this nephew was confronted with an occasion in which the cause for demonstration was clear and impelling, but whether to do so or not was still personally difficult. He was abroad, a U.S. citizen and student of African history at the University of Dar Es Salaam, Tanzania, when suddenly the Premier of Rhodesia declared its independence of Britain and thumbed his nose at a civilized world which has learned to abhor racial apartheid. Tall, deep mahogany in color, and Negroid in features, there my nephew was, a Watusi-looking American among the African students, who immediately and tumultuously set off to mass themselves before the British embassy and demand that the aged old lion bring himself to a roar again. He made his hard decision fast. Staying in street clothing and avoiding the university robes donned by the Africans, he promptly joined that demonstration, distinguishing himself as a Negro and American, while saving his black and kindred face among those of his fellow students.

Upon his return to Antioch, he and a fellow senior student organized a committee which went before the university's trustees on a mission much weightier than pressing for longer dating hours and less faculty surveillance of student activities and antics. The committee sought the withdrawal of Antioch's investments in apartheid-ruled South Africa, and was successful.[1]

The eleven months my nephew spent in Africa, even for a youngster without the inclination for international affairs to begin with, were so exciting and eventful as to have given him the hankering for it and especially at some "African desk." He professes to cherish every moment of his stay, many of which he summarized in long letters to friends, faculty members, and family members, asking the latter to retain his letters, as if they were certain to constitute a documentary of importance to a world which needs so hurriedly to enlighten itself about "the dark continent," its new nations and many peoples. How proud his Garveyite, great uncle would

1. Antioch fully divested from companies working in South Africa in 1978.

have been to hear so much of his "homeland" firsthand and from one in his own family. He would likely have caught the next Africa-bound plane.

One day, soon after his arrival in Dar Es Salaam, a big, black sedan drove up to his dormitory, from which he was summoned to report to the Tanzanian officials who were its occupants. Not only was the car a government vehicle, but its central, chauffeured occupant was Rugimbana, Commissioner of Prisons, who strode out, introduced himself, and demanded that my nephew identify himself. Then he said, "I hear that you have been having immigration difficulties. I must ask you to come with me to my office right away."

My young kinsman began quaking in his boots. He simply knew that he was in trouble of some kind and perhaps being placed under arrest. But as soon as the commissioner read upon my nephew's face a sufficiency of discomfiture for his amusement, he smiled and explained that it was all a farce. Rugimbana had recently been a guest of the Nesbitts in Chicago, where he had learned from the mother of my nephew that he was in school in Dar Es Salaam. He had promised thus first to frighten the nephew and then to befriend him, as he did also.

On his way back from Tanzania to classes at Antioch, and despite visa problems as well as those of his personal exchequer, he managed to see more of Africa than Tanzania. He touched down in Uganda, Zambia, Ethiopia, Sudan, Egypt, Somalia, and Kenya, where he was briefly under political arrest because of visa problems.

At the very least I am certain he will remain a student of African peoples.

Only a few days ago, as this is written, I visited with my youngest brother and his family in the Los Angeles metropolitan area.

For all of that vast distance between Chicago and Los Angeles, the style of living of the family branch in California is essentially much like that of those branches in Chicago. My brother, his wife, and their three children do not live in the Watts area of Los Angeles and instead have a rambler perched high on a lovely hillside in nearby suburban Altadena, with swimming pool, barn (though no riding horses), and an ample expanse of yard, landscaped with a great weeping willow, a hedge of natal plum, several orange and lemon trees, roses, hibiscus, poinsettias, cascading chrysanthemums, jade, cacti, and stretches of various ice plants and other succulents. Theirs is a rather lush abode, compared to that apartment house in the West Side ghetto of the city which Martin Luther King so aptly considers a classic illustration of Northern segregation. Yet my brother and his family deny neither themselves nor those from which they were cut.

As the other of the two brothers in self-exile from the clan's stronghold on the West Side ghetto of Chicago, I must confess to living in no Lawndale-like section of the District of Columbia.

My home is west of Sixteenth Street in Northwest Washington, near Rock Creek Park. The neighborhood is known as "Crestwood," an elegant enough name for the initial sale of its homes to whites only. However, some of my fellow Negro residents have by now unblushingly dubbed it "The Gold Coast," a reflection of relativity and "soul," I suppose, which hardly comforts, though it may amuse, the whites still in the area.

Many of my neighbors are among those Washington Negroes about whom the November 19, 1967, *New York Times* said, "The affluent doctors and lawyers can now get their children into the best prep schools and on to Yale and Harvard, Radcliffe and Vassar. Their sprawling homes in elegant neighborhoods are the envy of many middle-class whites. Beach homes and yachts, European trips, week-end golf, lavish dances and debuts are not new pleasures, but more and more Negroes now go to integrated parties, the embassies and White House receptions."

I can add that a goodly number of these people drive Cadillacs or other vehicles of class, contract out the maintenance of their yards, employ maids and day workers, and walk dogs of proper breeding, mostly the bigger type, to go along with their expansive yards: collies, German shepherds, boxers, and the like.

All of this is not for my interpretation, and some of those involved are among my good friends. It simply allows me better to say that my lifestyle is nevertheless not unlike that of my brothers in Chicago.

My wife and I have a simple though comfortable existence in a three-bedroom house. I wash its windows, cut its yard, pick and eat dandelions from it, all the while dressed like a "yardman." When I first moved in the neighborhood, a neighbor's visiting father passed by, saw me sweeping the gutter and addressed me as an employee of the city. (During the same period, the Negro garbage collector for the city advised my wife to tell "your lady" not to wrap the garbage in too much paper, or he would refuse to take it.) My wife and I drive a Dodge sedan, ride the buses, shop at the neighborhood supermarket, and carry clothing back and forth to the laundry and the dry cleaner. We buy from Sears and Montgomery Ward, soft goods as well as hard. We employ no maid or day cleaner, but know many of them who work in the neighborhood, because we have given them "lifts" to and from the bus line.

In one respect I cannot match my brothers. I give little or no service to the Washington community and its more disadvantaged members. I subscribe to U.G.F. and give to my favorite charities but do no leg work, no real service. I am fond of children but have not adopted a child, served as a foster parent, or been a Big Brother to a boy in a community in which 90 percent of its children are Negro, and thousands of them deprived. I do get on well with the children of my friends and am several times a godfather and many times called "Uncle," but this, of course, does little for them or me, in terms of our needs. In this area of omission, I feel especially remiss.

With another aspect of my life, I have lately, since this writing was begun, rejoined my brothers. I have re-activated my membership in the C.M.E. Church: I am prodigal son returned home. My church is one in which the message is modern but stirring and old style. My association with this church increasingly tempts me to embark on a venture which could busy me in self-redemptive service to the community.

I expect soon to retire from government service. Should I not flee the city and go live on my five acres in a Wisconsin village, I shall take the route which growingly tempts me. I shall seek and find a foundation to agree with me that the Negro church is uniquely situated to do within the racial ghetto something that in the final analysis cannot be done from the outside. It can engage and lead the ghettoed poor in self-improvement undertakings, meeting some of their most urgent needs but, in turn, bringing to them a sense of communal power, leaving them filled with pride and assured of respect.

There stands in the ghettos the Negro church—Baptist, Methodist, and their storefront splinterings. These churches have a glorious history, though few now know it, of having helped Negroes to win freedom from slavery and thereafter to put families together; find jobs for the newly freed; provide them with welfare services; organize them into savings, benevolent, and burial societies; and build schools for their children. They still meet with the Negro masses Sunday after Sunday and are yet first looked to by the newcomers to the city. They cannot avoid responsibility to them, know how to communicate with them, and have ever filled them with aspirations, hope, and faith. They organize endlessly, and each is an organization of organizations. They enjoy leadership, however limited its literacy level or low its sights, and the congregations are practiced in participation in the affairs of the church. Lastly, these churches are poor but property owners, however humble and heavily mortgaged their properties may be, and their properties are little used save for one day each week.

Here then, I am impressed, are resources for corralling resources of history and past achievement, mission and manpower, empathy and capacity for communication, organization, leadership, and plants little used. With these resources, and in the Negro churches, there can be founded one communal enterprise after another. They can range from the simple to the complex, from babysitting services, nurseries, clubs for the sub-teens, youth centers, and libraries of Negro history and culture to buying clubs, credit unions, group insurance plans, cooperative groceries, laundromats, rummage shops, cleaning and pressing agencies, car washes, and filling stations, and even to nonprofit and limited-dividend housing projects.

No Negro church able itself to survive, largely off the pennies and through communal undertakings of the poor, is unable to set up and operate one or two of at least those simpler enterprises I have suggested.

These churches mostly need a hard but trusted push, a set of what the bureaucrats call "guidelines," and the help of those young people who years ago were known by such club names as the "Willing Hands" and the "Busy Bees." Few of the latter are busy in the Negro churches, but they are around. Some are busy crying "black power" in the streets, and some serve the poor more quietly and productively in far away lands. But these young people share in common a compassion and a caring for the poor and disadvantaged. I believe that they can be brought to work in the ghettos and its churches. They are able to "get with" the ghettoed poor, speak their language, and accept them, despite all the dirt, disorder, and disability which go along with them.

There is one other mission which, in starry-eyed moments, I catch myself wishing upon black churches.

I would have black churches become apostolates of blackness, advancing in a systematic, thoroughgoing fashion the spread of black self-understanding and self-celebration. Traditionally and rather inevitably,

Negro Baptist and Methodist churches have contributed far more to the preservation of knowledge of the black past than is commonly realized. But what is now needed is a supplanting of their diffused and sporadic activities as repository of black history with a sustained and creative program of blackness that pervades black churchdom. Every Negro church of any consequence should have, as a strong, scholarly right arm of its minister, a rabbi-like master of blackness to carry forward the cause of black history, traditions, and culture.

The institutional weaknesses of these churches and the disfavor with which black youngsters view them present no insurmountable obstacles against the program I envision. They are nothing to fear, it seems to me, so considerable is the potential for the program inhering in certain attributes of black churches. Ghetto-bound, as they are, they are easily accessible to the masses of blacks. The latter, whatever the class, age, or literacy level, are welcome in the black church and know that it is theirs. The edifice contains ample, surplus space for teaching history, customs, and pride in every conceivable manner. Not the least of the given facilitative factors is the fervor abiding in the black church. What is learned there will constitute not mere knowledge but conviction. Moreover, the abundant presence of the elderly in black church congregations offers a firsthand resource for bringing alive the printed pages of history and exposing much that has too long been hidden or ignored.

When I forget little Fox Lake in Wisconsin, I keep seeing myself in some city somewhere in the center of a ghettoed church program such as I have sketched, that looks to the spirits of its people before they are called home.

Postscript

Nearly two years have passed since the lines above were written. During that brief period something not to be overlooked here has happened to my nieces and nephews. It has already unsettled them. It could conceivably go on to make them quite unlike their fathers and mothers, uncles and aunts, and unbecomingly so, in my view. And this is something to tell about with care.

My nieces and nephews are not going to pot by going for it, or anything of its kind. Still they are indulging a bit in the most heady form of recreation, recreation in essence, they have ever known. Not one has drowned himself, but all stick their toes in, wade in the waters, and take a deep dip now and then. They are excited by the black power movement. They are disenchanted and rebellious along with thousands upon thousands of their peers of whatever color. But they also have their special discomfiture with Whitey and what he has done to Negro self-esteem and self-image.

Not just one of the nephews is wearing his hair au naturel—all six of them are, even the youngest, who is not eleven years of age. All of the nieces but one keep their hair in a thick bush like Miriam Makeba's, and that holdout is really held back by the old-style system for training Negro girls practiced at the private school in the south she attends. Both boys and girls dress, talk, salute, and eat "soul." But deeper than the symbolism and showiness, one girl nearly adores a certain young black power spokesman; his wildest pronouncements seem music to her ears. Another, as a freshman in college, helped organize a bi-racial, integration-oriented race relations committee on her campus and became its president. But by the time she was a senior, she was all for black withdrawal, boosting a black students' union group, no whites wanted.

As for that nephew who delights in demonstrations, he has gone on from undergraduate days at Antioch College, where dissent is part of the training and trade, to graduate work at Columbia University, seemingly the eastern center of student disruptiveness. In April of 1968 he was one of the eighty-five Negro students who seized and made a fortress of Hamilton Hall for several days, in protest against the university's usurpation of park space which they felt was more badly needed for just that purpose by the poor and powerless of Harlem than by Columbia and its students for a gymnasium. How pleased I was to learn that the barricaded black students had accepted arrest for the trespassing charged against them and that the police had not beaten their heads. Both kept their cools; each accepted its obligation and behaved with some sense of propriety!

Now I am not too dismayed by these straws in a blowing wind.

The black power binge younger Negroes are on, I keep telling myself, I am expected to well understand. Some of them have been taught much about—and all of them have been bumped firsthand by—the hypocrisies and dishonesties of a society that shunts them aside. If they were not disenchanted and embittered young Americans, they would be less than deserving of the sympathy and support of young white civil rightists. For they and their elders have long been dealt a crooked hand, at school, on playground, at the plant, in the streets, by the police, and downtown. They must live hemmed-in and shut out but also must see and feel day in and day out the disparities between them and us in so many different ways and directions. The history that is theirs has been hidden from them and their fellows, to deny them self-pride, or it has been mis-told in ways to leave them doubting and ashamed of themselves. So they remain uncertain of self and struck with a sense of powerlessness at the most critical and thinnest-skinned stage of their lives. Even after they have joined in protest and struggle against racial wrongs, lent their youthful energies and incredible courage to bolder tactics, and quickened movement for equality and opportunity, they have seen promises made but poorly kept, evil systems remain intact, and must face the fact that they have many long miles yet to go.

There is little to wonder in it that they are embodied embitterment, exceedingly wrought, grabbing at what easily seems a panacea. "Black power" is for them a sweet slogan with a strong sound. People and places in America are already white and black, so complete is the arrangement with all else that counts: history and destiny, culture and custom, industry and jobs, position and power. If the game calls for mythology, stereotyping, sloganeering, slander, looting, and violence, we can play it too. Black racism is no worse than white, and hasn't been around as long or as much. We've a long way to go, and let's get on with it. So the tempting so easily runs.

But harder than understanding it all myself is helping my nieces and nephews to understand it for themselves,

I try never to rush in on them, declaring that black power when carried to its extremes adds up silly. It is in essence nothing really so new, but a mere resurrection; it can be ambiguous, irrational, full of inconsistencies, and is only here and there practical. My instinct tells me not to engage them head-on and too quickly, anyway, lest I irritate their rebelliousness and appear old fuddy-duddy, short on identity, and Uncle Tommish, all rolled together, for a quick write-off.

Certainly I am not upset by their dress styles, their au naturels, and their African-like adornments. Capriciously cut clothing, changed year after year; wigs, toupees, hair dyes and rinses; jewelry and other useless trappings are all commonplace in our society, to meet picayune, personal needs, from hiding age and appearance to showing off one's self, usually exaggerating one's standing in the process. The privilege ought also go to those trying to stick out and stand-up honestly and for causes beyond themselves, the white youngsters as well as the black ones. But especially aggrieved are those middle-class, middle-aged Negroes ill-put who squirm so to see young Negroes allow their hair to remain kinky. Here indeed the elders are confused and ashamed of themselves; they are the living proof of the youngsters' point.

Still, I often begin brushing with my young friends who hold high the black power banner in an easy, half-jesting, half-testing way, by questioning their studied conspicuousness. I can ask them one question after another for which most often they have no answer. They run like these: That beautiful African to-do you have on, is it continental, national, regional, or tribal? Is anybody to wear it anytime? You're not about to offend the brother, are you? Was it woven somewhere in Africa and shipped here? Or is there a chance that it has never been there?

Now the answers to my questions I don't have either. But then whenever a young one pitches such questions back at me, I can say, "Well, I'm not running so hard after the soul brothers so far away either."

Several times I've teased and troubled them a bit with this line: Now, how about your African brothers and sisters and the ways they treat and dress their hair? Are they now about to go your old ways, while you are busy trying to go theirs? Suppose some chemist comes up with a good-doing hair-kinker, Madison Avenue pushes it, and the whites go for it? They already suntan and Coppertone themselves blacker than some of us, you know. How will you keep whitey from pulling your rug out from under you?

With all their soul food, dress and jargon, I can have fun. I remind them that it is the big white packinghouses that really put out the chitterlings, fresh, frozen, and ready-to-eat. Maybe that soul delight will go the way of Southern fried chicken, which whites favor more than we do and some of them get rich raising (fairly manufacturing) them, not to speak of frying and dishing them up soul-style, like that pink-jowled Kentucky colonel does. Soul dress can't be kept soul either. What Sammy Davis wears, no matter how weird the cut or wild the color, the others will wear too. As for soul talk, it has never remained exclusively the brother's for long. And today it comes off the farm and out of the ghetto, hits the airways, and soon is long-gone everybody's, especially with soul brothers "telling it like it is," or making sport with it, sometimes for big money.

Upon occasion, as the young ones who are my kin or my friends bandy "soul" about, I can really dig them a bit. I'll suddenly say, "Who wrote *Souls of Black Folks* anyway?" I follow up with queries as to whether it has been read, how many times, and who owns copies. (Lately, I tell them about my recent lecture before a group of upper-class students at Howard University, bastion of black power talk and tirade. I quoted Du Bois a dozen times without revelation of my source and then said, "Now who's the fellow I've been quoting?" Only one student, a Jamaican, recognized Du Bois). I try to get to the point that soul is something a little deeper than eating, dressing, and talking. As Webster starts with it, soul is "the immaterial essence, animating principle, or actuating cause of an individual life." Then, if the young ones are in my home, I pull out my fingered copy of *Souls of Black Folk* and read selected passages from Du Bois's first essay. Here is my favorite selection:

> The history of the American Negro is the history of this strife — this longing to attain self-conscious manhood, to merge his double self into a better and truer self. In this merging he wishes neither of the older selves to be lost. He would not Africanize America, for America has too much to teach the world and Africa. He would not bleach his Negro soul in a flood of white Americanism, for he knows that Negro blood has a message for the world. He simply wishes to make it possible for a man to be both a Negro and an American, without being cursed and spat upon by his fellows, without having the doors of Opportunity closed roughly in his face.
>
> This then is the end of his striving, to be a co-worker in the kingdom of culture, to escape both death and isolation, to husband and use his best powers and his latent genius.

After such a passage from that thin little book of black American wisdom, Torah-like teachings for the Negro, I can declare, "Now that really is soul, black soul!"

Given a chance, I can then go on to make plain how far I go with the thrust for black power and where I must turn from it. It is not hard to do, for the core of black power is older and more familiar to many of my generation than our young realize. Even its seemingly new layers are not really new.

Certainly I am for knowing black history and having others have it straight and strong. I celebrate my Negro self, just as it is, and demand that it be respected, including its customs, strengths, and goodness. I claim in comfort and not without pride my own kind, in all their myriad being. I can even accept making the most of taller Negroes, puffing their deeds into the loftiness of heroism and legend, so long as they have indeed struggled against and surmounted the barriers raised against them. I like the idea too of being more the author of my own destiny, looking to myself for much of my salvation. I accept and understand the reality of power and believe black people ought to have it too. No people, no person, should be denied self-respect, esteem, and an equally counted voice in a civil and democratic society. All of this is of the essence of being somebody, and black besides, in America.

But I continue raising questions with all of my young friends, raising those running farther than my nieces and nephews are likely themselves to dare going—questions reaching after the lengths to which the voices of black power go. Questions are wonderful with the college-bred young. They are accustomed to producing answers and think their supply is far more ample than it is or can be. But when they lack quick responses or provide weak ones, they can admit as much far more readily than their elders. They can allow themselves to be put upon inquiry.

So I say to them: If the struggle for integration is to be replaced by self-separation, won't the result be a surrendering to disrespect from whites? Is it also a giving-up of the most glorious part of our history and tradition, what we've earned and are entitled to as part of humanity? Isn't it a little late to ask for segregation in a society so long at least bent on integration and which in fact subsists on interdependence? Isn't the timing of the worst, just as millions of young whites at home genuinely work for equality and approach their day of power, while a shrunken world judges our country by whether we are a democracy in fact and function?

If we blacks are to have a self-contained society and economy, do we have the wherewithal for all the self-sufficiency? Is a first-rate, separate society within a society any more easily and rapidly achievable than effective integration? Is an economy within an economy a practical thing? Can the economy of an all-Negro city or state, given Negro income levels, possibly provide the essential services of government for its population mix, without subsidy from outside? Can package houses and bars, barber shops and beauty parlors, "fish'n' chips" and "wings'n' things" places, laundromats and valet shops, make an economy? Doesn't an economy have to produce as well as distribute, distribute wherever and to whomsoever, and need to have had capital resources and management expertise to begin with?

If so, is it really separate and sustaining of itself? If black economies are to have their bases in the ghettos and to have as their opening wedge black workers and black retailers, and only so, why won't the exclusionism soon boomerang? Aren't black institutions, our economic mechanisms above all the rest, simply no more than realistic but passing means to an end—organizing unorganized resources where they are in the ghettos—but toward an end to ghettoism?

Don't we have always to watch hard our means and ends and avoiding confusing the two? Should we follow fellows who are against everything and for nothing? Shouldn't it always be asked, Where are you going? Will your course take you there? Why not this course, instead, that one, or the other? Which ways will attract needed allies and resources; which ask for increased opposition; which leave us better off on balance and long run?

What profit can there be in violence for those trying to go someplace? Stoning, looting, and burning will get attention, but what else? Violence is a tactic which easily becomes a goal, and who wants to negotiate with those who practice it? Violence is obviously a means of the very last resort; what's left to do next? Who can stand with and for those who are violent, and trying to be so, with what hope for success?

In this gentle, prodding fashion, I try to help young Negroes with whom I talk to bring themselves to a position which, in all honesty, is mine.

Black power is obviously a good rallying cry; it works because it conjures up before our eyes what Negroes have so little had. The overdue resurgence of self-celebration is nothing short of wonderful. The boldness and modernity of black power tactics, for the most part, make eminent sense to me—certainly the marching, the sitting-in, the mass lobbying confrontations, and the voter registrations. It takes drama, the psychological bludgeon, and a bit of disruption to get attention, cause embarrassment, and bring about change.

I do have a reservation about the out-shouting en masse, locking out teachers and administrators, the refusal to hear spokesmen for the establishment, and the like, that the youthful activists engage in. It is not the technical trespass sometimes involved, nor the impoliteness. The mistreatment of the responsible elders little matters, for most often they are no Voltaires themselves. My precaution is merely that those who are bent upon winning civil rights must busy themselves helping to keep civil liberties intact, lest they throw out the baby with the bath.

But I feel most certain of myself in abhorring three dimensions sometimes voiced as black power: black racism, black violence, and black self-separation.

Black racism is a stooping that holds no promise of conquering. It is ugly and demeaning in many ways. It simply reverses white racism and makes an enemy of the whole lump of those whose skins are white; equates goodness and beauty with black, and evil and ugliness with white; denies the equality and fraternity of man; travels on stereotyping, mythology, exaggeration, and lies; abandons the golden rule; lifts high "an eye for an eye and a tooth for a tooth"; and settles for the happenstance of skin color as reason enough for being and for deference from all mankind. In short, black racism is no better than white and would leave Negroes in America not only a physical minority but as morally weak as those it apes.

It has to fail, because arrogance breeds stupidity, results in an exaggerated sense of capacity, causes reaching beyond grasp, and makes for ignoring needed friends, allies, and resources.

The use, even the espousal and condoning, of violence, I also cannot accept. I am no subscriber to the philosophy of nonviolence. But I have been exposed to a lot of the New Testament and in many other ways taught to spurn dog-eat-dog behavior. However, completely aside from religious teaching and credo for living, violence makes no sense to me. It is rarely either a strategy or a tactic, for most often it is directed to no goal; it is simply reasoning forsaken, a spontaneous outbreak of desperation. When and if it is a tactic at all, it too much tends to become a goal, a self-demeaning if not also self-brutalizing way of living. If it is a tactic, it is a dangerous one, for violence begets itself and is a game any one with brute left in him can play. Negro violence is a two-edged sword which, swung forth in a land inured to violence and given to mass hysteria, can come back upon Negroes with a swift, terrible, and decimating effect. Worse yet, in the aftermath, faith in equality may be uprooted, and strong men privileged to substitute a social system devoid of those promises which have never been fulfilled.

And above all I have no use for those who see black power as a means to self-separation. As long as separation is in fact forced upon Negroes, I think that we are forced to use it as a base for power, a means to the undoing of the imposed segregation. But we should never set ourselves off and aside, giving up the struggle for integration and pretending that we like the isolation. For self-separation, black like white, confesses insecurity and reflects a sense of inferiority. Self-separation is sight lost, sight of the highest endeavor of man on earth, living in dignity and concerted oneness. The great religious, ethical, social, economic, and political systems of thought offer structures for this quest. Our democratic institutions, the Declaration of Independence, the Constitution, and especially its Bill of Rights, and the best fruit of the labors of the Supreme Court are so inclined. Equality, integration, and social plurality are the broad paths for all toward human dignity and social justice. Given the latter in the United States, only equality and integration can facilitate it. Inequality and separation can only frustrate and abort a social plurality.

All of this I would not be a party to abandoning for self-separation, not in any land, and never, never in that which is my own. I would not so disparage the strengths and history built up by Negroes over three hundred years of toil and troubles, struggle and suffering. I would not take from my country the hardest test and clearest measure of its most noble profession—to be a land of freedom for all and any of mankind. Nor shall I yield it all to stubborn resistance, which would keep us ditched and drag her down.

So much I would not join in doing, especially now. For at this time, darker peoples in a shrunken world outnumber and outgrow the fair-skinned and claim their places in the sun shining from the golden rule. The fair-skinned ones, colonizers and subjugators everywhere, are ridden and trembling with guilt. Their ugliness and hypocrisies no longer stay veiled and hidden but are soon discovered, and sometimes their perpetrators are seen in the midst of their misdeeds, caught in the act, by a watching world. The white young are disenchanted with their elders and clamor for justice and fairness. And the whole world fears a sudden sweeping holocaust, if its peoples do not soon learn to live together in peace and with equality.

Self-separation, here or anywhere, is for those Negroes who have neither faith in man nor the ultimate triumph of justice, nor sight and foresight enough to see what so plainly prevails around the world and approaches wherever injustice is seated.

I would have my young kinsmen and other blacks of their generation share in the exercise of community power and responsibility of all kinds but under systems that are not racially separated and with motives that are not first and last based on skin color and narrowed narcissism. I want them to have for themselves souls that are comfortably black but which freely reach for and feed upon excellence, wherever and whose ever it is. I want them to be somebodies among any people, anywhere. Only through cross contacts, movement of body, mind, and spirit wherever, unfettered by lines of color, race, nationality, or religious persuasion can they grow strong-souled and live rich lives. So away with blackness as the be-all and end-all of existence. Let the young, the black young, become people of intellectual and moral courage, filled with productive care and compassion for their fellows in a world that has become a neighborhood, and given not alone to a reach for black rights and power but for a social structure devoted to the practice of justice, love, and peace. Let them be bigger than black and able, to consider and pursue whatever is true as free and strong men and women, ". . . whatever is true, whatever is honorable, whatever is just, whatever is pure, whatever is lovely (and) whatever is gracious . . ."[1]

I doubt that any one of my nieces and nephews will go beyond temptation with the violent, racist, and separatist layers of black rage. They have been taught, and seen practiced by their elders, the brotherhood and plurality of man since they were little ones. Though it is yet made extremely difficult for them to do so, I like to think that each tries near instinctively to view each human being he or she encounters as deserving of respect and charity, if not because that being is God's wonderful work and can be one with him, then merely because he is unique, a being never before on earth nor again to be. I suspect that the determined black thrust which my young kinsfolk witness and share serves simply to strengthen the sense of self-comfort and self-celebration which their fathers exhibited before them, long before the anxious black rhetoric set in. What I lately hear and see of them, and sometimes draw from them, confirms my hope.

What does worry me is whether the society which is theirs, and which they question and challenge but would not help tear asunder, is prepared to live and let live with my nephews and nieces and the likes of them. For what they represent is a new "talented tenth," a better-trained, a more determined, a more activist elite among Negroes than in Du Bois's day. They are more certain of but less centered in themselves, committed to helping

---

1. Philippians 4:8.

meet the leadership needs not alone of Negroes but of the mistreated and disadvantaged at large in their country. Moreover, their allies among elite white youth are legion. Deep in the hearts of most of these young people, however threatening the rhetoric they repeat, they ask what they can do for their country and demand that they be allowed to do it.

Will they be permitted as much?

Acknowledgments

FROM PREXY: Bill Minter helped to bring this project together, giving a bit of needed momentum to both myself and Zeb that helped to set us in motion. Katherine Philipson performed the difficult task of a lengthy copyedit on scanned pages that had been typed up in the early 1970s, giving us something to work with. Martha Biondi and Barbara Ransby both provided early and important encouragement for this book.

Many thanks must be given to Elizabeth Branch Dyson, who championed this book and helped us shepherd it through publication. We must thank her for finding this book the home that it deserves. We're grateful too to Mollie McFee at the University of Chicago Press. To the anonymous reviewers who read the whole manuscript, thank you for your time and careful attention to detail.

Imani Perry's thoughtful foreword was exactly the kind of analysis we wanted for this book. Even after thinking about George Nesbitt's life for so long, she still managed to find new lenses to see him through that we had not yet considered.

Many thanks to the Drake family and to Sandra Drake in particular, who helped us secure permissions for her father's introduction.

FROM ZEB: To Prexy, thank you for giving me a chance to help publish this book. From your first description of George Nesbitt's memoirs, I was fascinated by them, and when I had a chance to read them, I was hopelessly drawn in. It's been a privilege to assist with this.

For all the love, photos, stories, and endless support from the Nesbitt family and extended family, we thank Carol Day, Boyce Brunson, Joyce Acklen, Twinkle Violet Ward-Barnes, Lea Adams, Rikki Zee, Karin Candelaria, Karen Maxwell, Kay Logan, Reese Nesbitt, Paul Nesbitt and Julie Harris, Marla Nesbitt-Laws, Phillip and Ginger Nesbitt, Julie Parson Nesbitt, David Lendor Nesbitt, Janet and Caterina MacLean, Samora Nesbitt, Donna Magdalina, and Josiya Jele Magdalina.

DATE DUE